Middle East Crisis

INTERNATIONAL CRISIS BEHAVIOR PROJECT

Editor: Michael Brecher

ALAN DOWTY

MIDDLE EAST CRISIS

U.S. Decision-Making in 1958, 1970, and 1973

University of California Press
Berkeley • Los Angeles • London

University of California Press
Berkeley and Los Angeles, California

University of California Press, Ltd.
London, England

© 1984 by
The Regents of the University of California

Library of Congress Cataloging in Publication Data

Dowty, Alan, 1940–
Middle East crisis.
"International Crisis Behavior Project"—
Bibliography: p.
Includes index.
1. Near East—Foreign relations—United States—
Decision-making. 2. United States—Foreign relations—
Near East—Decision-making. 3. United States—Foreign
relations—1953–1961—Decision-making. 4. United States
—Foreign relations—1969–1974—Decision-making.
5. International relations—Decision-making. 6. United
States—Foreign relations administration. I. Interna-
tional Crisis Behavior Project.   II.   Title.
DS63.2.U5D68   1983   327.56073   83–1396
ISBN 0–520–04809–1

Printed in the United States of America

1 2 3 4 5 6 7 8 9

To Gail
N.M.S.

Contents

Figures and Tables

FIGURES

TABLES

Foreword

THE STUDY OF international crises has gathered momentum in recent years. Several approaches have been adopted in an attempt to explain various dimensions of this ubiquitous phenomenon in world politics. Among them is structured empiricism which denotes the amassing of empirical data on a specific crisis (or any issue in foreign policy or the international system) and their integration into a structured analytical framework. There are several operational steps in this approach, and these are being applied in all the case studies of the International Crisis Behavior series.

The first is to designate the decision-makers and decisional units for the pre-crisis, crisis and post-crisis periods, along with the important decisions in each phase of the crisis. The psychological environment of the decision-makers is analyzed, both their perceptions of the setting for choices and their goals—for every decision-maker possesses a set of images and is conditioned by them in his behavior during an international crisis. This is followed by an inquiry into the decision process through time, a step which takes the form of a detailed description of the flow of decisions during the crisis, focusing on pre-decisional events, decisive inputs, and decisions. Apart from its intrinsic interest, this narrative provides the indispensable data to examine systematically the ways in which decision-makers cope with stress and choose among perceived options. In applying this stress-coping-choice framework, emphasis is placed on information processing, the consultative and decisional forums, and the search for and consideration of alternatives.

Among the merits of a common research design is that it facilitates a search for patterns in crisis behavior. Such knowledge, in turn, can assist in avoiding crises or in their effective management so as to achieve a stable world order. It is to this goal that the ICB project is directed.

The first volume in this series (*Decisions in Crisis,* 1980, Brecher with Geist) compared the behavior of a small state in two crises within a protracted conflict, namely, Israel in 1967 and 1973. The second (*The United States in the Berlin Blockade Crisis 1948–49,* 1982, Shlaim) analyzed the behavior of a superpower in another pivotal crisis, at the outset of the Cold War. In this, the third volume of the series, Alan Dowty compares U.S. behavior in three crises located in a region of persistent turmoil, the Middle East.

The result is a work of superior scholarship, with the added virtue of an admirably lucid style. Professor Dowty has, with impressive skills, integrated an array of research materials—documents, memoirs, interviews—into an engrossing reconstruction of American crisis behavior. His extensive interviews with officials at all levels in the Nixon administration have greatly enriched the narrative, with many fresh insights into U.S. policy towards the Middle East. Moreover, this volume provides a rigorous analysis of coping and choice under conditions of acute stress. And in testing a large number of hypotheses he has contributed much to the continuing quest for knowledge about international crises. In short, this is a valuable book.

Michael Brecher, Director,
International Crisis
Behavior Project

Preface

It is customary to say that a book "could not have been written" without the help and counsel of a particularly influential colleague or mentor. But this book literally could not, and would not, have been written without Michael Brecher, since it is part of an ambitious undertaking of which he is the progenitor in conception and the guiding spirit in execution. Were it not for his unexcelled powers of persuasion, I would never have been seduced into accepting an analytical challenge whose fascination is exceeded only by its complexity. In fact, Michael's imprint upon this study is so strong that I am tempted *not* to extend to him the customary exoneration from its shortcomings. Why not make him share the blame?

But as attractive as that might seem, I have probably contrived to commit sins that are originally and uniquely mine, and for which I must take sole credit. So be it. I only hope that the end result does not fall *too* short of the high standard that Michael himself has set in the initial studies of the International Crisis Behavior (ICB) project.

The ICB project, and the place of this volume in it, are described in Chapter One. What remains here is to acknowledge and thank the others whose help has been instrumental. In the first place, I am grateful to the many participants in U.S. foreign policy decision-making who agreed to be interviewed and tried to give honest answers to questions that must have often appeared somewhat arcane. The cooperation of interviewees—and very few participants declined to be interviewed—was a pleasant surprise and source of encouragement which more than offset the almost total failure, despite extended efforts, to secure the release of meaningful government documents under the Freedom of Information Act.

Other scholars working on related studies have also been generous in exchanging ideas, suggesting sources, and sometimes making their own work available before publication. I would like to acknowledge, in particular, Shlomo Aronson, William Quandt, Bernard Reich, Nadav Safran, Steven Spiegel, and Raymond Tanter.

A number of others have helped along the way by suggesting or arranging interviews or offering other useful advice. These include Nahum Barnea, Wolf Blitzer, Alvin Cottrell, Leonard Davis, Robert Harkavy, Ellen Joyce, Ariel Kerem, Walter Laqueur, Nissan Oren, Nathan Pelcovits, Richard Rosecrance, Aaron Rosenbaum, Max Singer, Paul Wolfowitz, Ken Wollak, and Robert Young.

The Social Science and Humanities Research Council of Canada, through its general support of the ICB project, made this study and others possible. Such large-scale commitments to ambitious academic undertakings, expressed in generous financial backing, need to be noted in an age when they are increasingly rare.

I am also grateful to the Ford Foundation for financial assistance in conducting the interviews, and to the School of Advanced International Studies of Johns Hopkins University, and its Director, Robert Osgood, for the use of SAIS facilities during the summer of 1977, when the interviewing in Washington was carried out.

At the University of Notre Dame, the College of Arts and Letters extended support in the summer of 1980, during a critical phase in the writing of the book. Peri Arnold and Michael Francis, both of whom served as Chairman of the Department of Government and International Studies while this work was in progress, were unusually understanding and helpful in lightening teaching loads at strategic times. I am also grateful to Michael Francis for his continuing interest in the research itself and his thoughtful comments on earlier drafts of the book.

Jihad Kassis, who served as my teaching and research assistant during most of the period of this book's gestation, was an extraordinarily strong source of support. He was, to begin with, a first-class researcher; and by the time the project was completed, he was more a colleague than an assistant. His own doctoral dissertation, which applies the ICB framework to a study of U.S. policy in the oil embargo of 1973–1974, nicely complements some of the work here on the 1973 crisis and is recommended to all students of the subject.

Finally, to the Window Co-op: *Baruch hashem, sof sof zeh nigmar.*

Alan Dowty
South Bend, June 1982

CHAPTER ONE

Crisis Decision–Making: A Research Framework

A MODEL OF INTERNATIONAL CRISIS BEHAVIOR

THE LITERATURE on U.S. foreign policy in Middle East crises is voluminous, but there are few studies that focus on the process by which
policy was made during these crises. This book is a case study of
decision-making under crisis conditions, taking as cases U.S. foreign
policy in the Lebanese crisis of 1958, the Syrian-Jordanian confrontation of 1970, and the Yom Kippur War of 1973. The question it
addresses, in common with other studies of the International Crisis
Behavior (ICB) Project, is: What is the impact of crisis-induced stress
on (a) the processes and mechanisms through which decision-makers
cope with crisis, and (b) their choices?[1]

Definition of Crisis

ICB researchers have evolved a definition of international crisis,
from the perspective of a state, based on extensive empirical work.
According to this definition:

> A crisis is a situation with three necessary and sufficient conditions,
> deriving from a change in its external or internal environment. All

1. For a definitive statement of the ICB Project, see the inaugural volume in this
series: Michael Brecher, *Decisions in Crisis: Israel, 1967 and 1973* (Berkeley, Los
Angeles, and London: University of California Press, 1980). Other related publications
by Brecher include: *The Foreign Policy System of Israel* (New Haven: Yale University
Press, 1972); *Decisions in Israel's Foreign Policy* (New Haven: Yale University Press,
1975); "Toward a Theory of International Crisis Behavior," *International Studies
Quarterly,* 21 (March 1977), 39–74; Brécher, ed., *Studies in Crisis Behavior* (New
Brunswick, N.J.: Transaction Books, 1979); Brecher and Jonathan Wilkenfeld, "Crises
in World Politics," *World Politics,* 34 (April 1982), 380–417.

three conditions are perceptions held by the highest-level decision-makers:

1. threat to basic values, with a simultaneous or subsequent

2. high probability of involvement in military hostilities, and the awareness of

3. finite time for response to the external value threat.

Though generally similar to other attempts to define international crisis, this definition differs in certain respects.[2] In the first place, a crisis may be initiated by a change in the internal as well as the external environment. Secondly, any threat to basic values—and not only to "high-priority goals," as in other widely-accepted definitions of crisis—may help to induce a crisis. Third, while most other definitions stress a "short" time period for response as a defining characteristic of crisis, the ICB definition holds that it is sufficient that policy-makers perceive the time available as limited (or finite). Fourth, "perceived high probability of war" (or at least a sharp increase in the perceived likelihood of war) is considered a necessary condition of crisis, in contrast to most previous definitions. Finally, while other definitions have included "surprise" as a defining attribute of crisis, the ICB definition does not.[3]

This definition of crisis was based, in part, on an effort to identify crises in the international system over the last half-century. One of the functions of the "vertical" ICB case studies, of which this book is one, is to test in depth the operational validity of the ICB crisis definition that has evolved from "horizontal" research.[4]

Model of Crisis Behavior

The independent variable in this research can be more precisely specified, therefore, as *perception of crisis,* based in turn on perceptions of threat, time pressure, and high probability of involvement in military hostilities. This composite perceptual variable, in turn, cre-

2. The best-known definition, from which the ICB definitions evolved, is that of Charles Hermann. See Hermann, *Crises in Foreign Policy: A Simulation Analysis* (Indianapolis: Bobbs-Merrill, 1969a), p. 414. Other recent definitions come strikingly close to the ICB definition; see Richard Ned Lebow, *Between Peace and War: The Nature of International Crisis* (Baltimore: Johns Hopkins University Press, 1981), pp. 9–12, and Glenn H. Snyder and Paul Diesing, *Conflict Among Nations: Bargaining, Decision Making, and System Structure in International Crises* (Princeton: Princeton University Press, 1977), pp. 6–9.

3. For a fuller explication and justification of the ICB definition of crisis, see Brecher, 1980, pp. 1–8.

4. For an extended discussion of the horizontal dimension of the ICB project, see Brecher and Wilkenfeld.

ates a sense of stress among decision-makers. Thus, the terms *stress* or *crisis-induced stress* are used here as code words for the perception of threat and/or time pressure and/or probability of war.

This calls attention to the importance of another element of the ICB model: the *psychological environment.* Like perceptions of crisis, all inputs into a foreign policy system from the operational (real) environment are filtered through the attitudinal prisms of decision-makers and can be described as their "images."

The intervening variable in the model is *coping,* or the processes and mechanisms through which decision-makers deal with the stress brought about by heightened perceptions of threat, time pressure, and probability of war. The four principal coping mechanisms are information search and processing, consultation, decisional forums, and the consideration of alternatives.

Finally, the dependent variable is *choice,* or the content of the decisions actually made.

The relationships among these variables, over time, is represented in Figure 1. Environmental changes at time t_1 trigger changes in decision-makers' perceptions of threat, time pressure, and war probability at time t_2, inducing a feeling of stress. In response, decision-makers adopt one or more coping strategies at time t_3, using the mechanisms of information search, consultation, decisional forums, and the search for and evaluation of alternatives. This leads to the decisional choice at time t_4. The decision itself, when implemented, changes the operational environment, which provides new stimuli or "feedback" for a second cycle of the same process.

Having specified the basic model, I will now elaborate the key variables and their possible interrelationships.

Coping Mechanisms

Each of the coping mechanisms has a broad range of variation, which may or may not be influenced by crisis-induced stress.

Information may be either sought or avoided; it may pass through channels; it may be openly received or reinterpreted to suit decision-makers' predilections; and it can be processed in a number of ways.

Consultation may involve only a small circle of senior policy-makers, or it may be broadened to include a large number of subordinates. Area experts, military advisors, and other bureaucratic specialists may or may not be drawn in. There may or may not be broad consultation with groups outside the executive branch: Congress, interest groups, competing elites, other governments. The

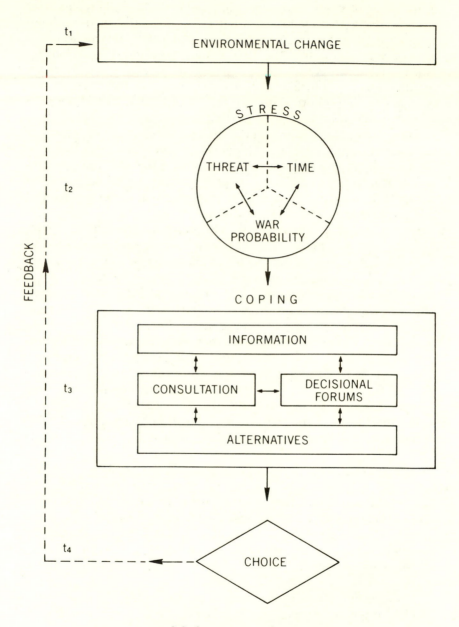

Figure 1. Model of International Crisis Behavior

form of consultation also varies; groups may be large or small, institutional or ad hoc.

Decisional forums—meaning the actual decisional unit—also vary in size, structure, and degree of institutionalization. There is a broad range of authority patterns, centralized or decentralized, that may characterize a decisional forum under either crisis or non-crisis conditions.

Search for and evaluation of alternatives may, like information, involve a genuine quest for new options, or premature closure on options. There may or may not be cognitive rigidity in seeking and evaluating alternatives. Decision-makers may be more or less careful in weighing the consequences of various options and making a choice based on a rational calculus rather than affective or emotional influences.

The first part of our basic research question asks, therefore, how perceptions of crisis affect these coping mechanisms. We ask nine specific questions regarding this linkage between our independent and intervening variables. What are the efforts of escalating and de-escalating crisis-induced stress . . .

on information:	1. cognitive performance.
	2. the perceived need and consequent quest for information.
	3. the receptivity and size of the information-processing groups.
on consultation:	4. the type and size of consultative units.
	5. group participation in the consultative process.
on decisional forums:	6. the size and structure of decisional forums.
	7. authority patterns within decisional units.
on alternatives:	8. the search for and evaluation of alternatives.
	9. the perceived range of available alternatives.[5]

Hypotheses on these relationships will be presented in the second section of this chapter.

Dimensions of Choice

Obviously, there is also a broad range in the possible content of decisions reached under crisis or non-crisis conditions. In order to

5. An earlier formulation of twenty-two ICB research questions can be found in Brecher, 1977, and in many of the studies in Brecher, ed., 1979.

identify patterns of choice, we must first find ways to measure and categorize the choices made. Brecher offers a list of "dimensions of choice" that is largely perceptual; that is, it is mostly based on how the decision-makers viewed the choice they made, after the evaluation of alternatives narrowed the options to the one that became the decision. These dimensions are:

Core inputs: the crucial stimuli to each decision as perceived by the decision-maker(s).

Costs: the perceived magnitude of the loss(es) anticipated from the choice that was made: human (casualties); material (equipment and economic); political (deterrence credibility, alliance potential); and intangibles, such as morale and unity.

Importance: the perceived value of the decision at the time of choice.

Complexity: the number of issue-areas involved in the choice, ranging from one to four—namely, Military-Security (M-S), Political-Diplomatic (P-D), Economic-Developmental (E-D), Cultural-Status (C-S).

Systemic
Domain: the perceived scope of reverberations of the decision, ranging from Domestic alone to Bilateral, Regional, Superpower, and Global—any one or all of which may constitute the Domain.

Process: the mental procedure associated with the selected options, as distinct—but not necessarily different—from the procedure attending the evaluation of all other options considered prior to choice; this can be Routine (following established procedures for response to similar challenges); Affective (an assessment dominated by reliance on past experience, ideology, rooted beliefs, emotional preference, etc.); and Rational (a calculus based upon the measurement of costs and benefits, qualitatively and/or quantitatively.)

Activity: the thrust of the decision: to act, to delay, or to not act; verbal or physical.

Novelty: the presence or absence of innovation, in terms of reliance on precedent and past choices.[6]

There are other possible measurements of decisions. In order to supplement Brecher's "dimensions of choice" with another measurement less dependent on decision-makers' perceptions, I will also examine the *coping strategies* embodied in the decisions made. As

6. Brecher, 1980, pp. 29–30, 380–381.

collated by Ole Holsti and Alexander George, theorists have identified a number of strategies by which decision-makers may cope with stress:

1. A "satisficing" rather than "optimizing" decision strategy.

2. The strategy of "incrementalism."

3. Deciding what to do on the basis of "consensus politics"—i.e., what enough people want and support—rather than attempting to master the cognitive complexity of the problem by means of analysis.

4. Avoidance of value trade-offs, by persuading oneself that a policy which is best on one value dimension is also best for all other relevant values.

5. Use of historical models to diagnose and prescribe for present situations.

6. Reliance on ideology and general principles as a guide to action.

7. Reliance on "operational code" beliefs.[7]

It is assumed that the content of decisions that policy-makers make will reflect their coping strategies (e.g., satisficing, incrementalism, etc.), and that we will thus be able to identify any consistent relationships between levels of stress and decisional choices as measured by coping strategies employed.

The second part of our research question asks, therefore, how perceptions of crisis affect dimensions of choice. In particular, what are the effects of escalating and de-escalating crisis-induced stress on the eight "dimensions of choice" and the seven "coping strategies" that have been specified above? In the second section of this chapter we will present some specific hypotheses on the first set of questions, i.e., on the relationships between stress and Brecher's "dimensions of crisis."

Crisis Periods

Since several choices will be made during a crisis, and since levels of stress will also vary, it is important to include in the model a means of differentiating stress levels. ICB studies posit a three-period model of crisis behavior, distinguishing a *pre-crisis period* (increased but still low stress), a *crisis period* (higher or highest stress), and a *post-crisis period* (low but still above-normal stress).

7. O. R. Holsti and A. L. George, "The Effects of Stress on the Performance of Foreign Policy-Makers," *Political Science Annual,* 6 (1975), 264. See this article for identification of the sources in which the various strategies were originally posited.

The word *crisis*, used alone or with a date, will be taken here to mean the entire phenomenon, from the first triggering event of the pre-crisis period to the return of all indicators to non-crisis levels at the end of the post-crisis period. The subdivisions of the total crisis are operationally defined as follows:

> The *pre-crisis period* is marked off from a preceding non-crisis period by a conspicuous increase in perceived threat on the part of decision-makers of the state under inquiry. It begins with the event (or cluster of events) that triggers a rise in threat perception.
>
> The *crisis period* is characterized by the presence of all three necessary conditions of crisis: a sharp rise in perceived threat to basic values, an awareness of time constraints on decisions, and a perceived probability of involvement in military hostilities (war likelihood) at some point before the issue is resolved. It, too, begins with a trigger event (or cluster of events). If war occurs at the outset of the crisis period or within its time frame, the third condition takes the form of a perceived decline in military capability vis-à-vis the enemy (or an adverse change in the military balance), i.e., increasing threat.
>
> The *post-crisis period* begins with an observable decline in intensity of one or more of the three perceptual conditions: threat, time pressure, and war probability. If the onset of this period is synonymous with the outbreak of war, the third condition is replaced by an image of greater military capability vis-à-vis the enemy (or favorable changes in the military balance), i.e., declining threat.

This periodization is incorporated in a three-stage elaboration of the basic model, presented in Figure 2. In this model, feedback from a decision made during any period, together with other environmental changes, may lead either to a repetition of the decision-making process on that level, or it may trigger the next level of crisis. For example, if feedback from a choice made during the pre-crisis period causes or is accompanied by an environmental change that is perceived as a sharp increase in threat, decision-makers will pass to the crisis period. It is posited—and will be tested in the case studies below—that this sharply increased perception in threat will be accompanied by perceptions of time pressure and likelihood of involvement in military hostilities.

Similarly, the decision process in the crisis period will repeat until feedback from the decisions, together with other environmental changes, brings about a de-escalation in one or more of the three crisis components. At this point the post-crisis period will begin. Finally, feedback and situational changes in the post-crisis period will lead to perceptions of "normal" threat, time pressure, and war probability, and the crisis ends.

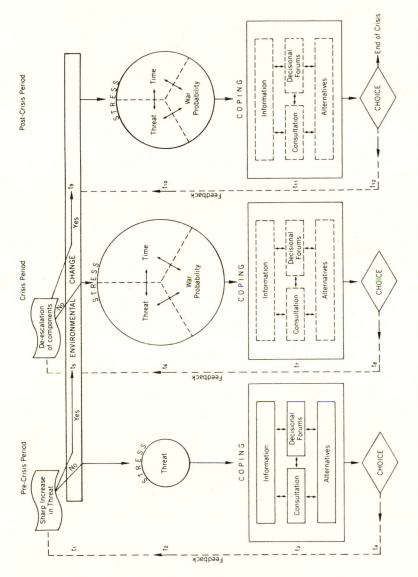

Figure 2. A Three-Stage Model of International Crisis Behavior

This dynamic model makes possible a more precise judgment on the relationship between stress levels and the other variables being examined than can be made from the single-stage model presented above (Figure 1). We can ask: Are there distinctive patterns of coping (as measured by our specific questions on coping mechanisms) in the pre-crisis, crisis, and post-crisis periods? And, of at least equal importance, are there distinctive patterns of choice (our "dimensions of choice" and "coping strategies") associated with the different crisis periods?

HYPOTHESES

Coping Mechanisms

It is possible to derive, from the behavioral literature, countless hypotheses on the relationship between stress and behavior in a decision-making context. One of the complications is the widely varying levels upon which the phenomenon has been studied; as Holsti and George point out, research has ranged from studies of laboratory animals at one end of the spectrum to entire social systems at the other.[8]

Research on foreign policy decision-making has usually focused on one or more of three levels of analysis: the individual, the group, or the organization. Interestingly enough, in studying the effects of stress, it is the individual level of analysis that has produced the most hypotheses and received the most attention. This may reflect the fact that cognitive psychologists have themselves focused more on questions clearly relating stress to (the individual's) performances, while social psychologists and organizational theorists have understandably tended to look more closely at pathologies associated with the group interactions and organizational peculiarities—and only secondarily at how these patterns change under stress. In addition, the effect of stress on the individual is perhaps more dramatic, and more easily isolated for analysis, than the more complicated relationships involving group interactions.

Thus, when Brecher surveyed the relevant literature in order to identify the most interesting and significant hypotheses on the relationship between crisis-induced stress and coping behavior in decisional forums, the major focus of the twenty-three hypotheses

8. Holsti and George, p. 272.

selected was on decision-making as a product of individual choice.[9] (These hypotheses, which Brecher tested for Israeli decisions in 1967 and 1973, are included in the hypotheses listed below.) The same could be said of the fifteen additional hypotheses that Brecher added on the basis of his own empirical findings.[10]

The tendency to focus on hypotheses drawn from studies of individuals under stress, as formulated by cognitive psychologists, has an important implication for the study of crisis decision-making, since research on the level of small groups or organizations has tended to produce less pessimistic conclusions about the impact of stress on decision-making. Holsti and George point out:

> As we shall demonstrate in this section, rather different diagnoses emerge from these three perspectives. Those who adopt a bureaucratic-organizational viewpoint tend to regard high stress as an impetus for reducing some of the pathologies of organizational behavior and they are, on balance, more sanguine about the consequences of stress. Analysts who focus upon a small group perspective tend to be considerably less optimistic about decision-making under such circumstances. Finally, those who conceive of decision-making as the product of individual choice are almost uniformly pessimistic about performance of complex cognitive tasks when stress is experienced.[11]

Thus, in order to test more fully the issue of whether stress has a dysfunctional influence on decision-making *in an organizational context,* this study will add to Brecher's hypotheses some additional propositions, suggested by Holsti and George's survey, that tend to focus on small group and organizational theory (a foreign policy bureaucracy being, among other things, a complex organization). As will be seen, these hypotheses do tend to have *optimistic* implications regarding the impact of crisis on decision-making.

The hypotheses to be examined will be grouped according to the coping mechanism involved:

INFORMATION

Of Brecher's thirty-eight hypotheses derived from the literature and his own crisis studies, eleven deal with information and communication patterns. Combining similar propositions leaves nine distinct hypotheses:

9. Brecher, 1980, pp. 343, 375–378.
10. Ibid., pp. 397–402.
11. Holsti and George, p. 272.

1. The greater the stress, the greater the conceptual rigidity of an individual, and the more closed to new information the individual becomes.[12]

2. The greater the crisis, the greater the propensity for decision-makers to supplement information about the objective state of affairs with information drawn from their own past experience.[13]

3. The greater the crisis, the greater the felt need for information, the more thorough the quest for information, and the more open the receptivity to new information.[14]

4. The greater the crisis, the more information about it tends to be elevated to the top of the organizational [decisional] pyramid quickly and without distortion.[15]

5. The higher the stress in a crisis situation, the greater the tendency to rely upon extraordinary and improvised channels of communication [and information].[16]

6. In crises, the rate of communication by a nation's decision-makers to international actors outside their country will increase.[17]

7. As crisis-induced stress increases, the search for information is likely to become more active, but it may also become more random and less productive.[18]

8. As crisis-induced stress declines, the quest for information becomes more restricted.[19]

12. This is a combination of Propositions 1 and 2 in H. B. Shapiro and M. A. Gilbert, *Crisis Management: Psychological and Sociological Factors in Decision-Making* (Arlington, Va.: Office of Naval Research, 1975), pp. 19, 20. The first half of the hypothesis is derived from J. W. Moffitt and R. Stagner, "Perceptual Rigidity and Closure as a Function of Anxiety," *Journal of Abnormal and Social Psychology,* 52 (1956), 355. The second half is derived from O. R. Holsti, *Crisis, Escalation, War* (Montreal: McGill-Queens University Press, 1972a), pp. 15, 19.

13. G. D. Paige, *The Korean Decision* (New York: Free Press, 1968), p. 295; T. W. Milburn, "The Management of Crisis," in C. F. Hermann, ed., *International Crises: Insights from Behavioral Research* (New York: Free Press, 1972), p. 274; and psychological findings cited in Holsti and George, p. 281.

14. Paige, 1968, p. 292; the hypothesis is modified to include Brecher's hypotheses on thorough information quest and receptivity, based on his own cases (Brecher, 1980, p. 397).

15. Paige, 1968, p. 292; Holsti and George, pp. 296–297.

16. O. R. Holsti, "Time, Alternatives, and Communications: The 1914 and Cuban Missile Crises," in Hermann, 1972, p. 75.

17. Hermann, "Threat, Time, and Surprise: A Simulation of International Crisis," in Hermann, 1972, pp. 202–204.

18. J. C. March and H. A. Simon, *Organizations* (New York: John Wiley, 1958), p. 116.

19. Brecher, 1980, p. 399.

9. As crisis-induced stress declines, receptivity becomes permeated by more bias.[20]

It will be noted that only one of the "cognitive" hypotheses above (No. 3) draws clearly optimistic implications regarding the impact of increased stress, while the "organizational" hypotheses (4, 5, and 6) tend as a group to posit less potentially dysfunctional effects. There are three additional ideas in Holsti and George's survey of the decision-making literature, linking increased stress to impaired cognitive functioning, that seem important enough to be tested in this study:

10. The more intense the crisis, the greater the tendency of decision-makers to perceive that everything in the external environment is related to everything else.[21]

11. The more intense the crisis, the less the sensitivity to, and learning from, negative feedback.[22]

12. The more intense the crisis, the greater the tendency to an overabundance of new information (information overload) and a paucity of usable data on decision-making levels.[23]

CONSULTATION

Brecher has identified six important hypotheses regarding consultation during crisis, based on the literature and his own case studies. These hypotheses are more closely linked to small group or organizational theory, and—as Holsti and George would lead us to expect—have more sanguine implications for the impact of stress on decision-making:

13. The longer the decision time [in a crisis], the greater the consultation with persons outside the core decisional unit.[24]

14. The greater the crisis, the greater the felt need for face-to-face proximity among decision-makers.[25]

15. As crisis-induced stress increases, the scope and frequency of consultation by senior decision-makers also increase.[26]

20. Ibid.
21. Holsti and George, p. 280, based on Milburn, p. 275.
22. Holsti and George, pp. 282–283.
23. Holsti, 1972a, pp. 104–117; Holsti and George, p. 298.
24. Paige, "Comparative Case Analysis of Crisis Decisions: Korea and Cuba," in Hermann, 1972, p. 52.
25. Paige, 1968, p. 288; and I. L. Janis, *Victims of Groupthink: A Psychological Study of Foreign Policy Decisions and Fiascos* (Boston: Houghton Mifflin, 1972), pp. 4–5.
26. Brecher, 1980, p. 399. This hypothesis combines two similar hypotheses (Nos. 5 and 7) in Brecher's list of new hypotheses suggested by his case studies.

16. As crisis-induced stress increases, decision-makers increasingly use ad hoc forms of consultation.[27]

17. As crisis-induced stress declines, the consultative circle becomes narrower.[28]

18. As crisis-induced stress declines, consultation relies heavily on ad hoc settings as high-level consultation reaches its peak.[29]

The link between organizational analysis and optimistic conclusions is made even more pointedly in another hypothesis on consultation derived from the Holsti and George survey:

19. The more intense the crisis, the less the influence of vested interests and other groups outside the bureaucracy.[30]

DECISIONAL FORUMS

Brecher offers eight hypotheses on decisional forums, most of them related to group or organizational theory, which are generally ambiguous on the issue of impaired decision-making:

20. The longer the crisis, the greater the felt need for effective leadership within decisional units.[31]

21. The longer the decision time, the greater the conflict within decisional units.[32]

22. The greater the group conflict aroused by a crisis, the greater the consensus once a decision is reached.[33]

23. The longer the amount of time available in which to make a decision, the greater will be the consensus on the final choice.[34]

24. Crisis decisions tend to be reached by ad hoc decisional units.[35]

25. In high-stress situations, decision groups tend to become smaller.[36]

27. Ibid.
28. Ibid.
29. Ibid.
30. Holsti and George, p. 297.
31. Paige, 1968, p. 289, and 1972, pp. 52, 305.
32. Paige, 1972, p. 52. This is also supported by U.S. Foreign Service officers' perceptions; see H. H. Lentner, "The Concept of Crisis as Viewed by the United States Department of State," in Hermann, 1972, p. 133. The Lentner proposition reads: "Crises raise tensions among the policy makers involved and heighten the stress and anxiety they experience."
33. Shapiro and Gilbert, p. 55, derived from findings on business and government decision-making groups, reported in H. Guetzkow and J. Gyr, "An Analysis of Conflict in Decision-Making Groups," *Human Relations,* 7 (1954), 367–381.
34. Shapiro and Gilbert, p. 56, derived from Paige, 1972, p. 52, and R. L. Frye and T. M. Stritch, "Effects of Timed versus Non-Timed Discussion Upon Measures of Influence and Change in Small Groups," *Journal of Social Psychology,* 63 (1964), 141.
35. Paige, 1968, p. 281.
36. Holsti and George, p. 288, and Hermann, in Hermann, 1972, p. 197.

26. In crises, decision-making becomes increasingly centralized.[37]

27. As crisis-induced stress rises, there is a heavy reliance on medium-to-large and institutional forums for decisions.[38]

28. As crisis-induced stress declines, there is a maximum reliance on large, institutional forums for decisions.[39]

Some other hypotheses from the study of groups and organizations have, however, clearer implications regarding their impact on decision-making, and are sufficiently interesting to be added here (many have been the subject of extensive discussion in both behavioral and political scientific literature). The first of these hypotheses has negative implications for crisis decision-making, but the others embody the Holsti and George premise that crisis may, to the contrary, reduce some of the "pathologies" of organizational behavior:

29. The more intense the crisis, the greater the tendency of decision-makers to conform to group goals and norms, and the less the dissent within the group.[40]

30. The more intense the crisis, the less the influence of "standard operating procedures."[41]

31. The more intense the crisis, the greater the role in decision-making of officials with a general rather than a "parochial" perspective.[42]

32. The more intense the crisis, the less the influence of vested interests in the bureaucracy ("bureaucratic politics").[43]

ALTERNATIVES

The eleven major hypotheses that Brecher has identified on the search for and evaluation of alternatives contain both positive and negative implications for the quality of crisis decision-making. Most focus, again, on the individual cognitive level, with some exceptions (e.g., Nos. 34 and 36):

33. As stress increases, decision-makers become more concerned with the immediate than the long-run future.[44]

37. Lentner, p. 130.
38. Brecher, 1980, p. 399.
39. Ibid.
40. Holsti and George, pp. 285–293.
41. Ibid., p. 296.
42. Ibid.
43. Ibid., p. 297.
44. O. R. Holsti, "The 1914 Case," *American Political Science Review*, 59 (June 1965), 365; Holsti, 1972b, pp. 14–17, 200; and G. T. Allison and M. H. Halperin, "Bureaucratic Politics: A Paradigm and Some Policy Implications," in R. Tanter and R. H. Ullman, eds., *Theory and Policy in International Relations* (Princeton: Princeton University Press, 1973), p. 50.

34. The greater the reliance on group problem-solving processes, the greater the consideration of alternatives.[45]

35. During crisis the search for alternatives occupies a substantial part of decision-making time.[46]

36. The relationship between stress and group performance in the consideration of alternatives is curvilinear (an inverted U)— more careful as stress rises to a moderate level, less careful as stress becomes intense.[47]

37. Despite the rise in stress, choices among alternatives are not, for the most part, made before adequate information is processed; that is, there is not a tendency to premature closure.[48]

38. As time pressure increases, the choice among alternatives does not become less correct.[49]

39. Decision-makers do not generally choose among alternatives with an inadequate assessment of their consequences.[50]

40. As crisis-induced stress increases, the search for options tends to increase.[51]

41. As crisis-induced stress increases, the evaluation of alternatives becomes less careful.[52]

42. As crisis-induced stress declines, the search for options tends to become less extensive than in all other phases of the crisis period.[53]

43. As crisis-induced stress declines, the evaluation of alternatives reaches its maximum care, more so when time salience is low.[54]

To this we shall add two additional hypotheses suggested by the Holsti and George survey, one (No. 44) a cognitive proposition with negative implications, and the other (No. 45) derived from the organizational level of analysis, with more positive projections:

45. Shapiro and Gilbert, p. 83, derived from Paige, 1972, p. 51.
46. J. A. Robinson, "Crisis: An Appraisal of Concepts and Theories," in Hermann, 1972, p. 26, based upon H. A. Simon, "Political Research: The Decision-Making Framework," in D. Easton, ed., *Varieties of Political Theory* (Englewood Cliffs, N.J.: Prentice-Hall, 1966), p. 19. Hermann, in Hermann, 1972, p. 210, and Holsti, 1972, p. 121, hypothesize that under stress the search for options is reduced.
47. Shapiro and Gilbert, p. 36; Milburn, p. 264; Holsti and George, p. 278.
48. Hermann, in Hermann, 1972, p. 210, and Holsti, 1972, p. 121.
49. Shapiro and Gilbert, pp. 36–37.
50. D. G. Pruitt, "Definition of the Situation as a Determinant of International Action," in H. C. Kelman, ed., *International Behavior* (New York: Holt, Rinehart and Winston, 1966), p. 411; and psychological findings cited in Holsti and George, pp. 278–279.
51. Brecher, 1980, p. 399.
52. Ibid.
53. Ibid., p. 402.
54. Ibid.

44. The more intense the crisis, the greater the tendency of decision-makers to narrow their span of attention to a few aspects of the decision-making task ("tunnel vision").[55]

45. The more intense the crisis, the more likely that decision-makers will be forced to make a clear choice rather than postponing choices or drifting into policy.[56]

Patterns of Choice

In a similar effort to identify the more significant and interesting ideas suggested by his own case studies, Brecher proposes seventeen hypotheses on the relationship between crisis-induced stress and the *dimensions of choice* already identified above.[57] Categorized according to the dimensions, these are:

CORE INPUTS

46. As crisis-induced stress begins to rise, the number and variety of core inputs to decisions increase sharply.

47. As crisis-induced stress declines, the number and variety of core inputs are reduced.

COSTS

48. When decision-makers operate under stress, they assess their decision as costly.

49. When decision-makers operate under low or declining stress, they perceive their decisions as of small cost.

IMPORTANCE

50. As crisis-induced stress rises, decision-makers tend to perceive their decisions as more and more important.

51. As crisis-induced stress declines, the perceived importance of decisions declines from the levels in all other phases of the crisis period.

COMPLEXITY

52. As crisis-induced stress rises, the complexity of issue-areas involved steadily rises.

53. As crisis-induced stress declines, the number of issue-areas involved in decision-making reaches its maximum.

55. Holsti and George, p. 279.
56. Ibid.
57. Brecher, 1980, pp. 402–403.

SYSTEMIC DOMAIN

54. In situations of peak crisis-induced stress, the heretofore steadily-broadening systemic levels of anticipated reverberations from decisions become narrower.

55. As crisis-induced stress declines, systemic domain rises from the peak crisis phase.

PROCESS

56. As crisis-induced stress rises, the selected option tends to be chosen by rational calculus and analysis of the issues, rather than by a process of bargaining and compromise.[58]

57. As crisis-induced stress declines, decision-makers resort mainly to rational procedures to ultimate choice.

ACTIVITY

58. As crisis-induced stress rises, there is a tendency for decisions to be continuously active.

59. As crisis-induced stress rises, the activity implied by the decisions moves from physical to verbal.

60. As crisis-induced stress declines, there is a sharp increase in decisions to delay or not to act.

NOVELTY

61. As crisis-induced stress rises, there is a steady increase in resort to choices without precedent.

62. As crisis-induced stress declines, unprecedented choices remain at their peak.

All of these hypotheses, together with those on coping mechanisms, will be tested in the concluding chapter, following the presentation of the case studies.

RESEARCH PROCEDURES

Case Studies

The cases chosen for analysis here are the Lebanese crisis of 1958, the Syria-Jordan crisis of 1970, and the Yom Kippur War of 1973. All three episodes involved U.S. decision-makers in crucial questions of

---

58. This combines Brecher's Hypothesis No. 26 (ibid.) with some suggestions of Holsti and George, p. 299.

diplomatic and military intervention, the survival of dependent regimes or states, and confrontation with the Soviet Union.

Since these three crises were chosen as part of a stratified sample of all international crises since 1938, there is no claim that they are in any sense "representative" of U.S. policy in Middle East crises. It was simply found convenient to put together in one book those three cases, from a sample of over thirty, that happened to involve Middle East crises in U.S. foreign policy. Though the cases span a fifteen-year period and cover two presidential administrations, a strong case could be made for including other crises (1948, or 1956, or 1967) if one were aiming for a sample that would best represent the range of U.S. crisis behavior in the Middle East.

Nevertheless, as the sample does represent three major cases from the rather small total of U.S. Middle East crises, the conclusions should be of interest from the perspective of a specialist on U.S. foreign policy or the Middle East, as well as that of a student of crisis. This should be especially true of observations that seem to hold for all three crises.

Organization

The body of this study is an analysis in depth of the three case studies. Each crisis is divided into four chapters, with the first three covering the pre-crisis, crisis, and post-crisis periods of the 1958, 1970, and 1973 cases, respectively. Within each of these substantive chapters, identification of the major decisions and decision-makers is followed by an extensive analysis of the psychological environment: the general attitudinal prism and the individual images of the senior decision-makers. Then the "decision flow"—the process by which the major decisions were made—is reconstructed.

The fourth chapter of each part of the book summarizes the conclusions to be drawn from that historic case regarding the impact of crisis-induced stress on decision-making, and makes a preliminary assessment of the findings from that case regarding the hypotheses stated above.

Part IV consists of two chapters, the first of which briefly compares the three crises with regard to crisis components. Finally, the concluding chapter draws together the evidence, examines the hypotheses on coping mechanisms and patterns of choice more systematically, and concludes with some general observations on both crisis decision-making and U.S. foreign policy in Middle East crises—as seen in the three cases studied.

Methodology

Research for all three crises was based, for the most part, on standard historical sources. For the 1970 and 1973 crises, extensive interviewing of participants in U.S. decision-making was carried out (see the list in the bibliography). By and large, interviewees were willing to be cited or quoted; those who preferred to speak "on background" have been identified by their general position at the time.

Other unpublished materials—oral histories and government documents—were in some cases available, especially for the 1958 crisis. Published memoirs were in all cases an important primary source. The amount of secondary material, especially for the 1973 war, is voluminous, though it is not always illuminating on the issues posed in this study.

While Brecher has made profitable use of content analysis of decision-makers' statements in identifying and describing the images of Israeli leaders, the much smaller quantity of public statements made by U.S. decision-makers during these crises made any sophisticated analysis of this sort impossible here. A relatively primitive content analysis has been carried out where possible, and has generally confirmed the conclusions reached by traditional methods.

PART I

THE LEBANESE CRISIS

CHAPTER TWO

1958: 8 May to 13 July

DURING THE 1950s, the focus of U.S.-Soviet clashes moved from the "central" area of Europe, where the crises of the late 1940s had occurred, to the "peripheral" areas of Asia, Africa, and Latin America. The search for an American policy appropriate to the new circumstances was nowhere more intense than in the Middle East, where a series of crises faced policy-makers with difficult judgments involving Soviet penetration and Arab nationalism. The Suez Crisis of 1956, in particular, raised the difficult issue of how to deal with the rising force of Nasserist Arab nationalism, with its radical and anti-Western tone, in the framework of a policy still oriented fundamentally to the containment—if not the total defeat—of Soviet and/or Communist power in the world at large. Suez also demonstrated some of the attendant dilemmas raised by the issue in relations with West European allies, with other Third World nations, and in the U.S. attitude toward the United Nations. The official response, after the crisis, was embodied in the "Eisenhower Doctrine," which in fact left a number of question marks by again defining the central problem as a struggle against "international communism."

One of these question marks was Lebanon, where a pro-Western government was faced with growing unrest during the year and a half following the Suez Crisis. The approach of Lebanese presidential elections, scheduled for mid-1958, brought this unrest to a high level; and on May 8, 1958, the assassination of an anti-government newspaper editor triggered the eruption of open civil war. With the United States's own allies largely out of the picture, and with "Nasserism" threatening to sweep the entire Middle East, U.S. policy-makers were forced to deal directly with a local situation that was under-

23

stood to have important implications for the entire region as well as for U.S.-Soviet relations and worldwide American prestige and credibility. During a lengthy pre-crisis period of two months, local, regional, and global considerations were intertwined in determining the American response to a situation in which the nature and extent of the threat were far from clear.

DECISIONS AND DECISION-MAKERS

There were two major decisions in the 1958 pre-crisis period:

Decision Number	Date	Content
1	13 May	In response to a Lebanese query, President Eisenhower responded that the United States would intervene as a last resort under specified circumstances and conditions, but not for the purpose of supporting Lebanese President Camille Chamoun's possible bid for re-election; light military equipment was airlifted to Beirut, and precautionary military moves were taken, including operational planning for intervention.
2	ca. 22 May	In line with the first decision, the State Department decided to support the Lebanese decision to turn to the UN Security Council.
3	ca. 11 June	Eisenhower decided not to respond favorably to a message from Egyptian President Gamal Abdel Nasser outlining a proposed resolution of the crisis.
4	15 June	Eisenhower and his advisors postponed a decision on direct action, in response to rebel success, pending further information.

The two major decision-makers for the United States in the pre-crisis period were President Dwight David Eisenhower and Secretary of State John Foster Dulles. Also participating in important deliberations were Neil McElroy, Secretary of Defense; General Nathan Twining, Chairman of the Joint Chiefs of Staff; and Allen Dulles, Director of the Central Intelligence Agency. The most influential second-level figures, who were often present in decisive meetings, were Christian Herter, Under Secretary of State; Robert Murphy,

Deputy Under Secretary of State for Political Affairs; Donald Quarles, Deputy Secretary of Defense; and Robert Cutler, Presidential Advisor for National Security (a role whose secondary importance should not be confused with the centrality it came to assume in later administrations). The U.S. Ambassador in Beirut, Robert McClintock, was also influential in policy deliberations by virtue of his personality and experience. Generally speaking, however, area specialists were not included in the higher-level policy debates and were not especially influential in the making of American policy during this period.[1]

PSYCHOLOGICAL ENVIRONMENT

Attitudinal Prism

Eisenhower and Dulles perceived the international situation in a generally similar fashion. At the heart of their shared perceptual universe was their *image of the Soviet Union*. Soviet leaders were seen as motivated by Communist ideology (as opposed to traditional Russian interests), implacably hostile to the West, and inherently expansionist. There could be little, if any, chance for meaningful accommodation between Communism and the West. Communism was seen as a monolithic international movement, and Communist parties as agents of Moscow. Against such a threat, all non-Communists were by definition part of the "free world," and should in their own interest unite to resist the common danger. Neutralism, in this context, was mistaken and immoral. Likewise, any program of long-range coexistence with such an enemy could not be entertained; the eventual goal of the free world must be the defeat, not merely the containment, of Soviet and Communist power. Unfortunately, the anti-Western nationalism and neutralism prevalent in the Third World made it difficult to rally these areas to the common effort, and furthermore made them, in American eyes, highly susceptible to Communist propaganda and subversion.[2]

1. According to one firsthand report, there were at this time no senior diplomats proficient in Arabic in either the Beirut Embassy or the Middle East division of the State Department. Charles W. Thayer, *Diplomat* (New York: Harper and Brothers, 1959), p. 14.

2. The definitive study of the Dulles world view is Ole R. Holsti, "Cognitive Dynamics and Images of the Enemy: Dulles and Russia," in David J. Finlay, Ole R. Holsti, and Richard R. Fagan, *Enemies in Politics* (Chicago: Rand McNally, 1967), Chapter 2. For a critique of the Eisenhower administration's perceptions as they related to the Middle East, see Leila M. T. Meo, *Lebanon, Improbable Nation: A Study in Political Development* (Bloomington: Indiana University Press, 1965), pp. 108–110.

Dulles, who prided himself on his knowledge of the Marxist scrip-
tures, saw a *Soviet Third-World strategy* that was using Asia and
Africa as the key to the ultimate destruction of the West, which was
in the meantime too strong to be attacked directly.[3] Thus, the
changes in Soviet policy that took place in the 1950s, with conciliatory moves in Europe and greater openness generally, were seen not
as moderation but as merely a change in tactics. The Soviets were
aiming to exploit unrest anywhere in the world as part of their overall scheme for weakening the West.[4]

State Department Arabists tended to share the prevailing view of
the Soviet Union's aims in the Middle East. Typical, if somewhat
more frankly expressed, was the assessment offered after the fact by
Parker Hart, Deputy Assistant Secretary of State for Near Eastern
and South Asian Affairs. Beginning with the premise that the Communists were planning to take over the Middle East, Hart identified
two methods: alliance with indigenous nationalist groups, and the
establishment of cohesive separate Communist parties. Both tactics
could be pursued simultaneously, and in Hart's analysis the distinction between the two does not appear to have been very important
on the operational level. In time of turmoil, the Communists would
seize power from the nationalists. Hart identified the Greek civil war
of 1946–47, the Turkish crisis of the same period, Iran in 1953, and
Syria in 1957 as examples of this pattern; all involved Communist
attempts to seize control of the government through alliance with
nationalist forces.[5]

U.S. policy-makers thus saw military intervention by the Soviet
Union as only one of the risks to be faced, and perhaps not the most
likely one. The danger of subversion by Moscow-allied elements was
perhaps a more immediate threat in the many unstable areas of the
world. Any instability could, in fact, create an opportunity that Communists could exploit, and the great instability of the Middle East was
therefore a focus of special concern. Jordan and Syria, as well as
Lebanon, were seen as highly vulnerable. Most Middle Eastern states
seemed to possess few organized groups comparable in cohesion and
discipline to the local Communist parties. Military establishments
were weak and highly susceptible to subversion from the inside. All
of these factors seemed especially marked in the "Fertile Crescent"

3. See, for example, Sherman Adams, *Firsthand Report: The Story of the Eisenhower Administration* (New York: Harper and Brothers, 1961), p. 293.
    4. Dwight David Eisenhower, *The White House Years: Waging Peace, 1956–1961*
(Garden City, N.Y.: Doubleday, 1965), p. 266.
    5. Hart's address was delivered on May 1, 1959, and is reprinted in *Department
of State Bulletin,* 40 (May 18, 1959), 117.

area from Israel to Iraq, in which there were few natural or univer-
sally respected national or ethnic borders, and in which the "spill-
over" of events from one country to its neighbors was especially
feared.[6]

Policy-makers paid an unusual amount of attention to the small
Communist parties of the Middle East. In the 1958 edition of its
annual survey of Communist party strength throughout the world,
the State Department estimated the Syrian Communist Party at only
12,000–15,000 members, but pointed out that Syria "is, in fact, gov-
erned by an alliance of pro-Soviet politicians, army officers, and opportunists." The outlawed Lebanese Communist Party was
estimated to have 8,000 members, and it was claimed that "Beirut
is a center for the preparation and dissemination of Communist
propaganda in the Near East. . . ." Regarding the Jordanian party,
which was said to have all of 300 members, the report claimed
5,000–6,000 active supporters and declared that "Communist and
front organization activity has increased considerably since the an-
nexation of former Arab Palestine. . . ." Ironically, only in the case of
the 500-member Iraqi party did the State Department feel that the
threat had been countered effectively—by the successful counterrevolutionary actions of the Iraqi government.[7]

Eisenhower administration officials demonstrated *hostility to radical Arab nationalism,* which they dealt with as a movement linked
to Communism. Whether they really perceived Arab nationalism as
necessarily tied to Communism is debatable.[8] But nationalist leaders
were seen as front men, consciously or unconsciously, for Moscow,
and their aspirations and programs seemed to Washington indistinguishable from a program of Soviet domination. The domestic context of their motives and actions was minimized; Arab leaders were
judged by the impact of their immediate moves on the vital struggle
to prevent the strengthening of the Soviet (or Communist) position
in the region. If an Arab government acted so as to give "aid and
comfort" to the enemy, then it became part of the opposition, whatever its true composition or whatever its actual motive. This was, in

6. Herbert K. Tillema, *Appeal to Force: American Military Intervention in the Era
of Containment* (New York: Crowell, 1973), pp. 74–75.

7. U.S. Department of State, Bureau of Intelligence and Research, *World Strength
of the Communist Party Organizations.* Annual Report No. 10. Washington, D.C.:
Department of State, 1958.

8. Townsend Hoopes, in *The Devil and John Foster Dulles* (Boston: Little, Brown,
1973), p. 431, hints that Dulles's tendency to identify Arab nationalism with Communism may have been a ploy to strengthen domestic support for a policy of intervention.
Even if true, of course, this only reaffirms the fact that Dulles was hostile to radical
Arab nationalism whether he perceived it as necessarily linked to Communism or not.

other words, a doctrine of judging by actions; as expressed by Dulles in the hearings over the Eisenhower Doctrine:

> The determination of whether a country is dominated by inter-
> national communism is a close question in some cases, and . . . is
> determined by a whole complex of actions or lack of actions which
> the government takes in its international and domestic affairs.[9]

The Eisenhower-Dulles attitudinal prism was also shaped by a certain preoccupation with the *analogy of the 1930s.* This was true of an entire generation of Western statesmen (Anthony Eden, Charles de Gaulle, etc.) for whom the struggle against Nazism had been their formative life experience. Consider a typical Dulles quotation, taken from a diplomatic cable during the pre-crisis period:

> The United States believes that the issue which confronts the
> United Nations is a grave one. If it is not met, the United Nations
> might go the way the League of Nations went when it failed to
> take effective action in defense of Manchuria and Abyssinia. Nor do
> we believe that the situation will be better if Lebanon is in effect
> coerced into Munich-like appeasement, which in effect is surrender
> to the UAR.[10]

The Eisenhower-Dulles approach was also known for its *focus on extended deterrence,* expressed popularly in one context as a doctrine of "massive retaliation." On a more conceptual level, this was basically the assumption that East-West issues were but part of a spectrum, and that by virtue of the linkage among these issues, the United States should not allow the Soviet Union to separate out those issues and battlegrounds where it enjoyed the best relative advantage. Instead, any issue would be regarded as part of the overall challenge, necessitating a full American response. By purposely putting the stakes high on seemingly minor questions, the United States would avoid piecemeal defeats. Of course, this strategy also assumed that the Soviet Union would behave in a rational fashion, just as deterrence theory generally assumes rationality. But the Eisenhower-Dulles view of Communism did not see Soviet leaders as irrational or wild; to the contrary, they were regarded as calculating and pur-

9. U.S. Senate, *Hearings Before the Committee on Foreign Relations and the Committee on Armed Services on Senate Joint Resolution 19 and House Joint Resolution 117,* Part I, January–February 1957 (Washington, D.C.: Government Printing Office, 1957), p. 29. See also Meo, pp. 111–112, and Melvin Gurtov, *The United States Against the Third World* (New York and Washington, D.C.: Praeger, 1974), pp. 38–39.

10. Dulles to U.S. Embassy Paris, June 24, 1958. *Declassified Documents Reference System* [henceforth *DDRS*], 1977. (Washington, D.C.: Carrollton Press, 1978).

poseful, and therefore as responsive to the logic of deterrence. As Eisenhower put it:

> Such operations [as the Korean War] had convinced me that if "small wars" were to break out in several places in the world simultaneously, then we should not fight on the enemy's terms and be limited to his choice of weapons. We would hold the Kremlin— or Peking—responsible for their actions and would act accordingly. These facts were not secret; they were well-advertised. The Communists had come to be aware of our attitude and there was reason to think that they respected it.[11]

A final element in the administration's outlook that should be noted is its *legalism*. Dulles himself was, of course, a lawyer with decades of practice, while Eisenhower has been described as something of a "Whig" when it came to constitutional issues, construing his own prerogatives on narrow legal grounds. The constitutional authority for Presidential action in Lebanon was a constant concern, and the Eisenhower Doctrine (like similar Congressional resolutions on other critical areas, such as Berlin or the Formosa Straits) was the favorite instrument for Middle East policy because of the Congressional approval that it carried. Both Eisenhower and Dulles were careful during the pre-crisis period to lay the legal groundwork for any possible U.S. military action, basically by "expanding" the Eisenhower Doctrine to cover more than blatant cases of overt aggression. There was also a strict attention to legal issues involving the United Nations, with Dulles stressing Article 51 of the UN Charter (the right of individual and collective self-defense) as justification for outside assistance to Lebanon, and resurrecting a 1949 UN resolution on "indirect aggression" as an instrument for the condemnation of UAR "aggression" in Lebanon.[12]

Images

Aside from their shared perceptions, what specific images were held by the two major decision-makers, and how—if at all—did they differ? The perceptual universe of John Foster Dulles has attracted much systematic scholarly attention, partly because of its distinctiveness and consistency as a model of a certain approach to international politics, and partly because Dulles is considered by many to have

11. Eisenhower, p. 291.
12. See especially Dulles press conferences of May 20 (*Department of State Bulletin* [henceforth *DSB*], June 9, 1958), June 17 (*DSB*, July 7, 1958), and July 1 (*DSB*, July 21, 1958).

been the real architect of Eisenhower-era foreign policy (a conclusion that is, incidentally, not valid for the 1958 crisis). Dulles's own
personal style is usually described as rigid and moralistic in a sense
that Eisenhower's was not. Ole Holsti's definitive study of Dulles's
belief system, as revealed in content analysis of all his public statements during his term in office, identifies the following central elements:

1. A "theological" world view that saw international politics as a
   struggle between the forces of good and evil.
2. A belief in moral power as the basic factor in political success.
3. Identification of "atheistic" Communism as the antithesis of
   Dulles's own core values, and opposition to Communism as a
   moral as well as a practical obligation.
4. An "inherent bad faith" model of the Soviet Union that
   consistently placed the worst interpretation on Soviet behavior.[13]

Dulles's public statements during this pre-crisis period, at four
press conferences, bear witness to his moralistic style. Analysis of his
statements leads to the identification of twenty-one different statements of belief; of these, thirteen dealt with legal and/or moral
justifications for U.S. action in defense of Lebanon. Typical of Dulles's
statements was his argument on "indirect aggression," as expressed
at a June 17 press conference:

> I would also recall the fact that, even though at the moment the
> disturbance assumes, in part at least, the character of a civil
> disturbance, it is covered by the United Nations resolution of 1949
> on indirect aggression.[14]

Dulles also was careful to reiterate more than once that "we do not
introduce American forces into foreign countries except on the invitation of the lawful government of the state concerned."[15] In this
way he also distinguished between a possible U.S. intervention in
Lebanon and the 1956 British-French action in the Suez crisis,
"where the armed intervention was against the will of the Government concerned."[16] Likewise, attention was paid to the domestic
legal basis for U.S. action, given the doubtful applicability of the
"international communism" provision of the Eisenhower Doctrine:

> That doesn't mean, however, that there is nothing that can be
> done. There is the provision of the Middle East resolution which
> says that the independence of these countries is vital to peace and

13. Holsti, 1967, pp. 36–46.
14. *DSB,* July 7, 1958.
15. Press conference of May 20, 1958; *DSB,* June 9, 1958.
16. Press conference of July 1, 1958; *DSB,* July 21, 1958.

the national interest of the United States. That is certainly a
mandate to do something if we think that our peace and vital
interests are endangered from any quarter.[17]

Eisenhower, while sharing the same basic perception of the Soviet
Union, was in some respects more open, more practical, and less
dogmatic in his approach to world politics. The best account of the
differences between Eisenhower and Dulles is that of Emmet John
Hughes, who worked closely with Eisenhower as a speechwriter
during various periods of his Presidency. Hughes draws a sharp contrast between Dulles's instinctive opposition to any dealing with the
Soviet Union, and Eisenhower's occasional willingness to pursue bold
initiatives aimed at reducing tensions. Hughes even attests to Eisenhower's "breadth and sensitivity of view" in international affairs:
"The drive for West European unity, the need for freer world trade,
the crucial importance of the Anglo-American alliance, the indis-
pensability of mutual security programs, the wisdom of greater
rather than less economic contact with the Communist world—all
these concepts were firmly anchored in his thinking."[18]

Characterizing Dulles as essentially a lawyer—"in effect, the prosecutor assigned to the historic labor of arraignment, condemnation,
and punishment of the Soviet Union for crimes against freedom and
peace"—Hughes argues that

> There was no anomaly in all the Eisenhower years so remarkable in
> nature, and so historic in consequence, as the official kinship of this
> President and this Secretary of State. Their differences in personal
> temper and world outlook attained an almost unblemished study in
> contrasts. Where the one was expansive, the other was suspicious;
> where the one was occasionally vague, the other was fastidiously
> precise; where the one valued the thrust of "instinct," the other
> lived by the rule of logic; where the one would warmly hail the
> hope of a new act or initiative, the other would stoically press the
> warning of its peril or cost; where the one might risk credulity, the
> other risked cynicism.[19]

Yet, as Hughes himself admits, despite the differences between
them in temperament and cognitive rigidity, Eisenhower and Dulles
worked together successfully for six years and molded a foreign policy that generally satisfied the inclinations of both. Nor was this
simply a matter of Dulles dominating, as some would have it. At least
in the 1958 crisis, as will be shown, Eisenhower's role was central in
fact as well as in theory.

17. Press conference of May 20, 1958; *DSB,* June 9, 1958.
18. Emmet John Hughes, *The Ordeal of Power: A Political Memoir of the Eisenhower Years* (New York: Atheneum, 1963), pp. 150–151.
19. Hughes, pp. 205–206. See also pp. 69–71, 109–110, 343–344.

Eisenhower, however, made few public statements about Lebanon during the pre-crisis period. In two of his three press conferences
during this time, he declined all comment on Lebanon because of the
delicacy of the situation—a reticence with which the assertive Dulles
was seldom afflicted. When Eisenhower did comment on Lebanon,
his statement, like Dulles's remarks, reflected concern over the legal
and procedural proprieties:

> Now we do know that the United Nations group has gone out
> there, and General *[sic]* Hammerskjold is taking this whole matter
> under his earnest and personal view. I should say that it would be
> dependent somewhat upon the judgments of the armistice team
> and the Secretary General as to what we might have to do.[20]

Recent Experiences

A number of specific events over the previous two years contributed
to the Eisenhower administration's sense of Middle East instability,
Soviet pressure, and the necessity of an American response. The Suez
crisis of 1956 had deeply sensitized administration officials to the
threat represented by radical nationalist leaders, even if the United
States had opposed intervention in that particular case. British Prime
Minister Harold Macmillan explained the changed American attitude toward intervention two years later as a result of experience:
"Fortunately the Americans have learned a lot since Suez, and the
Bermuda and Washington visits are beginning to show results."[21]
Dulles was, however, at pains to deny "any analogy whatsoever"
between Lebanon and Suez, on the grounds (as stated above) that in
the Lebanese case a lawful government was calling for assistance.[22]
Nevertheless, for American policy-makers, Suez and its aftermath
were part of their disillusionment with Nasser.

The unrest in Jordan in 1957 provided, in a sense, a rehearsal for
Lebanon in 1958. In February of that year, King Hussein had tried
to reorganize his Cabinet, setting off open opposition in the country
—instigated in part, according to CIA reports, by "Communists."[23]
Whether the Communist role was real or imagined, it was clear that

---

20. Press conference of June 18, 1958, *Public Papers of the Presidents of the
United States: Dwight D. Eisenhower, 1958* (Washington, D.C.: U.S. Government
Printing Office, 1958), p. 484. See also Eisenhower's comments on the applicability of
the Eisenhower Doctrine at his May 28 press conference (ibid, p. 438).

21. Harold Macmillan, *Riding the Storm, 1956–1959* (New York: Harper and Row,
1971), p. 506. Macmillan is quoting from the May 13, 1958, entry in his own private
journal.

22. Dulles press conference of July 1, 1958, in *DSB,* July 21, 1958.

23. Eisenhower, p. 194.

Nasserist influence was a strong threat to Hussein, and there was well-founded fear for his survival. In April the crisis erupted again, and this time Eisenhower moved the Sixth Fleet toward Jordan and issued a statement on the importance to the United States of Jordan's independence and integrity. The crisis abated and the fleet withdrew, with U.S. policy-makers perceiving their intervention as a success that had helped save a friendly regime from hostile forces.[24]

An even fresher experience was the Syria crisis in later 1957. The Syrian case seemed to show how radical nationalism and pro-Soviet orientation went hand-in-hand, as well as what could be expected if any other "traditional" regime in the area were overthrown. Even previously, Syria had been considered by administration officials to be essentially within the Soviet orbit.[25] But in August 1957, changes in the Syrian government had strengthened the pro-Soviet complexion of the regime even further. Tension rose on the Syrian-Turkish border, as the United States announced its concern over "Communist domination" of Syria, moved the Sixth Fleet, and speeded arms deliveries to Lebanon, Jordan, Iraq, and Saudi Arabia (even though most of these countries announced that they did not feel threatened by Syria and, in the name of Arab solidarity, tended to side with Syria against the Turks). The crisis passed, but one result of it was to set in motion military plans for the Fertile Crescent. A "shadow" command—Specified Command Middle East (SCME)—was established under Admiral James Holloway and directed to prepare contingency plans for intervention in Jordan and Lebanon.[26]

Finally, just as the Lebanese crisis came to a boil in May, Vice President Richard Nixon was attacked by a Caracas mob while on an official visit to Latin America. This added to the sense of the United States being under siege generally in the Third World. At his press conference the following day, Eisenhower interpreted the Caracas incident as part of a pattern around the globe, as "some kind of concerted idea and plan" instigated by forces that he did not choose to identify publicly.[27]

Image of Nasser

The union of Egypt and Syria as the United Arab Republic, in early 1958, had little impact on American perceptions of the Communist

24. Tillema, pp. 77–78. See also Gurtov, p. 32.
25. Eisenhower, p. 197; Adams, p. 289.
26. Tillema, pp. 78–79; Meo, pp. 191–192.
27. Peter Lyon, *Eisenhower: Portrait of a Hero* (Boston: Little, Brown, 1974), p. 769.

threat in the Middle East, since the American image of Nasser was almost as negative as the image of the "pro-Soviet" regime in Damascus. There was, moreover, concern over the increased appeal of Nasserism in Lebanon and elsewhere; Eisenhower recalls the "ominous" parade of Lebanese Nasserists who streamed across the border to attend mass rallies in Damascus.[28] Nasser was, in Eisenhower's view, working hard to exploit Lebanon's divisions. Consequently, his motives and independence came under a shadow: "If he was not a Communist, he certainly succeeded in making us very suspicious of him."[29] The "Communist incitement to revolt" was linked closely in official minds with "Nasser's ambition to extend the UAR at the expense of the still independent states, particularly those bordering on Syria."[30] Furthermore, Nasser's insidious influence was seen even in such events as the virtual abdication of King Saud, of Saudi Arabia, in favor of Crown Prince Faisal—with Saud defined as "a potential bulwark against Communist expansion efforts in the Middle East," and Faisal characterized as "pro-Nasserite."[31]

Perception of the Lebanese Situation

With the perceptions of key decision-makers dominated by regional and global factors, appreciation of the nuances of Lebanese politics was quite limited. Malcolm Kerr comments that "a reading of President Eisenhower's own memories of the Lebanese crisis makes it clear in what oversimplified, even caricaturized, terms he viewed the developments there."[32] Kerr agrees that Eisenhower "can readily be forgiven a lack of intense interest in the details of Lebanese clan politics," but describes as "startling" the following passage of Eisenhower's memoirs:

> Behind everything was our deep-seated conviction that the Communists were principally responsible for the trouble, and that President Chamoun was motivated only by a strong feeling of patriotism. He was the ablest of the Lebanese politicians and would undoubtedly agree not to be a candidate again for the Presidency if

28. Eisenhower, p. 263.
29. Eisenhower, p. 265.
30. Eleanor Lansing Dulles, *John Foster Dulles: The Last Year* (New York: Harcourt, Brace and World, 1963), p. 141.
31. Eisenhower, p. 264.
32. Malcolm Kerr, "The Lebanese Civil War," in Evan Luard, ed., *The International Regulation of Civil Wars* (New York: New York University Press, 1972), p. 77.

only he could be assured of a strong and sincere pro-Western successor.[33]

In addition to reflecting the Eisenhower-Dulles tendency to attribute responsibility for fomenting unrest to the Communists, this passage presents a picture of Chamoun that was not shared by many Lebanese. Few local observers felt in May 1958 that Chamoun was motivated principally by patriotism or that he would "undoubtedly agree" not to be a candidate again. In fact, had Chamoun communicated such agreement during that period, there might not have been a crisis.[34]

The dominant factor in Eisenhower's relationship to Chamoun and to Lebanese Foreign Minister Charles Malik was his perception of these two leaders as "pro-Western," and he saw their troubles as the price they paid for this orientation. The cost of their brave pro-Western stand, in Eisenhower's eyes, was that they earned the hostility of "pan-Arab, pro-Nasserite groups."[35] There was also, undoubtedly, a natural sympathy for Lebanese leaders as Christians and an expectation that Christians would normally be oriented to the West. The U.S. Embassy in Beirut assumed that U.S. military intervention would be welcomed by all Christians.[36] All of this was reinforced by Eisenhower's own personal ties to Chamoun, which had become "increasingly strong," especially after Chamoun had been "unusually solicitous" after Eisenhower's heart attack in 1955—a fact that Eisenhower deemed worthy of mention in his memoirs.[37]

Eisenhower did feel, however, that Chamoun had made a "political error" in allowing a movement to amend the Lebanese Constitution, and that he should have put an end to speculation over a reelection bid with a forthright public denial of such intentions.[38] In fact, Chamoun did not make such a statement until late June, in an interview with a foreign journalist. This was regarded by U.S. decision-makers as an important public announcement that confirmed

33. Eisenhower, p. 266.
34. Even the State Department's own analysis casts doubt on this benign view of Chamoun. A State Department Report dated June 25, 1958, said, speaking of Chamoun's interest in seeking reelection at the time of the June 1957 elections: "It is highly probable that [Chamoun] was then seriously considering such a move." Speaking of early 1958, the report baldly states that "although [Chamoun] has yet to make a public declaration of interest to succeed himself, he in fact was planning just that." *DDRS,* 1976.
35. Eisenhower, p. 264.
36. Unsigned (McClintock?) to Dulles, June 23, 1958, *DDRS,* 1976.
37. Eisenhower, p. 265.
38. Ibid.

their benign view of the Lebanese President, but in Lebanon it was too little and too late to divert the suspicions and opposition that Chamoun's long silence had engendered.[39]

The imperfect appreciation of Lebanese politics in Washington was not due to lack of reliable information from Beirut. McClintock's cables throughout the period give a detailed report of the local scene. The personal rivalries and clan politics behind the election, the developing organization of Moslem and Druze opposition, the dwindling support for Chamoun even in Christian circles, and the bargaining over the Presidential election scheduled for late July—all of these subjects were fully and accurately covered in the Embassy's reports to Washington.[40] By July 12, McClintock had even identified General Chehab as the likely Presidential candidate emerging from a developing compromise among major groups.[41] Even McClintock, however, was prone to see the threat to Chamoun as being largely external, and to define the choice as either support of Chamoun or the "loss" of the Middle East to radical forces.[42]

Generally, the significance of Lebanon's internal problems for American policy-makers lay in the opportunity these problems provided for outside interference—and the latter was seen as the real threat. There was no doubt in his mind, said Eisenhower, that Nasser was instigating the revolt in Lebanon, as evidenced in the inflammatory broadcasts of Radio Cairo.[43] As Dulles defined the situation in cabled instructions in late June:

> What is happening in Lebanon is that larger state in vicinity has seized upon Lebanese domestic political problems and is openly intervening therein with men, arms, and money to facilitate overthrow of constituted authorities of this small peaceful country. Admittedly the domestic political considerations may seem [to] present a confusing picture but basic issue is that a civil war is going on in Lebanon which would not be prolonged and might not have started without foreign intervention.[44]

39. McClintock reported to Dulles, in a cable dated June 24, 1958, that Chamoun denied any intention to seek reelection in an interview for the Scripps-Howard newspapers (*DDRS*, 1976). This is apparently the earliest public statement by Chamoun to this effect.

40. McClintock to Dulles, April 14, April 18, April 22, June 18, and June 21, 1958, all in *DDRS*, 1976. See also the State Department Report of June 25, 1958 (*DDRS*, 1976), cited above in note 34.

41. McClintock to Dulles, July 12, 1958, *DDRS*, 1976.

42. Thayer, p. 8.

43. Eisenhower, pp. 266–267.

44. Dulles to U.S. Embassy, Paris, June 24, 1958, *DDRS*, 1977.

Along the same lines, Eisenhower concluded that "it seemed likely that Lebanon occupied a place on Colonel Nasser's timetable as a nation to be brought under his influence."[45]

Outside intervention was therefore the crucial issue for U.S. policy; Dulles defined the Lebanese situation as a case of "indirect aggression," no less prejudicial to national sovereignty and no less in violation of international law than the direct variety. In this frame of mind, there was great preoccupation with the issue of infiltration into Lebanon from the Syrian region of the UAR. All top decision-makers felt that there was clear and substantial—though regrettably not "publicly usable"—evidence of large-scale movement of men, arms, and money across the border.[46] McClintock even claimed that the daily pay of the insurgent forces came by "subterranean channels" from the UAR.[47]

Interestingly enough, this perception—that extreme elements inside and outside Lebanon were the source of the trouble—contributed to an optimistic assessment of Lebanese capability to deal with the crisis unaided. American decision-makers tended to regard the dissension as marginal to the mainstream of Lebanese political life, and assumed that the Lebanese government's base of support was more than adequate to deal with such "extraneous" problems. On more than one occasion, Washington was clearly unimpressed by Chamoun's alarm, and McClintock found himself trying to calm the Lebanese President (whose perceptions, molded by weeks of living under siege in his steel-shuttered palace, may have erred in the opposite direction).[48] Eisenhower and Dulles saw that on paper the Lebanese army was perfectly adequate to cope with the situation, and found it hard to understand why the army was not used effectively. In fact, Dulles even went so far as to speculate on one occasion that "we are pawns in a political game we do not understand very well."[49] Eisenhower noted with wonder that Chamoun

45. Eisenhower, p. 265.

46. McClintock to Dulles, May 22, 1958, *DDRS*, 1976; McClintock to Dulles, July 12, 1958, *DDRS*, 1976; Memorandum of Conversation, Dulles with Manlio Brosio (Italian Ambassador), June 25, 1958, *DDRS*, 1976; Robert Murphy, *Diplomat among Warriors* (Garden City, N.Y.: Doubleday, 1964), pp. 396–397; Robert T. McClintock, *The Meaning of Limited War* (Boston: Houghton Mifflin, 1967), p. 101.

47. McClintock, 1967, p. 103.

48. Thayer, pp. 24–25.

49. Telephone conversation between Dulles and Assistant Secretary of State William Rountree, June 15, 1958, 2:05 P.M., summarized in *Minutes of Telephone Conversations of John Foster Dulles and of Christian Herter* (Microfilm) (Washington, D.C.: University Publications of America, Inc., 1980), Reel 7, Document No. 0990. Further references to this series are noted as *Minutes*, followed by the reel and document numbers.

had not relieved General Chehab of command despite this inaction, apparently not comprehending the Lebanese political constraints that made such a move unthinkable. And only in a footnote does Eisenhower refer to the basic problem of whether the Lebanese army could in fact be used in a civil war and remain intact, as though it were not itself part of the fragmented Lebanese scene.[50]

The preoccupation with external threats also shaped military planning, which focused on the armies of neighboring states (principally the UAR).[51] U.S. and British staff officers, meeting in Cyprus on May 22, adopted a plan for military intervention that identified the Syrian First Army as the major enemy force and concentrated on blocking invasion routes from Syria into Lebanon. The plan was subsequently accepted in Washington.[52]

DECISION FLOW

In the 1956 Suez Crisis, the United States found itself making common cause with the Soviet Union against its own allies, and coming to the defense of the nation whose actions had precipitated the crisis and whose intentions were regarded as hostile to American interests. The resulting confusion impelled decision-makers to seek a new definition of U.S. policy in the Middle East. Even before the dust of Suez had settled, Eisenhower, on January 5, 1957, submitted to Congress a request for a joint resolution that would put the Middle East into the administration's accustomed ideological framework by identifying "international communism" as the major threat. As subsequently signed into law on March 9, 1957, the joint resolution—known as the Eisenhower Doctrine—provided in part:

> The President is authorized to undertake, in the general area of
> the Middle East, military assistance programs with any nation or
> group of nations of that area desiring such assistance. Furthermore,
> the United States regards as vital to the national interest and world
> peace the preservation of the independence and integrity of the
> nations of the Middle East. To this end, if the President determines
> the necessity thereof, the United States is prepared to use armed

50. Eisenhower, p. 266; see also Tillema, pp. 112–113.

51. Albert P. Sights, Jr., "Lessons of Lebanon: A Study in Air Strategy," *Air University Review*, 16 (July–August 1965), 28–43. There is evidence, however, that Dulles did appreciate the fact that there might well be Lebanese opposition to an American landing; see telephone conversation with Deputy Secretary of Defense Quarles, June 14, 1958, 4:50 P.M., in *Minutes*, 7:0993.

52. Tillema, p. 79; Jack Shulimson, *Marines in Lebanon, 1958* (Washington, D.C.: Historical Branch, G-3 Division, Headquarters, U.S. Marine Corps, 1966), p. 8.

forces to assist any nation or group of such nations requesting
assistance against armed aggression from any country controlled by
international communism. . . .[53]

The Eisenhower Doctrine symbolized, perhaps, a greater U.S.
determination to act in the Middle East, but it did little to settle the
question of when and how such action would be carried out. The
restatement of the "vital" interest of the United States in the independence and integrity of Middle East states added nothing to the
Tripartite Declaration of 1950, which had committed the three
Western powers to the defense of existing borders in the area. There
were still no clear guidelines on policy toward Nasserism and radical
nationalist movements, as distinct from the threat of communism.
Nor was it clear what a "country controlled by international communism" meant in practice: Was it measured by the influence of the
Soviet Union on the government involved, or by some other standard? The Doctrine did not address the problem of internal instability, whether fomented by Communists or by others, nor did it cover
the case of intervention by a "Communist-controlled" country by
indirect methods that fell short of "armed aggression." Finally, the
use of force was implicitly tied to a request from a recognized government, without any indication of how the United States might
respond to critical situations where such a request, for one reason or
another, was not forthcoming.

Some of these issues had arisen already in the Syrian crisis of
August 1957, which, as noted above, was an important part of the
background to the Lebanese crisis. The Syrian government that had
been formed in January of that year was regarded in Washington as
leftist but not Communist.[54] But on August 6, Syria signed an economic and technical assistance agreement with the Soviet Union,
and a week later expelled three U.S. diplomats charged with plotting
against the Syrian regime. On August 17, the Syrian government
announced the appointment as Commander of Armed Forces of an
officer suspected of especially strong pro-Soviet leanings. Thus,
it appeared to American policy-makers that one Middle East country was, indeed, either already under the control of international
communism or about to become so. Eisenhower remarked
that "the entire action was shrouded in mystery but the suspicion
was strong that the Communists had taken control of the government."[55]

53. *DSB*, March 25, 1957.
54. Eisenhower, pp. 196–197.
55. Ibid.; see also Tillema, p. 76.

But a vigorous U.S. response, given the announced policy guide-lines, was problematic. Even if the Damascus regime were domi-nated by Communists, there was no open conflict in Syria, no requests for assistance from a Syrian government (nor, for that mat-ter, from any faction in Syria), and little evidence of a direct Soviet role in the takeover.[56] The principles so carefully and solemnly pro-mulgated in the Eisenhower Doctrine offered little scope for action related directly to events within Syria. Sherman Adams, the Presi-dent's chief of staff, later summarized the administration's dilemma:

> In contrast to the situation in Jordan, the Syrian government
> wanted nothing to do with any assistance from the West and there
> was therefore little that Eisenhower could do about it. . . . While we
> kept military aid moving into Jordan, Turkey, and Iraq, the
> President told the Congressmen there was little else that we could
> do except to make sure that the Russians themselves did not take
> over Syria.[57]

The administration did send Deputy Under Secretary of State Loy Henderson to confer with the governments of Turkey, Iraq, Jordan, and Lebanon, in addition to the demonstrative moves and contin-gency military plans already described. But Henderson reported that concerted action was unlikely because of lack of interest and rivalries among these states themselves. The United States did apparently goad Turkey in the border crisis that followed, but this only compli-cated matters further by rallying the Arab states—even the pre-sumed moderates—behind Syria.[58]

The Syria-Egypt union a few months later posed another dilemma to which the Eisenhower Doctrine had no clear response. The CIA reported to Eisenhower that the union had been engineered in part in order to *contain* Communist influence in Syria, although the Pres-ident's initial inclination was to believe either that it was "prompted by Communist influence" or that "the Communists were merely going along with Nasser's ambition eventually to unify the Arab world."[59] But again, even though the development was assumed to be advantageous to the enemy and a threat to U.S. interests, the only American response was to encourage closer cooperation among moderate Arab states, including in this case strong support for the Iraq-Jordan federation hastily erected as an answer to the UAR.[60]

56. Tillema, p. 76.
57. Adams, pp. 289–290.
58. Eisenhower, p. 262; Hughes, pp. 253–254; Tillema, p. 77.
59. Eisenhower, p. 262; see also Tillema, p. 77.
60. Eisenhower, p. 263.

Throughout early 1958, the apparent rising tide of Nasserism brought tension in the area to higher levels. This could not fail to have an impact on a country such as Lebanon, where internal tensions had in any event been on the rise for some time. In November 1956, President Chamoun had challenged the delicate Lebanese political balance by supporting Iraq at the Arab summit meeting that followed Suez; subsequently, the mildly pro-Egyptian government of Abdullah Yafi and Saeb Salam had resigned, and Sami Es-Sulh—like Yafi and Salam a Sunni Moslem, but pro-Western and tied to Chamoun—was appointed Prime Minister. In March 1957, Lebanon became the only Arab country to accept the Eisenhower Doctrine formally, thus further alienating Moslems and leftists. Rumors began to circulate that Chamoun intended to amend the constitution in order to seek reelection, and Chamoun's actions in the June 1957 parliamentary elections gave further currency to such reports. Using all the means at his disposal, the Lebanese President succeeded in these elections in gaining a strong majority, excluding from parliament such figures as Yafi, Salam, and even moderate opposition leaders—all of whom united in an extraparliamentary opposition to a regime increasingly regarded as illegitimate.

Following the formation of the UAR, the approach of Lebanese Presidential elections and the excitement engendered by the Nasserist movement for Arab unity brought the situation to the breaking point. On May 8, Nasib Matni, editor of the anti-Chamoun newspaper *The Telegraph* (although he was a Christian), was assassinated, and Chamounist forces were immediately blamed. Large parts of the country, including the entire Syrian border area, came under the control of armed opposition groups, while the control of the Lebanese army and the government was effectively limited to predominantly Christian areas.

On May 13, Chamoun asked the U.S., British, and French Ambassadors how their respective governments would respond to a Lebanese request for military assistance. Eisenhower met the same day with John Foster Dulles, Allen Dulles, and others, to decide on the U.S. response. As he later remarked, "we met in a climate of impatience because of our belief that Chamoun's uneasiness was the result of one more Communist provocation."[61]

Eisenhower nevertheless remained cautious, while his Secretary of State favored action. The President was apprehensive of adverse reactions throughout the Middle East, including the probable blocking of the Suez Canal and the interruption of oil pipelines and

61. Eisenhower, p. 265; Tillema, p. 47.

supplies generally. As in 1956, he was also worried about increased domestic pressures on moderate governments such as Iraq and Jordan. There was concern that the use of American forces would be construed as intervention in an internal conflict, even though Washington did not see it that way. In addition, there was apprehension that Lebanese armed forces, under General Chehab, might embarrass the United States by opposing an American landing forcefully. On the other hand, consideration of the Soviet response does not seem to have played a large role in American calculations.[62]

Eisenhower decided, therefore, to send Chamoun a reply that affirmed willingness to act, but with certain stipulated conditions (Decision No. 1). At the President's insistence, the message stressed the American preference that Lebanon attempt to maintain its own independence without outside help, and that U.S. intervention be seen only as the last resort. Also, it was stated directly that the United States would not intervene on behalf of Chamoun's reelection or any other internal Lebanese political issue, that Lebanon should first submit a complaint to the UN Security Council, and that Lebanon should secure the support of at least one other Arab nation.[63]

Eisenhower and his advisors also decided to take certain preliminary actions to bolster Lebanese morale and to signal American concern to hostile parties. Amphibious units of the Sixth Fleet were moved from Gibraltar to the eastern Mediterranean. Airborne battle groups in Europe that had been earmarked for possible use in the Middle East were placed on alert, and additional air transports were flown from the United States to Frankfurt. Shipments of police equipment and small arms that had already been promised were expedited. On May 16, it was announced that an agreement on the delivery of light tanks would be completed in the near future. On May 17, the State Department announced publicly that since "the integrity of the Lebanon was threatened by persons acting under alien influence," the shipment of arms and equipment had been speeded up in order to augment "the capacity of Lebanese security forces to control and prevent these subversive efforts. . . ."[64]

62. Eisenhower, pp. 266–267; McClintock, 1967, p. 106; Gurtov, p. 30.

63. Eisenhower, p. 267; McClintock, 1967, pp. 101–102; telephone conversation between Dulles and U.S. Ambassador to the UN Henry Cabot Lodge, May 21, 1958, 8:44 A.M., in *Minutes*, 7:0523.

64. Eisenhower, p. 267; John Donovan, ed., *U.S. and Soviet Policy in the Middle East, 1957–1966* (New York: Facts on File, 1974), p. 101; Thayer, pp. 13–14; Tillema, p. 47. According to minutes of telephone conversations held at the time, the tank shipment was part of the original decision on May 13; telephone conversations between Dulles and White House Staff Secretary Andrew Goodpaster, May 13, 1958, 8:01 P.M., in *Minutes*, 10:0526.

Eisenhower, in his press conference on May 14, the day following these decisions, refused to comment on Lebanon on the grounds that it was a delicate situation regarding which it was best to say nothing at the moment—thus conveying a sense of urgency in a different fashion. He repeated this formula at his next press conference on May 28, even though the situation had in his view improved as the month progressed. There was continuing concern, however, over the infiltration of hostile elements across the Syrian border.

Eisenhower and Dulles were, as noted, careful to prepare the ground legally and constitutionally for any eventuality. Recalling that in similar cases in the past the United States had been "unable to lend a hand" (a possible reference to the 1957 Syrian crisis), Eisenhower regarded Lebanon as an instance where "if the Lebanese government should call upon us for help, we might move firmly and in full accord with the local government and the principles of the United Nations."[65] Even with an invitation from a government, however, there remained the question of Presidential authorization under the Congressional resolution containing the Eisenhower Doctrine. As already outlined, Dulles dealt with this carefully in his May 20 press conference, stressing the Doctrine's clause on "preservation of the independence and integrity of the nations of the Middle East" rather than the provision for meeting the threat of "international communism." Dulles also claimed that the Congressional role in the Eisenhower Doctrine gave the President greater authority to act than he would otherwise possess by virtue of Presidential prerogatives or declarations alone, and the Secretary reiterated that the United States would not introduce forces into any area save at the invitation of a lawful government.[66]

As the stalemate continued into June, the United States supported Lebanon's decision to turn to the Security Council—in line with its stress on the issue of external interference in Lebanese affairs (Decision No. 2).[67] The Security Council took up the issue on June 6, with the United States and Britain supporting Lebanese complaints of interference from the UAR, and the Soviet Union backing the UAR

65. Eisenhower, p. 266.

66. *DSB*, June 9, 1958; on these legal points, see also McClintock, 1967, p. 102, and Meo, pp. 194–195. Dulles was also not above misrepresenting the decision actually made in order to minimize possible negative repercussions; in a telephone conversation with James Reston of the *New York Times*, who had published a reasonably accurate account of the administration's decision, Dulles claimed that nothing had been said to Chamoun "other than the possibility of moving troops in to protect American life and property" (conversation of May 19, 6:33 P.M., in *Minutes*, 7:0537).

67. Telephone conversation between Dulles and Rountree, May 19, 1958, 2:55 P.M., in *Minutes*, 7:0534.

in its denial of the charges. Despite the sharpness of the debate, both sides were able to agree on sending observers to the area, and a resolution establishing the United Nations Observer Group in Lebanon (UNOGIL) passed on June 11, with the Soviet Union abstaining.

Eisenhower, convinced of the truth of the infiltration reports, was "puzzled" that Nasser did not oppose a UN observation team in Lebanon.[68] Furthermore, at the same moment, Nasser quietly contacted the United States and suggested terms for ending the conflict that even Eisenhower described as "not wholly unreasonable." In fact, Nasser's terms—that Chamoun should finish his term, that he should be succeeded by Chehab, and that there should be a full amnesty for the rebels—were almost identical to the terms of the final resolution of the crisis months later. But in June the American suspicion of Nasser was still such that it was decided, in consultation with the British, simply to pass Nasser's proposals on to Chamoun, while making it clear that the United States was pressing no particular course of action and would support whatever move Chamoun made (Decision No. 3). As Chamoun chose to ignore Nasser's initiative, nothing came of it.[69] The failure to consider this diplomatic option seriously has been characterized by some observers as a missed opportunity, considering the intense diplomatic effort undertaken later, *after* U.S. intervention, to achieve a similar outcome.[70]

Direct military action was considered seriously a second time over the weekend of June 14–15, when opposition forces in Beirut threatened to overrun the Presidential palace. The Dulles brothers flew back to Washington on the 14th because of this development, and the Secretary held intensive consultations that day and the next with his advisors. On the basis of reports from McClintock, however, Dulles advised Eisenhower that the situation was not yet serious

68. In fact, there was a clear expectation before the event that the Soviet Union would (presumably at Egypt's behest) veto the pending Security Council resolution. Telephone conversation between Dulles and Twining, June 11, 1958, 8:59 A.M., in *Minutes*, 7:1005.

69. Telephone conversation between Eisenhower and Dulles, June 12, 1958, 11:-45 A.M. in *Minutes*, 10:0470.

70. Hoopes, p. 433, remarks: "In retrospect, Dulles's refusal to see these proposals as the ingredients of a reasonable settlement, and to use them as the point of departure for a serious negotiation between Chamoun and the rebels, perhaps with UN mediation, was rather clearly a missed opportunity. The final settlement consisted almost precisely of these terms, but there remained in Washington a basic antipathy to Nasser's Pan-Arabic aspirations, a state of mind which preferred military intervention to mediation." See also Eisenhower, p. 268; Macmillan, p. 509; and Miles Copeland, *The Game of Nations: The Amorality of Power Politics* (London: Weidenfeld and Nicolson, 1969), pp. 201–202.

enough to force the latter's return to Washington from Gettysburg, where he was spending the weekend.[71] On Sunday afternoon, June 15, Dulles was joined at home by his chief State Department advisors; and at 6:30 P.M., the President met with his chief advisors other than Dulles: Allen Dulles, Quarles, Twining, and Herter. It was finally decided to await further information (Decision No. 4). As the situation developed, it appeared less urgent than originally feared, and the idea of direct action faded from the agenda.[72]

The June crisis further prepared decision-makers for eventual action, however. Contingency plans became more fully developed. In addition, most of the earlier conditions for U.S. action had been met by this time: Lebanon had appealed both to the United Nations and to the Arab League, and had gained the support of two Arab states (Jordan and Iraq). Chamoun had also been authorized by his own Cabinet to request U.S. intervention whenever he deemed it necessary, thus guaranteeing a formal and lawful request from a recognized Lebanese government. The remaining constraint, and the reason for the deferral of action in June, was the belief that the Lebanese government could still cope with the threat. Should this view change, it was clear that the door was open for direct U.S. military action.[73]

Reflecting this state of mind, both Eisenhower and Dulles indicated publicly that military action remained a possibility. At his June 17 press conference, Dulles noted that the United States would be inclined to respond to a UN appeal for military support, but did not limit U.S. military intervention to UN-initiated actions alone: "There are other possible contingencies." Dulles refused to spell out these contingencies. On the following day, Eisenhower delivered a similar signal by stating that the United States could not make predictions on the conditions under which it would take military action.[74] At the same time, Eisenhower privately assured Chamoun that U.S. action was not dependent on the United Nations, while urging the Lebanese President to make every effort to resolve the problem without the need for foreign troops, which would create additional resentment in the Arab world.[75]

---

71. Telephone conversation between Eisenhower and Dulles, June 14, 1958, 3:41 P.M., in *Minutes*, 10:0466.
72. Tillema, pp. 113–114; E. L. Dulles, 1963, p. 132.
73. Tillema, pp. 119–120; E. L. Dulles, 1963, p. 132.
74. *DSB*, July 7, 1958.
75. Eisenhower, pp. 268–269.

Thus, at the end of June the United States was still waiting out the crisis. It was hoped that a UN presence would discourage infiltration, and in addition Chamoun's first public denial of a reelection bid stirred hopes for a political solution.[76] However, the first report of UNOGIL, on July 3, was a disappointment. Despite the small size of the group, its lack of access to the Syrian border area, and its inability to know of past border infiltration in any event, UNOGIL concluded that the reports of infiltration were exaggerated and that the fighting groups in Lebanon were largely Lebanese. The United States was reduced to pointing out the inadequacies of the UN observation, while continuing to encourage Chamoun to find a negotiated solution.[77] In early July, this latter possibility seemed entirely possible, as Chamoun announced that he would cooperate in a search for a Presidential candidate acceptable to all parties. As noted, the name of Chehab was coming to the fore.

This positive train of events was overwhelmed, however, by external events. On July 14, the overthrow of the Iraqi government put the Lebanese situation in an entirely new light and brought the pre-crisis period to a close.

76. Meo, p. 197.
77. Thayer, p. 24.

CHAPTER THREE

1958: 14 July to 31 July

AFTER TWO MONTHS of recurrent tension, the Lebanese situation in mid-July seemed headed for a resolution of sorts. A tenuous military stability, backed by the presence of UN observer forces, had been achieved. To be sure, the presence of UNOGIL did not resolve the issue of infiltration into Lebanon, but its presence apparently did help to reduce tension on the Lebanese-Syrian border. President Chamoun himself seemed to be backing off his earlier intention of seeking reelection, and a political resolution of the conflict seemed not only possible but likely.

This train of events was rudely upset by the brutal and unexpected coup in Iraq on July 14. The Iraqi regime had long served as a symbol of Western orientation and a model of "moderation" in an otherwise turbulent area. Its fall therefore raised fears for all "moderate" governments in the Middle East, and especially for Jordan, Saudi Arabia, and Lebanon. The sweeping tide of radicalism now seemed to threaten the few remaining bastions of pro-Western sentiment. In Lebanon this fear was reinforced by the already unsettled situation in that country and by the panic of the Lebanese government itself. On a broader scale, there were apprehensions about the impact of the Iraqi coup on the Arab-Israel conflict and on American prestige in the region and beyond it. Behind all of this, of course, was the perception that the coup was a major Soviet gain, with all the attendant implications for the global balance between the superpowers.

There was therefore a new sense of urgency in Washington on July 14. American policy-makers not only felt U.S. vital interests threatened more than formerly, but also saw themselves in a situation where time for response was limited and in which military involvement was a distinct possibility. Thus, the Lebanese crisis moved to the crisis period, beginning at peak intensity and winding down gradually over the following two-and-one-half weeks.

DECISIONS AND DECISION-MAKERS

There were five major decisions in the 1958 crisis period:

Decision Number	Date	Content
5	14 July	In response to a Lebanese request, President Eisenhower ordered the landing of U.S. troops in Lebanon.
6	16 July	Eisenhower sent Deputy Under Secretary of State Robert Murphy to Lebanon on a diplomatic troubleshooting mission.
7	17 July	Eisenhower decided not to join the British in sending troops to Jordan, but only to provide logistical support.
8	22 July	Eisenhower rejected a Soviet proposal for a summit conference, proposing instead that heads of state participate in a UN Security Council meeting.
9	17–31 July	In an important incremental change in policy, the President and the State Department accepted the recommendations of Robert Murphy, special Presidential envoy in Lebanon, first to work for early presidential elections in Lebanon, and then to support the choice of General Fuad Chehab as the new President.[1]

1. The relevant accounts, including Eisenhower's and Murphy's, are vague on the precise dates upon which Murphy's recommendations were approved. Nevertheless, it is clear that the overall result of Murphy's mission was to change the direction of U.S. policy in Lebanon quite sharply, leaving aside all the "international" issues— Communism, UAR infiltration, the repercussions of the Iraqi coup, etc.—and focusing almost exclusively on the resolution of Lebanese domestic divisions. This is seen in the outraged reaction of President Chamoun to Murphy's contacts and compromises with the Lebanese rebel leaders, which he later termed "le point de depart d'une politique nouvelle nettement en contradiction avec l'ancienne." Camille Chamoun, *Crise au Moyen-Orient* (Paris: Gallimard, 1963), p. 429. See also Dwight D. Eisenhower, *The White House Years: Waging Peace, 1956–1961* (Garden City, N.Y.: Doubleday, 1965), pp. 280–290; and Robert Murphy, *Diplomat among Warriors* (Garden City, N.Y.: Doubleday, 1964), p. 404.

A number of actions were taken to implement these decisions. In the first place, the Eisenhower administration immediately requested that the UN Security Council be convened, reported to it on its action in Lebanon as required by the UN charter, and proposed a resolution which would have replaced American forces with a UN force in Lebanon. The Eisenhower administration also exchanged letters publicly with Soviet Chairman Nikita Khrushchev, debating the terms for a summit meeting in the framework of the Security Council (the United States conceded little to Soviet demands for a special meeting, beyond willingness to have the Security Council convene somewhere other than New York).

Beyond landing troops and related military moves, the American government also implemented other military preparations and signals. On July 15, the President approved the stationing of Strategic Air Command tankers in forward positions, signaling the increased readiness of American strategic nuclear forces. Eisenhower also ordered the movement of a Marine regimental combat team to the Persian Gulf, as a precautionary measure, and the transfer of a Composite Air Strike Group from Europe to Turkey.[2]

It might be argued that a "decision" *not* to intervene in Iraq should be added to the above list. By one account, at least, the possibility of such intervention was seriously considered.[3] But evidence indicates that, in the absence of any real resistance to the new regime in Iraq, this was not a real option for American policy-makers. Intervention under such circumstances seemed hopeless, and the costs, both political and military, put it out of reach. As it became clear that the new Iraqi regime was in firm control, was stable, and was a nationalist Iraqi regime and not a puppet government, American decision-makers came to what could be called a "non-decision": no serious consideration was given to challenging the Iraqi regime, and by default the United States moved toward de facto acceptance of it.[4]

The major decision-makers were unchanged from the pre-crisis period, though Defense Secretary McElroy was vacationing on July 14 and Deputy Secretary Quarles took his place during the crucial decision-making phase. In addition, Deputy Under Secretary of State for Political Affairs Robert Murphy became an important figure in the policy-making process by virtue of his special mission to Lebanon

2. Eisenhower, pp. 275, 278.

3. Peter Lyon, *Eisenhower: Portrait of a Hero* (Boston: Little, Brown, 1974), pp. 775–776.

4. See summary in John C. Campbell, *Defense of the Middle East: Problems of American Policy* (New York: Harper and Brothers, 1960), p. 147.

on behalf of the President. The Commander-in-Chief of the Specified Command Middle East, Admiral James C. Holloway, also naturally had an important input into the decision-making process, together with Murphy.

PSYCHOLOGICAL ENVIRONMENT

Attitudinal Prism

The sudden shock of the Iraqi coup on July 14 transformed the psychological environment of American policy-makers. As Tillema summarizes the impact of these events:

> The suddenness and the unexpectedness of the blow in Iraq, especially since it occurred in the presumed stable core of the Baghdad Pact, seemed to raise doubts about the stability of all governments in the region. Most disturbing was that the coup appeared to have mob support. The psychological effect of the Iraq coup was immediate. The discussions among major American decision-makers began that morning with a shared assumption that action had to be taken. There was sudden and unanimous agreement among all members of the Administration that Lebanon could no longer protect itself.[5]

Eisenhower recalls his own reaction as being "shocked" and as fearing the "complete elimination of Western influence in the Middle East." He further recalls that "overnight our objective changed from quieting a troubled situation to facing up to a crisis of formidable proportions."[6]

Secretary of State Dulles indicated that previous to the events of July 14 he had expected a quiet resolution of the internal crisis in Lebanon, but that the Iraqi coup had completely changed his mind.[7] The brutality of the events in Iraq, with the Crown Prince reportedly torn limb from limb and various bodies dragged through the streets of Baghdad, also contributed significantly to the stunned reactions in Washington; decision-makers alluded to the violence and bloodshed in almost every reference to the coup.

The CIA's initial assessment was that the coup was essentially a military operation, supported by pro-Nasser civilian elements and

---

5. Herbert K. Tillema, *Appeal to Force: American Military Intervention in the Era of Containment* (New York: Crowell, 1973), p. 114.

6. Eisenhower, p. 269.

7. From a briefing of Latin American ambassadors, quoted in Eleanor Lansing Dulles, *John Foster Dulles: The Last Year* (New York: Harcourt, Brace and World, 1963), p. 147.

backed by the mob. Intelligence analysts noted the predominance of Ba'ath Party members in the new regime. There was no immediate report on the loyalty of army units outside Baghdad, which left some hope among observers in Washington that these units might support the Hashemites and even help to restore them to power.[8]

According to other reports, the Iraqi coup was part of a three-pronged operation aimed also at King Hussein of Jordan and President Chamoun in Lebanon, with the United Arab Republic backing if not instigating the entire plan.[9] The CIA reported the discovery of a "well-advanced" plot in Jordan, with the fate of King Hussein seeming to hang in the balance.[10]

American policy-makers tended to perceive the Iraqi coup as having a strong potential impact on the Lebanese situation in any event. They feared that the delicate balance being worked out would be shattered, with the morale of the rebels being immeasurably boosted by the Iraqi coup and the Lebanese government suffering not only psychologically but also in the direct loss of material aid.[11] This perception was strongly reinforced by the reaction of Lebanese President Chamoun, who condemned the Iraqi coup as part of an overall plot and argued that it proved his estimate of the threat of Nasserism in the Middle East to be essentially correct. Chamoun conveyed the desperate warning that without the presence of Western forces within forty-eight hours, his regime was doomed. The CIA tended to accept this appraisal.[12] Ambassador McClintock, who had reacted

8. Allen W. Dulles, Briefing Notes, Meetings at the White House with Congressional Leaders, July 14, 1958, *Declassified Documents Reference System (DDRS)*, 1979 (Washington, D.C.: Carrollton Press, 1980). Eisenhower, p. 270, gives an almost identical account of Dulles's briefing of top policy-makers.

9. Miles Copeland, *The Game of Nations: The Amorality of Power Politics* (London: Weidenfeld and Nicolson, 1969), pp. 202–203; Morton Berkovitz, P. G. Bock, and Vincent J. Fuccillo, *The Politics of American Foreign Policy: The Social Context of Decisions* (Englewood Cliffs, N.J.: Prentice-Hall, 1977), p. 108.

10. A. W. Dulles, Briefing Notes; confirmed by Eisenhower, p. 270 (and mentioned in general terms by Eisenhower in his public address on July 15, 1958; see *Department of State Bulletin (DSB)*, August 4, 1958). According to Ambassador McClintock, the Jordanian coup was scheduled for July 17; McClintock, *The Meaning of Limited War* (Boston: Houghton Mifflin, 1967), p. 107.

11. Alexander George and Richard Smoke, *Deterrence in American Foreign Policy: Theory and Practice* (New York: Columbia University Press, 1974), p. 348.

12. A. W. Dulles, Briefing Notes; Eisenhower, p. 270. Berkovitz et al. (pp. 107–108) claim that the CIA shaped information in such a way that military intervention seemed the only course; this overlooks the importance of the predispositions of Eisenhower and J. F. Dulles, who tended to accept theories (e.g., the complicity of Nasser) about which the CIA was in fact more cautious. In addition, the more influential alarms from Lebanon at this stage were not funneled through the CIA, but came directly from Chamoun and McClintock.

calmly to Chamoun's earlier alarms, now concurred in the latter's judgment that an army coup was likely at any moment.[13]

Washington still tended to place considerable stress on the issue of infiltration across the Lebanese-Syrian border. The Secretary of State's assessment, as expressed in cabled instructions on July 14, was that

> Indications have been that as result of UN action degree of infiltration lessened somewhat, but opposition activities carried out with help of substantial amounts of arms, ammunition and personnel brought into Lebanon prior to SC [Security Council] decision, combined with infiltrations which have taken place since then, have produced situation where continuing existence of Lebanon as sovereign and independent state is in grave jeopardy. In addition overthrow of Iraqi government by pro-Nasser elements has increased danger of hostile infiltration into Lebanon and likelihood that Lebanon as sovereign nation would go under unless it received more assistance than heretofore.[14]

American Ambassador to the UN Henry Cabot Lodge, in presenting the American case to the United Nations on the following day, claimed that, following the coup in Iraq, the problem of infiltration into Lebanon "has suddenly become much more alarming." On the following day, July 16, Lodge presented seven items of evidence to back up these claims, explaining that the evidence had not been produced earlier because of jeopardy to sources.[15] Also on July 16, Under Secretary of State Christian Herter presented a full account of the evidence on infiltration to a closed session of the Senate Foreign Relations Committee; following this session, a chronological summary of such infiltration during the period May 17–June 21 was released to the press.[16] That American decision-makers felt a strong need to believe in such infiltration, and that they in fact did believe it to be crucial to an explanation of events in Lebanon, is further buttressed by Ambassador Murphy's recalling of the tapping of the telephone line between Damascus and the rebel-held area in Beirut. This provided evidence, he claimed, conclusively proving that the rebels were receiving directions and support from the Nasserist regime in Damascus.[17]

Given the prominence of the issue in American public statements, the safety of American citizens in Lebanon as a consideration moving

---

13. McClintock to Dulles, July 14 and July 16, 1958, *DDRS*, 1977; Eleanor Lansing Dulles, *American Foreign Policy in the Making* (New York: Harper and Row, 1968), p. 275.

14. J. F. Dulles to American Embassy, Paris, July 14, 1958, *DDRS*, 1977.

15. *DSB*, August 4, 1958.

16. *New York Times*, July 17, 1958.

17. Murphy, p. 402.

U.S. policy-makers should also be weighed. On balance, however, it is difficult to see that this consideration played an important role in the decision-making process itself, as distinguished from the public justification of decisions. Even Eisenhower devotes only one sentence in his memoirs to a perfunctory mention of the fact that a "relatively large number of American citizens" were endangered by the strife in Lebanon.[18]

It is also clear that American policy-makers still possessed a rather simplistic perception of the Lebanese situation. President Eisenhower stated, as if the matter were not open to dispute, that "Mr. Chamoun has made clear that he does not seek re-election"—completely underestimating the continuing relevance of doubts on that score among Chamoun's opponents.[19] Just before U.S. troops landed, Ambassador McClintock found, contrary to the standard American appraisal, that General Chehab believed that no coup was imminent; further, Chehab warned that U.S. forces might be opposed if they attempted a forceable landing. This could conceivably bring about the defection of the Lebanese army to the rebel side and prevent a resolution of the conflict. McClintock forwarded this information, of which Washington seemed to be unaware, together with a proposal for a delay in landing until an accommodation could be worked out, but the warning was too late to affect the implementation of military plans.[20]

Uncertainty at the top decision-making level was reflected at the operational level as well. Officers in charge of the intervention reportedly had no idea what to expect upon landing. Troops were given live ammunition and were told to be prepared for any eventuality.[21]

It is possible, of course, to argue that the general perception of a threat to vital American interests was correct, even if some of the details were fuzzy. In the absence of American action, the prognosis for Chamoun or any pro-Western Lebanese government was presumably not good. According to one scholarly appraisal:

> This writer happens to be convinced that the Lebanon intervention was not a mistake, however foggy the thinking that determined it. Whether or not anyone in Washington spelled out for Eisenhower the precise nature of events that he would have to be prepared to witness if he did not send the Marines, such events can be readily

18. Eisenhower, p. 270.
19. *DSB*, August 4, 1958.
20. Jack Shulimson, *Marines in Lebanon, 1958* (Washington, D.C.: Historical Branch, G-3 Division, Headquarters, U.S. Marine Corps, 1966), p. 12; Charles W. Thayer, *Diplomat* (New York: Harper and Brothers, 1959), pp. 29–30.
21. Thayer, p. 31.

imagined in retrospect. Chamoun's prospect for finishing out his term until 23 September was fairly good on the eve of the Iraqi revolution, and so was the prospect that the Lebanese parliament would shortly agree on General Chehab as his successor and that with this, the violence would taper off appreciably. The events in Baghdad washed out those prospects at once, however, and replaced them with the opposite presumption: that Chamoun, unprotected from abroad, would find that what authority he held was dissolving all around him as various supporters deserted him and would end up, in a matter of days, being escorted out of the country by the Lebanese army or perhaps assassinated. Chehab might inherit the presidency anyway—or perhaps not—but would do so in circumstances that would propel Lebanese politics away from, rather than back toward, their traditional equilibrium, amidst all the euphoria of Sunni Moslem and pan-Arabic popular sentiment.[22]

Kerr projects further that the fall of Chamoun might well have doomed King Hussein, whose fall in turn would have precipitated another Arab-Israeli war as Israel intervened to keep the West Bank out of Nasserist hands (this fear was also prominent in CIA briefings).[23] In other words, the general perception of the dangers was not necessarily exaggerated, even though it was undergirded by a reading of Lebanese politics that could easily be criticized as misguided and oversimplified.

Given the prevailing American suspicion of Nasser, it was inevitable that decision-makers would search carefully for evidence of his complicity in the Iraqi coup. Events in Baghdad seemed part of the grand strategy that Nasser had presumably outlined in his book and elsewhere—a strategy that centered on control of the Suez Canal and Persian Gulf oil as a key to bringing pressure on the West.[24] Since this strategy had obviously been advanced by the coup in Baghdad, led by pro-Nasser elements, it seemed improbable that Nasser and Egyptian forces had not been involved in its planning or execution. Yet, there was no hard evidence to support this suspicion, as CIA Director Allen Dulles himself admitted:

22. Malcolm H. Kerr, "The Lebanese Civil War," in Evan Luard, ed., *The International Regulation of Civil Wars* (New York: New York University Press, 1972), p. 79.

23. Kerr, 1972, p. 80; A. W. Dulles, Briefing Notes.

24. *U.S. News and World Report,* July 25, 1958. As Dulles remarked to U.S. Ambassador to the UN Henry Cabot Lodge, "it looks like a plot by Nasser to take over the whole thing." Telephone conversation between Dulles and Lodge, July 14, 1958, 7:20 P.M., in *Minutes of Telephone Conversations of John Foster Dulles and of Christian Herter* (Microfilm) (Washington, D.C.: University Publications of America, 1980), Reel 7, Document No. 0854. Documents from this series are hereafter referred to as *Minutes,* followed by the reel and document numbers.

There is some question, however, as to whether the methods and timing of the present coup in Iraq were dictated from Egypt. The timing seems a little out of gear with what might have been expected, as well as the manner and brutality of carrying out the coup. Nasir is still absent, completing his visit to Yugoslavia.[25]

Nevertheless, whether the Egyptian government could be held directly responsible for the Iraqi coup or not, the effect of the Iraqi revolution was to heighten the American fear of Egyptian interference in Lebanon.

This fear naturally extended to other countries. In Saudi Arabia, King Saud privately demanded the intervention of the Baghdad Pact nations, and warned that Saudi Arabia would not be in a position to oppose the United Arab Republic if Iraq and Jordan were not saved —and that in this case the United States and Britain would be finished as Middle East powers.[26] Among other countries in the Middle East, Kuwait was also thought to be especially threatened by the change of government in Baghdad, given the long-standing Iraqi threat to annex Kuwait. The impact of the coup on Iran, Turkey, and Pakistan was also considerable, given the fact that these three Moslem nations, as members of the Baghdad Pact, had placed their reliance on a Western alliance in opposition to the same nationalist currents that had brought down their ally in Baghdad so brutally and unexpectedly. In summary, as the CIA saw the situation:

> If the Iraq coup succeeds it seems almost inevitable that it will set up a chain reaction which will doom the pro-West governments of Lebanon and Jordan and Saudi Arabia, and raise grave problems for Turkey and Iran.
> The Soviet Union will undoubtedly welcome these developments and do what it feels it safely can without direct involvement in overt hostilities to support this chain reaction.[27]

A similar assessment was reached unanimously among the senior advisors within the American government, who concluded that American inaction following the Iraqi coup would have the following results:

1. Nasser would take over the whole area.

2. The United States would lose influence not only in the Arab states of the Middle East but in the area generally, and our bases throughout the area would be in jeopardy.

3. The dependability of the United States commitments for

25. A. W. Dulles, Briefing Notes.
26. Ibid.; Eisenhower, p. 270.
27. A. W. Dulles, Briefing Notes.

assistance in the event of need would be brought into question throughout the world.[28]

This line of thinking suggests that American policy-makers felt impelled to act in Lebanon more out of regional and global considerations than in reaction to the situation in Lebanon itself.[29] The third point in particular embodies a set of considerations that later policymakers would define as the "credibility" problem: the question of belief in American commitments. As in later crises, these considerations were to prove central in 1958. What would the effect of American action or inaction be on other American allies, who would begin to question whether American commitments could be trusted?

More concretely, events in Iraq raised, in the minds of Eisenhower administration officials, the alarm of Soviet expansion. This was predictable in an administration that tended to interpret events everywhere as a function of East-West competition. There was concern that, with the cooperation of Nasser and Iraq, the Soviet Union would succeed in rendering vulnerable all major oil routes to Europe, and in putting itself in a position of being able to strike at all loading ports on the Persian Gulf.[30] John Foster Dulles in particular made repeated references during the crisis to the "growing Soviet practice of indirect aggression," comparing the train of events to the earlier losses of Estonia, Latvia, Lithuania, and Czechoslovakia. Although he admitted that there was no direct evidence that the Iraqi coup had been directed from Moscow, Dulles also felt strongly that inferences drawn from this pattern of past behavior were of direct relevance and should put the West on its guard concerning current developments in the Middle East.[31] What Dulles saw in the events in Iraq and Lebanon was a concrete instance of the Soviet "Third World strategy" described in Chapter Two.

28. Memorandum for the Record, "Meeting re Iraq," July 14, 1958, Department of State (declassified 1975), quoted by William B. Quandt, "Lebanon, 1958, and Jordan, 1970," in Barry M. Blechman and Stephen S. Kaplan, eds., *Force Without War: U.S. Armed Forces as a Political Instrument* (Washington, D.C.: Brookings Institution, 1978), p. 231.

29. Manfred Halpern, "The Morality and Politics of Intervention," in James Rosenau, ed., *International Aspects of Civil Strife* (Princeton: Princeton University Press, 1964), pp. 258–259.

30. As Tillema (p. 83) points out, "A threat of Communist government and a threat to oil . . . are not mutually exclusive perceptions. The policy-makers probably perceived both threats at the same time."

31. E. L. Dulles, 1963, pp. 148–149. Secretary Dulles gave full expression to the "global" view of Lebanon when he briefed the Cabinet on July 18; his statement began with a quotation from Stalin that the Communist road to victory lay in Asian and African nationalism. *Minutes and Documents of the Cabinet Meetings of President Eisenhower* (Microfilm) (Washington, D.C.: University Publications of America, 1980).

It has been said that Dulles and other top policy-makers were, in the case of Lebanon and other Middle East crises, motivated as much by antinationalism as by anticommunism.[32] In truth, given the prevailing attitudinal prism, there was little operational distinction between the two attitudes. In the minds of Dulles and others, nationalism had proved itself hostile to American interests by serving the interests of the Soviet Union. Thus, as Townsend Hoopes says of Dulles, his preoccupation with what might be termed an "abstract macro-effort"—that is, the worldwide ideological struggle with the Soviet Union—led to a deep-set inability to come to terms with Arab nationalism for what it was.[33] Dulles's overall view of the world posited a "zero-sum" view of the American-Soviet conflict; Iraq was a Soviet gain and therefore an American loss. Any other radical coup would by definition be the same.

Thus, in summary, the general objectives of American policy in reaction to the Iraq coup were (in Quandt's formulation):

1. Prevent the spread of instability (Nasserism, communism) to the remaining pro-Western Arab regimes of Lebanon, Jordan, Kuwait, and Saudi Arabia.

2. Deter Soviet adventurism in the area.

3. Develop the capability to act in or against Iraq should circumstances require.

4. Enhance U.S. credibility as an ally and as a superpower.[34]

The urgency in achieving these aims was reflected in what Kerr calls "a generalized feeling on the part of the highest officials that 'something had to be done.' " The United States had to establish a military presence, even without precise guidelines, in order to buy time and retain some control over future events in the area. Otherwise it could not expect to exercise any effective influence or enjoy any credibility throughout the Middle East. To put it bluntly, "doing something" was better than "doing nothing."[35] Or in Eisenhower's own words: "The time was rapidly approaching, I believed, when we had to move into the Middle East, and specifically into Lebanon, to stop the trend toward chaos."[36]

32. Melvin Gurtov, *The United States Against the Third World* (New York and Washington, D.C.: Praeger, 1974), p. 23.

33. Townsend Hoopes, *The Devil and John Foster Dulles* (Boston: Little, Brown, 1973), p. 439.

34. Quandt, 1978, p. 234.

35. Kerr, 1972, p. 78.

36. Eisenhower, p. 270.

Furthermore, it was clear to policy-makers that such action must be immediate. There was a general consensus that Lebanon could fall while the Security Council debated and deadlocked on the issue.[37] By that time, the momentum of the sweep of Arab nationalism could well be irreversible, and both Jordan and Saudi Arabia would be lost irretrievably. As Eisenhower said in his public address justifying the American intervention: "We reacted as we did within a matter of hours because the situation was such that only prompt action would suffice."[38]

Despite the decision to act before consulting the United Nations, the administration's attitudes were still colored by legalism. The United States was careful to convene the Security Council immediately, as required by the Charter, and to announce that American forces would be withdrawn as soon as UN forces took their place. Considerable stress was laid on the fact that the American action came in response to a proper request from a legal government—unlike the British and French action at Suez in 1956—though Secretary of State Dulles warned that some observers and nations would not be able to grasp this vital distinction.[39] Attention was also called to the fact that Lebanon, alone among the Middle East nations, had accepted the Eisenhower Doctrine. Of course, it remained difficult to show that the Chamoun government had been threatened by a "country controlled by international communism." Therefore, in public statements covering this part of the legal defense, stress was laid not on this clause of the Eisenhower Doctrine, but rather on the Mansfield amendment which stated that "the United States regards as vital to the national interest and world peace the preservation of the independence and integrity of the nations of the Middle East."

Constraints on military action were also an important, though not critical, part of the perceptual framework. Eisenhower claimed that the American landing in Lebanon demonstrated the ability of the United States to react swiftly in "brushfire" situations around the globe.[40] But U.S. policy-makers also perceived certain limits to military intervention. This was especially true with regard to Iraq, which was among the Middle Eastern states least accessible to American military action. In addition, the swift and definitive nature of the coup in that country meant that in purely military terms "any reversal of the action was impossible."[41] Military constraints in Lebanon were also apparent. American strategic bombers were deployed at

37. Tillema, p. 110; *U.S. News and World Report,* July 25, 1958.
38. *DSB,* August 4, 1958.
39. Eisenhower, p. 271.
40. Ibid., p. 290.
41. E. L. Dulles, 1963, p. 142.

a considerable distance (in Spain and Morocco), and their usefulness was correspondingly limited. In naval terms, the United States was faced with the need to maintain a supply line stretching 3,800 miles from its Atlantic bases. The army intervened with the knowledge that half a million French troops had not been able to control Algeria.[42] There was also a perception that Lebanon stretched American resources thin at a time when other problems threatened, thus creating an apprehension of increased vulnerability and invitation to attack elsewhere. In the summary of one analyst:

> Despite President Eisenhower's reduction of conventional forces after Korea, the only overt military intervention that he undertook —in Lebanon—seemed to occur smoothly. Some military men did not see the incident in such complacent terms, though, pointing out that if any heavy fighting had occurred, reinforcement of the United States expedition would have been problematic. The navy's Military Sea Transport Service had lost a hundred ships to budget cuts and had none ready in the Atlantic when landings were ordered. Even if the ships had been available, the navy would have needed nearly a month to load and move an army division from the United States to the eastern Mediterranean. At the same time, tension in the Taiwan Straits left military leaders fearful that United States conventional capabilities were inadequate to cope with threats in both theaters. The low level of conventional ammunition stocks in the Far East and the small number of combat aircraft rigged to carry nonnuclear ordnance alarmed Pacific Commander Harry Felt, who warned that in the event of conflict in the Pacific, United States forces would have to use nuclear ammunition at an early stage.[43]

The constraints of domestic politics were another element in the psychological picture, though again not a major one. Congressional elections were to be held shortly, and the Suez crisis of 1956, along with other Middle Eastern developments, had alienated some sectors of the voting public. Eisenhower also felt clearly, after his meeting with Congressional leaders on July 14, that Congress would not support broader American action in the Middle East beyond the Lebanese landing. Very few Congressional leaders were outspoken in support of the Lebanese action, while some were vocally opposed.[44] As anticipated, the legal distinctions by which the Eisenhower administration justified its action in Lebanon did not curtail or substantially moderate domestic opposition to that action, and the public response to the Lebanese intervention was mixed. On the other

42. Hughes, p. 263.
43. Richard K. Betts, *Soldiers, Statesmen, and Cold War Crises* (Cambridge: Harvard University Press, 1977), p. 101.
44. Eisenhower, p. 272; see also John Donovan, ed., *U.S. and Soviet Policy in the Middle East, 1957–1966* (New York: Facts on File, 1974), p. 105.

hand, the landing was not opposed by any major interest group or organized public body, a fact that in the minds of some observers "freed the administration from the need to convince the public of the correctness of its decision."[45] The administration therefore bore these constraints in mind, but proceeded anyway with its contemplated action in Lebanon.

The crucial question was, of course, the expected Soviet reaction. On this topic the prevailing confidence in the extended deterrent theory was decisive. Eisenhower believed, as he often stated, that the Soviets were not likely to undertake impulsive actions, but would be circumspect in their behavior: "Personally I had always discounted the probability of the Soviets doing anything as 'reaction.' Communists do little on impulse; rather their aggressive moves are invariably the result of deliberate decision."[46]

At the critical morning meeting on July 14, Secretary of State Dulles also affirmed that the Soviet Union would, in all likelihood, make threatening gestures, but stop short of any direct challenge. The CIA view, as expressed by Allen Dulles, was in concurrence.[47] The principal military advisors were also agreed that nuclear deterrence would work effectively against the Soviets. The Chairman of the Joint Chiefs of Staff, General Nathan Twining, later recounted:

> John Foster Dulles personally asked my view as to the probability of Soviet reaction to such United States support. Speaking for the Joint Chiefs of Staff, I assured him that the Soviets would do no more than wring their hands and deliver verbal protests. We knew this because U.S. military forces could have destroyed the USSR— and Russia knew it.[48]

Finally, this view was supported by U.S. Ambassador to the Soviet Union Llewellyn Thompson, who cabled from Moscow that the Soviet Union would in all likelihood exploit the American action in propaganda, but would be cautious in action. Thompson also predicted, prophetically, that the Soviet leaders might make a dramatic gesture such as demanding an immediate summit meeting.[49]

45. Berkovitz et al., p. 103.
46. Eisenhower, p. 282.
47. Ibid., pp. 270–271; Tillema, p. 95.
48. Nathan Twining, *Neither Liberty Nor Safety* (New York: Holt, Rinehart and Winston, 1966), p. 64; Tillema, p. 95.
49. Thompson to Dulles, July 15, 1958, *DDRS*, 1977. These estimates turned out to be accurate; as Mohammed Heikal later described Khrushchev's talks with Nasser, the Soviet leader refused to issue an ultimatum to the West because of the risks, and warned the Egyptians that the most the Soviets could do was hold maneuvers on the Bulgarian-Turkish border. And this is in fact what transpired. Heikal, *The Cairo Documents* (Garden City, N.Y.: Doubleday, 1973), p. 134; see also Donovan, pp. 108–109.

At the Congressional briefing later on July 14, administration leaders were asked if they were prepared to "go the distance" with the Soviet Union. Both Dulles brothers, Twining, and the President all responded that they were ready to run this risk, but all discounted the danger of an actual military confrontation with the Soviets.[50] Thus, while the risk of involvement in military hostilities seemed high, especially given the lack of knowledge regarding the Lebanese situation into which American forces were to be inserted, the danger of escalation beyond the Lebanese context was felt to be considerably less and quite affordable. In a sense, as others have pointed out, this was the crucial perception, since in the absence of a Soviet military response there was no military problem that American forces could not meet and overcome, given sufficient time.[51]

American decision-makers were also occupied to some extent with other likely reactions around the globe. They anticipated a highly negative reaction in the Arab world: John Foster Dulles predicted that the Syrians might well cut the pipeline that crossed their territory, and the closing of the Suez Canal was also considered possible. It was assumed that most of the nations of Asia and Africa would vocally oppose the American action.[52] Despite these negative

50. Tillema, p. 95; *U.S. News and World Report*, July 25, 1958; *Time*, July 28, 1958.

51. The fact that the United States enjoyed a great margin for error, in light of its local military superiority, so long as the Soviets reacted passively as predicted, has been expressed lucidly by Malcolm Kerr (Kerr, 1972, pp. 79, 81):

> The very large powers can afford to stumble in the dark on a good many occasions, however, as long as the other great powers are not there in the same room. Even assuming the vaguest and most ill-founded rationales for American intervention on the part of the President, in one essential respect his estimate that the Soviets would do nothing in response was all that really mattered: in the absence of the Soviet Union in the Eastern Mediterranean, an American exercise in military deployment, not devoted to outright assault on anyone (unlike Suez), ran no great risks. In this respect it might be compared to the American landings in the Dominican Republic in 1965, which was a messier operation involving some loss of life but involved no threat of the outbreak of war. Apparently, on that occasion also, the decision to intervene was made from one moment to the next by a President possessing only the skimpiest of information and the crudest image of the local realities. A mistake? Quite possibly; but one that the intervening power could rather easily afford to indulge in.

· ·

> These alternative risks were not equal: American inaction would leave the initiative and the ability to influence events entirely to others; American intervention might turn out to be messy and expensive, but not downright disastrous, given the clear superiority of American armed forces over those of anyone else in the area (the chance of a Soviet decision to intervene having been readily dismissed in Washington). The worst that might happen was that American forces would actually have to be used, but not that they would not prevail. The best that might happen was that they would not be employed in combat, but that their presence would calm and stabilize a deteriorating situation and enable Lebanese life (and with it that of surrounding states) to return to normal. And that is precisely what happened.

52. Eisenhower, p. 271.

projections, the political costs of American action internationally were obviously not regarded as a price too high to be paid.

Perceptual Changes During the Crisis Period

The perceptions described above underlay the key decisions made on July 14 and immediately following (see below). But once these decisions were made, the perceptions behind them were modified by new inputs. As there was no armed opposition to American forces in Lebanon, the threat to stability within the country receded. The Iraqi situation also appeared increasingly stable, with a government dominated neither by Communists nor by hard-line Nasserists but rather by genuine Iraqi nationalists. A number of accommodating gestures from the new government also helped to soften its image. But above all, a decisive input in the perceptual changes in Washington was the reporting by Deputy Under Secretary of State Murphy from Beirut.

Murphy, who was highly trusted by both Eisenhower and Dulles, sent a stream of messages on the Lebanese internal situation during the two weeks of his mission in that country. He described President Chamoun as tired and worried, as a "self-made prisoner," and as a "victim of his own political excesses."[53] Murphy also came to a better understanding of General Chehab's position, including why the Lebanese commander would not and could not use the Lebanese army to quell the disturbances, and why at the same time he could not easily be replaced. Murphy also quickly recognized Chehab's possible role as a compromise candidate for the presidency. In extended conversations with leaders of the rebel forces, Murphy found the opposition interested in a compromise resolution of the Lebanese crisis, and came to consider their attitude as basically anti-Chamoun rather than as pro-Nasser or pro-Communist. In short, Murphy conveyed a new perception of the Lebanese situation that had its focus on the local forces within the country, rather than the international currents sweeping the Middle East. In Tillema's words:

> The rapid change in perception once intervention had begun demonstrates . . . that the impressions of the top leaders of American government are fortunately not immutable. They can sometimes be affected by information and events.[54]

---

53. Murphy, pp. 400, 407–408; Eisenhower, p. 280.
54. Tillema, p. 83; see also pp. 74, 80–82.

Images

The personal images of senior decision-makers, as revealed in their public statements, fill in the above picture and highlight differences of nuance between the two main American decision-makers. On July 15, Eisenhower made three public statements justifying American intervention, including a general radio-TV address to the American nation; in addition, he sent a public message to American forces in Lebanon on July 19, and made public two letters to Soviet Chairman Khrushchev later in the month. These documents contain ninety-three statements of belief, which include the following most frequent themes in declining order of importance:

1. *Danger to Lebanon.* Lebanon was seen as menaced by external forces beyond its control; without outside help, the Lebanese government was likely to collapse, and therefore the integrity and independence of the Lebanese state was the central issue of the crisis. There were twenty-seven references along these lines.

2. *Indirect Aggression.* In this perception, the pattern of fomenting civil strife in order to penetrate and/or control other nations was seen as a central element in the behavior of the United Arab Republic and/or the Soviet Union, and it applied to the Lebanese case. Fourteen statements can be so classified.

3. *Positive Statements about Lebanon.* Eisenhower made repeated references to Lebanon as a small (and therefore inoffensive and vulnerable) state, or to its being a peaceful, democratic nation traditionally friendly with the United States. Stress was also placed on the presence of a freely elected parliament. There were nine such statements.

4. *Accordance with the UN Charter.* American actions were defended as consistent with the UN Charter, including the collective right of self-defense, and with the general aim of promoting effective international organization and respect for international law. Nine statements.

5. *Defense of American Lives.* This traditional justification for intervention was invoked—perhaps *pro forma*—but nevertheless in solemn public declarations. Seven statements.

6. *Consequences of Inaction.* Six statements asserted that lack of American reaction would lead to further challenges, or that the present threat was in fact part of a larger threat, or that the current case fit the pattern of past Soviet thrusts, or called attention to the consequences of inaction during the appeasement period of the 1930s. The centrality of this perception was backed by a number of other observations that make it seem more significant than numbers alone would indicate. As Eisenhower himself stated, lack of American

response could result in "a complete elimination of Western
influence in the Middle East."[55] According to Emmet John
Hughes, Eisenhower "was impelled by awareness that the whole
Western position in the Middle East, so perilously poised since
Suez, now could crumble."[56] According to Ambassador Murphy's
account of the President's oral instructions, Eisenhower
commented that some had come to believe that the United
States was afraid of the Soviet Union, that American inaction
would lead to irreparable losses, and that it was therefore time
to demonstrate that the United States could support its friends.[57]

7. *Negative Reactions to the Iraqi Coup.* The shock over "the
   lawlessness," bloodshed, and brutality of the revolution in
   Baghdad was reflected in four statements in the public
   documents.

It is possible to see in the public statements of decision-makers
more focus on Lebanon itself than was apparent in their underlying
perceptions, even though this focus on Lebanon still defined the
problem in terms of external threats to that nation. Otherwise, the
account of Eisenhower's images in public documents simply underlines features of his thinking that have already been noted: concern
for following proper procedures and legal forms, the recoil to the
unexpected and brutal liquidation of friendly leaders, and the need
to demonstrate American resolve and boost American prestige.

On this last issue, as mentioned, a series of anti-American incidents
had considerable impact on the American President, who was increasingly irritated with the insults to the United States. The attacks
on Vice President Nixon in Latin America were very much on Eisenhower's mind. As one contemporary account put it, "these things did
not rest lightly upon a man who got his start as a soldier in an age
when respect for American citizens was backed up by gunboats and
landing parties."[58]

Eisenhower also tended to fall back into his old role as a soldier
during the crisis. Once the decision to intervene had been made, he
was able to occupy himself with the technical aspects of the landing.
As a close observer noted at the time:

> It was good to see him so relaxed. There was no hurling of thunder
> bolts, nor was there uncertainty. I realized as never before why a
> President is so important—to be able to give to others, at such a

55. Eisenhower, p. 269.

56. Hughes, p. 263.

57. Murphy, p. 398. Eisenhower later indicated his belief that Nasser had demonstrated a new respect for the United States after the Lebanese crisis (Eisenhower, p.
290).

58. *U.S. News and World Report,* July 25, 1958.

time, an impression of unruffled assurance and confidence. This was Eisenhower at his best.[59]

Secretary of State Dulles made only two public statements during the crisis period of the 1958 Lebanon crisis. On July 18, he appeared before the Senate Appropriations Committee to present testimony on behalf of the administration's foreign aid request for the upcoming fiscal year. In addition, he held an important press conference on the last day of the month. These two public documents contained twenty-four statements of belief, including the following major themes:

1. *Indirect Aggression.* Dulles laid special stress on the theme of subversion and exploitation of internal instability as a "pattern of conquest." This theme accounted for fully half of his public references during the period.

2. *Orderly Procedures and Effective UN Action.* In five statements, Dulles defended the need for following established rules in international bodies, while hoping that such bodies could take effective action against threats to the international peace.

3. *Legality of U.S. Actions.* Three statements emphasized the importance of the request of a legal Lebanese government, and reaffirmed the principle of nonintervention in the internal affairs of sovereign states.

4. *Consequences of Inaction.* Dulles also twice dwelt on the need to demonstrate that the West would resist aggression, making the same arguments that Eisenhower made in his references to the 1930s. It can again be argued that the importance of this theme is not adequately indicated by the frequency of its mention. For example, in cabled instructions sent on July 14, Dulles emphasized that "failure by West to respond to appeal from small, peaceful, traditionally Western-oriented Middle East state, especially when viewed within context coup d'etat in Iraq, would deal most grave blow to Western position in Middle East and in all countries which looked to West for support and assistance."[60] At the Congressional meeting on July 14, Dulles is reported to have declared that if the United States did not act, its prestige would be totally undercut and it would lose not only the Middle East but Africa and Asia as well.[61]

It is clear that Dulles shared Eisenhower's legalism, his stress on the external threats to Lebanon, and his felt need for American action to avert dire consequences to the U.S. world position. But

59. *Time,* July 28, 1958.
60. J. F. Dulles to American Embassy, Paris, July 14, 1958, *DDRS,* 1976.
61. *Time,* July 28, 1958.

Dulles's statements are also marked by the total absence of a Lebanese focus, or concern regarding the nature of Lebanese society and government. The theme of danger to American lives is also absent. Instead, there is an almost total obsession with the theme of "indirect aggression," which in practice meant an almost exclusive focus on the Soviet Union. Consider, for example, the following passage from Dulles's testimony before the Senate Appropriations Committee, which is unlike any statement made by Eisenhower:

> The Middle East is especially an area of change and instability. There are tensions between the Arab states and Israel and ambitions based on pan-Arabism. The Soviet Union seeks to exploit these in pursuit of its "revolutionary alliances," a strategy to which I have alluded. It hopes to gain control in this area of great natural richness where three continents meet. For the most part, its hand is hidden.[62]

Thus, even though Dulles professed sympathy to Arab nationalism (as did Eisenhower), in practice the focus on the Soviet Union again led him to an instinctive hostility toward the United Arab Republic on the basis of what some would call a misperception of Arab nationalism. In the words of one critic:

> Fearing or misperceiving the Pan-Arabic movement, [Dulles] seems to have acted out of unresolved contradictions within himself and within the fabric of American opinion: convinced that colonialism must come to an end, he was drawn in logic to an active sympathy for the rising forces of Arab nationalism, yet such a move was inhibited, not only by his Wilsonian insistence on a universal order, but more specifically in this case by the interests and judgments of his British ally. They were judgments that reinforced his own stubborn belief that Nasser was, wittingly or not, the principal agent of Soviet Communist expansion in the Middle East.[63]

DECISION FLOW

News of the Iraqi coup reached Washington in the early hours of July 14. Allen Dulles informed John Foster Dulles at 7:00 A.M., and Eisenhower was apprised of the situation at 7:30. Early information was, of course, incomplete, but was quickly followed by the Lebanese request for American intervention. Though the request was made verbally, McClintock transmitted it immediately without waiting for

---

62. J. F. Dulles, Statement in Support of Appropriation Request for FY 1959, Senate Committee on Appropriations, July 18, 1958, *DSB*, August 11, 1958.
63. Hoopes, p. 439.

a formal written request, and it reached the Secretary of State shortly
before 9:00 A.M. (thus indicating McClintock's changed perception of
the situation, in view of his earlier refusal to transmit verbal requests).[64]

Government machinery immediately moved into action, with military planners consulting contingency plans that had already been
drawn up. In particular, the plan for troop deployment that had been
drawn up during the May and June crises (BLUEBAT) was ready at
hand and stood planners in good stead in July. Also, in May the
number of marine battalions with the Sixth Fleet had been increased
to two; and on July 14, as one battalion had just been relieved and
had scarcely started homeward, there were in fact three available in
the area. Two landing teams were already stationed in the eastern
Mediterranean, where they had been deployed a few days earlier.
Thus, when the Joint Chiefs of Staff met at about 9:00 A.M., they
needed only to adjust existing contingency plans and military deployments.[65]

Eisenhower, after a briefing from military aide General Andrew
Goodpaster at 7:30 A.M., held a long phone conversation with John
Foster Dulles. Afterwards he consulted with a number of other officials.[66] Dulles also, by one account, consulted some seventy people
during the next five hours.[67] At 8:15, the Secretary of State met with
the State Department Middle East experts to hear their evaluations
and recommendations. At around 9:00 A.M., this meeting was expanded to include military figures, including General Twining and
Deputy Secretary of Defense Quarles. Two Deputy Under Secretaries of State, Robert Murphy and Loy Henderson, also joined this
group, and Allen Dulles came in later to provide the latest CIA
assessment of events in Iraq.[68]

This early meeting systematically considered the options available
to the United States in response to the Iraqi coup. One possibility
considered was acting through the UN, combined with other diplomatic efforts (possibly including a summit meeting of heads of state).
Alternatively, the United States could employ verbal warnings and
/or economic measures to put pressure on hostile elements. Another

64. Thayer, p. 28; Tillema, pp. 118–119.
65. Tillema, p. 100; *Time*, July 28, 1958; E. L. Dulles, 1963, p. 132.
66. Fletcher Knebel, "Day of Decision," *Look*, 22 (September 16, 1958), 17–19;
U.S. News and World Report, July 28, 1958. The Eisenhower-Dulles conversation,
which expressed fear for loss of the entire Arab World, is summarized in *Minutes*,
10:0418.
67. E. L. Dulles, 1968, p. 275.
68. E. L. Dulles, 1963, p. 143; Tillema, pp. 94–95; Knebel, pp. 17–19.

possibility was simply to wait for further developments, allowing the situation to clarify itself. But throughout the meeting the clear trend was in favor of direct action in response to the Lebanese request. Other options seemed too weak, too slow, and inadequate in light of the need for a determined response. As one participant put it: "Within an hour I think each of us there reached the conclusion that action was the only course. That meant landing troops and taking the risk."[69]

At 10:30 A.M., the group meeting with Secretary of State Dulles joined Eisenhower, Vice President Nixon, Secretary of the Treasury Robert Anderson, and others at what was afterwards labeled a "National Security Council" meeting. At this time, the Secretary of State presented the three major options developed in the earlier meeting, which were then discussed at length. Again, however, the trend was toward direct action.[70] Eisenhower reportedly insisted, however, on full discussion of all alternatives, even though he left the clear impression among those present that he had already decided on the preferred American response. This was later confirmed by Eisenhower himself, who recalled that "this was one meeting in which my mind was practically made up regarding the general line of action we should take, even before we met."[71] In any event, by noon the participants in the meeting had reached a consensus in favor of intervention. Eisenhower, however, announced no decision at this time, pending consultation with Congressional leaders, which had been scheduled for the afternoon.

The military input during these meetings was consistently in favor of action, though military advisors expressed concern over the adequacy of warning time for implementation of intervention plans. Admiral Arleigh Burke, Chief of Naval Operations, had originally asked for twenty-four hours, but in the event had to settle for considerably less lead time.[72] But the general attitude among the top military advisors was reflected in a later statement by Chairman Twining:

> It was only when the Soviets pushed "too far" and really high-level decisions had to be made that America toughened its hand. The

69. Quoted in Knebel, p. 18; see also E. L. Dulles, 1968, p. 276; and Tillema, pp. 103–104.

70. Knebel, p. 18; Tillema, p. 104; E. L. Dulles, 1963, p. 143; *New York Times*, July 15, 1958; *U.S. News and World Report*, July 28, 1958.

71. Eisenhower, pp. 269–270. The impression that Eisenhower had already made up his mind was shared by Sherman Adams, Robert Cutler, and Special Assistant Karl Harr; see Adams, p. 291; Cutler, *No Time for Rest* (Boston: Little, Brown, 1966), p. 363; and Karl Harr interview in the Dulles oral history collection, Princeton University Library, cited in Hoopes, p. 435.

72. Betts, p. 90; Shulimson, p. 10.

unflinching decisions which were taken in dispatching troops to Lebanon and our deployment for defense of the Quemoy-Matsu islands are examples. These decisions were taken at the very top level, and the Eisenhower-Dulles team had to make them against all manner of timid and overcautious advice. The results, of course, speak for themselves.[73]

The Joint Chiefs of Staff met a second time at about 1:00 P.M., and issued an alert to American forces in readiness for orders to move into Lebanon.

Other preparatory moves were made on the diplomatic level through consultations with allies. Lord Hood, the British Chargé d'Affaires, and Charles Lucet, Minister in the French Embassy, both met with the Secretary of State following the crucial morning meeting, as did Lebanese Foreign Minister Charles Malik.[74]

At 2:30 P.M., top administration officials met with twenty-two Congressional leaders. Eisenhower was careful not to present the issue as already having been decided, but the inclination to intervene was apparent to all present. The two Dulles brothers both presented briefings summarizing the situation and the arguments on behalf of the various alternatives, and General Twining presented the unanimous recommendation of the Joint Chiefs for direct military action. The President asked the Congressional leaders present for advice, and received some skeptical comments based primarily on the argument that the Lebanese situation was a civil war and not Communist-inspired. This skepticism, together with the virtual absence of enthusiastic support, seems to have impressed upon the President that Congressional support of American action beyond Lebanon would be uncertain.[75]

Nevertheless, it was clear to all participants that the President intended to respond positively to the Lebanese request. As Sherman Adams recounted, "the President put before the Congressmen the decision which faced him and left no doubt in their minds how it was going to go." And though most Congressmen were not enthusiastic about the proposed American intervention, tending rather to disassociate themselves from it, they also made it clear that the decision was the prerogative of the President. There was in this an element of self-abnegation, in which the President's responsibility was understood to be exclusively his.[76]

73. Twining, p. 74.
74. E. L. Dulles, 1963, p. 144.
75. Eisenhower, pp. 271–272; see also *Time,* July 28, 1958; Tillema, pp. 104–105.
76. Adams, pp. 291–292; see also *U.S. News and World Report,* July 28, 1958; *New York Times,* July 15, 1958.

Following the Congressional meeting, and despite the fact that only a few Congressional leaders had indicated outspoken support, Eisenhower felt that "in any event the issue was clear to me—we had to go in."[77] According to another account: "The president turned to General Twining. 'All right,' said he. 'We'll send 'em in. Nate, put it into operation' " (Decision No. 5).[78]

The plan that Eisenhower implemented was essentially BLUE-BAT, with some changes and adaptations. The first landing was ordered for the following day, July 15, at 3:00 P.M. Lebanon time. Only the airfield and the capital were to be occupied, contrary to some military advice in favor of a broader operation.[79] Eisenhower also decided not to ask for British participation in the intervention, though such participation had been a part of the original plans, on the ostensible grounds that American forces would be adequate and that the British forces on Cyprus would best be held in reserve.

As indicated, the United States also moved immediately to convene the Security Council in order to offer the United Nations a chance, at least formally, to take over the American role in Lebanon.[80] Realistically speaking, this action was of course designed primarily to cover the American flank legally and diplomatically.

Eisenhower later described his decision as the "least objectionable of several possible courses of action," comparable to the difficult decisions that he had made on the D-Day landing in Europe in 1944. Despite the acknowledged costs in terms of U.S.-Arab relations, and the risks of a confrontation with the Soviet Union, it was clear in his mind that doing nothing was the worst alternative.[81]

Eisenhower also tried to present the intervention as a redeployment of troops rather than as a military action, consistent with the official picture that the United States was merely responding to the request of the Lebanese government for the stationing of American troops in Lebanon. In Eisenhower's words:

> The basic mission of the United States forces in Lebanon was not primarily to fight. Every effort was made to have our landing be as much a garrison move as possible. In my address I had been careful to use the term "stationed in" Lebanon rather than "invading." If it had been prudent, I would have preferred that the first battalion ashore disembark at a dock rather than across the beaches.

77. Eisenhower, p. 272.
78. *Time*, July 28, 1958; see also Knebel, pp. 17–19.
79. Eisenhower, p. 275.
80. Telephone conversation between Dulles and Lodge, July 16, 1958, 9:45 A.M., in *Minutes*, 7:0843.
81. Eisenhower pp. 273–274.

However, the attitude of the Lebanese army was at that moment unknown, and it was obviously wise to disembark in deployed formations ready for any emergency.[82]

Following this final meeting of the President with his chief advisors, General Twining convened a third meeting of the Joint Chiefs of Staff in order to implement the President's decision. Eisenhower and Dulles, during the same period, telephoned British Prime Minister Harold Macmillan and began another round of diplomatic contacts.

The execution of the American decision was, however, marred by the same misperceptions that had preceded it. Ambassador McClintock, as noted, discovered that American forces might well be allowed to disembark in port if an agreement could be worked out with General Chehab. But in the event, U.S. and Lebanese forces almost clashed, due to the lack of coordination with or consideration for the Lebanese army, together with the rigidity of American military orders for an immediate forward advance. The Lebanese army was deployed and prepared to resist the entrance of American forces into Beirut, and only heroic efforts by McClintock, in cooperation with General Chehab, prevented the actual outbreak of hostilities. An agreement on an unopposed entry into Beirut was finally reached, and American forces were allowed to deploy peacefully in the areas designated in their orders.[83]

Another military-civilian clash on the American side took place over the deployment of short-range nuclear howitzers, which were carried as standard equipment by the marine and army groups deployed. Due to strong State Department opposition, these weapons, even without their nuclear armament, were not landed or deployed by U.S. forces in Lebanon. The military resentment of this decision was shown in General Twining's reaction:

As the circumstances developed in Lebanon, we did not have to fight, but, if we had, the absence of these primary weapons from the battlefield, in the hour of need, could have been most serious.[84]

Since the United States was still trying to operate legally and in accordance with the UN Charter, the relationship to UNOGIL had

82. Ibid., p. 275.

83. In McClintock's words, the troops thus "gained the hard way the objective whose unimpeded attainment they had rejected." McClintock, 1967, p. 113; see also pp. 109–114 and Thayer, pp. 31–33.

84. Twining, p. 65; see also Tillema, pp. 101–102.

to be considered carefully. Following the American landing, UNO-GIL commanders threatened to quit, while the United States was anxious to have them remain in order to demonstrate American readiness to have the UN safeguard Lebanese independence. UN Secretary General Dag Hammarskjold, exploiting this American anxiety, was able to obtain the agreement of the U.S. government that the marines would not move further inland nor interfere in any way with the operation of the UN observer forces.[85] At the same time, the United States formally proposed that a UN force replace the U.S. troops, and, as expected, encountered a Soviet veto of this resolution in the Security Council. As the Security Council quickly deadlocked over any resolution dealing with the Lebanese situation, the hope of any compromise solution through that channel receded.

The American landing in Lebanon was accompanied by other preparatory military moves, partly as a signal to other parties. General Twining had recommended the deployment of Strategic Air Command tankers in forward positions, as part of an increased alert for SAC forces. At the same time, he warned Eisenhower that the tanker deployment could not be concealed from the Soviet Union, and might therefore be subject to misinterpretation. But Eisenhower regarded the move as a useful signal to the Soviet Union that affirmed the seriousness of American intentions.[86] The President also dispatched a marine regimental combat team from Okinawa to the Persian Gulf, in order to contain any threat to Kuwait or other friendly governments in the area (including Saudi Arabia, where there was fear of an internal coup). But at the same time, Eisenhower decided against the movement of forces from the continental United States; part of the 82nd Airborne Division was held in readiness, but no further measures were taken.

Other proposals for broader action were also rejected, including plans to "unleash" Israeli forces against Nasser's Egypt. According to an account based on interviews with involved officials, General Twining urged Israeli action against the West Bank of Jordan as part of an overall scheme for reestablishing the Western position in the Middle East, including British action to restore the Hashemite regime in Iraq and Turkish action against Syria. Such plans, however, never reached a serious level of consideration.[87]

85. Rajeshwar Dayal, "The 1958 Crisis in the Lebanon—the Role of the UN and the Great Powers," *India Quarterly*, 26 (April–June, 1970), 130. Dayal was one of the members of the UN observer team.
86. Eisenhower, p. 276.
87. Quandt, 1978, p. 232.

Even more importantly, there was never serious consideration of intervention in Iraq, though events in that country were the trigger of the crisis. As already indicated, such action was seen to be too risky and too costly, there was no easy access to Iraqi territory, and above all there was no faction to support within the country. The firm control by the new regime in Baghdad was a decisive consideration in ruling out serious contemplation of a military move. The regime also moved quickly to demonstrate that it was neither a Soviet nor a Nasserist puppet, thus providing some reassurance to American decision-makers. Ambassador Murphy, when his mission finally took him to Baghdad, concluded that the new ruler of Iraq, General Kassem, "was grimly determined to maintain Iraqi independence."[88] In this atmosphere, American policy-makers began gradually to pursue a tactic of cultivating the new government and attempting to limit its ties to Egypt and the Soviet Union. This line received backing at a meeting of the Baghdad Pact powers on July 28–29, during which America's Moslem allies pushed for recognition of the new regime. By the time of Secretary of State Dulles's press conference on July 31, it was clear that such recognition was imminent.[89]

The second important operational decision, taken on July 16, was to send Robert Murphy to Lebanon (Decision No. 6). According to Eisenhower, the aim of this mission was "to achieve the best possible coordination between United States officials on the spot and Lebanese authorities."[90] Yet, Murphy was given very broad instructions that went far beyond this modest aim. The general scope of the instructions may have reflected the President's lack of close familiarity with the Lebanese situation. In any event, Murphy later recalled that "my oral instructions from the president were conveniently vague, the substance being that I was to promote the best interests of the United States incident to the arrival of our forces in Lebanon."[91] As it turned out, the Murphy mission, beginning as a perfunctory move to coordinate policy among American officials, ended by changing American policy in Lebanon considerably.

American policy-makers next had to decide on a response to a Jordanian request, parallel to the Lebanese request, for the deployment of Western troops. The British were inclined to respond favorably to the Jordanians, leaving the United States with the question

88. Murphy, p. 414; see also sources cited in notes 3 and 4, above.
89. *DSB*, August 18, 1958.
90. Eisenhower, p. 279.
91. Murphy, p. 398.

of whether to back the British or participate with them in a military intervention. There were hesitations in Washington regarding cooperation with the British, as the British appeared to have far broader aims than merely protecting the status quo in Jordan (such considerations may also have influenced the decision to decline British assistance in Lebanon).[92] American hesitations were also reinforced by the perceived lack of public and Congressional support for American actions beyond Lebanon.

British Foreign Secretary Selwyn Lloyd was sent to Washington on July 16 in order to secure American participation in a Jordanian intervention. Prime Minister Macmillan also spoke to John Foster Dulles at least twice by telephone on the same day. Eisenhower and Dulles finally refused to commit American troops to the operation, but promised logistical support and backup in case the British encountered serious trouble (Decision No. 7). In this way, they made it clear to the British and others that U.S. aims in the Middle East were limited to the protection of Jordan and Lebanon. In explanations made to the British, stress was placed on the need for a Congressional commitment, which at the moment was not forthcoming. As Eisenhower explained in a letter to Macmillan: "The introduction of our ground forces [into Jordan] raises much more difficult problems. Our public opinion in Congress would, I know, be extremely averse to seeing us take this further step."[93]

The British went ahead with an airlift of troops to Jordan on July 17. Subsequently, the United States was called on to help, particularly in providing airlift capacity and in dealing with the Israeli government, whose consent was required for the overflights to Amman. A week after the British intervention, Eisenhower agreed to the use of U.S. Globemasters to fly in supplies for the British troops, and exerted American influence on Israel regarding Israeli restrictions on the size and hours of the airlift to Jordan. At the same time, Eisenhower repeated his warning that no American ground troops were to be committed to the Jordanian operation.[94]

On July 18–19, the Lebanese situation stabilized somewhat. There was little fighting in Lebanon itself, and world reactions to the American and British military moves were calm. Aside from maneuvers on the Turkish border, there were no Soviet military moves. On

92. On this point see Quandt, 1978, pp. 252–253.
93. Eisenhower, p. 279; Macmillan quotes Dulles as saying that "no operational support could be considered until Congressional leaders were consulted" (Macmillan, p. 519; see also Tillema, p. 81).
94. Eisenhower, p. 282; see pp. 279–282 generally.

July 19, as the Security Council deadlocked over the issue, Khrushchev sent a letter to Eisenhower and the other relevant heads of state proposing an immediate summit conference of the Soviet Union, the United States, Britain, France, and India, in order "to take urgent measures to stem the beginning military conflict." Khrushchev indicated willingness to meet at any time or place, but specifically proposed meeting in Geneva on July 22.

This initiative put the United States in an uncomfortable position, given the general appeal of such a proposal. As Eisenhower put it, "this proposal was attractive on the surface and, I understand, made a strong impression in the United Nations."[95] Nevertheless, he had no hesitation in rejecting it in the form made. An ad hoc summit meeting would have provided a forum considerably inferior, for American purposes, to the Security Council itself—with Nationalist China replaced by neutralist India, and with no veto power available. It was inevitable that such a meeting would focus on American actions, giving the Soviet Union a chance to embarrass the United States in the full glare of world publicity. There was also the general opposition of the Eisenhower administration to hastily convened and inadequately prepared summit conferences. Eisenhower and Dulles had long insisted that any such conference be preceded by enough prior agreement to guarantee that it would not serve simply as a propaganda exercise. Also, the American administration argued that Khrushchev's proposal bypassed the United Nations and its established procedures. In the view of the American government, UN resources for resolving the conflict were "far from exhausted." Finally, it was pointed out that the ad hoc summit meeting would exclude smaller powers that were affected by events in the Middle East, such as Israel.

Thus, the American response, set at a White House meeting on July 20, laid considerable stress on the need to follow established procedures in the United Nations (Decision No. 8).[96] The rejection of Khrushchev's proposal was framed as a defense of the United Nations; Eisenhower pointed out, among other things, that heads of government could represent their states in the Security Council, thus providing a forum for a summit meeting without going beyond established procedures.[97] Eisenhower was taken aback, however, when

95. Eisenhower, p. 283.
96. See the discussion between Lodge and Dulles, July 20, 1958, 8:50 A.M., in *Minutes*, 7:0807. The statement was released on July 22; see also telephone conversations between Lodge and Dulles on July 21, 8:46 A.M. (7:0802), 9:07 A.M. (7:0798), and 11:00 A.M. (7:0796), and between Dulles and Eisenhower, July 22, 11:32 A.M. (10:0388).
97. *DSB*, August 11, 1958.

Khrushchev "accepted" this proposal on the following day (July 23), though still pushing for participation of India and Arab states in the debate and generally trying to make the contemplated Security Council summit meeting resemble his original proposal. Eisenhower rejected this ploy in his answer of July 25, again taking a line of defense behind established Security Council procedures. There was, he pointed out, no prior agreement on additional participants in a Security Council debate, and the Soviet leader could not take it upon himself to add participants without the agreement of other Council members. Eisenhower also stressed that such a meeting, if convened, would also discuss Soviet misdeeds in the Middle East, and not limit itself to a discussion of the American and British interventions.[98]

In the meantime, however, a more fundamental decision in U.S. policy was being made in practice (Decision No. 9). Murphy's close contact with the Lebanese situation, his long daily reports (often backed up by those of McClintock and Holloway), and his closeness to Eisenhower were all having a cumulative impact on views in Washington, as recounted in the previous section. A new view of President Chamoun, of the internal roots of the Lebanese conflict, of chances for its resolution, and of General Chehab as the potential key to such a resolution was recasting U.S. objectives in Lebanon. Already on July 19, Murphy and Holloway had agreed that "Communism" was not a direct participant in the conflict. Subsequent input from Lebanon to Washington, and its influence on American policy, is best recounted by Murphy himself:

> We [Murphy and Holloway] agreed that much of the conflict
> concerned personalities and rivalries of a domestic nature, with no
> relation to international issues. Communism was playing no direct
> or substantial part in the insurrection, although Communists no
> doubt hoped to profit from the disorders as frequently happens
> when there is civil war. The outside influences came mostly from
> Egypt and Syria. From talks with Chamoun, McClintock, Holloway
> and others, my estimate of the situation was that arrangements
> should be made for an immediate election of a new president. Such
> election would be conducted by the single-chamber Parliament
> according to the constitution, and I urged Chamoun and the head
> of Parliament, whom I visited promptly, to hold an election
> without delay. I hoped this would bring about relaxation of the
> prevailing tensions and permit the withdrawal of American forces.
> The United Nations group would remain in Lebanon as observers.
> This, then, was the United States objective which was reported to
> and approved by the State Department.[99]

---

98. See the discussion of U.S. strategy between Eisenhower and Dulles, July 24, 1958, 8:29 A.M., in *Minutes*, 10:0379.
99. Murphy, p. 404; see also Tillema, p. 82.

Murphy also, as reported, paid extensive visits to the chief rebel leaders and conveyed to them the reassurances of the American government that the United States was not attempting to keep President Chamoun in power.[100] Finally, in the last stage before the Lebanese election on July 31, the United States moved behind the compromise candidacy of General Chehab and used its influence on his behalf as part of a compromise solution designed to end the internal turbulence.[101]

The extent to which this represented a change in the American attitude is demonstrated by the hostile reaction of Chamoun and his supporters to the Murphy mission and its results. In one account, written by an American operative in Lebanon, reference is made to the "statesmanship of Great White Fathers," and the author goes on to recount that

> I pleaded with Mr. Murphy that on the anti-Government side he should confine his dealings to those who were clearly representative of their constituencies, and stay away from those whose status was in doubt, especially those who were known to be in the pay of the UAR. He listened politely, and less than an hour later he was on his way to meet with the leading UAR agent in Lebanon, in this way reviving his influence which had been falling since the arbitration effort.[102]

This new American position meant, as one observer put it, that in some sense the United States accepted the fact of Arab neutrality and nonalignment—since a compromise government was destined to reject the Eisenhower Doctrine and declare its neutrality in the East-West struggle.[103] In any event, the changed American policy posited a much more limited set of ends than those associated with the decision to intervene. As Quandt puts it:

> The driving force behind the decision [to intervene] was a desire to stop the spread of Communism and Nasserism, but the U.S. action was incapable of achieving such nebulous purposes. It was able to help restore order in Lebanon; U.S. diplomacy was able to help mediate the Lebanese internal conflict; the United States was able to assist the United Kingdom in providing aid to King Hussein. These were reasonable, legitimate objectives. Viewed dispassionately, they also contributed to the stability of the Arab-Israeli balance. And yet these were not the terms in which the issue of intervention was discussed. Instead, a much more ambitious set of goals was initially articulated, and only after the

100. Murphy, pp. 404–406.
101. Tillema, pp. 50–51.
102. Copeland, pp. 204–205.
103. Leila M. T. Meo, *Lebanon, Improbable Nation: A Study in Political Development* (Bloomington: Indiana University Press, 1965), p. 200.

decision had been made to commit U.S. forces were the objectives of the operation consciously scaled down, in part to counter British pressures to expand the scope of intervention.[104]

Operationally, this new policy, much more tuned to local politics, was expressed in a more active American role in the elections. As Chamoun recounts with some dismay, the United States even threatened the withdrawal of U.S. troops immediately if the scheduled election were not held on July 31.[105] As it turned out, the election was held as scheduled, and Chehab was elected as the new Lebanese president. His election was followed by an immediate drop in the tension in Lebanon, with less urgency and less need for the continued presence of American forces. With the decreasing perception of threat to American interests, the lessened sense of time pressure, and the reduced risk of further military involvement, the crisis passed into the post-crisis period.

104. Quandt, 1978, pp. 255–256.
105. Chamoun, p. 428.

CHAPTER FOUR

1958: 1 August to 14 October

THE ELECTION of General Fuad Chehab as President of Lebanon on July 31, 1958, drained most of the tension out of the Lebanese crisis. During the following three months, the internal stabilization of Lebanon was achieved and a diplomatic formula satisfying most of the governments involved in the crisis was successfully devised. In accord with its expressed intentions, the United States consequently wound down its involvement, withdrawing the last American troops from Lebanon in late October.

DECISIONS AND DECISION-MAKERS

There were six significant decisions in the 1958 post-crisis period:

Decision Number	Date	Content
10	1 August	Eisenhower instructed the U.S. Ambassador to the United Nations to seek a meeting of the UN Security Council on or about August 12, and informed Khrushchev in a public letter.
11	2 August	The State Department, with the President's approval, announced U.S. recognition of the revolutionary regime in Iraq.
12	5 August	Eisenhower acquiesced in Khrushchev's move to place the Lebanese issue before a special session of the UN General Assembly.

13	13 August	Eisenhower authorized withdrawal of one Marine battalion from Lebanon as a signal of intentions.
14	30 September	Ambassador McClintock decided, in a move subsequently approved by the State Department, to mediate actively in the Lebanese Cabinet crisis that followed the installation of General Fuad Chehab as President.
15	8 October	Eisenhower approved a U.S. government announcement that all U.S. forces would be withdrawn from Lebanon by the end of the month.

There was no change in the identity of the decision-makers during the post-crisis period, except that with the return to routine procedures, roles created by the crisis itself faded. This was true to some extent of military figures, such as Admiral Holloway, and was even truer of special envoy Robert Murphy, who returned to Washington in early August, resuming his usual position as Deputy Under Secretary of State, and ending his unique role as a bridge between the President and the Lebanese situation.

PSYCHOLOGICAL ENVIRONMENT

Attitudinal Prism

The basic perception of the causes of the Lebanese crisis held by American policy-makers remained unchanged in the post-crisis period: the Lebanese situation had developed because of *outside instigation.* Charges of "indirect aggression" and "fomenting civil strife" still dominated American discussion. The stress was still on the need for the United States and other supporters of international law to protect small and weak states, in particular, against inflammatory propaganda, subversion, and infiltration that threatened their integrity and independence. The Lebanese government, a legitimate, democratically elected regime, had made a legal request for outside assistance to meet such a threat. The United States had acted because the United Nations could not, but the United States government would defer to the world body whenever it took over protection of Lebanese independence, or when the threat itself terminated. All of this had, of course, important global implications, as it was an important indication of the determination of the free world to resist the pressures of totalitarianism and hostile ideologies.

The *reaffirmation of legalism* in American thinking was even stronger during this period, reflecting the movement of the debate to the United Nations. There were repeated statements defending the consistency of U.S. actions with the Charter and principles of the United Nations, agreeing on discussion of the issues in the Security Council or the General Assembly, and urging UN action that would make the American presence in Lebanon unnecessary. American policy-makers invoked the inherent right of collective self-defense, and underlined the fact that the action had been taken upon an invitation from the Lebanese government (and that the continued presence of American troops in that country was dependent upon the continuation of that invitation). There was also considerable stress on the principle and fact of nonintervention in internal Lebanese affairs.[1]

But against this background of relatively consistent basic attitudes, perceptions of the immediate Lebanese situation, and the threat it represented, shifted in *response to changing events.* The first of these events was the election of Chehab on July 31. This seemed to resolve the immediate issue in Lebanese politics, as it was a solution acceptable to both sides; Eisenhower noted that "things were now beginning to stabilize in the Middle East."[2] The remaining problem appeared to be simply holding on until the end of Chamoun's term, on September 23, and this was not expected to require any urgent measures so long as the presence of U.S. forces seemed to deter any challenge to Chamoun and to discourage widespread hostilities generally.

A further *relaxation of tension* followed the UN General Assembly adoption, on August 21, of a resolution cosponsored by all the Arab UN members, including Lebanon, Iraq, and Egypt. Representing a delicate compromise among the opposed parties, the resolution included a strong statement on noninterference by Arab states in each other's affairs, and requested the UN Secretary-General to make "such practical arrangements as would adequately help in upholding the purposes and principles of the charter in relation to Lebanon and Jordan in the present circumstances, and thereby facilitate the early withdrawal of the foreign troops from the two countries."[3]

1. The themes of "legalism," "indirect aggression," and other elements of basic perceptions that remained strong in the post-crisis period are documented and analyzed further in the following section *(Images).*
2. Dwight D. Eisenhower, *The White House Years: Waging Peace, 1956–1961* (Garden City, N.Y.: Doubleday, 1965), p. 285.
3. *Department of State Bulletin (DSB),* September 15, 1958.

Since the United States had consistently indicated its willingness to withdraw from Lebanon whenever the United Nations acted, this was acceptable in Washington and in fact constituted a convenient legal framework for what the United States planned to do in any event. More importantly, it was perceived as an important signal of *change in the political atmosphere;* Egyptian acceptance of a restatement of the principle of nonintervention, and of something less than an outright call for the withdrawal of U.S. forces from Lebanon, seemed to indicate a remarkably moderate shift in Cairo's position. Eisenhower noted that "fundamentally, this action in the United Nations terminated the Lebanon crisis, although American troops were to stay there for another two months."[4]

Earlier apprehensions of a chain reaction following the Iraqi coup, engulfing not only Lebanon but most of the Middle East, were no longer current. Whether this was credited to the presence of U.S. forces in Lebanon or to other developments, U.S. policy-makers sensed that the danger had passed. Initial fears about the role of Nasser or the Soviets in Iraq were allayed, and the subsequent behavior of both parties seemed relatively circumspect. American perceptions of an external threat to Lebanon also declined as the internal situation stabilized. There was little mention of infiltration across the Syrian-Lebanese border. There was an improved perception of the extent to which the crisis was actually Lebanese in origin or content, due largely to the impact of the Murphy mission, the consequent opening of contacts with opposition elements within Lebanon, and the U.S. military presence, which required ongoing contacts and negotiation with the Lebanese army and other forces in the country.

It was clear to U.S. decision-makers that the troubles in Lebanon had not ended, but they now saw these events as largely internal in source and implication. The general strike, not ended until early September, was, for example, attributed by Eisenhower to the effort of Lebanese opposition leaders to force Chamoun to resign before the end of his term—and it collapsed, in Eisenhower's estimation, when it became clear that the Lebanese President, backed by U.S. troops, could not be forced to do so.[5]

Another minor crisis, in late September, was likewise seen in domestic Lebanese terms. This followed Chehab's succession to the Presidency, when rightist forces objected to his initial cabinet, which was composed entirely of anti-Chamounists who had been active in the "rebellion." Consequently, the pro-Chamounists staged a "counterrevolution." As McClintock wired Washington:

4. Eisenhower, p. 288.
5. Ibid.

Present incidents in Beirut are of a political-confessional character
and entirely indigenous origin. They are not inspired from outside
as was the case when Syrian-Egyptian arms and money were
pouring into Lebanon. They definitely have no anti-United States
tinge as phalangist opposition to Karame government is a Christian
one and Americans are still greeted with applause when they go
about Beirut.

Security situation elsewhere in Lebanon is generally quiet although,
as we have predicted, there will continue for some months to come
to be sporadic acts of individual vengeance and violence. These
acts, however, will be Lebanese against Lebanese.[6]

The *decreased perception of threat* was reflected in a perception
that the number of troops could safely be reduced. U.S. forces in
Lebanon reached a numerical peak in early August, immediately
following the Lebanese election. Eisenhower explained the total
number of troops (14,357) as a result of "uncertainty during the early
stages of the operation." But now "we had more troops there than
were needed," and withdrawals were possible.[7] This was reinforced
by the overall perception, repeated in all public statements, that the
presence of U.S. troops was a temporary measure designed to meet
a temporary, external threat, and that so long as the remaining problems were internal, there was no need to prolong their presence in
the country.

There was also a perception of improved conditions in Iraq. The
new government there was obviously in firm control of the country,
had announced that it would honor all international obligations, and
was even "showing traces of friendliness to the West" in Eisenhower's eyes.[8] Murphy's visit to Baghdad in early August, following
the completion of his mission in Lebanon, reinforced the view of
Iraqi ruler General Abdul Karim Kassem as essentially an Iraqi nationalist, pro-Nasser but not a puppet of either Egypt or the Soviet
Union. Murphy, as already mentioned, saw Kassem as "grimly determined to maintain Iraqi independence."[9] It was increasingly clear
that the Iraqi coup was of domestic origin, and not part of an overall
plot extended through the Middle East. Consequently, it was considered necessary to deal with Iraq in its own terms. Eisenhower saw
the withdrawal of troops from Lebanon as, among other things, a
means of reassuring Kassem that the U.S. intervention had been only
for purposes of guaranteeing the security of Lebanon.[10] Iraq thus

6. McClintock to Dulles, September 29, 1958, *Declassified Documents Reference
System (DDRS)*, 1977 (Washington, D.C.: Carrollton Press, 1978).
7. Eisenhower, p. 286.
8. Ibid.
9. Robert Murphy, *Diplomat among Warriors* (Garden City, N.Y.: Doubleday,
1964), p. 414.
10. Eisenhower, p. 286.

became the object of solicitation rather than a target for intervention.

As U.S. decision-makers saw it, in fact, the major aims of American policy had been achieved. As Eisenhower said, "with a duly constituted government, elected by legal means, the independence and integrity of Lebanon were preserved."[11] In the longer run, senior policy-makers credited themselves with rendering Nasser less aggressive, with making the Middle East more stable for a period of several years, and with giving a salutary demonstration of U.S. willingness and capability to intervene in "brushfire" situations around the globe—thus deterring such challenges in the period that followed.[12]

The reduced perception of threat also enabled government officials to *focus on broader issues* that had not been visible during the peak of the crisis. They now turned to "positive" measures for ensuring the peace and stability of the Middle East, including controls on inflammatory propaganda and agreement on limiting arms transfers to the area. There were increased expressions of support for indigenous regional forces, including Arab nationalism and unity. There was a new stress on the need for economic development and a profession of willingness to assist in this endeavor, including a suggestion to establish a regional Arab development authority. Aside from reflecting a shift in perspectives on the region, this new stress also served to undercut domestic American opposition to the intervention in Lebanon and to the military thrust of Eisenhower's policy. Such criticism was never perceived by the administration as a serious constraint, but a surge of Democratic opposition in early August was successfully stemmed by Eisenhower's August 12 speech in the General Assembly, which embodied the proposals described above.[13]

Images

EISENHOWER

During the post-crisis period, President Eisenhower made one public address (to the United Nations General Assembly), released two public statements, held two press conferences, and wrote one public letter to Soviet Premier Nikita Khrushchev. These six documents contain eighty statements of belief, coinciding generally with

11. Ibid., p. 288.
12. Ibid., pp. 288–291.
13. Bernard G. Browne, "The Foreign Policy of the Democratic Party during the Eisenhower Administration" (Ph.D. dissertation, University of Notre Dame, 1968), p. 260.

the observations in the preceding section and providing an interest-ing comparison with the prevalent images of the crisis period. The most frequently occurring themes were:

1. *Vulnerability of Small Nations.* Eisenhower made seventeen references to the problems of small or weak nations in resisting the pressures and domination of powerful states, and to the need to protect the independence and integrity of such states and their right to be heard.

2. *Legality of U.S. Actions.* Eisenhower repeatedly argued that U.S. intervention was in accord with the UN Charter, or that the United States was following proper procedures within the United Nations, or invoked the inherent right of collective self-defense, or defended the legality of the Lebanese invitation of U.S. intervention. There were seventeen statements of this type.

3. *Indirect Aggression.* In nine statements of belief, the President developed the concept of indirect aggression, calling attention to the danger of external exploitation of internal unrest, inflammatory propaganda, and other techniques of destabilizing governments.

4. *Danger to Lebanon.* Eisenhower made eight references that expressed concern about the integrity and independence of Lebanon, describing the danger to that state as one of external forces beyond its control.

5. *Need of Economic Development.* Eisenhower made seven statements on the general need for economic and social development in the Middle East, pledging U.S. support in this effort and blaming many of the region's problems on unsatisfied material aspirations.

6. *No Permanent U.S. Presence.* In four statements, Eisenhower repeated his assertion that the United States had no designs on any other state, that American forces were sent to Lebanon only to accomplish limited ends, and that these forces would be withdrawn as soon as the situation justified.

7. *Need of Arms Control.* There were three statements on the need to control the influx of arms into the Middle East.

These public statements reflect a predictable need to justify U.S. actions. They also reflect or enlarge upon certain attitudes described above: concern with legality and indirect aggression. The theme of small states subjected to external threats was picked up and general-ized, as the need for justification apparently led to an effort to frame these thoughts in terms of the general features of international rela-tions rather than simply the immediate case at hand. There is also ample expression of the larger themes that were introduced in the post-crisis period: economic development and arms control.

On the other hand, as compared to the crisis period, the perception of danger to Lebanon from without is considerably less evident. There are likewise fewer specific statements about Lebanon as a democratic, peaceful, or friendly state. But, above all, there is little expression of the fear of broader consequences of inaction: the fall of friendly regimes, the loss of Western influence in the Middle East, the general issue of credibility, or the fear of Soviet gains. Also missing are the concern over U.S. lives (which may in any event have been *pro forma*) and the earlier shock over the brutality and bloodshed of the Iraqi coup.

On the whole, then, Eisenhower's images, as expressed in his public statements, fit into the observations regarding the attitudinal prism: the basic perception of causes remained unchanged, and there was continuing concern over the justification for U.S. actions taken during the crisis, but there was a greatly lessened sense of threat in the immediate situation and lessened fear of broader consequences, with more attention now being paid to some of the background issues obscured at the peak of the crisis.

DULLES

During the post-crisis period, Dulles touched on Lebanon in three public addresses (one of these to the special session of the UN General Assembly on Lebanon) and two press conferences. These included forty-four statements of belief, with the following major themes:

1. *Indirect Aggression.* Dulles made thirteen statements developing the theme of indirect aggression, including the previously noted new stress on the need to contain inflammatory propaganda across national borders.

2. *Legality of U.S. Actions; Support of UN Action.* There were also thirteen references to the legality of the U.S. intervention in the framework of the UN Charter, most of them including the assurance that the United States would withdraw when the UN acted effectively.

3. *Vulnerability of Small Nations.* Dulles referred five times to the problems of weak or small nations in resisting subjugation by outside forces.

Again, as in the crisis period, Dulles seemed especially preoccupied with the threat of "indirect aggression" as a form of Soviet expansion through client states. He shares Eisenhower's legalism. But again, there is a surprising lack of focus on Lebanon itself, along with a striking tendency to read the Lebanese situation in terms of general themes. And while Dulles, like Eisenhower, obviously felt less of an immediate or broad threat than during the crisis period, there seem to have been many fewer changes in Dulles's images than in Eisenhower's. His preoccupations remain basically the same, with some adjustment to the changed situation but no new themes such as appear with Eisenhower.

DECISION FLOW

At the end of July, American and Soviet leaders were still maneuvering over the proposed summit meeting. Eisenhower, as described in Chapter 3, had written a public letter to Khrushchev on July 25, repeating his suggestion that heads of state simply attend a special session of the UN Security Council, and rejecting Khrushchev's efforts to include India and some Arab states in the Security Council proceedings. Khrushchev answered this on July 28 by accusing Eisenhower of delaying the meeting through niggling procedural argument, and the Soviet leader seized on a proposal made by French President Charles de Gaulle that a summit meeting of the five powers be held in Europe.

At this point, in Eisenhower's words, the correspondence over a meeting of the heads of state "was becoming fruitless."[14] It was also becoming increasingly irrelevant, given the Murphy mission and the election of a new Lebanese President on July 31. Eisenhower therefore decided to act, on August 1, by instructing the U.S. Ambassador to the United Nations, Henry Cabot Lodge, to seek a special session of the Security Council on August 12, as the United States was entitled to do (Decision 10). As he informed Khrushchev, Eisenhower intended to represent the United Nations at this Security Council session, and hoped Khrushchev would also attend.[15]

But the course of events in Lebanon, and changing perceptions of the area, were at the same time setting new policy trends in motion. As early as July 25, there were press reports of U.S. and British agreement on a policy of reconciliation with the new Iraqi government, and a final ruling out of military action against that regime, given the lack of counterrevolutionary activity within Iraq itself.[16] This policy was reinforced, as described above, by the growing perception of Kassem as an Iraqi nationalist rather than as an Egyptian or Soviet puppet, and by conciliatory gestures from Baghdad. Also,

14. Eisenhower, p. 285.
15. Ibid.; *DSB*, August 18, 1958.
16. *U.S. News and World Report*, July 25, 1958.

when Dulles attended the ministerial meeting of the Baghdad Pact
in London on July 28–29, other Moslem members (Turkey, Iran, and
Pakistan) urged him to recognize the new Iraqi government. At a
press conference on July 31, Dulles acknowledged this pressure: "It
was the combined judgment of our friends . . . that the recognition
was on the whole desirable." He further indicated that this pressure
was influential: "Therefore we shall probably ourselves go along in
that judgment. . . . If they think that under the circumstances recognition is the wise and prudent course, we would give a great deal of
weight to their judgment in the matter."[17]

Eisenhower concurred in this shift of policy. Given all these facts,
as he put it, "there was no overriding reason for the United States
to withhold recognition any longer."[18] Official announcement of U.S.
recognition of the Kassem regime was made on August 2 (Decision
11).

In the meantime, Eisenhower's call for a Security Council meeting
did not end the maneuvering on that topic. Not to be finessed by the
United States, Khrushchev sent another message blaming the American government for the failure of the proposed summit conference,
and skirted Eisenhower's call for a Security Council meeting by
announcing that the Soviet Union would convene the General Assembly. This caused some consternation among the British, who
feared embarrassment in a General Assembly debate over their intervention in Jordan. But nothing could be done to prevent a General Assembly meeting anyway, and Eisenhower could see "no real
reason for embarrassment" there, given the perceived legality of
U.S. and British actions. Furthermore, as Dulles remarked privately,
"we cannot seem to be afraid of a meeting of the General Assembly."[19] Accordingly, the United States acquiesced in the transfer of
the debate from the Security Council to the General Assembly, issu-
ing a public announcement on August 5 that "welcomed" Khrushchev's decision to place the issue before the United Nations,
regretted his not accepting the Security Council as the appropriate
forum, but agreed on a debate in the General Assembly. This was
made easier by the fact that the United States had proposed a Gen-

---

17. *DSB*, August 18, 1958.
18. Eisenhower, p. 286.
19. Telephone conversation between Dulles and Under Secretary Herter, August
5, 1958, 6:40 P.M., *Minutes of Telephone Conversations of John Foster Dulles and of
Christian Herter* (Microfilm) (Washington, D.C.: University Publications of America,
1980), Reel 8.

eral Assembly debate on July 18, when the Security Council had deadlocked during its first Lebanese debate, and thus needed merely to move the previous resolution (Decision 12).[20]

The impact of the impending General Assembly debate, together with the relaxation of tension in Lebanon following the election of Chehab, led to a reconsideration of U.S. troop strength. As indicated, Eisenhower felt that the earlier buildup, decided when the extent of armed opposition in Lebanon was uncertain, was now excessive in view of the calm situation there. There were also signs of growing Congressional resistance to the size of the force already deployed.[21] In addition, there was a feeling that the United States should seize the initiative on withdrawal in order to establish its good faith, clarify its ultimate intentions, and avoid the appearance of submitting to Soviet pressure. As McClintock put it:

> From the diplomatic point of view it seemed essential that the initiative for withdrawal should remain in American hands. Nationalistic Arab radio and press attacks could not in that case successfully allege that the American landing was an exercise in imperialism. As a matter of fact, if the Americans kept the initiative, they would prove to the world that this was a case of "imperialism in reverse."[22]

Eisenhower felt that it was particularly important to avoid the appearance of responding to Soviet demands that were certain to be made in the course of the General Assembly debate. Consequently, "we arranged for sufficient troops to depart to attract some public notice before the convening of the Assembly."[23] On August 13, as the General Assembly convened, the United States announced the withdrawal of one marine battalion from Lebanon (Decision 13). At the same time, behind the scenes, Admiral Holloway and the Joint Chiefs of Staff were authorized to begin planning the eventual withdrawal of the remaining U.S. forces.[24]

The General Assembly debate thus took place one month after American intervention in Lebanon, with the situation in that country

20. Ibid., pp. 285–286; U.S. President, *Public Papers of the Presidents of the United States: Dwight D. Eisenhower, 1958* (Washington, D.C.: U.S. Government Printing Office, 1958), p. 585.

21. Telephone conversation between Dulles and William Macomber, Assistant to the Secretary of State, August 2, 1958, 10:55 A.M., in *Minutes*, Reel 8.

22. Robert T. McClintock, *The Meaning of Limited War* (Boston: Houghton Mifflin, 1967), p. 117.

23. Eisenhower, p. 286.

24. Ibid.; Herbert K. Tillema, *Appeal to Force: American Military Intervention in the Era of Containment* (New York: Crowell, 1973), p. 51.

relatively calm, a new Lebanese President elected, and U.S. withdrawal already inaugurated. As noted, in this atmosphere Egypt and
Lebanon were able to agree on a compromise resolution, also acceptable to the United States, that provided a general formula for resolving the issue. The United States also tried to put its intervention in
the best light by broadening its defense to include general Middle
East issues. Eisenhower's speech to the UN General Assembly on
August 13 included proposals for monitoring radio broadcasts to control inflammatory propaganda across borders, for the creation of a
standby UN peace force (which would presumably make such actions
as the U.S. landing in Lebanon unnecessary), for the creation with
U.S. aid of an Arab development institution, and for international
controls on arms shipments to the area.[25]

Whether intended seriously or not—and the Eisenhower administration clearly knew the problems involved in such proposals as
monitoring propaganda or creating an effective UN police force—
these ideas were not pursued seriously afterward by either the
United States or other nations.

A final flurry of activity occurred when Chehab, upon assuming
office on September 24, chose a cabinet consisting entirely of leftist
figures who had been active in the rebellion against the Lebanese
government. This set off a reaction among the Christian parties,
threatening a renewal of violence and an upset of the delicate compromise that had been achieved. Consequently (Decision 14),
McClintock cabled Washington on September 30 that

> I have decided to move more energetically in taking up Gemayel's
> request for my good offices reported Embassy telegram 1724. I
> have asked Prime Minister Karame, Foreign Minister Takla,
> Gemayel and two of his Henchmen, Kamal, Junblat, Henri
> Pharaon, Maurice Zwein, Pierre Edde, Takieddine Solh, Ghassan
> Tweini, Joseph Skaff and Adel Osseiran to meet at my house at six
> this evening to see if some formula cannot be found which will end
> general strike in Beirut and, in effect, terminate this civil war.[26]

McClintock proposed a formula based on a widening of the Lebanese cabinet to include some pro-Chamoun loyalists. In the Department's reply, McClintock's "commendable influence . . . on Lebanese
political scene" was noted, but the Ambassador was urged to keep his
role out of the public eye: "We should seek avoid creating public
impression of U.S. interference in Lebanese internal affairs."[27]

25. Eisenhower, p. 286; *DSB*, September 1, 1958.
26. McClintock to Dulles, September 30, 1958, *DDRS*, 1977.
27. Dulles to McClintock, October 1, 1958, *DDRS*, 1977.

While McClintock mediated, planning for U.S. withdrawal, put in high gear after Chehab's assumption of office, continued unchanged. In fact, there is some indication that the public announcement of the final withdrawal was not only *not* withheld, but purposely carried out during this mini-crisis in order to bring pressure on Chehab and others to compose their differences.[28] In any event, the United States announced on October 8 that the remaining American troops in Lebanon would be withdrawn by the end of the month (Decision 15).

Subsequently, on October 14, the Lebanese cabinet crisis was resolved along lines proposed by McClintock. With full calm restored to the country, and with a government acceptable to all major parties functioning and in control, American withdrawal proceeded on schedule and the last troops were withdrawn on October 25—almost, as Eisenhower noted, without public notice.[29] With the Lebanese situation fully restored to normal, the final period of the 1958 Lebanese crisis came to a close.

28. Tillema, pp. 51–52.
29. Eisenhower, p. 288.

CHAPTER FIVE

Decision-Making in the Lebanese Crisis

HAVING RECONSTRUCTED the psychological environment and decision flow of U.S. policy-making in the 1958 Lebanon crisis, I will now summarize the implications of this treatment for the central questions of this study. This means, first, identifying the impact of the crisis on the coping mechanisms through which decision-makers deal with uncertainty and stress; and, secondly, discussing how the content of decisions—the "dimensions of choice"—changed under crisis conditions. In both cases, we will make a preliminary assessment of the validity of the hypotheses presented in Chapter One.

COPING MECHANISMS

The coping mechanisms posited at the outset were changes in information processing, patterns of consultation, decisional forums, and consideration of alternatives. What changes in these four areas can be noted during the 1958 Lebanon crisis?

Information Processing

In the pre-crisis period, there was increased demand for accurate and up-to-date intelligence. Policy-makers were especially eager for evidence on UAR assistance to leftist rebels in Lebanon. Consequently, there was some tapping of new sources. The U.S. Embassy in Beirut entertained a stream of emissaries from the warring factions, who kept American diplomats abreast of their thinking. The embassy also gained information from patrols sent out to locate U.S.

citizens, and from exchanges of information with other Western diplomats in Lebanon. Basically, however, policy-makers in Washington remained dependent on the same sources of information they had had previously: embassy reporting backed up by the usual intelligence estimates.

The changes in the processing of this information were also minor. More of the intelligence was presented orally, given the greater frequency of face-to-face meetings. Allen Dulles was a regular participant in Eisenhower's meetings with advisors. Information moved to the top a bit more rapidly, and to some extent in a more "undigested" or unanalyzed form. It is apparent from his own testimony, however, that Eisenhower was no more influenced by the detailed and accurate embassy reporting on the internal Lebanese situation, at the end of the pre-crisis period, than he had been at the outset.

During the crisis period, the unexpectedness of the coup in Iraq left policy-makers in a state of uncertainty and intensified the demand for accurate intelligence. There was confusion regarding the nature of the new regime in Iraq and the role of various forces in the instigation of the coup, and there was even lingering hope for restoration of the Hashemite regime. Likewise, policy-makers were uncertain about the impact of outside events on the situation in Lebanon, and this was reflected in a greater demand for accurate information on that country. The general state of uncertainty that surrounded intelligence estimates upon which the Lebanese intervention was based is indicated by the lack of knowledge regarding the likely reaction of the Lebanese army to the presence of American troops.

In reaction to these felt needs, policy-makers sought new and often unconventional sources of information, and channeled it more directly to the top. The search was reasonably thorough, and could not be described as random. The primary expression of this was the dispatch of Presidential emissary Robert Murphy, who provided a new and direct source of information from the field to the President himself. This contributed to a change in the perceptions of senior policy-makers, beginning with Eisenhower. As seen in their altered perceptions of internal Lebanese politics and the new regime in Baghdad, American policy-makers were not insensitive to these inputs, but in fact demonstrated considerable responsiveness to negative feedback from the external environment.

There was also, during the crisis period, a pronounced increase in communication with external actors: consultation with allies, exchanges with the Soviet Union, negotiations at the United Nations, etc.

On the other hand, Eisenhower and Dulles did exhibit a greater tendency to rely on past experience as a guide during the peak of the crisis; the frequency of references to the 1930s and to the major events of the Cold War is striking, in both public and private statements. There was also a clear tendency to see more relationships among various elements of the external environment when tension was highest. The Soviet connection became stronger in decision-makers' minds; the mental distances between Communism, Nasserism, and Lebanese opposition parties became (at least initially) even fuzzier; and there was an immediate urge to relate Lebanese events to the potential "loss" of the entire Middle East (as seen in the certainty that the Iraqi coup was part of a "three-pronged" plot to overthrow pro-Western regimes).

In a sense, there was indeed information "overload" at the top, in the form of raw, undigested intelligence, but this proved to be at least in part functional, as it was Murphy's cables that taught Eisenhower to appreciate the subtleties of Lebanese politics.

During the post-crisis period, there was still a larger than usual amount of information being processed, and to great extent being transferred directly to the top of the decision-making structure. On the other hand, there was clearly less of a strongly felt need for information than at the height of the crisis, given the fact that there were no rapid developments that might leave decision-makers uncertain about the basic facts. There was a return to routine procedure in information processing, with more time to analyze and digest the intelligence gathered before it was transmitted to senior policy-makers. It was notable, however, that the new receptivity to information on the internal Lebanese situation, demonstrated by Eisenhower and others in response to the Murphy mission, seems to have remained characteristic of the post-crisis period as well.

In conclusion, analysis of the 1958 Lebanese crisis seems to confirm the following hypotheses on information processing, from among the twelve hypotheses posed in Chapter One:

2. The greater the crisis, the greater the propensity for decision-makers to supplement information about the objective state of affairs with information drawn from their own past experience.

3. The greater the crisis, the greater the felt need for information, the more thorough the quest for information, and the more open the receptivity to new information.

4. The greater the crisis, the more information about it tends to be elevated to the top of the organizational pyramid quickly and without distortion.

5. The higher the stress in a crisis situation, the greater the tendency to rely upon extraordinary and improvised channels of communication.

7. In crises, the rate of communication by a nation's decision-makers to international actors outside their country will increase.

8. As crisis-induced stress declines, the quest for information becomes more restricted.

10. The more intense the crisis, the greater the tendency of decision-makers to perceive that everything in the external environment is related to everything else.

On the other hand, three of the hypotheses on information processing are rejected in the Lebanese case:

7. As crisis-induced stress increases, the search for information is likely to become more active, but it may also become more random and less productive.

9. As crisis-induced stress declines, receptivity becomes permeated by more bias.

11. The more intense the crisis, the less the sensitivity to, and learning from, negative feedback.

Finally, in two cases, hypotheses on information processing were only partially confirmed:

1. The greater the stress, the greater the conceptual rigidity of an individual, and the more closed to new information the individual becomes.

This hypothesis is confirmed, at least in part, regarding cognitive rigidity, but is rejected in regard to closure to new information.

12. The more intense the crisis, the greater the tendency to an overabundance of new information (information overload) and a paucity of usable data on decision-making levels.

As indicated above, there does seem to have been some "overload" in the 1958 crisis, but it is not clear that this was dysfunctional or that there was a "paucity of usable data" at the top level.

Patterns of Consultation

As with information processing, patterns of consultation were not basically altered by the onset of pre-crisis tension levels. The circle of those consulted was not significantly enlarged or constricted, nor were procedures of consultation transformed. But within this framework there were some shifts of focus or emphasis.

First, there was greater volume and speed in consultations, with more of them taking place in formal meetings. During the two major decisional periods, in mid-May and mid-June, large-scale meetings— of Dulles and his advisors, of the military advisors, and of Eisenhower and all his advisors—were the norm. This only brought together those within the executive branch who would normally be consulted, but it did intensify the consulting process. It also gave area experts more opportunity than they usually had to proffer their advice to Dulles in face-to-face meetings.

Secondly, there was more consultation with military advisors. This of course reflected the need for contingency planning covering possible military options, as well as the execution of the precautionary military moves carried out during the pre-crisis period. Military judgments and cooperation were essential, even where the inputs were not decisive on the policy level. Policy-makers needed precise information on U.S. interventionary capabilities, and contingency planning for military intervention reached an advanced stage during the pre-crisis period.

Finally, consultation was focused more narrowly within the executive branch, with less tendency to seek or to accept outside advice. Though not yet as pronounced as it later became, this is the beginning of a trend that led to closure of the decision-making process to outside influences during the crisis period. It was expressed in Eisenhower's refusal to discuss Lebanon publicly, and by his failure to consult Congressional leaders on the issue.

When the crisis broke, the first reaction of decision-makers was wide-ranging consultation within the government, involving area experts, intelligence officials, military advisors, and others. Consultation with military advisors, in particular, was much more evident. Consultations in general were more frequently on a face-to-face basis, and the entire procedure was less formal. The fact of consultation should not, however, be taken as an indication of influence or of full participation in the decision-making process; in fact, the tendency on the part of both Eisenhower and Dulles (particularly the former) was to hear out as large a number of advisors as possible, but to play the actual decision closer to the chest than before.

The only outside consultation before the decision for intervention was taken was a *pro forma* meeting with Congressional leaders, who were given to understand that the die had already been cast. There was generally a closing out of domestic pressures on decision-making, though consideration of public or Congressional reactions did serve as a constraint upon policy-makers to some extent (for example, in the decision not to dispatch American forces alongside the British in

Jordan). Nor was this lack of outside consultation solely a matter of available time; the decision that took the most time to make (the gradual shift of American policy toward Lebanese internal politics) was in fact the most hidden from public view or external constraints.

During the post-crisis period, there was a drop in the rate of consultation with persons outside the core decisional unit, including those within the executive branch who had participated in meetings during the crisis period. Fewer extraordinary meetings were held. Consultation with the military was reduced to planning for the eventual withdrawal of American forces. On the other hand, a high level of consultation with American allies and other governments continued, as illustrated by Dulles following the advice of Baghdad Pact members on the matter of recognition of Iraq, and by the close consultation with the British on the UN debate and other issues.

Of the seven hypotheses on patterns of consultation, then, four seem to be confirmed in the Lebanese case:

14. The greater the crisis, the greater the felt need for face-to-face proximity among decision-makers.

16. As crisis-induced stress increases, decision-makers increasingly use ad hoc forms of consultation.

17. As crisis-induced stress declines, the consultative circle becomes narrower.

19. The more intense the crisis, the less the influence of vested interests and other groups outside the bureaucracy.

One additional hypothesis is confirmed insofar as it relates to consultation within the executive branch and with foreign governments:

15. As crisis-induced stress increases, the scope and frequency of consultation by senior decision-makers increases.

The two remaining hypotheses are rejected for the 1958 Lebanese crisis:

13. The longer the decision time, the greater the consultation with persons outside the core decisional unit.

18. As crisis-induced stress declines, consultation relies heavily on ad hoc settings as high-level consultation reaches its peak.

Decisional Forums

In U.S. foreign policy-making, important decisions are ultimately made by the President. There is no collective responsibility; the Cabinet, the National Security Council, and other such bodies are technically advisory groups and do not make decisions by majority vote. Thus, all fifteen of the decisions identified during the Lebanese crisis were, in the final analysis, Presidential decisions. Nevertheless, Presidents make use of different forums in reaching decisions, and advisors enjoy varying degrees of participation in the decisional process. In this sense, how did increasing levels of crisis affect the character and functioning of decisional forums in the Lebanese case?

During the pre-crisis period, the structure of decisional groups remained close to routine procedures, and largely institutionalized rather than ad hoc. It might appear that the two major decisions of the period—the decisions of May 13 and June 15—were departures from routine, since in both cases Eisenhower convened a large "ad hoc" meeting of advisors to air the pros and cons of intervention in his presence, prior to reaching a final determination. But this sort of procedure was actually fairly routine for important decisions in the Eisenhower administration (based perhaps on the model of military staff meetings). And the label of "ad hoc" obscures the fact that, with the inclusion of all the President's principal advisors, the meeting took on a large and formal character not so different from an "institutionalized" NSC meeting.

The immediate reaction to peak crisis on July 14 was to convene a series of large meetings of advisors in an ad hoc fashion. But then, and later, the real decisional unit was the President himself, or the President in consultation with one or two close advisors (usually Dulles). On July 14, as Eisenhower himself said, his mind was made up before the meetings were convened. There was thus less representation of regional and military expertise in the *decisional* unit, as opposed to the consultative circle. Decisions were taken without the direct participation of area experts; the higher the tension, the more dominant the role of the "generalists" at the top of the hierarchy. The process was less formal, and there was even less room for bureaucratic politics. There was a pronounced tendency to consensus both in the decisional unit and among advisors, reflecting perhaps the respect for strong leadership expressed by more than one observer. Nor was the high level of consensus a function of the time available, since in the Lebanese case there seems to have been almost no dissent on any of the important decisions throughout the entire crisis.

During the post-crisis period, the return to routine procedures meant a tendency to move decision-making back to lower-level bodies and to larger decisional units. The bureaucracy was again included more directly in the formulation of decisions taken, which were usually passed through the formal channels that had been bypassed at the peak of the crisis. There was even a decision taken on the spot by the U.S. Ambassador to Lebanon, Robert McClintock, when he moved on his own to mediate in the September-October cabinet crisis.

Of the thirteen hypotheses on decisional forums, therefore, eight seem to be confirmed by the evidence of the Lebanese crisis:

20. The greater the crisis, the greater the felt need for effective leadership within decisional units.

24. Crisis decisions tend to be reached by ad hoc decisional units.

25. In high-stress situations, decision groups tend to become smaller.

26. In crises, decision-making becomes increasingly centralized.

29. The more intense the crisis, the greater the tendency of decision-makers to conform to group goals and norms, and the less the dissent within the group.

30. The more intense the crisis, the less the influence of "standard operating procedures."

31. The more intense the crisis, the greater the role in decision-making of officials with a general rather than a "parochial" perspective.

32. The more intense the crisis, the less the influence of vested interests in the bureaucracy ("bureaucratic politics").

Four of the initial hypotheses on decisional forums do not, however, hold true in the Lebanon case:

21. The longer the decision time, the greater the conflict within decisional units.

23. The longer the amount of time available in which to make a decision, the greater will be the consensus on the final choice.

27. As crisis-induced stress rises, there is a heavy reliance on medium-to-large and institutional forums for decisions. (Large institutional settings were used in the Lebanese crisis, but not as decisional units.)

28. As crisis-induced stress declines, there is maximum reliance on large, institutional forums for decisions.

Finally, the remaining hypothesis on decisional forums is not testable in the Lebanese case because of the uniformly low level of group conflict in all major decisions:

22. The greater the group conflict aroused by a crisis, the greater the consensus once a decision is reached.

Alternatives: Search and Evaluation

There seems to have been little search for new options in U.S. Lebanese policy during the pre-crisis period. U.S. policy-makers saw the

situation as defined by the enemy threat, which called for a direct—
and presumably military—response. Diplomatic approaches, such as
following through on Nasser's proffered compromise solution, were
not seriously weighed. The basic assumptions of U.S. policy—that
Nasserism and Communism were the issue in Lebanon, and that
Nasserism anywhere was a basic threat to U.S. interests—were not
reexamined. Thus, the option of dealing with the Lebanese situation
as a "local" problem (e.g., mediating among the factions) was also not
considered. On the other hand, the options considered—all variants
on an interventionary theme—were carefully and soberly evaluated
in terms of costs, risks, and prerequisites, both locally and globally.
This is especially apparent in the cautious and measured responses
made to the Lebanese government in response to Beirut's queries
about possible American action.

Certain "routine" military moves (such as bringing the Sixth Fleet
closer to the arena of action) have tended to become reflexive in
Middle East crises; this was no less true in Lebanon in 1958 than at
other times. These moves, typical of the pre-crisis period, do not
involve the search and evaluation associated with "rational" decision-making.

The legalistic approach characteristic of the Eisenhower-Dulles
administration did not, apparently, serve as a real limit on the search
for and evaluation of alternatives. At the same time, it does not seem
to have lessened to any appreciable degree with the onset of pressing
political and diplomatic problems.

During the crisis period, there was a wider formal search for
alternatives; decision-makers were careful to examine all the options
that presumably lay at their disposal. This must, however, be seen
against the fact of a shared common presumption that the United
States had to act forcefully in reaction to the events in Baghdad.
Discussion therefore focused more on the method and tactics of
intervention than on the need to intervene, leading to a stress on
military and tactical options rather than on the basic choices to be
made. The legalism of the Eisenhower-Dulles approach was just as
intense as before, also, as seen in the drawn-out negotiations over a
summit meeting in the framework of the Security Council.

There was, consequently, no serious weighing of diplomatic or
political options as an alternative to a more forceful response. The
UN was employed as a means of ratifying American intervention, the
idea of high-level diplomatic contacts (such as a summit meeting) was
held in disfavor throughout the crisis, and the option of taking diplomatic initiatives within Lebanon itself only appeared gradually in the
course of events. In fact, the weighing of nonmilitary alternatives

came only as a response to inputs into the decision-making process from the Murphy mission. On the level of consideration of military and tactical options, some miscalculations and omissions might be noted, and in particular the lack of planning regarding possible clashes with the Lebanese army. Nevertheless, it can be said that the decision-making process followed a careful procedure of weighing options and reaching a rational and analytic judgment on this level, with a serious, if not totally correct, assessment of the likely consequences of different courses of action. The comment on Eisenhower's calm and "soldier-like" conduct of the crisis as a military exercise is indicative of the tactical rationality that characterized the American response.

In particular, military and political decision-makers alike were careful to reject, on the grounds of impracticality, all proposals for more ambitious actions, such as intervention in Iraq itself, or the instigation of broader Middle East conflict (either by encouraging Israel to act against Egypt or by goading Turkey to intervene on the Syrian border of the UAR). It should also be noted that estimates of Soviet reactions appear, in retrospect, to have been sober, clearheaded, and accurate. The crisis also seems to have forced clearer choices, where there had been a notable tendency in the May and June cases to postpone final choices or to make incremental changes in policy. And the decisions taken under the highest stress seem, finally, to have been no less "correct"; in any event, the immediate American aim was achieved, and it can be argued that the response was appropriate to the circumstances and needs of the case, even if it was based on questionable premises.

Evidence on the consideration of alternatives during the post-crisis period is mixed. There appears to have been considerable openness to new possibilities after the Lebanese election. The United States demonstrated considerable flexibility toward the forum of international discussion (Security Council or General Assembly) and was able to incorporate the General Assembly resolution into its own posture. There was also a tendency to consider a number of broad proposals for the Middle East that had been submerged during the crisis period. On the other hand, it is not clear that the evaluation of alternatives essentially differed from evaluations made in earlier periods, and in particular the U.S. role in the September-October cabinet crisis in Lebanon seems to have come about as a result of McClintock's own initiative rather than any carefully considered overall American policy. Basic beliefs and predispositions—the definition of U.S. aims, legalism, etc.—remained strong, but there was some tactical subtlety, and a clearer perception of the internal

Lebanese situation remained with the policy-makers (as in Eisenhower's analysis of the significance of the general strike). The general sensitivity on tactical matters is also demonstrated in the careful
consideration of the factors favoring an American reduction in
troop numbers prior to the General Assembly session.

In conclusion, the evidence of this case study leads to the tentative
confirmation of nine of our thirteen hypotheses on the search for and
evaluation of alternatives:

34. The greater the reliance on group problem-solving processes,
    the greater the consideration of alternatives.

35. During crisis the search for alternatives occupies a substantial
    part of decision-making time.

36. The relationship between stress and group performance in the
    consideration of alternatives is curvilinear (an inverted U)—
    more careful as stress rises to a moderate level, less careful as
    stress becomes intense.

37. Despite the rise in stress, choices among alternatives are not,
    for the most part, made before adequate information is
    processed; that is, there is not a tendency to premature
    disclosure.

38. As time pressure increases, the choice between alternatives
    does not become less correct.

40. As crisis-induced stress increases, the search for options tends to
    increase.

43. As crisis-induced stress declines, the evaluation of alternatives
    reaches its maximum care, more so when time salience is low.

44. The more intense the crisis, the greater the tendency of
    decision-makers to narrow their span of attention to a few
    aspects of the decision-making task ("tunnel vision").

45. The more intense the crisis, the more likely that decision-
    makers will be forced to make a clear choice rather than
    postponing choices or drifting into policy.

Three additional hypotheses are *partially* confirmed in the Lebanese case:

33. As stress increases, decision-makers become more concerned
    with the immediate than the long-run future.

39. Decision-makers do not generally choose among alternatives
    with an inadequate assessment of their consequences.

41. As crisis-induced stress increases, the evaluation of alternatives
    becomes less careful. (This does not seem to be the case with
    moderately increasing levels of tension, but does seem to hold
    for the period of peak stress.)

The final hypothesis on consideration of alternatives is rejected for the 1958 Lebanese crisis:

42. As crisis-induced stress declines, the search for options tends to become less extensive than in all other phases of the crisis period.

DIMENSIONS OF CHOICE

In considering the impact of crisis conditions on the content of decisions made during the 1958 Lebanese crisis, we shall proceed by considering as a group the decisions made during each of the three crisis periods, respectively.

Pre-crisis Period

During this period, it will be recalled, four major decisions were taken:

1. On May 13, conditions were set for American intervention in Lebanon.
2. On about May 22, it was decided to support a Lebanese appeal to the UN Security Council.
3. Around the date of June 11, Eisenhower decided not to respond favorably to Nasser's suggested compromise.
4. On June 15, Eisenhower and his advisors again postponed any direct action.

In each of these decisions, there was a single, dominant *core input* or crucial stimulus: a Lebanese request in Decison 1, a pending UN debate in Decision 2, an Egyptian "feeler" in Decision 3, and sudden Lebanese rebel military success in Decision 4.

The perceived *costs* of the choices made, as coded on a three-point scale (low, medium, high), seem to have been low in all four cases.

The *importance* or perceived value of the decisions at the time of choice, measured on a five-point ordinal scale, appears by the evidence discussed to be 1 (marginal) for Decisions 2 and 3, and 3 (important) for Decisions 1 and 4.

In terms of *complexity*, only Decision 1 seems to have involved more than one issue area (Military-Security and Political-Diplomatic). Decisions 2 and 3 were Political-Diplomatic only, and Decision 4 seems to have been Military-Security only.

The *systemic domain*—the perceived scope of reverberations from the decision—was both Bilateral and Regional in Decisions 1 and 4, primarily Regional in Decision 2, and primarily Bilateral in Decision 3.

The dominant *process* or mental procedure associated with the selected option was Rational in Decisions 1 and 4, Routine in Decision 2, and Affective in Decision 3.

Regarding *activity,* the thrust in Decisions 1, 3, and 4 was either not to act or to delay, while in Decision 2 (taking up the issue in the Security Council) it was to act. The action contemplated was in two cases (2 and 3) verbal, in one case (1) verbal and physical, and in one case (4) physical.

Only one decision, Decision 1, clearly possessed *novelty*—i.e., was innovative in the sense of being nonreliant on precedent and past choices.

The *coping strategies* employed by decision-makers in the 1958 pre-crisis period were fairly consistent. In all four decisions, reliance on *ideology* and on *operational code* beliefs seems to have been significant. In all but Decision 3, the use of *historical models* was clearly a factor; in all but Decision 2, there was a tendency to *"satisficing"* rather then "optimizing" behavior—i.e., choosing the non-problematic rather than the best solution. In Decision 3, there was also a marked tendency to *avoid value trade-offs,* in that decision-makers seem to have persuaded themselves that what best preserved good relations with Chamoun was also best on other value dimensions (resolving the conflict, dealing with Nasser, etc.).

Crisis Period

There were five significant decisions taken during the crisis period:

5. Eisenhower ordered the landing of U.S. troops in Lebanon on July 14.

6. Eisenhower sent Murphy to Lebanon on July 16.

7. Eisenhower decided not to send U.S. troops to Jordan (July 17).

8. On July 22, the United States rejected a Soviet proposal for a summit conference.

9. During the last two weeks of July, the United States evolved a policy of supporting the election of Chehab as a compromise solution.

There was some increase in the number and variety of *core inputs* during this period. Decision 5 involved both external events (the Iraqi coup) and a strong input from prevailing ideology; Decision 8 also involved both an external stimulus (the Soviet proposal) and an internal input (the Eisenhower-Dulles operational code). Decisions 6, 7, and 8 involved single, but new, core inputs: respectively, the need of coordination with Lebanon, pressure from the British, and the Murphy mission.

The anticipated *costs* of the decisions rose to high in Decision 5 and medium in Decision 8, remaining low in the other three cases.

The perceived *importance* of the decisions rose sharply. Decision 5 was regarded as decisive (5), Decision 9 seems clearly to have been seen as significant (4), and the other three decisions still ranked as important (3).

The *complexity* of the decisions also increased, with all but Decision 8 involving two issue-areas (Military-Security and Political-Diplomatic). Decision 8, on the Soviet summit proposal, involved only the Political-Diplomatic.

The anticipated scope of repercussions or *systemic domain* also expanded. Decision 5, at the peak of the crisis, seems to have involved all five levels, from Domestic to Global. Decision 7 involved three levels (Domestic, Bilateral, Regional), as did Decision 8 (Regional, Superpower, Global) and Decision 9 (Bilateral, Regional, Global). Decision 6 was limited (initially) to the Bilateral level.

In terms of the decisional *process*, Decision 5 must be judged to have been predominantly Affective with some Rational elements. By the same token, the other decisions were predominantly Rational, though with some elements of Routine processes in Decision 6 and of Affective processes in Decision 8.

Regarding *activity*, the thrust of all the decisions but Decision 7 was to act. Decisions 6, 8, and 9, however, involved only verbal action, while Decision 5 involved both verbal and physical. Decision 7 was a decision *not* to act, but contemplated physical action.

There was more *novelty* in the crisis period decisions. Decisions 5, 8, and 9 were all basically innovative, not relying predominantly on past patterns, while Decisions 6 and 7 were not "novel."

As for the Holsti and George *coping strategies*, there was slight change in the crisis-period decisions. Strong use was still made of the "operational code" (all decisions), of ideology (all but Decision 6), of historical models (all but Decision 9), and of "satisficing" behavior (Decisions 7, 8, and 9). The other three strategies were each employed once: "incrementalism" in Decision 9, "consensus politics" in Decision 7, and the avoidance of value trade-offs in Decision 9. There was thus somewhat greater variety in the use of coping strategies, but the pattern was basically the same as in the pre-crisis period.

Post-crisis Period

The six decisions of the 1958 post-crisis period were:

10. On August 1, Eisenhower decided to convene the UN Security Council on about August 12.

11. On August 2, the United States recognized the new regime in Iraq.

12. On August 5, Eisenhower agreed to a General Assembly debate on Lebanon.

13. On August 13, Eisenhower authorized the withdrawal of one Marine battalion from Lebanon.

14. Ambassador McClintock, in late September, moved to mediate in a Lebanese cabinet crisis.

15. On October 8, Eisenhower approved public announcement of the withdrawal of the remaining U.S. troops from Lebanon.

Except in one case (Decision 11, in which both normalization within Iraq and pressure from allies served as crucial stimuli), there was a single dominant *core input* to post-crisis decisions. These inputs were: Decisions 10 and 12, Soviet pressure; Decision 13, the impending UN debate; Decision 14, Lebanese instability; and Decision 15, the successful transfer of power in Lebanon.

In all six decisions, the perceived *cost* was low, and the perceived *importance* ranged from marginal (1) in Decision 12, to consequential (2) in Decisions 10, 11, and 14, to important (3) in Decisions 13 and 15.

The *complexity* of the decisions also declined, with only Decisions 13 and 15 involving more than one issue-area (in both cases, Military-Security and Political-Diplomatic). The other decisions were all limited primarily to the Political-Diplomatic area.

The *systemic domain* was also reduced. Three of the decisions (10, 12, and 13) were perceived to have reverberations on two levels (Global and Superpower), while Decision 15 was perceived to be of importance on the Global and Bilateral levels. Decisions 11 and 14 seem to have had perceived repercussions only on the Bilateral level.

The *process* associated with post-crisis decisions was predominantly Rational in all cases, with some elements of Affective processes in Decision 10 and of Routine processes in Decision 11. There was also fair consistency in activity, with all decisions being to act, and with the implied action being verbal in all but two cases (Decisions 13 and 15, involving physical action).

None of the decisions can be regarded as novel; all seem to fit well into past patterns and precedent.

With one exception, patterns in coping strategies remained consistent. The one exception was value trade-offs, which in the post-crisis period seem to have been a part of half of the decisions (12, 13, and 15). Apart from this, historical models (all cases), ideology (all cases but Decision 11), and operational code (all cases) all remained central elements in the decision-makers' approaches to dealing with crisis. "Satisficing" strategies also remained important, in this case characterizing three decisions (10, 11, and 12). Incrementalism can be observed in one case, Decision 13.

Hypotheses

In Chapter One, I introduced seventeen hypotheses on the relationship between stress levels and decisions, as measured on the above dimensions (apart from coping strategies). On the basis of the discussion there, we can now test these hypotheses for the 1958 Lebanese crisis.

Ten of the hypotheses are confirmed by the evidence presented:

46. As crisis-induced stress begins to rise, the number and variety of core inputs to decisions increase sharply.

47. As crisis-induced stress declines, the number and variety of core inputs are reduced.

48. When decision-makers operate under stress, they assess their decision as costly.

49. When decision-makers operate under low or declining stress, they perceive their decisions as of small cost.

50. As crisis-induced stress rises, decision-makers tend to perceive their decisions as more and more important.

51. As crisis-induced stress declines, the perceived importance of decisions declines from the levels in all other phases of the crisis period.

52. As crisis-induced stress rises, the complexity of issue-areas involved steadily rises.

57. As crisis-induced stress declines, decision-makers resort mainly to rational procedures to ultimate choice.

58. As crisis-induced stress rises, there is a tendency for decisions to be continuously active.

61. As crisis-induced stress rises, there is a steady increase in resort to choices without precedent.

The evidence at hand leads, however, to the rejection of the other seven hypotheses posited at the outset:

53. As crisis-induced stress declines, the number of issue-areas involved in decision-making reaches its maximum.

54. In situations of peak crisis-induced stress, the heretofore steadily-broadening systemic levels of anticipated reverberations from decisions become narrower.

55. As crisis-induced stress declines, systemic domain rises from the peak crisis phase.

56. As crisis-induced stress rises, the selected option tends to be chosen by rational calculus and analysis of the issues, rather than by a process of bargaining and compromise. (This hypothesis is clearly not supported by evidence regarding the decision taken at the peak phase of the crisis, but it is supported by other decisions made during the crisis period.)

59. As crisis-induced stress rises, the activity implied by the decline moves from physical to verbal.

60. As crisis-induced stress declines, there is a sharp increase in decisions to delay or not to act.

62. As crisis-induced stress declines, unprecedented choices remain at their peak.

PART II

THE JORDANIAN CRISIS

CHAPTER SIX

1970: 6 September to 15 September

THE 1970 Jordanian crisis bore a number of similarities to the Lebanese crisis twelve years earlier.[1] Once again, the issue for U.S. policymakers was the survival of a friendly and moderate regime in a small Middle Eastern state. Once again, this regime was threatened in a civil war by forces controlling large areas of its territory. Once again, the "real" problem was assistance to anti-government forces from a neighboring radical regime—a radical Syrian regime, to be specific. Finally, in both cases Damascus was seen as the agent or the collaborator of the Soviet Union, and in both cases the United States decided on the use of military force, if necessary, to save the threatened regime.

But there were, of course, important differences. The international context had changed considerably over twelve years: American fears of radical Third World nationalism had abated somewhat, but at the same time the Soviet Union had in many ways achieved rough parity as a rival. In the Middle East in particular, there was more superpower involvement: a greatly increased Soviet role in Egypt and Syria since the 1967 war, an enlarged Soviet naval presence in the Mediterranean, and greater polarization of Middle East conflicts along Cold War lines. The dangers of direct U.S.-USSR confrontation were more apparent; the American President himself habitually referred to the Middle East as a "powder keg."

---

1. For suggestive comparisons of the two crises, see William B. Quandt, "Lebanon, 1958, and Jordan, 1970," in Barry M. Blechman and Stephen S. Kaplan, *Force without War: U.S. Armed Forces as a Political Instrument* (Washington, D.C.: Brookings Institution, 1978), pp. 222–288; and Yair Evron, *The Middle East: Nations, Superpowers, and Wars* (New York: Praeger, 1973), pp. 159–162.

Regionally, the threat of Nasserism had receded, but the Arab-Israeli conflict had become more turbulent. The 1967 war had added new issues and pressures, while enlarging the Soviet role in the conflict, not only in military aid but also diplomatically. This was illustrated in the 1969–1970 "war of attrition" between Israel and Egypt, which was terminated by a cease-fire in August 1970.

The Jordanian crisis also differed in that direct Syrian intervention became a reality, while, despite this greater "provocation," direct U.S. military involvement did not. The closer tie to the Arab-Israeli conflict was reflected in American contemplation of Israeli action as a substitute for its own intervention. Finally, while the threatened regime was "saved" in both Lebanon and Jordan, in the former case this was part of a diplomatic compromise along rather traditional Lebanese lines and marked a restoration of the *status quo ante*, while the latter case was a military "victory" that constituted a turning point in Jordan and in the region.

This "victory" was in turn made possible by certain differences between the internal situation of Jordan as compared to that of Lebanon. In contrast to the fragmented and complex Lebanese internal scene, King Hussein of Jordan faced a single opposition force—the Palestinian guerrilla organizations in Jordan—which was in many ways an alien body. The Jordanian population, by and large, was uninvolved in the struggle. "Nasserism" as a force was no longer a major threat to the internal cohesion of Jordan, and Hussein enjoyed the undivided allegiance of an army which had clear military superiority over the Palestinian forces.

The crisis in Jordan had developed gradually, as the Palestine Liberation Organization (PLO) and its constituent groups rose to prominence after the 1967 war and sought to use Jordan as a base and a staging area. As the various Palestinian factions came to function as a state within a state, defiant of governmental authority, tensions between them and the Jordanian army rose. By mid-1970, violent incidents had become commonplace, and there was widespread expectation of an imminent showdown—if Hussein decided to risk the almost certain hostile reactions of radical Arab states to any move to assert his authority over the Palestinians. On the other hand, it was clear that Hussein would lose authority altogether if he did not act, and there were indications that his army—led by fiercely loyal and traditional Beduin officers—would soon act to reassert its authority over the PLO camps, with or without Hussein's orders. In this context, the simultaneous hijacking of three Western airliners on September 6, as part of a Palestinian effort to sabotage the cease-fire on the Suez Canal and the peace initiative linked to it, marks the onset of a short pre-crisis period that escalated within ten days into a struggle over the future of Jordan. U.S. policy-makers immediately perceived these events as a threat to American interests and credibility in the Middle East and global systems.

DECISIONS AND DECISION-MAKERS

There were four major decisions in the 1970 pre-crisis period:

Decision Number	Date	Content
1	7 September	In coordination with other threatened states, President Nixon and his advisors set a policy of no capitulation to hijackers and unified negotiations with the International Red Cross as an intermediary; proposals for military rescue operations were deferred.[2]
2	9 September	Nixon ordered Sixth Fleet movements, the deployment of C-130s and F-4s to Turkey, and a semi-alert for the 82nd Airborne Division.[3]
3	11 September	The United States announced a comprehensive program of anti-hijacking measures for U.S. airports and airlines.[4]
4	12 September	Nixon authorized resumption of economic aid, and an increase in military aid, to Israel; this was announced by Secretary of State Rogers.[5]

Rescue operations were proposed and studied on various levels throughout the following week, but never reached the point of serious discussion requiring an explicit decision on proceeding.[6]

2. Henry Kissinger, *White House Years* (Boston: Little, Brown, 1979), p. 601; Henry Brandon, *The Retreat of American Power* (New York: Dell, 1973), pp. 129–133; interviews with Admiral Thomas Moorer, Chairman, Joint Chiefs of Staff; U. Alexis Johnson, Under Secretary of State for Political Affairs; and Robert Pranger, Deputy Assistant Secretary of Defense for Near Eastern and South Asian Affairs (all positions are those held during the 1970 crisis).
3. Kissinger, 1979, p. 605; Quandt, 1978, pp. 272–274.
4. U.S. President, *Public Papers of the Presidents of the United States: Richard Nixon, 1970* (Washington, D.C.: U.S. Government Printing Office, 1970), pp. 742–743.
5. Quandt, 1978, p. 274.
6. Kissinger, 1979, pp. 601–609; Quandt, 1978, p. 278; interviews with Johnson; Pranger; Samuel Hoskinson, National Security Council Staff; Talcott Seelye, Country Director, Lebanon, Jordan, Syria, and Iraq, Department of State; Walter Smith, Deputy Director, Egyptian Affairs, Department of State; and L. Dean Brown, U.S. Ambassador to Jordan.

The major decision-makers in the pre-crisis period were President Richard Nixon and his Assistant for National Security Affairs, Henry Kissinger. Other participants in high-level discussions included William Rogers, Secretary of State; Melvin Laird, Secretary of Defense; Admiral Thomas H. Moorer, Chairman of the Joint Chiefs of Staff; Richard Helms, Director of the Central Intelligence Agency; U. Alexis Johnson, Under Secretary of State for Political Affairs; Joseph Sisco, Assistant Secretary of State for Near Eastern and South Asian Affairs; and David Packard, Deputy Secretary of Defense. L. Dean Brown, Ambassador to Jordan, also made important contributions to the decision process.

The core decisional units during this period were the Washington Special Actions Group (WSAG), a sub-body of the National Security Council (NSC) chaired by Kissinger, and higher-level meetings either among the "principals" (Nixon, Kissinger, Rogers, and Laird) or between Nixon and Kissinger alone. Generally present at WSAG meetings were Kissinger, Moorer, Helms, Johnson, Sisco, and Packard, together with lower-ranking officials in State and Defense (such as Rodger Davies, Sisco's deputy; G. Warren Nutter, Assistant Secretary of Defense for International Security Affairs; and Nutter's deputy for the Middle East, Robert Pranger). WSAG met daily during the pre-crisis period and prepared recommendations for the President on major issues, as well as making decisions itself on matters of implementation. Kissinger served as the link between WSAG and the President, and generally meetings with the Secretaries of State and Defense—either ad hoc or as a formal National Security Council meeting—were held only if there was serious disagreement within WSAG. No formal NSC meetings were held during the 1970 pre-crisis phase, though there were at least two informal meetings on the Secretary level. The major decisions were made by the President, either in consultation with his National Security Advisor or as confirmation of WSAG deliberations.[7]

7. My description of WSAG functioning is based on interviews with participants, including Moorer, Johnson, and Pranger. Kissinger describes the procedures in these terms:

> In the preliminary phase of the Jordan crisis I submitted daily at least two, and on occasion three, situation reports to the President. These informed him of WSAG recommendations, events in Amman, and the progress of negotiations for the release of hostages. Since all relevant agencies were represented on the WSAG, it could be assumed that full reports reached the appropriate Cabinet officers, who of course had the opportunity to appeal any disagreement to the President.

During the actual phase of the crisis (i.e., after September 15), in contrast, Nixon found it necessary to meet with the "principals" to review WSAG recommendations. Kissinger, 1979, p. 604.

PSYCHOLOGICAL ENVIRONMENT

Attitudinal Prism

Nearly every observer, and nearly every policy-maker as well, has noted the *global focus* that characterized the Nixon-Kissinger perspective on foreign policy. Local and regional events and forces were seen as functions of the basic themes and rivalries of world politics; relevance was measured in terms of impact on superpower relations. In the eyes of some participants—especially the area experts, needless to say—this meant insufficient appreciation of local conditions and considerations in policy-making. At least one such expert felt that the 1970 crisis fared relatively well in this regard, and that local factors were more adequately weighed and decisions better adapted to local conditions than in the 1973 Middle East crisis, for example, in which he was also involved.[8] But there is still no doubt that Nixon, Kissinger, and their top aides tended to see the Jordanian crisis primarily through the prism of U.S.-Soviet relations.

The Nixon-Kissinger philosophy, as expressed in every major foreign policy document produced by the administration, stressed the ordering of relations among the superpowers (perhaps including China) as the need of the hour. Building a "structure of peace" meant involving the Soviet Union in a process of fixing rules of the game that would moderate and civilize superpower rivalries. This was not to imply that administration officials took an optimistic view of Soviet intentions and cooperativeness. But, as Kissinger put it, excesses of truculence would be as much in error as excesses of conciliation (and in this way, Kissinger by implication distinguished *his* "global" view from that of John Foster Dulles). In a businesslike way, the United States would deal with the Soviet Union on the basis of three principles: (1) concreteness (dealing with specific issues rather than "general atmospheres"), (2) mutual restraint as opposed to pursuit of unilateral advantages and exploitation of areas of crisis, and (3) the recognition of "linkage"—i.e., that cooperation in one area was predicated on progress across a broad front of U.S.-Soviet issues.[9]

Part of this stabilization of superpower relationships involved the *redefinition of the American role*. Nixon and Kissinger agreed that, given basic changes in the world, the United States could no longer expect to carry the burden it had once easily assumed. The economic revival of other powers, the erosion of U.S. strategic superiority, and

---

8. Interview with Brown, who described 1973 decision-making as "global" and "confused."

9. Kissinger, 1979, pp. 123–129.

the implications of Vietnam all indicated a need to come to terms with a relative decline in the American position, with regard to allies, rivals, and neutrals alike. Nixon had already attempted a new formulation on future military commitments in the "Nixon Doctrine" of July 1969 (elaborated in the first Presidential Foreign Policy Report of February 18, 1970), according to which the United States would keep its treaty commitments and would extend both the nuclear umbrella and military aid to threatened allies, but would expect the threatened state to supply the manpower for its own defense.

But no local conflict could be judged, for all that, simply in a local context. Such conflicts still had great significance in their impact on the global balance and on the changing texture of U.S.-Soviet ties. Defeat in a local struggle would encourage further challenges, since it was part of a global test of wills. This led to a tremendous *stress on credibility* and to an interpretation of local conflicts as Soviet probing actions, as "tests" of American resolve. One had to "stand up" to the Soviets in instances where the issue might appear inconsequential; few if any local issues could be judged in terms of their inherent importance. Withdrawal from Vietnam was made conditional on a settlement that would preserve U.S. credibility. Kissinger, and after the fact Nixon himself, criticized themselves for responding feebly in their own first crisis—the North Korean downing of a U.S. reconnaissance plane in April 1969—not because of the impact on North Korea, but because of the message of "weakness" conveyed to the Soviet Union.[10] At times this thinking bordered on a cult of toughness or an assertion of masculinity, fixated on the image of strength or weakness that each action signaled, and obsessed with avoiding any outcome that might be labeled "defeat." In any event, the words *will, credibility, test, humiliation, strength, resolve*, etc., occur with striking regularity in Nixon administration documents.

With this orientation, it is not surprising that Soviet complicity in local threats was readily assumed. In the 1970 crisis, American decision-makers credited Moscow, despite its denials and a lack of real evidence, with an active role in instigating Syria's intervention into Jordan. This fit in with the general *image of Soviets as ruthless opportunists.* While Nixon and Kissinger did not share the theological outlook of John Foster Dulles, they clearly expected that Soviet leaders would exploit any opportunities, and that successful negotiation with the Soviets was possible only if such opportunities were vigorously denied to them. Soviet cooperation could not be purchased by charm or by demonstrations of American moderation and restraint;

10. Ibid., pp. 320–321.

to this extent, the image of an inexorable ideological drive reflected Soviet reality. Gestures of goodwill or other such measures were futile. The analogy often heard among administration officials was of the thief who tests hotel doors in hopes of finding one unlocked.[11]

Furthermore, in the context of 1970, the Soviet Union seemed to be in the midst of a forward thrust, pushing the rules to their limits and testing the new administration. It was necessary, therefore, that the United States respond to this challenge vigorously and force some caution on the other side. Nixon and Kissinger felt strongly that they could not permit the image of the U.S. being immobilized.[12]

This *perception of a Soviet offensive* was compounded of a number of issues. The Soviets seemed to be stalling in negotiations over Berlin, over strategic arms limitations, and over a European security conference. They seemed uncooperative over Vietnam, despite a major administration effort to persuade Soviet leaders that their help in finding a Vietnam resolution was a condition for American cooperation on issues of importance to them. In the Washington perspective, the Soviets perhaps found the continuing American involvement in Vietnam of convenience, since it tied down American forces and gave the Soviets a freer hand elsewhere. The fact of American forces being spread thin made it seem only too likely that the Soviets would choose that moment to test American resolve.

The planned opening to China was another aspect of the global perspective. Although gestures had been made (privately) by this time, matters were proceeding slowly. In the view of American policy-makers, this was another reason for a vigorous response to the Soviet forward thrust. The Chinese were unlikely to be interested, it was thought, in closer relations with an American government that could not stand up to Soviet threats.[13]

Soviet actions in the Middle East in 1970 were therefore regarded as part of a general challenge facing the United States. Nixon was quoted in late 1969 as saying that "the summit and trade they [Moscow] can have but I'll be damned if they can get the Middle East."[14] The President's 1970 foreign policy report charged, in connection with the Middle East, that "we have not seen on the Soviet side that practical and constructive flexibility which is necessary for a successful outcome," and noted "evidence ... that the Soviet Union seeks a position in the area as a whole which would make great power

11. Interview with a senior CIA official.

12. Interviews with Helmut Sonnenfeldt, Harold Saunders, and William Hyland, all from the National Security Council staff.

13. Quandt, 1978, p. 285; interviews with Sonnenfeldt and Saunders.

14. Kissinger, 1979, p. 369.

rivalry more likely."[15] Tying Jordan to simultaneous crises in Cuba
and Chile, Kissinger declared that "they all represented—or seemed
to us to represent—different facets of a global Communist challenge."[16] That challenge was of course particularly acute in the Middle East, as Washington saw it, and the instability of the area was
directly attributable to Soviet mischief. Kissinger argues that "the
Soviet military thrust into Egypt and its incitement of radical Arabs
spawned the crisis in Jordan."[17] More generally, Richard Nixon told
Israeli Ambassador Yitzhak Rabin on August 17, 1970, that "I completely agree with you that the Soviets are the main cause of Middle
East tensions. . . ."[18]

During the pre-crisis period, on the other hand, a direct Soviet
role in instigating events was difficult to identify. The Soviets could
not be blamed for the hijacking, nor could they be held responsible
for instigating any specific threatening actions (as they were held
responsible for the Syrian incursion later in the crisis).[19] They could,
however, still be charged with general culpability for the state of
affairs that engendered the crisis, and most decision-makers assumed
that they would in every event try to capitalize on the situation as
well as they could.[20] Kissinger assumed at least some Soviet control
over the situation when he argued that the Soviets missed a bet by
not ending the crisis during this period:

> If the Soviet Union had around September 10 pressed for the
> release of hostages and a cease-fire, the gain for the fedayeen
> would have been massive; the authority of the King would have
> been gravely weakened. Instability in Jordan would have been
> added to insecurity along the Suez Canal; Soviet prestige would
> have been demonstrated and reinforced. But by getting too greedy
> —by not helping to rein in their clients—the Soviets gave us the
> opportunity to restore the equilibrium before the balance of forces
> had been fundamentally changed.[21]

Clearly, for Kissinger the local aspects of the situation were of secondary importance; the Jordan crisis of September 1970 was primarily a confrontation between Soviet and American power—and one

15. Ibid., p. 159.
16. Ibid., p. 594.
17. Ibid.
18. Richard Nixon, *RN: The Memoirs of Richard Nixon* (New York: Grosset and
Dunlap, 1978), pp. 482–483.
19. Interviews with Sonnenfeldt and Johnson.
20. Admiral Elmo Zumwalt, Chief of Naval Operations, recalls that the general
tenor of meetings during this period was that "the Soviets were up to mischief"
(personal interview).
21. Kissinger, 1979, p. 609.

which worked to American advantage because the Soviets did not help to "rein in their clients," which they presumably had the capability of doing.

When Nixon and Kissinger did think in regional terms, *concern for stability in the Arab-Israeli conflict* was their primary interest. Of course, this also was not unrelated to Cold War considerations. The Arab-Israeli impasse not only threatened the peace and stability of the area and such interests as access to oil, but it also created leverage that the Soviet Union could exploit. Moreover, there was the continual danger that the volatile Middle East conflict might catalyze hostilities between the superpowers; both Nixon and Kissinger were prone to repeatedly use the analogy of the pre-World War I Balkans to describe what they obviously saw as the frightening risk of being dragged by Middle East clients into a clash with the Soviets.

Thus, in the Nixon administration, as in past American governments, there was a clear perception of an American interest in preventing the outbreak of another Arab-Israeli war and in contributing to diplomatic solutions of the underlying issues. Regarding the methods of promoting stability, there were, also as in the past, differing views within the government. According to one view, stability was best promoted by the active pursuit of diplomatic initiatives, which in practice meant leaning on Israel to make concessions that would win Arab favor and cooperation. This approach, which was practically "conventional wisdom" in the bureaucracy (especially in the Near Eastern Bureau of the State Department), was tied to perceptions of Israel as an impediment to U.S.-Arab ties rather than as a strategic asset, and preferred a more "evenhanded" policy which, it was argued, would defend U.S. interests by giving less leverage to the Soviet Union.[22] Some in the bureaucracy were even more negative toward Israel—suspecting, for example, that Israel's readiness to intervene in the Jordan-Syria confrontation was an expression of Israeli desire to annex the Irbid area.[23]

During the early period of his Presidency, Nixon often tended to accept the recommendations of this school of thought, even while agreeing with critics (such as Kissinger) who argued that, in the circumstances of 1969–1970, bold American initiatives would be counterproductive. There were a number of reasons for Nixon's ambivalence. Having centralized foreign policy-making in the White

22. Quandt, in *Decade of Decisions: American Policy Toward the Arab-Israeli Conflict, 1967–1976* (Berkeley: University of California Press, 1977), p. 120, describes this thinking and its influence on Nixon and Kissinger in the period preceding the Jordanian crisis.
23. Interviews with Hoskinson and Pranger.

House, Nixon wanted to leave some prerogatives for the State Department. In addition, he sought to avoid direct confrontations with
Rogers, his old friend, as much as possible. Furthermore, precisely
because he felt that the chances of success were slim, and that the
domestic costs of failure were high, he wanted to get the White
House out of the line of fire. Finally, the fact that Kissinger was
Jewish added another complication to direct Presidential control
through his personal assistant. Thus, at least until the 1970 Jordan
crisis, Nixon often yielded to the importunities of the Middle East
bureaucracy in pursuing active diplomatic initiatives and pressuring
Israel—even when he himself was dubious about such moves and
undercut them in his own later actions.[24]

Thus, in early 1970, Nixon adopted the "evenhanded" approach
when he postponed the delivery of Phantom jets to Israel only days
after it became public knowledge that the Soviet Union had introduced combat personnel into Egypt. This was done, in Nixon's words,
in order to encourage Israel to be more forthcoming diplomatically,
to slow down the arms race, and to improve relations with Egypt and
Syria in order "to construct an entirely new set of power relationships in the Middle East. . . ." This brought the President into conflict
with what he described as "the unyielding and shortsighted pro-
Israeli attitude" of some segments of American opinion (Jewish and
non-Jewish); and in a revealing memorandum to Kissinger, he argued
that Israel should nevertheless rely on him, rather than on anti-
Vietnam liberals, because only a President willing to stand up to the
Soviets throughout the world would be a real support: "Unless they
[the Israelis] understand it and act as if they understand it beginning
now, they are down the tubes."[25]

This is not, however, the whole picture, for, as indicated, Nixon
himself at times, and even more his National Security advisor and
some of the military establishment, tended to the second approach
on promoting Arab-Israeli stability. This second view emphasized
military balance as the key to stability in the Middle East, and was
more closely linked to "global" thinking in that it saw the frustration
of Soviet schemes—not diplomatic progress per se—as the first priority in the area. The success of Soviet arms in any theater would, it
was feared, increase Soviet prestige and lead other states to seek
Soviet aid. In this perspective, there was strategic value in a strong
Israel that would block Soviet designs and counter the Soviet pres-

---

24. For a full account of this ambivalence, see Kissinger, 1979, Chapter 10 (especially pp. 348, 372, 377–379); and Steven Spiegel, *The War for Washington: The Other
Arab-Israel Conflict* (forthcoming), Chapter 6.
    25. Nixon, pp. 480–482.

ence in Egypt and elsewhere. Finally, this deterrence of Soviet-backed provocations was also seen as the key to diplomatic progress, since it was assumed that Arab states would negotiate if, and only if, military options were convincingly closed off.

Nixon and Kissinger had initially allowed the State Department to pursue the "evenhanded" approach, through the Two-Power and Four-Power talks and the Rogers Plan in 1969, as well as the decision to postpone further plane deliveries to Israel. But as the Soviet involvement in Egypt grew during the year, the two top policy-makers became increasingly dubious about the approach and increasingly persuaded by the strategic arguments advanced by Israel and Israeli supporters. Soviet and Egyptian violations of the standstill cease-fire in August (discussed below) contributed significantly to this change of climate, and William Quandt concludes that even without the Jordan crisis, Nixon would have renewed arms aid to Israel soon.[26] Of course, the crisis provided a decisive impetus for the immediate effectuation of this move.

American attitudes were also shaped by an *image of Arab irrationality.* The behavior of Arab leaders—at least those heading radical regimes—often seemed wild, irresponsible, and self-defeating to U.S. policy-makers, the Middle East experts no less than the "generalists." In fact, Kissinger refers to "the conventional wisdom of the Middle East experts that Arabs were so excitable that any public warning was likely to drive them into frenzy." On these grounds, Arabists tended to oppose strong measures directed at hostile Arab leaders or groups; Kissinger, on the other hand, argues that this cautionary attitude "confuses volubility with erratic behavior; in crises I found most Arab leaders to be circumspect and calculating."[27]

Whatever the exceptions, however, there was general agreement that the regimes of Syria and Iraq, with which the United States had no relations at the time, were populated by fanatics who were out of touch with reason—though, somewhat contradictorily, the same leaders were assumed to be docile in their relations with Moscow. Attitudes to Syria were molded by the perception of the regime there as "wild men," a view that subsequent Syrian behavior in the Jordan crisis did little to change.[28] As a senior intelligence officer stated frankly, Syrian leaders appeared then as a "bunch of

26. Quandt, 1977, pp. 121–122.
27. Kissinger, 1979, p. 598; also, interviews with officials in the Bureau of Near Eastern and South Asian Affairs, Department of State.
28. Interviews with Hoskinson and Smith.

brigands," and Nixon himself demonstrated an antipathy to them that was almost visceral.[29]

The radical Palestinian organizations, as well, seemed in American eyes to behave in an often inexplicable fashion. Hijackings and other acts of terror seemed not only inhumane and uncivilized, but unproductive in terms of the Palestinians' professed goals. Kissinger confesses himself puzzled by PLO actions in the Jordan crisis: "By overplaying their hand, they destroyed their own prospects and ended up expelled to Lebanon." In Kissinger's view, the diplomatic situation after the August cease-fire offered a good opening to the Palestinians—though he recognized that many of them were not seeking a compromise solution but the destruction of Israel, and "in this sense their attempt to thwart diplomatic progress had a rational basis." But even on this basis, Palestinian extremists behaved irrationally by forcing the issue in Jordan just as they were gaining ground and approaching de facto autonomy within the country. In the end, they defeated themselves, losing their base in Jordan, contributing to a stronger U.S. position in the Middle East, and opening the road for the diplomatic efforts they opposed.[30]

Insofar as radical Palestinian groups represented a threat to negotiating efforts and to moderate regimes, American decision-makers would in any event see them as hostile elements and try to contain them. But their choice of tactics added another dimension to the reaction in Washington. The Nixon administration was especially sensitive on issues of violence and terrorism that challenged the existing norms of civilized society. The anti-war demonstrations at home, racial riots, rising crime rates, and the explosion of political terrorism using new tactics such as hijacking had all combined to create a sense of siege within the government that has been well documented in the massive literature covering the eventual results of that mental attitude. A recurring theme in all of Nixon's public utterances was the threat of anarchy and the breakdown of law and order in Western societies. Even Kissinger, with his sense of the tragic and his innately conservative and pessimistic view of man and history, put a high value on stability as a goal in itself and tended to identify any extralegal source of instability as a threat to American interests and to civilization itself.[31] There was nothing in the basic attitudes of either decision-maker that might lead him to empathize

29. Interview with a senior CIA official.
30. Kissinger, 1979, pp. 600–601.
31. On Kissinger's attitudes see John Stoessinger, *Crusaders and Pragmatists: Movers of Modern American Foreign Policy* (New York: Norton, 1979), p. 242.

in the slightest degree with those who resorted to guns and dynamite.

Thus, in an administration that saw itself as a protector of "law and order" domestically and internationally, the *antipathy to terrorism* was especially marked. Hijacking was seen as an act of barbarism akin to piracy, and was lumped together with domestic violence as part of a growing challenge to the elementary decencies of civilized existence. In a later public statement about the September 6 hijackings, Nixon tied the incident to a law-and-order context, as part of a "spreading disease of violence and terror and its use as a political tactic."[32] The administration had long taken a hard line toward all hijackings and hostage-takings, maintaining that any concessions only encouraged additional acts of terrorism and undermined the maintenance of law and order.[33] Of course, this line of action assumed that the terrorists were not completely irrational, that they would not act rashly or out of spite so long as they hoped to achieve their ends—and indeed Washington acted on this assumption during the pre-crisis period by ignoring deadlines and similar threats, arguing (correctly, as it turned out) that the hijackers wanted to negotiate and would not trigger a showdown.[34]

The strongly negative perception of the "fedayeen" was matched by a strikingly *favorable image of Jordan and King Hussein.* The commitment to Hussein's survival had long since become axiomatic in U.S. Middle Eastern policy, but since 1967 the rated importance of Hussein and Jordan had increased.[35] The continuation of a moderate regime in Amman was regarded as crucial to the stability of the region and to prospects for peace negotiations, as Hussein seemed the most promising partner for Israel in any resolution of the "Palestinian issue." There was some skepticism among Middle East experts over Hussein's future viability or his capacity to play a major stabilizing role in the region, but the weight of opinion was highly favorable to him and would have regarded the radicalization of Jordan as a major blow to peace prospects, stability, and American interests.[36]

32. *Public Papers of the Presidents, 1970,* pp. 758–759.

33. Interview with Johnson.

34. See the account in Tad Szulc, *The Illusion of Peace: Foreign Policy in the Nixon Years* (New York: Viking, 1978), p. 323.

35. For an incisive analysis of the background and development of the U.S. commitment to Jordan, see Stephen S. Kaplan, "United States Aid and Regime Maintenance in Jordan, 1957–1973," *Public Policy,* 23:2 (Spring 1975), 189–217.

36. Interviews with government officials, especially Sonnenfeldt, Saunders, a senior CIA official, and Granville Austin, Executive Assistant to Senator Clifford Case (on leave from the Bureau of Near Eastern and South Asian Affairs, Department of State).

Kissinger's summary of his own feelings at this time reflected general sentiment:

> I felt a bias toward supporting Hussein if at all possible. Just as I had sought to thwart Nasser as long as he relied so heavily on his Soviet connection and supported all radical movements, so it now seemed to me important to demonstrate that friendship with the United States had its benefits. Hussein had always advocated moderation, resisted the radical tide, and avoided fashionable anti-Western slogans. He was in difficulty because of his reluctance to permit the guerrillas free rein. His collapse would radicalize the entire Middle East. Israel would not acquiesce in the establishment of guerrilla bases all along its Jordanian frontier. Another Middle East War would be extremely likely. Thus, Jordan, in my view, was a test of our capacity to control events in the region.[37]

Much, then, was seen to depend on Hussein's continuation in power: demonstration of the value of friendship with the United States (especially, in light of the "Nixon Doctrine," with friends who would fight), blocking the radicalization of the Middle East, and preventing another Arab-Israeli war. Added to this was the admiration for Hussein personally—the "plucky little king," a "fine little guy"—that was felt by most policy-makers, and especially by Nixon.[38] All together, American policy-makers saw a threat to Hussein almost as a threat to the United States itself.[39]

American reactions were, however, likely to be tempered by *perceptions of constraints on military action.* The continuing involvement in Vietnam, and the public reaction to the Cambodian operation in May, led policy-makers to think very cautiously about further military actions abroad. Also, it was feared that intervention on behalf of Hussein would totally discredit him in the Arab world.[40] In addition to the political constraints, moreover, there were doubts about the U.S.'s military capability to act effectively. Kissinger notes that "in the more than ten years since our 1958 landing in Lebanon we had lost either the staging areas available then . . . or the right to use them for Mideast conflicts." It was estimated that only four U.S.

37. Kissinger, 1979, p. 596. Kissinger also says (p. 362) that "Hussein was one of the most attractive political leaders I have met. . . . [He] sought with dignity and courage to reconcile the roles of Arab nationalist and America's friend." Brown, at his September 11 meeting with Nixon and Kissinger, was told to do what was necessary to save Hussein (interview with Brown).

38. Quandt, 1978, pp. 265–266; interviews with a senior CIA official and Austin.

39. At an NSC meeting on June 17, President Nixon had said: "Let us suppose late in the summer we get a request from Lebanon or Jordan for assistance. . . . There comes a time when the U.S. is going to be tested as to its credibility in the area. The real question will be, will we act. . . . We must be ready. . . ." Quoted in Kissinger, 1979, p. 597.

40. Kissinger, 1979, p. 596.

brigades could reach Jordan quickly, and this would commit the entire strategic reserve. Even this would require overflight rights or ground access. And even if such an operation could be mounted, there was no guarantee that it would be effective in rescuing the hostages held in Jordan; in fact, the prognosis for a military solution to the pre-crisis situation was uniformly dismal.[41]

Finally, the attitudinal prism of Nixon-Kissinger foreign policy included a shared *belief in private diplomacy*. Both principal figures had a deep distrust of the foreign policy bureaucracy, and sought to centralize control of important issues—Soviet relations, China, Vietnam, SALT—in the White House. Not only policy-making, but even the implementation, often bypassed the normal channels within the government (as in Kissinger's own secret diplomacy on China and Vietnam and his direct channels to many world leaders). Both Nixon and Kissinger had a high regard for the leadership style embodied in solitary decisions—and the more so if the decision "courageously" went against a tide of adverse opinion inundating the oval office from below. A leader needed to "stand alone" so as not to become a prisoner of his own bureaucracy, which was in any event too entangled in its own routines and petty interests to perceive the overall picture with any clarity. In addition, successful diplomacy required secrecy, which was clearly impossible in any large bureaucracy and especially where there was opposition, and thus a motive to sabotage, within the bureaucracy. In sum, Nixon and Kissinger regarded the foreign policy apparatus of the American government as another of their adversaries, and were guided by a conception similar in many ways to the classical model of diplomacy, with its focus on the discreet interaction of small elites, well insulated from the vagaries of bureaucracies or domestic constituencies.[42]

Images

The decision-makers whose personal images were most relevant to the shaping of U.S. policy in late 1970 were Nixon and Kissinger. Aside from the shared attitudes outlined above, each held particular perceptions of world politics and crisis management that have been dissected and evaluated extensively by various analysts. Without attempting to paint a comprehensive psychological portrait, what

41. Ibid., pp. 596, 605; confirmed in interviews with Moorer, Pranger, and other Department of Defense officials.

42. These attitudes permeate the memoirs of both Nixon and Kissinger, and are sketched even more starkly by critical accounts of Nixon-era foreign policy. See, for example, Kissinger, 1979, pp. 38–48.

features of their respective perceptual worlds seem most significant in this context?[43]

As opposed to Kissinger, Nixon does not seem to have had a fully developed conceptual system that "mediated between him and his psychological impulses."[44] Nixon acted directly on the political system as his impulses dictated; there was no intellectualization that transformed disparate events into a coherent world view, but rather instinctive reactions expressed generally in tactical language. In fact, Nixon's approach might be seen as primarily *tactical*, interpreting the Great Power game in more immediate terms rather than in relation to the structure of international or other concepts or abstractions. Thus, for Nixon, as Coral Bell notes, even detente "may have been more of a tactic than a strategy," since it remained tied to essentially hard-line instincts and was seen primarily as a way of coping more efficiently with the Soviet Union, rather than as a structural change in the international system.[45]

In addition, Nixon was undoubtedly more attuned to domestic political considerations in foreign policy—not in the sense of seeking broader consultation, but as an input into his own thinking. Thus, his concept of detente, in addition to being more tactical, was also more political, as Kissinger himself remarks: "Nixon had come to the problem by a more political route than I. . . . He understood that as President he would need to stretch his political base toward the political center; indeed, he shrewdly saw in East-West relations a long-term opportunity to build his new majority."[46]

Nixon also tended to put considerable stress on personal relationships in diplomacy, partly because he was personally acquainted with many world leaders. Nixon had traveled widely as Vice President and

43. The conclusions of this section, except as otherwise noted, are consensual observations drawn from the Nixon and Kissinger memoirs and from the following accounts:

On Nixon: David Abrahamsen, *Nixon vs. Nixon: An Emotional Tragedy* (New York: Farrar, Straus and Giroux, 1976); Lloyd C. Gardner, ed., *The Great Nixon Turn-Around* (New York: New Viewpoints, 1973); Bruce Mazlish, *In Search of Nixon: A Psychohistorical Inquiry* (New York: Basic Books, 1972).

On Kissinger: Coral Bell, *The Diplomacy of Detente: The Kissinger Era* (New York: St. Martin's Press, 1977); Peter W. Dickson, *Kissinger and the Meaning of History* (Cambridge, England: Cambridge University Press, 1978); Marvin Kalb and Bernard Kalb, *Kissinger* (New York: Dell, 1975); Bruce Mazlish, *Kissinger: The European Mind in American Policy* (New York: Basic Books, 1976); Roger Morris, *Uncertain Greatness: Henry Kissinger and American Foreign Policy* (New York: Harper and Row, 1977); John G. Stoessinger, *Henry Kissinger: The Anguish of Power* (New York: Norton, 1976).

44. Mazlish, 1976, p. 285.

45. Bell, pp. 43–44.

46. Kissinger, 1979, p. 126.

as private citizen, and enjoyed a firsthand knowledge of countries and leaders that was almost unmatched. He took pride in his own expertise on places and people, often correcting intelligence briefers on matters of detail. He saw foreign affairs as the area in which he would make his contribution to history, and in some estimations was determined to outdo Eisenhower—a father figure about whom he had ambivalent feelings—as a peacemaker.

But whatever his interest in peace, Nixon's view of the human condition was anything but benign. The siege mentality of the Nixon White House reflected an image of a hostile outside world that bordered on paranoia (some claim it crossed that border). But whether Nixon was paranoid or not, he clearly believed the external environment was basically inimical, and saw his own life as a series of challenges or crises to be met and mastered. His first autobiographical writing—*Six Crises*—embodied in its very conception this confrontational view of the world. Conflict was for Nixon the essence of politics; he thrived on opposition and interpreted his career in terms of victories and defeats.[47]

But while Nixon may have regarded crises as the high point and *raison d'être* of politics, it was not because he reveled in the excitement and drama they provided. In fact, Nixon's philosophy of crisis management was to insulate the crisis as much as possible from public hysteria and to maintain a low level of excitement and emotion. The model was cool unflappability and detachment rather than the relish of total involvement; in fact, Nixon sought to distance himself from anything that would distract from cold calculation. Control—self-control and control of the situation—was his byword and his forte. (One is reminded of his earlier reputation as a formidable poker player and—unlikely as it sounds—a consummate actor in college and amateur dramas.)

As a decision-maker, Nixon was also noted for his "instinct for the jugular" and his relative disinterest in the specifics of particular policy proposals.[48] He had a sense for the basic issue involved and would focus on it to the exclusion of other considerations. Kissinger credits him, in this regard, with a great capacity for decisiveness when required.[49] In fact, Nixon had a predilection for dramatic public moves as the outcome of decision-making (as opposed to dramatizing or publicizing the decision-making process itself). He valued the bold stroke, as shown in his oft-noted admiration for General George

47. See Hugh Sidey, "Anybody Seen Patton?" in Gardner, pp. 183–186 (especially p. 185).

48. Kissinger, 1979, pp. 142, 148, 163, *inter alia*.

49. Ibid., p. 45.

Patton.[50] He typically rejected "halfway" measures in a crisis, on the grounds that necessary steps should not be carried out so as to convey hesitation, but the chips should fall where they may. Above all, one must not appear weak; Nixon was determined that the United States should never appear as a "pitiful, helpless giant."

This assessment of Nixon cannot be illustrated by words from the pre-crisis period, since Nixon made no public statements during these days. But only four months earlier (on April 30, 1970), Nixon delivered his address to the nation in defense of the Cambodian incursion, which is by all accounts one of the purest public samples of Nixonian imagery and rhetoric. Nixon apparently refused almost all bureaucratic input into the speech, working on it until 4:15 A.M.; what emerged was an unusually lucid statement of his view of the world and America's place in it. It is, in short, vintage Nixon, and readily illustrates many of the points made above.

In the speech, Nixon returns repeatedly to the theme of avoiding defeat, repeating the words *defeat* and *humiliation* in close conjunction three times and vowing not to see the U.S. "accept the first defeat in its proud 190-year history." He notes with regret the "counsels of doubt and defeat" from public figures in the country. In a world where only the United States deters aggression, an ineffective response to threat would destroy American credibility in every area of the world: "It is our will and character that is being tested tonight." In Nixon's view, "we live in an age of anarchy, both abroad and at home." The destruction of great universities at home is mentioned in the same breath as attacks on small nations all over the world. Everything depends on the United States rising to the test: "If . . . the United States of America acts like a pitiful, helpless giant, the forces of totalitarianism and anarchy will threaten free nations and free institutions throughout the world." And "plaintive diplomatic protests" would be a confession of defeat; only the use of force will meet the challenge.

Finally, Nixon indicates that in his view he is putting principle above popularity: "It is tempting to take the easy political path. . . . I have rejected all political considerations in making this decision. . . . I would rather be a one-term President and do what I believe is right. . . ." He states his belief that, while there are differences of opinion in the country, "the decision I announce tonight transcends those differences."[51]

50. Sidey, pp. 183–186.
51. *Public Papers of the Presidents, 1970*, pp. 405–410.

Thus, only weeks before the Jordan crisis, Nixon put on record his preoccupation with victory or defeat, his perception of American will and credibility being at issue in local conflicts, his sense of growing anarchy and lawlessness in the world, his contempt for weak verbal responses, his self-image as a lonely fighter for the hard but correct course, and his scorn for popular defeatism and misjudgment. These perceptions proved to be as central for the Middle East in September as they were for Cambodia in April—with allowance for the regional factors described above.

To this, one might add a word on Nixon's personal images of Middle East actors, which differed from Kissinger's primarily on one topic: Jews. Nixon was capable of mildly anti-Semitic remarks in private, and he often reacted angrily to American Jewish pressure and attacks, as seen in the memorandum quoted above (p. 120).[52] (Another illustration is the March decision to delay plane shipments to Israel, which was apparently influenced in large part by Nixon's rage over American Jewish demonstrations against visiting French President Georges Pompidou.)[53] One might expect such feelings to be balanced by domestic political considerations, to which Nixon would presumably be sensitive—and indeed, Nixon often had Attorney General John Mitchell (his main domestic political advisor) sit in on Middle East discussions for this reason. But Nixon also stated frequently that he owed nothing to the Jewish vote, and that therefore he paid little attention to the "Jewish lobby."[54] But what did balance things out, and lead him to essentially the same position on Israel as his National Security Advisor, was an "unsentimental geopolitical analysis" that stressed reduction of Soviet influence, the weakening of Arab radicalism, and—by extension—maintenance of Israel's security. In Kissinger's words, "Nixon and I often travelled different roads for part of the way, but at points of decision in the Middle East we met, agreed, and acted in mutual support."[55]

In many ways, Nixon and Kissinger shared personality traits that made their "styles" in policy-making compatible: a tendency to solitude, admiration of strength and manliness, a penchant for secrecy, assumption of a hostile environment, a sense of being tested continuously, and an acute concern about how history would record their

52. Kissinger remarks laconically that Golda Meir's greeting Nixon as an old friend of the Jewish people was "startling news to those of us more familiar with Nixon's ambivalences on that score." Kissinger, 1979, p. 370.

53. Ibid., p. 565.

54. Nixon, p. 435.

55. Kissinger, 1979, p. 564.

actions.[56] But Kissinger went far beyond Nixon in the scope, elaboration, and explicitness of his conceptualization of foreign policy. Because of this high level of intellectualization, Kissinger's cognitive
universe has attracted more scholarly analysis than that of any other
modern U.S. foreign policy-maker.

What were the basic elements of this universe, apart from those
discussed as part of the general attitudinal prism in the Nixon administration? In the first place, Kissinger was concerned with the broad
sweep of history and tended to place current affairs in a much longer-
range perspective than was customary among his present-minded
contemporaries (studying, for example, the Congress of Vienna in
order to shed light on the post-war problems of his own age). As one
study has sought to show, Kissinger was genuinely concerned with
the meaning of history and was influenced by his broader perceptions of it in his actions.[57]

Kissinger's perception of international relations was state-cen-
tered and traditional, focusing on the interplay of the Great Powers.
The domestic dimensions of foreign policy—internal political systems and values—interested him less. Nor was the role of ideology
stressed, though Kissinger saw the role of Marxism in modern times
as an exceptional case. Marxism did influence the Soviet perception
of the world, and by a turn of historical irony it also presented an
attractive answer to the needs for political legitimacy and cohesion
in the unstable areas of the contemporary world—despite its univer-
sally inferior performance as an economic system.[58] As a result of this
attraction and the tie of Marxism to a superpower, Kissinger saw the
modern world as one in which internal upheavals in small states
could in fact play an integral role in the overall balance of power.[59]
This led to what some observers saw as an anomaly in Kissinger's
attitudes: relative tolerance of Communism in the Soviet Union, but
extreme sensitivity and antagonism to local Communist movements
in more remote areas.[60]

Morality, like ideology, was relative to overall stability. Kissinger
distrusted moral claims, and argued that the statesman, unlike the
outsider, could not afford the luxury of defining morality in terms of
absolutes:

56. For a psychological comparison of Nixon and Kissinger, see Mazlish, 1976, pp.
218–222.
57. Dickson, passim.
58. Kissinger, 1979, p. 69.
59. Ibid., p. 68.
60. For example, Stoessinger, 1976, p. 241.

> Any partial step is inherently morally imperfect and yet morality
> cannot be approximated without it. . . . The statesman's test is not
> only the exaltation of his goals but also the catastrophe he
> averts. . . . The dialogue between the academic and the statesman is
> therefore always likely to be inconclusive. Without philosophy,
> policy will have no standards; but without the willingness to peer
> into darkness and risk some faltering steps without certainty,
> humanity will never know peace.[61]

Stability for Kissinger rested on equilibrium, on a balance among opposing forces, and thus power had to be a central concern of policy. This is not to say that the essence of world politics was conflict alone. The relations among the Great Powers were found somewhere on the spectrum between pure conflict and pure cooperation; it was the task of the statesman to move these relations in a more cooperative direction by stressing the common interests that coexist with the inevitable conflict. The model was negotiation, not victory. The nineteenth-century "Concert of Europe," by which the Great Powers legislated solutions to diplomatic disputes, was in Kissinger's mind worthy of emulation.[62] Detente, which Nixon saw tactically, was thus for Kissinger strategic or even structural, creating a new basis for the conduct of international relations.[63]

Peace could not, however, be sought directly, but only as a function of overall stability—which depended on confrontation as well as conciliation. States that made conciliation their sole method would only put themselves at the mercy of the most ruthless.[64] The correct posture was a combination of firmness and willingness to negotiate, maintained patiently over the long run without reverting to either unrelenting opposition (for which Kissinger criticized Dulles) or unilateral retreat (of which he accused his critics on Vietnam policy). The inability to conceive of such a policy as an ongoing effort, without overreacting to either conflictual or cooperative signals, was what accounted for the wild historical fluctuations in U.S. policy from one extreme to the other. Americans sought an end-point to international conflicts and thus swung in frustration between pursuit of total victory and embittered withdrawal. In truth, Kissinger argued, there is no end-point; policy-makers must accept an ambiguous role for an indefinite period of time. But at the end of the 1960s, Kissinger was concerned about the self-doubt engendered by the Vietnamese War

61. Kissinger, 1979, p. 55.
62. Bell, pp. 25 ff., stresses this rather than "balance of power" as the key to Kissinger's thinking. The two concepts are of course clearly linked.
63. See especially Kissinger, 1979, pp. 126–127.
64. Ibid., p. 70.

and feared a new American isolationism that would tempt the Soviet Union into further challenges and upset the already tenuous stability of the world order.[65]

Kissinger criticized the American tendency to divorce military power from diplomacy, which exacerbated the fluctuations in policy. Those who pursued diplomatic initiatives without linking them to power realities were in his mind doomed to futility and failure. Those who, like Eisenhower and Dulles, stressed military balance without exploiting diplomatic openings were guilty of shortsightedness (Kissinger also criticized the "empty legalism" of the Eisenhower-Dulles approach).[66] But Kissinger was also sensitive to changes in the nature of power, arguing (again in opposition to Dulles) that strategic nuclear power, because of the superpower deadlock, was not adequate as a military deterrent on all levels, and was increasingly unusable as a form of influence politically and diplomatically (for example, in relations with allies, in economic and global issues, in Third World conflicts, etc.).[67] More subtle instruments, better attuned to the complexities of mid-twentieth-century international relations, would have to be forged.

Kissinger's views on crisis management followed from his criticism of divorcing power from the pursuit of peace. Passivity in a crisis, he argues, "leads to mounting impotence. . . . By contrast, the side that seizes the initiative can occupy its opponent's energies in analysis." Furthermore, one should not seek to reassure the enemy, but rather make him feel the risks that his continued opposition entails: "For maximum effectiveness one's actions must be sustained; they must appear relentless, inexorable; hesitation or gradualism invites an attempt to test one's resolution by matching the commitment."[68] There was even value, in accord with the well-known theory of the "rationality of irrationality," in appearing somewhat irresponsible in order to force caution on the other side.[69] Kissinger contrasts this approach with that of Rogers in the 1970 Jordanian crisis: Rogers sought to calm the atmosphere in order to further a solution, while Kissinger believed "it was the danger that the situation might get out of hand which provided the incentive for rapid settlement." When Rogers publicly dismissed military options, Kissinger regretted the

65. Ibid., especially pp. 56–61, 65.
66. Mazlish, p. 203; Kissinger, 1979, pp. 61–64.
67. Kissinger, 1979, pp. 66–67.
68. Ibid., p. 604.
69. Mazlish recounts Kissinger's admiration for an earlier lecture by Daniel Ellsberg (in his more hawkish days) entitled "The Political Uses of Madness" (Mazlish, 1976, pp. 185–186). The value of a calculated image of unpredictability in crisis bargaining was a staple of 1960s strategic literature.

reassurance this provided to the Palestinian hijackers—and was relieved that they apparently did not believe Rogers.[70]

Regarding the Middle East, Kissinger's views follow logically from his general premises. By all accounts, what Kissinger refers to as "my Jewish origin" was of little import to his approach; he was committed to the survival of Israel and admired Israeli achievements, but such general sympathy was shared by most non-Jewish policy-makers, past and present. In introducing the Middle East in his memoirs, Kissinger refers to "a people, sustained by faith through two millennia of persecution, come to reclaim dreams that for all this time had been more powerful than their tragic reality." But he also warns that "the meaning of this faith must not be exhausted in the heroic defense of a country that threatened to turn into another beleaguered ghetto."[71] His entire account is similarly "balanced" and written from an "outside" perspective. Most importantly, it treats the Middle East, and the Arab-Israeli conflict, basically as functions of U.S.-Soviet rivalry.[72]

Thus, for Kissinger the main fact of Middle East diplomacy in 1970 was the expanded Soviet presence in Egypt, which dominated his perception of the area. Understanding the causes of this involvement was not as important as coping with the consequences of it. This Soviet probe had to be met; the Russians had to be faced down. Judging from past patterns of Soviet use of a military presence, Kissinger reasoned, this presence would escalate unless the West reacted at once, vigorously and effectively, to the initial threat.[73]

In Kissinger's view, the indecisiveness of U.S. policy in 1969–1970 tempted such Soviet probes. The State Department's inclination to pursue negotiations at all costs, combined with other signals of anxiety to placate Soviet and radical Arab opinion, only served, in his mind, to invite further challenges. He was especially critical of the first American reaction to the introduction of Soviet SA-3 missiles and combat personnel into Egypt, when weak verbal protests were undercut by the dramatic postponement of Israeli arms requests, by a Sisco mission that seemed to indicate intensified diplomatic efforts, and by Nixon's simultaneous pursuit of a summit meeting with Soviet leaders. Similarly, Kissinger felt that the hesitant American response to evidence of Soviet and Egyptian violation of the standstill cease-fire, in August, also encouraged further Soviet adventurism.[74]

70. Kissinger, 1979, pp. 607–608.
71. Ibid., p. 341.
72. See the discussion in Kalb and Kalb, pp. 215, 220–221.
73. Kissinger, 1979, pp. 562 ff., 569 ff., 581.
74. Ibid., pp. 560, 586–588.

As Kissinger saw the situation, there was little point in pursuing a comprehensive settlement in 1969–1970, and even less in the United States taking the lead in such an enterprise. Conditions were not suitable for a successful negotiation; the two sides were too far apart on basic issues. And so long as the Soviets were simply backing the radical Arab position, any American diplomatic initiative would simply involve getting concessions from Israel in order to placate the other side. Not only would this, he argued, complicate U.S.-Israeli relations with little compensatory gain, but it would vindicate the Soviet and radical Arab strategies. The Soviet Union would gain the credit for forcing the United States to pressure Israel, and Arab states would lose any incentive to make reciprocal concessions. Kissinger therefore opposed the presentation of American comprehensive designs, such as the Rogers Plan, and argued—in opposition to the Middle East experts—that diplomatic stalemate might actually work to U.S. benefit. It would, he reasoned, demonstrate to the Arabs that only by cooperating with the United States would they make diplomatic progress, and this would undercut rather than bolster the tendency to rely on the Soviets—who actually could supply little other than arms.[75]

Kissinger argued, in fact, that one prerequisite to any successful Middle East diplomacy was a prior reduction in the Soviet role. In addition, the issues should be broken apart into manageable segments rather than tied into one package whose success depended on the solution of the least tractable problems. But even then, he was not optimistic; Nasser and the other radical leaders did not seem ready to make any real concessions. And even if progress could be made on Arab-Israeli negotiations, it would not solve the problems of U.S. policy in the area to the extent that State Department personnel seemed to feel. Arab radicalism, and the opening it offered to Soviet intrusion, was not a product of the Arab-Israeli conflict and would continue to plague the area even if that conflict should be miraculously resolved.[76]

As for Israel, Kissinger felt at this time that the secret to obtaining meaningful concessions was by strengthening the Israeli sense of security, rather than by creating greater apprehension and insecurity as the State Department approach did.[77] On the other hand, Kissinger was not entirely charmed by his exposure to negotiation

75. Ibid., pp. 349 ff., 360–361, 367, 376. On the evolution of U.S. Middle East policy and the differences between Kissinger and the State Department, see also Kalb and Kalb, pp. 216–219.
76. Kissinger, 1979, pp. 351, 558.
77. Ibid., p. 578.

with Israelis; speaking of his first diplomatic dealings with them, at about this time, he characterized the Israeli negotiating style as "a combination of single-minded persistence and convoluted tactics [that] preserve in their interlocutor only those last vestiges of sanity and coherence needed to sign the final document."[78]

Nixon and Kissinger were clearly the key decision-makers in U.S. foreign policy, but the outlooks of the Secretaries of State and Defense were also relevant in the crisis. William P. Rogers had been appointed Secretary of State in part because of his past close relationship with Nixon, but this tie became problematic when Nixon sought to centralize policy-making in the White House while at the same time trying to avoid direct confrontations with his old friend. Rogers was a lawyer who had no previous experience in foreign affairs; apparently, Nixon viewed that as an asset, since a Secretary with no strong views would be less likely to resist White House direction. On the other hand, Nixon (according to Kissinger) described Rogers as "one of the toughest, most cold-eyed, self-centered, and ambitious men he had ever met." This was also felt to be advantageous in that Rogers would "give the Soviets fits" as a negotiator and would ride herd on a willful State Department bureaucracy that the President distrusted.[79]

In practice, matters did not work out this way. Rogers, who had earlier been the psychologically dominant partner in his relationship with Nixon, found it difficult to accept the role assigned to him and insisted—understandably, as even Kissinger admits—on the prerogatives due the office of Secretary of State. Furthermore, though a shrewd analyst by all accounts, Rogers tended to adopt a tactical and episodic view of the issues, treating each case "on its merits," as his legal background prepared him to do. As principal foreign policy spokesman, he was also more closely attuned to the immediate reactions of Congress, the media, and the general public. He therefore found himself frequently in conflict with the overall Nixon-Kissinger strategy, with its stress on longer-range perspectives and linkage among issues (as illustrated in the above discussion of 1969–1970 Middle East policy), while his emphasis on specificity and immediacy, combined with his lack of expertise, made him more dependent on the bureaucracy he was expected to dominate. Thus, during the 1970 Jordanian crisis (and generally), Rogers's substantive views were usually indistinguishable from those of the foreign affairs bureaucracy;

78. Ibid., p. 569.
79. Ibid., p. 26. Despite their rivalry, Kissinger's description of Rogers and the Nixon-Kissinger-Rogers relationship (pp. 26–32) is a dispassionate and revealing account.

rather than serving as the instrument of the White House in disciplining the State Department, Rogers tended to be the latter's spokesman in the highest-level debates.

Melvin Laird, Secretary of Defense, was first and foremost a politician. His skill at political maneuvering and bureaucratic infighting, and his connections throughout Washington (he had served for sixteen years in Congress), gave Laird greater leverage than Rogers in dealing with the White House.[80] Laird had less substantive conflict with the White House, however. Thoroughly familiar with defense issues from long experience on the Defense Subcommittee of the House Appropriations Committee, he shared the administration's supportive position toward the military and its concern about the public "assault" on the military and defense budgets as a result of the Vietnam War. As part of this battle, Laird supported the move to defuse public opposition through the withdrawal of American troops from Vietnam. His general sensitivity to political currents was reflected, in fact, in a cautious attitude toward any use of American troops, a posture that did sometimes bring him into opposition to the White House (often in alliance with Rogers). Laird had opposed, for example, the Cambodian invasion, and in the Jordanian crisis also demonstrated general reluctance to envision further American military involvement in unpredictable local conflicts.

Recent Experiences

The state of U.S.-USSR relations in late 1970 was critical in conditioning American decision-makers to regard the Jordanian crisis as a Cold War confrontation rather than as a localized Middle East conflict. As already noted, there was at this time a general perception of a Soviet forward thrust, both globally and in the Middle East.[81] This perception was strengthened by a number of recent events, some of which have also been described above:

1. The Soviet rejection of the Rogers Plan in December 1969, which seemed to indicate the uselessness of joint diplomatic efforts.[82]

80. Kissinger notes, not disapprovingly, that "Laird acted on the assumption that he had a Constitutional right to seek to outsmart anyone with whom his office brought him in contact." The struggles between Nixon and Laird over credit for Vietnam withdrawals "were conducted with all the artistry of a Kabuki play, with an admixture of the Florentine court politics of the fifteenth century" (pp. 32–33).

81. Interviews with Hoskinson, Hyland, Johnson, Saunders, Sonnenfeldt, and a senior CIA official.

82. See especially comments by Kissinger, 1979, pp. 373 ff., and Quandt, 1978, p. 259.

2. The Soviet introduction of surface-to-air missile systems into Egypt in early 1970, as part of a deepening direct Soviet involvement there.[83]

3. The forward movement of SAM missiles in violation of the standstill cease-fire in August 1970, which was seen by Nixon and Kissinger as additional evidence of Soviet perfidy and raised further suspicions regarding Soviet intentions.[84]

4. The continuing drain of Vietnam, which, it was feared, tempted the Soviets to move at a time when American resources were spread thin.

5. What was seen as Soviet stalling in negotiations over Berlin, at the SALT talks, and at the European Security Conference.

6. The simultaneous crisis in September 1970 over Russian construction of what was identified as a nuclear submarine base at Cienfuegos, Cuba, which for a time raised echoes of the 1962 missile crisis.[85]

To this, one must add the unstable situation in Jordan during the year preceding the crisis, which sensitized U.S. policy-makers to the threat to Hussein's survival. Twice already in 1970—especially after a June 9 assassination attempt—it had appeared that Hussein was ready to crack down on the Palestinian organizations, but in both cases he had backed down. Harold Saunders, of the NSC staff, reported to Nixon in early June that "the authority and prestige of the Hashemite regime will continue to decline. The international credibility of Jordan will be further compromised. . . . Greater fedayeen freedom of action will inevitably result in more serious breaches of the cease-fire in the Jordan Valley. . . . Hussein faces an uncertain political future. . . ."[86] Reports from Amman indicated that the Jordanian army would soon take matters into its own hands if the King did not act, thus further increasing pressures on Hussein.[87] The feeling in Washington was that a final denouement could not be postponed much longer, and that much else hung on a successful outcome. In Kissinger's words:

83. In addition to interviews cited in note 81, above, interviews with Pranger and Smith.

84. This is especially stressed by Edward R. F. Sheehan, *The Arabs, Israelis, and Kissinger: A Secret History of American Diplomacy in the Middle East* (New York: Reader's Digest Press, 1976), p. 20, who quotes a former aide saying that, in reaction to the missile movement, "for the next two years Kissinger was 100 percent pro-Israeli —and the flow of American arms to Israel proved it."

85. Kalb and Kalb, pp. 241–244.

86. Quoted in Kissinger, 1979, p. 597.

87. Interview with Brown; Kissinger, 1979, p. 603.

Each successful inconclusive crisis had weakened Hussein a little
further; matters were drifting toward showdown. Either Hussein in
desperation would move against the fedayeen or the fedayeen
would overthrow him. Until that challenge was resolved no peace
initiative had any chance; Israel would never discuss new borders
with a government not in control of its own country.[88]

Based on the recent train of events, therefore, it seemed to Nixon
and Kissinger in September 1970 that the Russians—and their clients
—were not taking the United States very seriously. The Jordanian
situation merely tied in with Indochina, SALT, Egypt, and the rest.
Furthermore, it reportedly aroused in Kissinger a dark foreboding
that Jordan might be "the Balkans of 1970."[89] In this atmosphere,
Nixon, Kissinger, and others came to the conclusion that the United
States was being purposely tested by the Soviet Union and that the
time had come to demonstrate American resolve by standing firm
against Soviet moves. Diplomatic approaches, for the time being,
were likely to be seen as a sign of weakness. In this light, furthermore, the distinction between regional and global factors had little
significance; as Under Secretary Johnson expressed it, regional and
global factors did not run counter to each other. The Soviet Union
had to be contained in the Middle East and elsewhere.[90]

One historical experience, however, did exert a cautionary influence on policy-makers. The Cambodian incursion only four months
previously, and the intense domestic reaction to it, made the use of
U.S. troops abroad seem less inviting. Laird, who had opposed the
Cambodian decision, was, as noted, especially cautious about any
further U.S. interventions.[91] The Cambodian experience may also
have been instrumental in the decision to keep the Syria-Jordan crisis
as muted as possible, rather than going before the nation to galvanize
public support.[92]

DECISION FLOW

Contingency planning for a crisis in Jordan had proceeded as the
situation in Amman had worsened. Following the June 9, 1970, attempt on Hussein's life, the U.S. Embassy had been authorized to
evacuate dependents from Jordan, and Kissinger had convened
WSAG to consider both evacuation plans and the American response

88. Kissinger, 1979, p. 605.
89. Kalb and Kalb, p. 226.
90. Interview with Johnson.
91. Interview with Laird.
92. Kalb and Kalb, p. 235.

to a possible plea from Hussein for assistance against either the Palestinian groups or the forces of Syria or Iraq. Despite great reluctance to consider military action (the Cambodian operation was still at its peak), planning undertaken at this time laid the basis for later decisions.[93]

In the two months following, American Middle East policy was focused on "Rogers Plan B": an American proposal for an immediate cease-fire in the Suez Canal war and for resumption of negotiations through UN mediator Gunnar Jarring. The cease-fire went into effect on August 7, but Israeli charges of Egyptian and Soviet violations of its standstill provisions complicated the realization of the second half of the proposal. The State Department, reluctant to see its long-planned negotiations torpedoed by such developments, downplayed the cease-fire violations, and it was only on September 3 that the U.S. government publicly confirmed the violations. At the same time, Rogers and the State Department continued to urge immediate resumption of the Jarring talks, despite the violations. But the episode clearly strengthened the hands of Rogers's critics—primarily Kissinger—and set the stage for a more sympathetic response to Israeli claims. On September 6—the same day that the multiple hijackings triggered the Jordanian crisis—Israel announced that it would not, for the moment, participate in the Jarring talks. From this point on, the issue of resuming negotiations in the Arab-Israeli conflict converged with the dramatic developments in Jordan.

Tension had already risen in Amman on September 1, when Palestinian terrorists again attempted to assassinate Hussein. Fighting broke out between the Palestinians and the Jordanian army; and Iraq —which had 17,000 troops stationed in Jordan—threatened to intervene on behalf of the Palestinians. Hussein then appealed for a strong American statement, but the State Department, preoccupied with keeping its peace initiative alive, responded with what Kissinger termed "an amazingly noncommittal reply."[94] At the same time, the U.S. Ambassador in Moscow was instructed to ask for Soviet help in restraining Iraq—only to receive a noncommittal reply from that quarter. The threat of Iraqi action receded as the days passed, though on September 14 Nixon received the new U.S. Ambassador to Jordan, L. Dean Brown, in San Clemente, as a signal of American concern over events in that country.

The hijackings on September 6 were not initially aimed at Hussein, actually, but were rather a reaction to the cease-fire and peace initiative, which the Palestinians opposed and sought to upset. This

93. Kissinger, 1979, pp. 596–597.
94. Ibid., p. 598.

further tied the two issues together in American minds and helped
to reduce the splits within the administration: both the State Department (concerned over its initiative) and Kissinger (focusing on Hussein's survival) put high priority on frustrating the hijackers' designs.

The hijackers, from the Popular Front for the Liberation of Palestine (PFLP), seized a TWA 707, a Swissair DC-8, and a Pan American
747 (an attempt on an Israeli El Al airliner was foiled). The Pan
American plane was flown to Cairo airport and blown up after the
passengers had been evacuated; the other two aircraft were flown to
a deserted airstrip about thirty miles from Amman, where planes and
passengers were held as hostages for the release of Palestinian terrorists held in Swiss, German, British, and Israeli jails. A British VC-10
was hijacked on September 9 and added to the other two planes. The
hijackers initially set a 72-hour deadline for a favorable response to
their demands.

Nixon's initial response to the hijacking was a "gut reaction": a
tough and uncompromising determination not to yield, which set the
tone for U.S. policy during the pre-crisis period. It was, says one
observer, "Nixon at his law-and-order, no-capitulation-to-blackmail
best."[95] Kissinger concurred, describing the U.S. position as roughly
identical to Israel's known policy of never yielding to blackmail; in
addition, he was concerned to prevent the retention of American
(and Israeli) citizens after other hostages had been released, and put
a high priority on maintaining a united negotiating position with the
countries holding Palestinian prisoners.[96]

Given the sadly increasing frequency of terrorist incidents, the
treatment of hijacking was, to a great extent, institutionalized by this
time. Task forces were established, contacts with other states instituted, and the International Red Cross activated, all in almost
routine fashion. Rogers met on September 7 with representatives of
West Germany, Switzerland, Britain, and Israel, pushing the American insistence on a common front and a firm position against the
hijackers' demands. As the hijackers were trying to negotiate separately with each country, and as the European nations tended to a
more conciliatory posture (urging the United States to put pressure
on Israel to be less rigid), the task of "strengthening spines" was one
of the preoccupations of U.S. diplomats in the following days.[97]

Possibilities of military action were considered throughout this
period, but were rejected as impractical (the hijackers had placed

95. Quandt, 1977, p. 112; see also Brandon, pp. 129–133; interview with Johnson.
96. Kissinger, 1979, p. 601.
97. Interviews with Johnson and Smith; Brandon, pp. 129–133; Szulc, 1978, pp.
322–323.

explosives on the planes, where the passengers were still held). Rescue operations were under intense review by the Joint Chiefs of Staff
for some time, but received little support; Laird, the military establishment, and the top intelligence observers were in agreement that
no military options looked promising.[98] There was some feeling that
a successful rescue operation might have the added benefit of aiding
Hussein, but as chances of success seemed negligible, this was not a
decisive consideration.[99]

One reason military options seemed too risky was simply the lack
of information needed to plan any rescue attempt. This was especially true after September 11–12, when the hijackers removed some
of the hostages to undisclosed locations, released the others, and blew
up the planes. But even before then, the lack of direct communication with, or good field intelligence on, the Palestinian organizations,
Syria, or Iraq, combined with the generally confused situation within
Jordan, circumscribed the choices of decision-makers. In fact, the
lack of information was a serious constraint on U.S. policy-making
throughout the crisis, perhaps even more in later stages than in the
pre-crisis period.[100]

The initial American reaction, then, was a middle-of-the-road posture: negotiation rather than military action or threats, but refusal to
make substantial concessions, and strong pressure to prevent others
from doing so (Decision 1). Negotiations were to be conducted
through the International Red Cross, with an ad hoc committee of
involved countries to coordinate policies. As Secretary of State Rogers later described the U.S. position:

> We had to steer a quiet course and rescue the people in the
> airliners held by the guerrillas. Our people considered every
> possible solution to the rescue problem, some of them pretty
> far-out: landing troops, getting people to infiltrate the areas where
> the planes were downed and sending men in by parachute. But all
> these ideas were rejected as unworkable.

Consequently, Rogers explained, Nixon adopted a policy of quiet but
unyielding diplomacy:

> He was resolute in his warnings so that there would be no doubt
> about our willingness to play a role and our absolute refusal to pay
> ransom.[101]

98. Interviews with Hoskinson, Laird, and a senior CIA official; confirmed in interviews with Johnson, Brown, and Pranger. See also Quandt, 1978, p. 266.
99. Quandt, 1978, p. 266.
100. Interviews with Johnson, Pranger, and other senior officials.
101. Quoted in Frank Van der Linden, *Nixon's Quest for Peace* (New York: Robert
B. Luce, 1972), p. 78.

Another possibility, however, was to apply milder forms of military and psychological pressures to back up the tough negotiating stance. Direct military options were still being considered on September 8–9, but the idea of demonstrative moves began to receive more favorable attention. On September 8, a morning meeting called by Rogers, and including Kissinger, Laird, Helms, Johnson, and Sisco, ended a discussion of what Kissinger termed "wild ideas" (such as use of nerve gas) by concluding that nothing could be done.[102] An afternoon meeting with the President made no further progress, though Nixon was reported to have remarked privately that the hijacking "should be used as a pretext to crush the fedayeen. . . ."[103]

On September 9, Kissinger activated WSAG, which met at least once a day, nearly every day, for the next two and a half weeks. At this point, Kissinger felt that the United States had to begin exerting pressure on the hijackers, in order to prevent negotiations from dragging out. There was also concern that the incident might trigger a showdown between Hussein and the Palestinian organizations. For both reasons, precautionary military moves were considered. Following the WSAG discussion, Nixon ordered the movement of elements of the Sixth Fleet (an aircraft carrier and six destroyers) eastward in the Mediterranean, and the positioning of six C-130s at Incirlik air base in Turkey (Decision 2). These steps were not to be announced publicly, but it was expected that Soviet intelligence would quickly pick them up and convey the information to its clients. In the meantime, contingency planning, and preparations for higher alert status for selected U.S. forces, were also set in motion.[104]

These moves were not taken without opposition. In the view of Middle East experts in the State Department, moving the Sixth Fleet was a "reflex" response to Middle East crisis that in this case was inappropriate to the circumstances and even risky, given the psychology of the hijackers. These arguments were overruled.[105] But enthusiasm for military signals was not unqualified in the Defense Department either, given the cautious attitude toward further military interventions then prevailing. Laird indeed authorized the Sixth Fleet movements ordered by the President, but then reported that "bad weather" did not permit the use of the aircraft carrier. In discussions of available options, military spokesmen such as Moorer and Packard argued forcefully against military options; at one JCS

102. Kissinger, 1979, pp. 601–602.
103. Ibid., p. 602.
104. Ibid., pp. 604–605.
105. Interview with Seelye.

meeting on September 11, the Joint Chiefs warned Sisco and Johnson that the United States did not really have a "credible deterrent" to Soviet military intervention in the Middle East.[106]

Contingency planning for future developments raised additional issues. Like the military advisors, Kissinger did not want another large-scale military operation while the United States still had several hundred thousand troops in Vietnam. He therefore favored Israeli intervention, if major intervention should be required, with the American role limited to neutralizing Soviet threats to Israel. Nixon disagreed at this time, favoring American military actions and the exclusion of Israel.[107] The State Department also opposed backing an Israeli operation because of the political complications. Kissinger dealt with the division in the short run by having two contingency plans prepared so that the President would still have both options available at the moment of decision.

U.S. policy-makers were also concerned about the Soviet response to the crisis. No one accused the Soviet Union of complicity, and in fact the Soviet Chargé d'Affaires in Washington, Yuli Vorontsov, informed American officials on September 9 that his government was urging restraint on its clients. But at the same time, Kissinger felt the Soviets were exploiting the crisis:

> In my view, the Kremlin was playing the Jordan crisis as it had the cease-fire. It made formally correct noises but did nothing constructive to reverse the drift toward crisis. . . . Moscow obviously did not yet believe that it was running a serious risk.[108]

For this reason, the signals decided upon were aimed at the Soviet Union as well as the hijackers.

On September 11, the remaining hostages were moved to secret locations, and threats were made to kill them if the United States took military action. Nixon and Kissinger were inclined to issue a counterthreat, but there was intense opposition in the State Department to any statement likely to "excite" the hijackers. Consequently, the prepared message was not sent, but Kissinger attempted to increase the impact of American actions by telling Admiral Moorer to have the Sixth Fleet break radio silence.[109]

---

106. Interview with Laird; Adam Morris Garfinkle, "United States Foreign Policy and the Jordan Crisis of 1970: A Cognitive Approach" (Ph.D. dissertation, University of Pennsylvania, 1979), pp. 234–235, 237–238 (based on interviews conducted by Garfinkle and on the account in Elmo Zumwalt, *On Watch: A Memoir* (New York: Quadrangle Books, 1976), pp. 296–297).

107. Kissinger, 1979, pp. 605–606.

108. Ibid., p. 606; see also p. 609.

109. Ibid., p. 608.

As indicated, on September 11 the White House also announced a comprehensive anti-hijacking program, and on September 12 the freeze on new arms deliveries to Israel was lifted (Decisions 3 and 4).[110] The latter action was, of course, in part a direct response to Egypt's cease-fire violations, but it also reflected the pressure of events in Jordan and, in Kissinger's words, "the increasing likelihood that our contingency plans would have to be activated."[111] By September 13–14, negotiations with the hijackers were making little progress, there were disturbing signs that West Germany and Britain might break the united negotiating front, and Soviet behavior gave little cause for reassurance.

But, most importantly, Nixon and Kissinger clearly anticipated that the situation in Jordan might explode (though others, such as the NSC staff, were less pessimistic).[112] The dramatic insult to Hussein's sovereignty presented by the hijackings would, it was feared, finally ignite the long-expected showdown. Under pressure of threatened mutiny in his own army, which reacted to the defiance of the Palestinians with growing rage, Hussein would have to move to save his regime. And that is precisely what happened on September 15–16, ending the pre-crisis period of the 1970 Jordanian crisis.

110. See above, p. 113.
111. Kissinger, 1979, p. 608.
112. Interview with Brown; interviews with participants; Garfinkle, p. 240.

CHAPTER SEVEN

1970: 15 September to 23 September

ON SEPTEMBER 15, the hijacking crisis was still unresolved. The hijacked aircraft had been destroyed, but fifty-four hostages were still being held at unknown locations. There was increasing difficulty in holding together the unified diplomatic front with the other affected states. But American policy-makers still felt no urge to act quickly: military measures were considered impractical, and the extension of the crisis was not seen to endanger the safety of the hostages or any other important American interest directly related to the hijacking.

The Jordanian aspect of the situation was, however, another matter, and there the denouement could not be postponed for long. The focus was shifting to the internal struggle between King Hussein and the Palestinian military organizations in Jordan. The defiance of the Jordanian government by the PFLP hijackers was an embarrassment to Hussein and put an end to his efforts to establish a workable modus vivendi with the PLO groups operating as a state-within-a-state. The restiveness of his own military, alone, was forcing the King to act. And when Hussein did move against the irregular Palestinian fighting organizations, an entirely new situation was created.

Late on September 15, Washington received word that Hussein intended to establish a military government and impose martial law. Such a program, if fully implemented, would, in the expectations of most observers, bring on a full-scale military confrontation with the PLO forces. In such a conflict, the support of his own population—roughly half of which were "Palestinian" by the accepted definition—was a question mark. There was also the risk of intervention by Syria or Iraq, heightened by the presence in Jordan of an Iraqi expeditionary force of some 17,000 troops deployed there since the 1967

145

war; and behind this were the unpredictable responses of Nasser's Egypt and of the Soviet Union, patron of radical Arab causes. The news from Amman thus rang a number of alarm bells in Washington.

In the hijacking crisis, U.S. policy-makers had perceived a threat to the lives of U.S. citizens, plus an implicit potential threat to Arab-Israeli diplomatic negotiations and to Middle East stability generally. But they now perceived a clear and present threat to stability, involving the questioned survival of a friendly and moderate regime and an almost certain civil war that could easily spread into a general Middle Eastern war and trigger a superpower confrontation. Thus, the regional, and even the global, balance of power was at stake.

In addition, the time to act was limited as it had not been before Hussein had decided to act. Vital interests turned on military outcomes that shifted rapidly and could become irreversible before outside intervention could make an impact. Furthermore, the possibility of American military involvement was now taken seriously, and was from this moment a major focus of policy-makers' deliberations.

The message received on September 15 thus immediately created crisis conditions in Washington, according to the criteria employed here. Four days later, the crisis was intensified when Syria intervened in Jordan, making one of the major fears of U.S. policy-makers a reality. But the Syrian withdrawal on September 23, combined with the Jordanian army's demonstrated superiority over PLO forces, led to an immediate and almost total decline in perceptions of threat, time urgency, and probability of war, and therefore marks the end of the crisis period.

DECISIONS AND DECISION-MAKERS

There were eight identifiable decisions in the 1970 crisis period:

Decision Number	Date	Content
5	15 September	The President confirmed the WSAG recommendation that the readiness of the Sixth Fleet and of U.S. airborne troops in West Germany be increased.
6	17 September	The President confirmed further precautionary military moves.
7	17 September	The President approved $500 million in military aid and the speeding up of F-4 aircraft deliveries to Israel.

8	20 September	The President approved Kissinger's recommendation to return the airborne brigade in West Germany to its base embarkation point.
9	20 September	The President confirmed WSAG recommendations that the alert states of the airborne brigade in West Germany be further improved, that the 82nd Airborne Division be put on full alert, and that a reconnaissance plane be flown from the Sixth Fleet to Tel Aviv.[1]
10	20 September	The President approved the recommendation of advisors that, in response to an urgent Jordanian plea for air support, the United States endorse an Israeli air strike on Syrian forces in Jordan.
11	21 September	The President decided, in the framework of an NSC meeting, to back Israeli ground action against Syrian forces in principle, subject to determination of the Jordanian attitude and further U.S.-Israel consultation before actually taking action.
12	21 September	In response to Israeli requests for clarification, the President reportedly approved a U.S. guarantee of Israel against an Egyptian or Syrian attack in response to Israeli action against Syria (see discussion below, pp. 168–173).

In addition to these major decisions, minor military moves were made almost continuously during the crisis: units of the Sixth Fleet were moved, additional C-130s were sent to Turkey, etc. A number of public and private warnings were delivered through various channels, and there was nearly continuous consultation and military planning with Israel.

The identity of decision-makers did not change from the pre-crisis

1. The account in Marvin Kalb and Bernard Kalb, *Kissinger* (New York: Dell, 1974), p. 231, dates the improved alerts of the 82nd Airborne Division and the German-based airborne brigade on September 19. Other accounts, such as William Quandt, *Decade of Decisions: American Policy Toward the Arab-Israeli Conflict, 1967–1976* (Berkeley: University of California Press, 1977), p. 115, have accepted the Kalbs' dating. But Henry Kissinger, in *White House Years* (Boston: Little, Brown, 1979), pp. 617–622, puts these moves a day later. In such cases of contradiction in factual detail, the Kissinger version has generally been preferred, since it presents a more thorough and consistent picture of such detail, being based, to all appearances, on direct access to records of the events in question.

period. But with the WSAG meeting almost continuously, its members (Kissinger, Johnson, Sisco, Packard, Helms, and Moorer) were most intimately involved in the crisis. At the peak of the crisis, there was a shift to an "NSC" focus, meaning that the President was present and that the Secretaries (Rogers and Laird) replaced the Under Secretaries (Johnson and Packard). But this was largely on the formal level; in practice, deliberations became more ad hoc, there were more intimate consultations (often by phone) with selected advisors, and the Nixon-Kissinger axis became more dominant.

PSYCHOLOGICAL ENVIRONMENT

Attitudinal Prism

Policy-makers clearly perceived the Jordanian situation as potentially explosive, and from the beginning had feared that the hijacking would spark the long-expected detonation. But this was tempered by the very fact that the situation was of long standing, and that there had been several previous "showdowns" that had not been decisive. Twice earlier in 1970, Hussein had appeared ready to crack down on the rebellious Palestinian factions, but on both occasions he had backed down. Thus, while the announced intention to establish a military government and impose governmental authority was taken seriously, there was also a note of wariness in the reaction of knowledgeable officials. Ambassador Brown cabled Washington that Hussein was closer to a showdown than before, but that he could also be bluffing. One school of thought in the bureaucracy felt that Hussein's move might be nothing more than a political and psychological gesture aimed at the PLO groups.[2]

There was, however, little disagreement on the importance of ensuring Hussein's survival in case of a showdown. The consequences of his overthrow seemed stark. In Kissinger's words:

> I considered it essential to preserve Hussein's rule; it was important
> to demonstrate that friendship with the West and a moderate
> foreign policy would be rewarded with effective American support.
> It was necessary to arrest the progressive radicalization of the
> Middle East, which had been accelerated by the dispatch of Soviet
> missiles and combat personnel to Egypt. Nasser's technique of
> blackmailing the United States with Soviet threats had to be shown
> as futile.[3]

2. Kissinger, 1979, pp. 609–610; *New York Times*, September 17, 1970.
3. Kissinger, 1979, p. 611.

The survival of Hussein's government was also considered vital to any long-term hopes for a settlement of the Arab-Israeli conflict, since it was axiomatic that Israel would not negotiate with the kind of radical Palestinian government most likely to take Hussein's place. In fact, his downfall might even set off another Arab-Israeli war: Israel would intervene to prevent the establishment of a radical regime in Amman, possibly catalyzing a general war and dragging in the superpowers. All in all, as described by a senior Middle East specialist, Nixon and Kissinger considered the maintenance of the Jordanian regime important enough to save Hussein at all costs, except perhaps the actual deployment of U.S. troops.[4]

As the military situation was perceived in Washington, conflict with PLO forces in Jordan would present a serious threat to Hussein. Given the growing boldness of the armed PLO irregulars and their entrenched position in key areas, a campaign to subdue them would mean full civil war, which would be bloody and possibly prolonged. Nevertheless, the general feeling was that Hussein could handle the military challenge if there were no outside intervention on behalf of the PLO groups. The Jordanian army, with 50,000 troops, far superior equipment (the PLO having only small arms), better organized and disciplined, and apparently loyal to the King, should easily overwhelm the few thousand hastily trained, undisciplined, and ill-equipped "guerrillas" organized in uncoordinated and often mutually hostile organizations. There were some doubts in the State Department among those who assumed that all Palestinians were anti-Hussein and that the Jordanian army would therefore operate among a hostile population. The fact that the British took a more pessimistic view of Hussein's military prospects also influenced some observers. But most U.S. government sources, including the Department of Defense, felt that the Jordanian army could handle the situation.[5]

This perception was reinforced by the early results of the fighting after civil war erupted. By September 18, when Nixon met with Golda Meir, discussions between the two centered on other problems, since both felt that Hussein was winning and that the crisis would soon be over.[6] On the following day, both Laird and Moorer

---

4. Tad Szulc, *The Illusion of Peace: Foreign Policy in the Nixon Years* (New York: Viking, 1978), p. 326; *New York Times,* September 17, 1970; interview with Talcott Seelye, Country Director, Lebanon, Jordan, Syria, and Iraq, Department of State.

5. *New York Times,* September 17, 1970; Henry Brandon, *Retreat of American Power* (New York: Dell, 1973), p. 134; interviews with L. Dean Brown, U.S. Ambassador to Jordan; Admiral Thomas Moorer, Chairman, Joint Chiefs of Staff; Harold Saunders, National Security Council staff; and senior Defense Department officials.

6. Kissinger, 1979, p. 615.

publicly expressed confidence that the Jordanian army was gaining control and could handle the situation unaided.[7]

The crucial question was whether either Syria or Iraq would intervene. Initially, this threat was taken seriously, but on balance was not considered likely. Kissinger recalls Brown's assessment that Iraqi or Syrian action was unlikely and records his own disagreement on this point.[8] But in the intelligence community, the State Department, and even among the NSC staff working with Kissinger, most experts tended to Brown's view of the probabilities.[9] And to the extent that the threat was taken seriously, it was the Iraqis rather than the Syrians who were the main focus of concern, since Iraqi troops were already present in Jordan. In Kissinger's words, "for some unknown reason no one in either Amman or Washington expected Syrian intervention." This needs to be qualified; Hussein did indicate to Brown that he was more apprehensive of Syrian action than of Iraqi, but this message made little impression on Washington when Brown relayed it.[10] Furthermore, even the Iraqi threat seemed to recede as the fighting continued and the Iraqi troops in Jordan remained immobile. Nixon's public warning on September 17 against interference was viewed as directed at Iraq, among others—and Kissinger carefully noted later the same day that Iraqi troops were standing by as the Jordanian army attacked PLO forces near them.[11]

Views of both the Syrians and the Iraqis were influenced, of course, by the global perspective. This was especially true of Nixon and Kissinger, who tended to view both Syria and Iraq (with scant attention to the split between these two countries) as proxies for the Soviet Union. The crisis was seen as a U.S.-Soviet confrontation, and the local sources of conflict were correspondingly de-emphasized. As one observer put it:

> Mr. Nixon saw the situation in its broadest implications. Jordan to him was a microscopic spot on the map and yet he viewed it as having far-reaching implications on the worldwide stage and on American relations with the Soviet Union.[12]

7. *Washington Post,* September 20, 1970.

8. Kissinger, 1979, p. 610.

9. Quandt, 1977, p. 113; interviews with Saunders and with Walter Smith, Deputy Director, Egyptian Affairs, Department of State; also confirmed in interviews conducted by Adam Garfinkle, "United States Foreign Policy and the Jordan Crisis of 1970: A Cognitive Approach" (Ph.D. dissertation, University of Pennsylvania, 1979), p. 249.

10. Kissinger, 1979, pp. 611, 612; interview with Seelye.

11. Kissinger, 1979, p. 615.

12. Brandon, 1973a, p. 139.

Middle East experts in the Departments of State and Defense were very critical of this approach. Though framing the crisis as a U.S.-Soviet confrontation might suit White House political needs, they suggested, it overrated the Soviets' control of their clients and their interest in Jordan, while overlooking important U.S. interests in the Middle East that were independent of Soviet relations.[13] This lack of appreciation of local dimensions led, it was said, to a situation in which Nixon and Kissinger could be manipulated by local parties (Israel and Hussein). In short, facing down Moscow might be useful in the short run, but left behind a policy ill-suited to regional trends and to the maintenance of healthy U.S.-Arab relations. These experts would argue later that this global fixation had contributed to the conditions out of which the 1973 Arab-Israeli war developed.[14]

This is, of course, disputed by Nixon and Kissinger, and by other policy-makers in the 1970 crisis as well, who have argued that there was no contradiction between the regional factors and the global considerations. A firm response to Soviet pressures was required everywhere; containment was as relevant in the Middle East as it was elsewhere. Operationally, therefore, the American response to the 1970 crisis was appropriate even if there was a tendency to exaggerate Soviet control of Syrian actions.[15]

The feeling was not that the Soviets had initiated the crisis or that they were masterminding events, but rather that they were supporting disruptive forces from the first moment, trying to accelerate and exploit the crisis.[16] Warning the Soviets off was therefore a principal preoccupation. Kissinger, for example, noted with satisfaction that the Soviet note of September 18 showed that "Moscow had heard us." The note was free of the usual bombast, urged prudence on all parties, and promised to use Soviet influence to bring the civil war to an end. Simultaneously, Soviet Chargé Yuli Vorontsov reassured Washington that the Syrians were not going to intervene. Kissinger interpreted all of this to mean that the United States had successfully deterred the Soviet Union.[17]

13. Interviews with Smith and Seelye; interview with Robert Pranger, Deputy Assistant Secretary of Defense for Near Eastern and South Asian Affairs; interview with a senior State Department official; Quandt, 1977, p. 124.

14. See especially Quandt, "Lebanon, 1958, and Jordan 1970," in Barry M. Blechman and Stephen S. Kaplan, eds., *Force without War: U.S. Armed Forces as a Political Instrument* (Washington, D.C.: Brookings Institution, 1978), p. 288.

15. Interview with Johnson.

16. Interview with Moorer.

17. Kissinger, 1979, pp. 616–617; Szulc, 1978, p. 328.

Given this Soviet assurance, there was special anger when the Syrians invaded on September 19–20. The recent experience with the Russians in the violations of the Suez standstill cease-fire agreement, only the month before, made Washington specially sensitive to evidence of Soviet duplicity. Kissinger, in particular, concluded that the Soviet assurance, given only one day before the invasion, was a deliberate act of deception.[18] While Middle East specialists questioned the degree of Soviet control over Syria, Kissinger held Moscow responsible and berated the Soviets during the remainder of the crisis—telling Vorontsov on September 22, for example, that he took all new Soviet promises skeptically, in light of the earlier assurance that the Syrians would not intervene.[19]

There was little doubt in Kissinger's mind that the Soviets were instigating the Syrians. As he told Nixon, "the Soviets are pushing the Syrians and the Syrians are pushing the Palestinians."[20] All of this was seen as part of a pattern that began with Soviet rejection of the Rogers Plan and the dispatch of large numbers of Soviet troops to Egypt, and which might well culminate in a Soviet-backed effort to overthrow Hussein.[21] The Soviets were in fact pushing to the limit; accordingly, they had to be taught a lesson.

By September 21, Kissinger thought that the Soviets had begun to learn the lesson. A Soviet note on this date was yet more conciliatory than the September 18 note. The Russians indicated that they had opposed Syrian intervention into Jordan, and made it clear that they were pressing the Syrians to withdraw.[22] When the Syrians did indeed withdraw, this of course helped to confirm the perception of strong Soviet influence in Damascus. As Nixon and Kissinger saw the outcome, it showed that "though Moscow was willing to take advantage of a promising situation, it was not willing to run intolerable risks." The Soviets would in fact shrink, in the American view, from a genuinely dangerous course of action. Earlier, Nixon had "snorted" in disbelief when informed of a Defense Department apprehension that the Soviets might launch air attacks on Israel in response to Israeli air strikes on the invading Syrians.[23]

18. Kalb and Kalb, p. 231; interviews with Helmut Sonnenfeldt and William Hyland, National Security Council staff; interview with Smith.

19. Interview with Seelye; Kalb and Kalb, pp. 238–239.

20. Richard Nixon, *RN: The Memoirs of Richard Nixon* (New York: Grosset and Dunlap, 1978), p. 483.

21. Interview with Johnson; Nadav Safran, *Israel: The Embattled Ally* (Cambridge: Harvard University Press, 1978), p. 455. Garfinkle (pp. 264–265) analyzes the cognitive aspects of the conviction, on Nixon's and Kissinger's part, that the Soviets were behind the Syrian invasion.

22. Kissinger, 1979, p. 627.

23. Szulc, 1978, p. 331; Kissinger, 1979, p. 624.

The absence of direct evidence of Soviet complicity in the Syrian action had little influence on perceptions. There was even, in fact, some information that cast doubt on the theory of Soviet instigation of the Syrians.[24] But participants do not recall any sophisticated discussions of Soviet-Syrian relations or of Syrian domestic politics.[25] Some, reacting to the lack of direct evidence, justified the focus on the Soviet role as a preferred strategy whatever the truth of Soviet-Syrian relations: given the Soviet support of Syria, the Russians should be held responsible as a working hypothesis. In this view, it is more effective to deal with the stronger ally in some crises. Putting pressure on the Soviet Union was the best recourse under the circumstances, and the actual degree of Soviet responsibility for Syrian actions was of secondary importance.[26]

Policy-makers also lacked a clear picture of how Syrian policy was shaped, beyond their image of Syrian leaders as fanatics. There were, for example, splits within the Syrian leadership that were important in the eventual outcome of the crisis. These splits were reported to Washington, but did little to alter perceptions: not enough was known about them, and there was no understanding of their relationship to Soviet influence or to decisions on intervention in Jordan.[27] Again, the perception of local forces as secondary or marginal led to minimization of those limited inputs that were available. Even though regarded as madmen, the Syrians were not expected to take the risks inherent in an invasion of Jordan; and when they nevertheless did so, it seemed improbable that they would have acted without the encouragement and backing of their Soviet patrons.

The Syrian intervention triggered an explosive reaction in Washington, given the unexpectedness of the move, the linkage in the minds of policy-makers to broader issues, and the immediate threat posed to Hussein (with the last point reinforced by Jordanian reports described as "panicky" by most observers).[28] Nixon's immediate reaction, as he later recalled it, was that "they're testing us. . . . The testing was continuing, moving a few notches higher each time. We would have to decide what to do very soon, or it might be too late

24. Interview with Seelye.
25. Interviews with Melvin Laird, Secretary of Defense; Samuel Hoskinson, National Security Council staff; and a senior Defense Department official.
26. Interviews with Joseph Sisco, Assistant Secretary of State for Near Eastern and South Asian Affairs, and with Sonnenfeldt.
27. Interviews with Brown, Hoskinson, Smith, and a Middle East specialist in the Department of Defense.
28. Interviews with Brown, Hoskinson, Johnson, and a Middle East specialist in the Department of Defense.

to do anything."[29] One observer said that Kissinger saw the Syrian invasion as a "serious and direct challenge to the balance of power in the area, and to the West in general," and that "he knew the Russians were involved, and he knew therefore that we had to be involved."[30] In Kissinger's own words:

> I had no doubt that this challenge had to be met. If we failed to act, the Middle East crisis would deepen as radicals and their Soviet sponsors seized the initiative. If we succeeded, the Arab moderates would receive a new lease on life. On the whole, I was optimistic. The balance of forces was in our favor both locally and overall. I expressed the view to the President late that evening that the Soviets were "either incompetent or forcing a showdown. If they are incompetent we will have an easy victory." I did not need to add that if they had decided on a showdown we had no choice in any case.[31]

Nixon and Kissinger thus saw the crisis as a test of their resolve in the global confrontation. The United States had to establish its credibility with the Kremlin, or it would find itself in increasingly mortal danger. The stakes went far beyond the survival of one friendly government.

But top policy-makers also continued to perceive important constraints on U.S. action. As recounted in Chapter Two, there was apprehension of the domestic reaction to any use of force, especially in light of the reaction to the Cambodian incursion only four months earlier. Laird, in particular, was opposed to further commitment of American troops abroad, just as he had opposed the Cambodian decision.[32] Senator Richard Russell, the Chairman of the Appropriations Committee and a senior member of the Armed Services Committee, also let his opposition be known.[33] Newspaper reaction to the President's September 17 remarks in Chicago was described by Kissinger as "a storm warning of what we would face if we sought to implement the President's strategic preference for a unilateral American move."[34] Approaching Congressional elections increased the general sensitivity to public opinion. Thus, facing a situation in which he anticipated having to take a highly controversial action, Nixon chose to keep the Jordanian crisis as muted as possible: there was no speech to the nation, in fact no dramatic public statement of

29. Nixon, p. 285.
30. Quoted in Kalb and Kalb, p. 232.
31. Kissinger, 1979, pp. 618–619.
32. Interview with Laird.
33. Kissinger, 1979, p. 616.
34. Ibid., p. 615.

any kind after the September 17 remarks (which were actually leaked, with Presidential acquiescence, from an off-the-record briefing; see below, p. 164).[35]

The likely international reaction was also a factor to be taken into account, even if it was not influential in the final decision. The climate of world politics was even more hostile to superpower intervention in the non-Western world than it was in 1958. Any U.S. action, it was anticipated, would incur a heavy cost in relations with allies and with the Third World. Western European allies had already made their opposition to American intervention in Jordan clear.[36] There was, in particular, fear of violent anti-U.S. reactions in the Arab world, with the interesting result that some officials not noted for sympathy to Israel nevertheless preferred Israeli over U.S. action, should it become necessary for one or the other to act in order to save Hussein. The viewpoint was especially marked among State Department Arabists; Assistant Secretary Sisco shared it and argued effectively for it in higher-level discussions.[37]

Added to these constraints were, of course, the risks inherent in any U.S. military operation in a sensitive area. Again, it was no longer 1958: the Soviet role was both more extensive and more intensive, their military capability in the region was incomparably better, and with parity on the nuclear level the effectiveness of nuclear deterrence of nonnuclear military moves—tenuous as it had been even in the 1950s—was of increasingly doubtful credibility. Even if a direct military challenge was still regarded as unlikely, some kind of Soviet response seemed more likely than before. At the least, any introduction of U.S. forces would create a precedent, if not an immediate excuse, for the introduction of "matching" Soviet forces. The risks in superpower relations were therefore not insignificant.[38]

Given these considerations alone, it is not surprising that officials publicly ruled out any repetition of 1958.[39] But behind this was a yet more compelling constraint: the perception of inadequate American military capability. Already in 1969, the Department of Defense had concluded that the United States was inadequately prepared and deployed for any future Middle East conflict.[40] The problem began with the lack of a secure base structure in the region. The nearest

35. Kalb and Kalb, p. 235.

36. Ibid. A senior intelligence official involved in the highest-level discussions has said that the political costs of U.S. intervention would have been "disastrous" (personal interview).

37. Interview with Seelye.

38. Interviews with Moorer and other Defense Department officials.

39. *New York Times*, September 17, 1970.

40. Interview with a senior Defense Department official.

available base was on Cyprus, but this depended on the British, whose attitude under given conditions was uncertain. NATO bases in Greece or Italy, or even American bases in Spain, were unlikely to be available for most Middle East contingencies such as the Jordanian crisis. The Turks made it clear during the 1970 crisis that the use of the Incirlik air base would be restricted to "humanitarian" missions (meaning the rescue of hostages or the evacuation of U.S. citizens, but not intervention in the civil war).[41]

There were problems even with regard to an American air strike, which some military advisors thought might suffice against the Syrian tanks. The United States could fly fifty sorties daily from Cyprus if the British permitted use of their base there, and two hundred sorties from the Sixth Fleet. But the question was whether this would be adequate; and in any event, the Israelis could do much more.[42] Furthermore, despite superior American naval power in the area, one intelligence analyst later reported that the Soviets had trebled the missile capacity of their fleet within thirty hours during the crisis, while it had taken the United States ten days to assemble the Kennedy aircraft carrier group. There was also serious concern over the Soviet naval configuration during the crisis, which employed new tactics of intermingling Soviet combat vessels with U.S. forces in order to keep every major American vessel within firing range of surface-to-surface missiles.[43]

Getting ground forces into Jordan in time to be effective was even more of a problem. The Marines deployed with the Sixth Fleet lacked adequate helicopter transport, though a helicopter carrier (the *Guam*) was en route. The transport of troops by C-130s from West Germany, or of the 82nd Airborne Division by C-141s from Fort Bragg, would be slow and in inadequate numbers.[44] In any event, with the Syrians employing a large tank force in Jordan, sending in troops without armor would be suicidal. And if the United States had been pressed, additionally, to back Israel against a Soviet threat, its resources would have been yet more inadequate, in the minds of key military advisors.[45]

Largely because of this perception of limited American capability, the Joint Chiefs of Staff consistently opposed U.S. intervention during

41. David Schoenbaum, "Jordan: The Forgotten Crisis (2)," *Foreign Policy*, 10 (Spring 1973), 177.
42. Quandt, 1977, p. 118.
43. Joseph Churba, *The Politics of Defeat: America's Decline in the Middle East* (New York and London: Cyrco Press, 1977), p. 45; Garfinkle, pp. 284–285.
44. Schoenbaum, p. 176.
45. Interviews with Admiral Elmo Zumwalt, Chief of Naval Operations, and with a senior Defense Department official.

the 1970 Jordanian crisis.[46] Though there was disagreement over the likely effectiveness of an American air strike, there was a generally shared perception that the option of using American ground forces to meet the Syrian thrust did not exist.[47] The military argument was in this case reinforced by a political argument which may or may not have been a rationalization: that if only American military action could save Hussein, then he was in any event lost, since such action would bring about his final discrediting in the eyes of his own population and the Arab world.[48] In any event, no key advisor argued seriously for U.S. ground action, given the fact that those unpersuaded by other negative arguments had to contend with the consistent judgment of military planners that it simply could not be done (and that even an air strike alone was at best a risky venture). This feeling was clearly conveyed at a later date by Under Secretary of State Johnson:

> The other side of the equation was, those of us who were involved in planning and working on that contingency were appalled at the —let's say the inadequacy or limited resources and capabilities that we had to bring to bear if we had been called upon to do so. I cannot predict here, how and in what numbers American forces might be used, or required in the area, but I can say with confidence that our availability will continue to be important and that managing our political, military and diplomatic resources to maintain an acceptable position in the Middle East will be a challenge of the highest order for all of us.[49]

The advice that Nixon and Kissinger received on the other leading option—backing an Israeli move—was not so unanimous. To a certain extent, the Israeli option gained the support even of those generally cool toward Israel, due to the high costs and military impracticality of American action. There was a strong feeling, especially in the State Department, that the U.S. position in the Arab world would suffer less from backing Israel than from a direct American intervention. This was thought to be especially true if military action could be restricted to an air strike, thus avoiding the need for the use of Israeli ground forces in an Arab country, with all the problems and risks that this involved.[50]

---

46. Interviews with Moorer, Zumwalt, Laird, Pranger, and other Defense Department officials. See also Richard K. Betts, *Soldiers, Statesmen, and Cold War Crises* (Cambridge: Harvard University Press, 1977), p. 102.
47. Interviews with Johnson, Smith, and a senior intelligence official.
48. Interview with Sisco.
49. Johnson in a speech at CINCSTRIKE Command Conference, Puerto Rico, February 24, 1971, quoted in Schoenbaum, p. 171.
50. Interviews with Johnson, Sisco, and Brown.

But this was complicated by other, long-standing perceptions of Israel and the Arab-Israeli conflict, especially among area specialists. First, of course, there was the simple fear that the introduction of Israeli forces would create a whole new set of problems, expand the conflict, and destabilize the region over the long run, if not precipitate a general Middle East war in the short term.[51] More specifically, some analysts feared Israeli intentions, believing that the Israelis would exploit such a situation to gain more territory and/or to press the United States for future favors. Though some State Department Arabists took this line, it was strongest among Middle East specialists in the Department of Defense, some of whom felt that doing nothing was preferable to "letting the Israelis in."[52]

But the suspicion of Israel could also be used as an argument for working closely with, and thus controlling, the Israeli government. To the extent that policy-makers feared unilateral Israeli action, they had a motive for heading it off by forcing Jerusalem into joint planning and response. And it was this argument that seems to have been decisive at the top. At the onset of the crisis period, Nixon's biggest concern, reportedly, was the fear that Israel would attack the hijackers.[53] The Syrian invasion brought to a head the feeling that Israel would act if the United States did not, and thus fostered the feeling that it was necessary "to bring Israel into the tent."[54]

The result was far from what the area specialists had counseled. By collaborating with Israel on a common program of action, and basing U.S. policy on threatened Israeli military action (see below), Nixon and Kissinger came out of the crisis with a new perception of Israel. Israel now seemed more of a strategic asset, having shown itself ready to save Hussein and having been instrumental in forcing a Syrian retreat. This new appreciation of the potential value of U.S.-Israeli ties, as Quandt points out, led to stronger cooperation between the two countries in the period to follow.[55]

51. Interview with Moorer; Brandon, 1973a, p. 134.
52. Interviews with Seelye, Smith, Pranger, a senior Defense Department official, and a Defense Department Middle East specialist. An interesting confirmation of these attitudes among State Department Arabists can be seen in the cognitive mapping (based on a June 1970 simulation), and a follow-up interview three years later, of an unnamed Middle East specialist by G. Matthew Bonham and Michael Shapiro, "Explanation of the Unexpected: The Syrian Intervention in Jordan in 1970," in Robert Axelrod, ed., Structure of Decision: The Cognitive Maps of Political Elites (Princeton: Princeton University Press, 1976), p. 138.
53. "The Mid East: Search for Stability," Time, October 5, 1970, p. 11.
54. Interviews with Johnson, Brown, and Sonnenfeldt; Benjamin Welles, "U.S.-Israeli Military Action in Jordan was Envisioned," New York Times, October 8, 1970.
55. Quandt, 1977, p. 122. For a definitive discussion of this shift in U.S. policy and its implications, see the forthcoming work by Steven Spiegel, The War for Washington: The Other Arab-Israel Conflict, Chapter 6; also Garfinkle, pp. 306–309.

But this was the later outcome. The dominant perceptions in Washington during the crisis period in 1970 were: (1) the perception of a serious threat to King Hussein, with the view that his downfall would in turn threaten other moderate regimes, Arab-Israeli peace, overall Middle East stability, and the U.S. position in the area relative to the ongoing Soviet thrust; (2) apprehension of Syrian or Iraqi intervention that Hussein could not overcome and that would test U.S. ability to act in time, and suspicion of the role of the Soviets in instigating or supporting such intervention; and (3) the perception of serious constraints on U.S. military action, given limited military capabilities, the likelihood of strong domestic opposition, and the expected negative regional and international reactions.

Images

On the level of personal images, the statements and behavior of Richard Nixon during the crisis period confirm the previous analysis of his pre-crisis images and provide some nuances in relation to the general attitudes described in the preceding section.

Surprisingly, Nixon's first reaction to the Jordanian crisis was to denigrate its importance. But, as Kissinger points out, in all likelihood this is attributable to Nixon's greater sensitivity to domestic politics:

> That morning [September 16], too, I sent a report to the President outlining the conclusions of the previous night's WSAG meeting. Unexpectedly, his reaction was vehement. He had an election campaign on his mind and was still hopeful of a Moscow summit. He questioned whether there had been any need for an emergency WSAG meeting and covered my report of the WSAG's views with angry scribbled comments. He wrote that he preferred no confrontation at all; if it was unavoidable he wanted American forces used; he opposed any Israeli military moves unless he specially approved them in advance, which he strongly implied he would never do. I was not surprised by his preference for demonstrating American power directly and unilaterally; this had been his consistent view. I was convinced that once he had studied its implications and our resources he would have second thoughts.[56]

Kissinger was correct, in that Nixon did quickly come to take the crisis seriously, and did eventually overcome his original instinct to use U.S. power directly and forcefully. His antipathy to the "terrorists" who flouted civilized standards came out quickly and sharply on September 16 and 17 in two public statements. In a tough "law and order" speech at Kansas State University, on the 16th, Nixon tied the Palestinian hijackers into the broader issue, as he saw it, of increasing

56. Kissinger, 1979, p. 612.

lawlessness and violence around the world. The vehemence of his statement is especially noteworthy:

> When Palestinian guerrillas hijacked four airliners in flight, they brought to 250 the number of aircraft seized since the skyjacking era began in 1961. And as they held their hundreds of passengers hostage under threat of murder, they sent shock waves of alarm around the world to the spreading disease of violence and terror and its use as a political tactic.
>
> The same cancerous disease has been spreading all over the world and here in the United States. . . .
>
> Those who bomb universities, ambush policemen, who hijack airplanes, who hold their passengers hostages, all share in common not only a contempt for human life, but also the contempt for those elemental decencies on which a free society rests—and they deserve the contempt of every American who values those decencies.[57]

The next day, in remarks at a Citizenship Day reception in Chicago, Nixon called attention to the fact that in dealing with the hijacking the United States had rejected any distinctions among U.S. citizens, since all citizens were strictly equal in the eyes of the government and entitled to the same protection.[58] The two statements of September 16–17 were the only public references to the Middle East made by the President during the crisis.

By this time, Nixon had moved from domestic preoccupations to a confrontational view of the crisis, to an extent that threatened to undermine his normal stress on "keeping cool." Kissinger reported that, when he telephoned Nixon on September 17 to get confirmation of military movements recommended by WSAG:

> He approved all the deployments enthusiastically; they appealed to his romantic streak: "The main thing is there's nothing better than a little confrontation now and then, a little excitement." He could be dissuaded only with difficulty from having all our military movements announced, which would have created too much of a crisis atmosphere; the announcements would have backfired because they would have required too many public reassurances, draining our deployments of some of their effect. By late in the day Nixon had changed his mind. He now agreed that it was best to issue no warning, to continue to move forces and treat the Soviets with cool detachment.[59]

Nixon continued to see the crisis basically in confrontational terms, as can be seen in his reaction to the first reports of Syrian

57. U.S. President, *Public Papers of the Presidents of the United States: Richard Nixon, 1970* (Washington, D.C.: U.S. Government Printing Office, 1970), pp. 758–759.
58. Ibid., p. 765.
59. Kissinger, 1979, p. 614.

incursions and partial withdrawal: " 'They're testing us,' I said to Kissinger, 'and the test may not be over yet.' "[60] But this was balanced by the cult of coolness: "I felt it was important to keep as cool as possible. . . . We decided to pursue a very hard but very quiet line."[61] Another Nixon trait that Kissinger comments on was the former's decisiveness, tempered by a certain fatalism. Referring to Nixon's change of mind in favor of Israeli rather than U.S. action, Kissinger writes:

> Once the point of decision was reached, Nixon acted with a kind of joyless, desperate courage—torn between his insights and understanding of the international reality and his fatalistic instinct that nothing he touched would ever be crowned with ultimate success. The biggest problem at that point was to keep the courage from turning into recklessness and the firmness into bravado. In these situations he would not be concerned with short-term political advantage; he would do what he thought was required by the national interest as he perceived it.[62]

Kissinger made no public statements during the crisis, but his own account makes it clear that he shared the attitudes outlined in the previous section. Of particular note, however, is his stress on his philosophy of crisis management—usually presented in contrast to that of Secretary of State Rogers. Discussing the decisions made on September 20, Kissinger argues:

> In my view what seems "balanced" and "safe" in a crisis is often the most risky. Gradual escalation tempts the opponent to match every move; what is intended as a show of moderation may be interpreted as irresolution; reassurance may provide too predictable a checklist and hence an incentive for waiting, prolonging the conditions of inherent risk. A leader must choose carefully and thoughtfully the issues over which to face confrontation. He should do so only for major objectives. Once he is committed, however, his obligation is to end the confrontation rapidly. For this he must convey implacability. He must be prepared to escalate rapidly and brutally to a point where the opponent can no longer afford to experiment.[63]

Pursuing this view of how to deal with the Syrians and the Soviets, Kissinger recounts an argument with Rogers at the NSC meeting on the following day. While Rogers wanted to take a conciliatory move, "Nixon and I held that if we wished to avoid confrontation with the Soviets we had to create rapidly a calculus of risks they would be

60. Nixon, p. 485.
61. Ibid.
62. Kissinger, 1979, p. 621.
63. Ibid., p. 622.

unwilling to confront, rather than let them slide into the temptation to match our gradual moves."[64]

Kissinger's focus on the superpower chess game, his appreciation of the military underpinning of power, his philosophy of firm crisis management, and his conception of leadership in crisis are all reflected in other observers' perspectives of the same decision-making:

> Did Kissinger "enjoy" the manipulation of American power? another top official was asked. "Enjoy?" the official exclaimed, a look of astonishment on his face. "Henry adores power, absolutely adores it. To Henry, diplomacy is nothing without it." A Pentagon aide related how Kissinger leaned over large maps, moving toy battleships and aircraft carriers from one end of the Mediterranean to the other, arguing with admirals, expounding on military tactics and then picking up the phone to order the JCS to change the deployment of the Sixth Fleet. The World War II sergeant had become all at once a general and an admiral and, during that crisis, a kind of deputy Commander in Chief.[65]

DECISION FLOW

On the evening of September 15, most top U.S. officials were at a dinner honoring Defense Secretary Laird at Airlie House in Warrenton, Virginia. While en route to the dinner, Kissinger received from Ambassador Brown a cable announcing that King Hussein was about to establish a military government, reaffirm his authority, and use force if the PLO groups resisted. Shortly thereafter, there was a phone call from London: the British wanted to know the American reaction to the news from Amman, and added that Prime Minister Edward Heath might call President Nixon later that night. Sensing the gravity with which the British viewed the situation, and needing to consider the American response, Kissinger gathered the available members of WSAG (Moorer, Helms, Packard, and Sisco—all but Johnson) and returned by helicopter to the White House.[66] The initial reaction of U.S. policy-makers is described by Kissinger:

> The WSAG convened from 10:30 to close to midnight in the White House Situation Room and continued afterward in my office upstairs. Still elegant in our dinner jackets, we reviewed the possible contingencies: outbreak of war between the King and the fedayeen; Iraqi involvement (for some unknown reason no one in either Amman or Washington expected Syrian intervention); or armed intervention by the United States at least for purposes of

64. Ibid., 626.
65. Kalb and Kalb, p. 232.
66. Kissinger, 1979, pp. 609–610; Kalb and Kalb, p. 227.

evacuation. The meeting confirmed the judgments of the previous week. The King would probably defeat the fedayeen. Israel would almost certainly intervene if the fedayeen seemed to gain the upper hand; it would surely do so if Iraq moved. If Israel acted, everyone agreed that the United States should stand aside but block Soviet retaliation against Israel. To show our support, material help should be offered to the King immediately. Whatever happened, our readiness would have to be intensified.[67]

The only immediate decisions related to the last point. WSAG recommended, and the President confirmed, a number of military moves (Decision 5). The carrier *Saratoga* was sent to the eastern Mediterranean, airborne units in West Germany were put on semi-alert, and more C-130s were sent to Turkey.[68] In Kissinger's view, the massing of military power was important to deter radical Arab states, to restrain the Soviet Union, and to provide reassurance to Hussein.[69]

With Nixon and Kissinger committed to preserving Hussein's rule, the question was what action would be taken if deterrence failed. Hussein could hold his own against the PLO, but not against other Arab states. At this stage, there was still some support, apart from Nixon himself, for American as opposed to Israeli action.[70] But there was no immediate need for a decision on this choice; the task at the moment was defined as encouraging Hussein to act ("holding his coat" in the words of one participant), and restraining Israel but at the same time using the threat of U.S. and/or Israeli action to help deter Iraq, Syria, and the Soviet Union.[71]

WSAG met again briefly on the morning of September 16, following which Kissinger ordered the preparation of contingency plans for aiding Jordan in case of Arab or Soviet intervention, including the options both of U.S. action or of U.S. acquiescence in Israeli action.[72] But Nixon, as already described, reacted angrily to Kissinger's report of WSAG activities, questioning the degree of urgency and disagreeing sharply with those favoring the Israeli option should a confrontation develop. In any event, Nixon decided to keep to his schedule, and departed on a planned two-day trip to Kansas City and Chicago.[73]

Later that day, Nixon delivered his "law and order" speech at Kansas State, in which he vigorously denounced the hijackers but did

67. Kissinger, 1979, pp. 610–611.
68. Quandt, 1977, pp. 112–113; Quandt, 1978, p. 273.
69. Kissinger, 1979, p. 611.
70. Brandon, 1973a, p. 134; Szulc, p. 326.
71. Quandt, 1977, p. 113; interview with a WSAG member; see also Kalb and Kalb, pp. 227–228, and *Time*, October 5, 1970, p. 11.
72. Kissinger, 1979, pp. 611–612.
73. Ibid., p. 612; Nixon, p. 483.

not refer to Hussein's moves, the danger of civil war in Jordan, or warnings against the intervention of other parties. Kissinger and Sisco also traveled to Chicago to brief a group of midwestern editors in a "background" session. Sisco stated in response to a question that the United States had no present intention of intervening in Jordan, but "obviously, it is normal, routine planning to cover every contingency and to weigh what the pros and cons are."[74] So long as the situation in Jordan did not actually explode, policy-makers were taking a "wait and see" position.

But this changed quickly on September 17, when Hussein ordered his army into Amman and civil war broke out. Kissinger, having returned to Washington, wakened Nixon at 3:00 A.M. The President decided not to dramatize the crisis by returning to Washington, but it was agreed that the United States would have to issue a warning to the potential interveners.[75] An opportunity presented itself later in the morning when Nixon met the editors of the *Chicago Sun-Times* and the *Chicago Daily News* for a (presumably) off-the-record briefing. According to Kissinger's version of the event:

> When his meeting began, Nixon had just learned of the outbreak of civil war in Jordan. Though usually his self-discipline was monumental, it could be breached by emotion at moments of high tension. Charged up by the news and the military movements he had just approved, Nixon proceeded to tell the amazed editors that if Iraq or Syria intervened in Jordan only the Israelis or the United States could stop them; he preferred that the United States do it. (It was also his way to get a message to me without confrontation.) Carried away by the spirit of the occasion, Nixon added that he would make the Russians pay dearly for their adventures with the missiles along the Suez Canal. "We will intervene if the situation is such that our intervention will make a difference." It was too much to expect that such sensational news could be kept off the record. The *Sun-Times* ran the exact quote in an early edition. Though it was then withdrawn when Ziegler insisted on the off-the-record rule, this only heightened its foreign policy impact.
>
> Though Nixon was contrite after the event, I considered his statement on the whole helpful.[76]

Kissinger also notes that Nixon later congratulated the author of the article for his handling of the story. Nor does Nixon's own account of the affair indicate any displeasure that his off-the-record comments had been "leaked."[77]

74. Kalb and Kalb, pp. 228–229.
75. Schoenbaum, p. 172; *Time,* October 5, 1970, pp. 11–13.
76. Kissinger, 1979, pp. 614–615; see also *Chicago Sun-Times,* September 17, 1970, and *New York Times,* September 19, 1970.
77. Nixon, p. 483.

Kissinger also convened WSAG twice during the day. WSAG recommended a number of further military deployments, which were approved by the President from Chicago (Decision 6). A third aircraft carrier was dispatched to the Sixth Fleet from Puerto Rico, the amphibious task force in the Mediterranean was ordered to remain thirty-six hours off the Lebanese coast, and the helicopter carrier *Guam* with its task group was ordered to the Mediterranean.[78]

Following Nixon's return to Washington in the evening, there was a meeting with top advisors, including Rogers and Laird as well as the WSAG members.[79] The general feeling was that U.S. warnings had been effective; Iraqi troops were standing by, and there was as yet no real fear of Syrian intervention. But as the President was due to meet Golda Meir the next day, and as U.S.-Israeli relations were at a low ebb due to the cease-fire controversy, it was thought advisable to make a gesture to Israel. Nixon therefore decided to approve an Israeli request for $500 million in military aid, and to expedite the delivery of Phantom jets (Decision 7). Though this decision basically grew out of the cease-fire situation and Arab-Israeli diplomacy generally, the timing was clearly related to events in Jordan, as the possible need for Israeli cooperation there was still on decision-makers' minds.[80]

On the following day, September 18, events seemed to confirm American expectations. The Jordanian army was gaining the upper hand, the Iraqis were still not intervening, and the Syrians were only making threatening noises. There was also the conciliatory note from the Soviet government already mentioned above. The Soviet message was notably free of accusations and warnings, written in a tone described as "plaintive," with the Soviets counseling caution on all sides and reportedly urging the governments of Jordan, Iraq, Syria, and Egypt to end the civil war. The Russians added that "we are searching for ways of bringing our viewpoint also to the attention of the leadership of the Palestine movement," which was interpreted by Kissinger as Moscow's way of distancing itself from the PLO and especially from the hijackers.[81] All in all, the Soviet message was reassuring enough that Nixon told Senator Mike Mansfield that,

78. Kissinger, 1979, p. 614. Kissinger also dates the decision to have the carrier *Saratoga* moved to the eastern Mediterranean on September 17, but other sources include this as part of the initial military movements set in motion (though not made public) on September 15.

79. Quandt, 1977, p. 114; Kalb and Kalb, p. 229.

80. Quandt, 1977, p. 114; Kalb and Kalb, pp. 229–230; interview with Pranger.

81. Kissinger, 1979, p. 616.

"based on the note, I was optimistic that we could work things out without a confrontation."[82]

This optimism was reflected in the meeting with Golda Meir later in the day. The focus was on the Suez Canal cease-fire and the renewal of diplomatic negotiations. Jordan was discussed, but intervention was not seriously weighed, since Hussein seemed to be gaining control. Both leaders agreed that it was preferable to have the problem solved by the Jordanian army unaided, and Meir promised that in any event Israel would not move "precipitately" into Jordan.[83]

On September 19 came reports that a small number of Syrian tanks had crossed the border and taken positions some 250 yards inside Jordan. But U.S. policy-makers, still focused more on Iraq than Syria, did not react strongly—especially as the report had come from a British official in Cairo, and neither London nor Amman had contacted Washington directly on the incident. "Despite all the communications difficulties," Kissinger notes, "we believed that Hussein would have found a way to notify us had he been deeply concerned."[84]

There was also further reassurance from the Soviets. Soviet Deputy Foreign Minister Vasily Kuznetsov had a conversation with U.S. Ambassador Jacob Beam that reinforced Kissinger's conviction that the Soviets were looking for a way out, and that "we were approaching the end of the crisis with much of our credibility established." Nixon, however, was less sanguine. When Kissinger called him at Camp David late on the nineteenth to report the Soviet message, the President responded with the "gut" feeling that whenever the Soviets offered reassurance they were up to something.[85]

Nixon's suspicions seemed confirmed the next day, September 20, when a serious Syrian invasion was reported. At 6:00 A.M., Washington time, Hussein himself reported to Brown that there had been two incursions of Syrian tanks (with the markings of the Palestine Liberation Army, a branch of the PLO). Around noon, two more armored brigades crossed the border; this was confirmed by U.S. sources dur-

82. Nixon, p. 484; the optimism at this stage is analyzed by Garfinkle, pp. 253–254.

83. Nixon, p. 484; Kissinger, 1979, p. 615; Kalb and Kalb, p. 230. The Kalbs state that the first reports of Syrian tank movements across the border were received late on September 18, but Kissinger himself (p. 618) firmly dates these reports on September 19. Other sources and circumstantial evidence tend to confirm Kissinger.

84. Kissinger, 1979, p. 618. Again, Kalb and Kalb (pp. 230–231), and others such as Szulc, 1978 (pp. 328–329) and Quandt, 1977 (p. 115), who apparently rely on the Kalbs' account, anticipate Kissinger's account by one day, locating on September 19 events and decisions that Kissinger clearly places on September 20. See note 1, above.

85. Kissinger, 1979, p. 617.

ing the afternoon. Jordan asked for U.S. help in general terms, but the only specific request at the moment was for reconnaissance on possible Syrian reinforcements.[86]

With the Syrian invasion, the focus in Washington shifted to the question of Hussein's survival. Nixon and Kissinger had already made the essential commitment here: preserving Hussein was an assumed basic aim of U.S. policy. In Kissinger's words, "I had no doubt that this challenge had to be met."[87] Operationally, this meant action on two fronts: (1) bringing pressure on Syria (primarily through the Soviets) to withdraw its forces from Jordan, and (2) developing a credible military option to save the Jordanian government in case the first course of action failed.[88]

The campaign to bring pressure on the Syrians was inaugurated at once. A peremptory statement demanding Syrian withdrawal was issued over Rogers's name.[89] More to the point was action directed at the Soviet Union, given the anger among policy-makers over the "deceptive" Soviet assurance before the event. Sisco called in Vorontsov and delivered a "blistering" message, formally a reply to the Soviet note of September 18, which warned of "serious consequences which could ensue from a broadening of the conflict" if Syrian forces were not withdrawn, and called upon the Soviets "to impress upon the Government of Syria the grave dangers of its present course of action."[90] During the course of the afternoon, Kissinger also recommended, and Nixon approved from Camp David, returning the airborne brigade in West Germany to its base embarkation point, thus reducing its alert time from ten to four hours (Decision 8). The brigade was instructed to move openly so that Soviet intelligence would pick up the signal more quickly.[91]

Aside from bringing pressure, diplomatic options—activating the UN, negotiating through the Soviets, diplomatic approaches to Syria,

86. Ibid., p. 618.
87. Ibid.
88. Quandt, 1978, p. 268.
89. *Department of State Bulletin,* October 12, 1970, p. 412. The statement reads as follows:

> We have been informed that tank forces have invaded Jordan from Syria during the night and have moved toward Ramtha. We have also been informed that Jordanian armor is resisting this invasion.
>
> We condemn this irresponsible and imprudent intervention from Syria into Jordan. This action carries with it the danger of a broadened conflict. We call upon the Syrian Government to end immediately this intervention in Jordan, and we urge all other concerned governments to impress upon the Government of Syria the necessity of withdrawing the forces which have invaded Jordan.

90. Kissinger, 1979, p. 619.
91. Ibid.

Egypt, or the Palestinian organizations, etc.—were not seriously considered. Attention focused on the second line of defense as defined above: developing a credible military option, hopefully as a deterrent but if necessary for execution. The discussion moved around two interrelated questions: Would air strikes alone suffice, or would ground operations also be needed? And should such operations, on either level, be carried out by U.S. or by Israeli forces? (There was agreement that it should be one or the other, and not both.)

On September 17, Kissinger had already conveyed to the President WSAG's preference that the United States not intervene with its own forces, but rather back up Israeli action. This preference was reaffirmed at the WSAG meeting convened at 7:00 P.M. on September 20 to make a final recommendation. The decisive considerations in this preference, as recounted above (pp. 154–157), were:

1. A general reticence to take on a new military involvement in the prevailing circumstances, with Vietnam still raging, the Cambodian invasion still fresh, and a growing anti-militarist and isolationist mood in public opinion.

2. The military judgment that the United States lacked the capability for successful ground operations in Jordan, and that air strikes, while possibly effective, could be carried out better by the Israeli Air Force.

3. Anticipated heavy political costs in U.S. relations with Arab countries and with the Third World generally.

4. The risk that U.S. involvement would lower the threshold for Soviet involvement in the Middle East sooner or later.

The consensus in favor of Israeli action brought together nearly all governmental actors: Kissinger and the NSC staff, the career and political levels of the State Department, and most of the Defense establishment except some military advisors who preferred a U.S. air strike to Israeli air operations, if it appeared that air attacks alone would be enough.[92] Kissinger describes the sense of the WSAG meeting as follows:

> A quick review of the pros and cons of American military intervention strengthened our conviction that our forces were best employed in holding the ring against Soviet interference with Israeli operations. To be effective unilaterally we would have to commit our entire strategic reserve; we would then be stretched to near the breaking point in two widely separated theaters and

92. This summary of views on the U.S. versus the Israeli option is based on interviews with Sisco, Seelye, Brown, Hoskinson, Laird, Zumwalt, and a senior Defense Department official. See also Quandt, 1978, p. 272; Brandon, 1973a, p. 136; and Schoenbaum, p. 173.

naked in the face of any new contingency. Our forces would have to go in without heavy equipment and with air support only from carriers. Our only overland supply route was across Israel, linking us with Israel when separation was the principal reason for an American action. If we got into difficulties, we would have to call on Israel for help. In short, if the situation in Jordan got out of control it could be remedied only by a massive blow against Syria, for which Israeli armed forces were best suited.[93]

The major dissenter on the preference for the Israeli option had been the President himself. But just before the WSAG meeting, Nixon (who had just returned from Camp David) revealed to Kissinger that he had changed his mind. Kissinger then asked Nixon to meet with the senior WSAG members without revealing his new opinion, so that WSAG could then review the options again without Presidential pressure. Following this, a formal decision could be made. The WSAG meeting was interrupted at about 8:00 P.M. for this purpose, with Kissinger, Johnson, Moorer, Helms, Packard, and Sisco moving to the President's office for a brief "pep talk."[94]

As WSAG reconvened, at about 8:20 P.M., an urgent message was received from Hussein, via the British, requesting immediate air strikes to halt the deterioration in his military situation. This changed the debate over U.S. or Israeli action from contingency planning to operational decision-making. Hussein apparently did not specify whose air support he was requesting or was willing to accept; the request was directed to the United States, but he obviously could not turn to Israel directly even if he were willing to have Israel act.[95] In any event, U.S. policy-makers moved to conclude the issue of which air force would intervene if the Syrian advance continued,

93. Kissinger, 1979, p. 620.

94. Ibid., pp. 620–621. According to *Time* (October 5, 1970, p. 13), Nixon and Kissinger war-gamed the options during this period.

95. King Hussein vigorously denies that he ever appealed for Israeli assistance, and Ambassador Brown (personal interview) states that the request was for American action. The claim by Kalb and Kalb (p. 233) that Hussein *specifically* asked for Israeli air support seems, in light of other evidence and his own known preferences, to be unlikely. A more plausible account is that of Peter Snow in *Hussein: A Biography* (New York: Robert B. Luce, 1972), pp. 228–229, which asserts that Hussein, in desperation, indicated that he would accept any intervention to save his throne, without specifically asking for Israeli action. Snow attributes his information to an unnamed source close to the King, who had "no reason to discredit Hussein," and says it has been confirmed by two other disinterested authorities. Kissinger tends to confirm this version, noting merely (p. 621) that "the King was requesting immediate air strikes," and then recounting the continuing debate in the U.S. government over which air force should carry out such strikes. There is little suggestion in the account of this debate that U.S. policy-makers anticipated any problem with Hussein regarding an Israeli action in the *air*, in contrast to the suggestion of Israeli intervention on the ground (as will be seen below).

under the impetus of Hussein's urgent plea but on the basis of the same considerations and options debated previously. But before finalizing the debate, WSAG turned to other measures designed to give Jordan timely assistance (there being, in any event, insufficient target information to launch U.S. air strikes at once).

WSAG recommended a further set of preparedness measures, including further improvement in the alert status of the airborne brigade in West Germany, putting the 82nd Airborne Division on full alert, and flying a reconnaissance plane from the Sixth Fleet to Tel Aviv to get targeting information. It was expected that these moves would be detected quickly by the Soviet Union, thus conveying an important signal of U.S. determination.[96] Kissinger and Sisco then tracked Nixon down to a bowling alley in the basement of the Executive Office Building and got his approval of the WSAG recommendations (Decision 9).[97]

At about 10:00 P.M., Kissinger returned to his office and telephoned Israeli Ambassador Yitzhak Rabin, who happened to be in New York at a dinner honoring Golda Meir. Kissinger asked only for Israeli help in reconnaissance at this point—there being no final decision yet on approval of an Israeli air strike—but Rabin pressed the issue by asking what the American attitude toward Israeli action would be if the reconnaissance showed the Syrians gaining the upper hand. The discussion was interrupted by another urgent message from Hussein; Kissinger promised to call Rabin back.[98]

Hussein's second message had an added tone of desperation: Irbid was occupied and Jordanian forces were no longer in contact with each other. Immediate air strikes were imperative. WSAG moved, therefore, to conclude its debate on U.S. versus Israeli intervention, having already reached virtual consensus on the second option. Kissinger and Sisco phoned Rogers, who agreed to a joint recommendation that the United States endorse and back an Israeli air strike. Finding their way back to the bowling alley, Kissinger and Sisco received Nixon's confirmation of this recommendation and his authorization to convey the decision to Rabin (Decision 10).[99]

Kissinger then phoned Rabin again, informing him that "if Israeli reconnaissance confirmed what he had told me, we would look favorably upon an Israeli air attack." Kissinger added that the United States would replace Israeli losses in material and neutralize any

96. Kissinger, 1979, pp. 621–622; Kalb and Kalb, pp. 230–231; Szulc, 1978, pp. 328–329.

97. Kissinger, 1979, p. 622.

98. Ibid., pp. 622–623; Kalb and Kalb, p. 233; Yitzhak Rabin, *The Rabin Memoirs* (Boston: Little, Brown, 1979), p. 187.

99. Kissinger, 1979, p. 623; Nixon, p. 485.

Soviet threat. Rabin called back later, however, to say that the Israeli military were not persuaded that air operations alone would suffice, and that intervention on the ground might be necessary. Rabin also wanted to know exactly what the United States would do if either Egypt or the Soviet Union intervened. Finally, Israel would study the results of the reconnaissance scheduled for first light, Middle East time, and would not act without further consultation.[100]

U.S. decision-makers thus faced two questions: first, the question of Israeli ground operations, which raised sensitive issues that air strikes did not; and second, they had to respond to the Israeli query regarding American support against Soviet or Egyptian reactions to any Israeli move, on the air or on the ground. Consideration of the first question was again pressed by Rabin at 5:15 A.M. on September 21, when he called with a report that Israeli military leaders definitely did not think air strikes alone would contain the Syrian advance. The American view of this dilemma was requested within hours.

Nixon was inclined to approve Israeli ground action, but was reportedly persuaded by Kissinger to defer a decision until meeting with his senior advisors, given the fact that any Israeli movement by land across an Arab border was a much more serious move than air strikes alone and involved the risk of triggering a general Middle East war.[101] Kissinger also felt that the United States need not respond to the Israeli query quite so rapidly, since Israel could not move on land in any event without undertaking a serious mobilization. In fact, he was even hopeful that the Israeli mobilization in itself would help resolve the crisis without the necessity of actually approving military operations:

> I did not think the issue required an immediate resolution because the Israeli reply, while adding the complicating threat of a ground war, also provided a political opportunity. If Israel considered a ground action essential, it would have to mobilize. Mobilization would take at least forty-eight hours. And Israel could not afford *not* to mobilize because it could not permit a Syrian victory, whatever our ultimate reaction. Thus we had a breathing space—if the King could hold on—during which pressures on Syria would mount and perhaps to the point where the crisis resolved itself without war.[102]

At 8:45 A.M., an NSC meeting was convened. (Aside from the presence of Nixon, the difference between this and a WSAG meeting

---

100. Kissinger, 1979, pp. 623–624; Rabin, pp. 187–188.
101. Kissinger, 1979, pp. 624–625.
102. Ibid., p. 625.

lay mainly in the attendance of the two Secretaries, Rogers and Laird.) There was suspicion that Israel had "its own reasons" for pushing ground attack, and there was a general apprehension of the risks involved. But since U.S. ground operations appeared impractical, military advisors favored giving the Israelis the green light—if ground action seemed essential. The discussion thus turned around the basic need for ground action, including the question of whether to intervene only if the Syrians continued advancing or to do so if they simply refused to withdraw from positions to which they had already advanced. Fortunately, the "breathing space" afforded by the need of prior Israeli mobilization made it possible to decide "conditionally" on the matter. Nixon finally resolved the debate temporarily by authorizing a response to Israel that approved ground action in principle, but made the actual operations subject to consideration of Hussein's views and final consultation before attack (Decision 11). Kissinger was also authorized to work out a joint plan of action with Rabin.[103]

This qualified U.S. approval led Israel to submit a set of questions regarding U.S. policy in case of hostilities, the response to which took the better part of the day. This again suited Kissinger's purposes, as he recounts the matter, since Israeli mobilization was continuing in the meantime and pressure on Syria was presumably mounting. There was also the further reassurance of a Soviet message that seemed to show that the Kremlin was very worried and was using all its influence to get the Syrians to withdraw.[104]

By the end of the day, Rabin and Kissinger had worked out a two-stage plan for an Israeli air strike and, if that did not turn the Syrians back, an armored thrust into Jordan and Syria to cut off the Syrian force. The plan was to be executed if Syrian tanks drove toward Amman, or if the Iraqi troops in Jordan joined the fight.[105] The crucial question that remained was the American "umbrella" protecting Israel against Soviet or Egyptian counterattacks. According to some reports, during the evening, as the Syrians sent some additional forces across the border, Nixon made the final decision:

103. Interviews with Moorer, Laird, Johnson, Seelye, and a Defense Department official; *Time,* October 5, 1970, p. 13; Kissinger, 1979, p. 626; Quandt, 1977, p. 117; Kalb and Kalb, pp. 235–236; Rabin, p. 188.

104. Kissinger, 1979, pp. 626–627.

105. Details of the plan, which apparently remained unwritten, are described by Safran, p. 454, and Welles. Safran and Welles state that the plan was to include an American airborne seizure of Amman airport; other sources fail to confirm this (Quandt, 1977, p. 117; Kalb and Kalb, pp. 237–238; interviews with participants). Neither Kissinger nor Rabin, in their respective memoirs, mentions the content of the plan.

the United States would unequivocally guarantee Israel against Egyptian or Soviet attack (Decision 12). In other accounts, however, the final commitment was never given, or was never given in the form of a specific guarantee, but was instead "inherent" in the fabric of the crisis.[106] In any event, whether because they were excluded from the decision or because there was no decision, senior advisors cannot confirm the extension of the final formal commitment, and some maintain that none was given.[107] Also, there was little planning on the operationalization of the guarantee of Israel, aside from some routine procedures set in motion by the Defense Department.[108]

When WSAG met at 8:30 A.M. on September 22, however, the news was encouraging. Hussein had committed his air force against the Syrian tanks, which had no air cover, and had destroyed an estimated 120 of them.[109] In addition, there were clear signs that the Soviets were indeed forcefully pressing the Syrians to withdraw. U.S. policy having been set, Nixon and Kissinger waited on events. Hussein conveyed his objections to Israeli ground action in Jordan, but as the day progressed this contingency seemed less immediate in any event.[110] In the evening, Kissinger met Vorontsov at a diplomatic reception and renewed his warning to the Soviets, in line with his belief in unrelenting pressure at decisive junctures of crisis. The Russian stressed in response that the Soviet government was doing all in its power to stop the Syrians.[111]

Kissinger continued this line the following day, September 23, although there were increasing signs that the Syrians were beginning to withdraw. Kissinger, however, feared that the Syrian force might

106. Reports of the decision are in Safran, pp. 453–454; Quandt, 1977, pp. 116–117; Quandt, 1978, p. 21; and Kalb and Kalb, pp. 237–238. Kissinger's book (1979, pp. 626–627) is inconclusive on the point, as were most interviewees (though Brown and Sisco maintained that there was at least an understood commitment to Israel). On the other hand, Adam Garfinkle, in his dissertation (pp. 291–293) and in personal correspondence with the author, has argued persuasively that the evidence is not conclusive (most of it seems to be derived from a single source: Henry Kissinger), and that in fact both Nixon and Kissinger had strong motivations after the event to leave the impression that a firm guarantee had been given, when actually Nixon had hesitated to take the final step. Garfinkle has some strong contextual evidence, and, of course, considerable negative evidence in the large number of advisors who disclaim knowledege of such a formal decision (with many of them denying forthrightly that there could have been such a conclusion without their knowledge).

107. Interviews with Moorer, Hoskinson, and a senior intelligence official.

108. Interviews with Zumwalt and with a senior Defense Department official.

109. Kissinger, 1979, p. 628. Both Kissinger and Quandt (1978, p. 282) attribute Hussein's bold use of his air force to the security provided by the U.S.-Israeli contingency plan, but Ambassador Brown (personal interview) describes it as an act of desperation.

110. Kissinger, 1979, p. 628.

111. Ibid., pp. 628–629; Kalb and Kalb, pp. 238–239.

dig in where it was already established and declare a "liberated zone," thus still leaving the threat to Hussein's survival and the danger of Israeli intervention. WSAG continued its contingency planning. Under pressure from Rogers, who feared sudden Israeli action on the basis of the approval given two days earlier, the United States asked for and received a renewed Israeli assurance that no action would be taken without final consultation. Finally, at 2:50 P.M., policy-makers received conclusive word that the Syrian tank force was being totally withdrawn from Jordanian territory.[112]

The Syrian withdrawal broke the tension at once, as Hussein had already established his dominance over the unaided PLO factions. There was no longer any perceived likelihood of U.S. involvement in military hostilities, nor any perception of an urgent need for an American response within a limited time. The threat to Hussein having passed—and his position now appearing stronger than it did prior to the crisis—the only remaining threat to U.S. values was the safety of the remaining hostages, whose fate had been obscured by the Jordanian civil war and the Syrian invasion. To this, policy-makers redirected their attention in the post-crisis period.

112. Kissinger, 1979, pp. 629–630.

CHAPTER EIGHT

1970: 23 September to 29 September

DECISIONS AND DECISION-MAKERS

THE JORDANIAN CRISIS of 1970 was marked by a rapid return to normal conditions following the critical turning point: the withdrawal of Syrian forces from Jordan on September 23. The Syrian withdrawal made possible the quick subjugation of Palestinian fighting organizations by the Jordanian army, leading in rapid succession to an Arab summit conference, a cease-fire confirming the guerrillas' defeat, and the release of the remaining hostages. All these developments took place in less than a week, so that by September 29 the post-crisis period could be said to have passed.

Given this telescoped succession of events, U.S. decision-makers perceived no major threats and no urgent need of action during these six days. Only one decision of note was made during this period:

Decision Number	Date	Content
13	25 September	The State Department sent Israel a message canceling the understandings on Israeli intervention against Syria and the U.S. guarantee of Israel against retaliation.

There was basically no change in the decision-makers during the post-crisis period, but with the return to routine procedures, members of the Washington Special Actions Group (WSAG) became less central, and the Nixon-Kissinger dyad became less dominant. The State Department was to some extent restored to its normal position in the foreign policy decision-making machinery.

175

PSYCHOLOGICAL ENVIRONMENT

The overwhelming fact regarding the attitude and images of decision-makers in the few days of the post-crisis period was that they
experienced a sharp drop in the tension level. What explains the
sudden passage to a non-crisis atmosphere, with little perception of
a remaining threat and no sense of urgency?

One factor was the fact that the crisis had been muted. The public
had not been aroused, so there was no need to deal with it afterwards.
The crisis was over when the key decision-makers decided that it was
over.

A second factor was a simultaneous crisis—the Cienfuegos crisis
over a Soviet submarine base in Cuba—which *did* go public (to some
degree) only two days after the Syrian withdrawal from Jordan, on
September 25. This diverted attention from the remaining issues in
Jordan and Syria to what seemed like an even more important test
of wills with the Soviet Union.

But, above all, the relaxation in Washington reflected a perception
that the United States had achieved a smashing victory in forcing the
Syrians to withdraw. The crisis appeared to have been resolved on
U.S. terms; there were no ambiguities to mar the sense of triumph.
The very extent of this success removed most elements of crisis from
the post-crisis period and guaranteed a quick transition from post-
crisis to non-crisis.

In Kissinger's account, after receiving conclusive news of the
Syrian withdrawal on September 23, "there remained only the pleasant aftermath of success."[1] In this air of finality, Kissinger called all
members of WSAG to thank them, and arranged for Congressional
and press briefings (finally) to recapitulate what had been achieved.
In his mind, "the Jordan crisis was over."[2]

There was no doubt in Washington that the Syrians had suffered
unmitigated defeat. It was also assumed that the Soviets had suffered
defeat, though there was still no exact knowledge regarding the
Soviet role in the Syrian incursion. In the minds of some officials, this
was of no consequence; in any event, the effect of the firm American
stand on the Soviets would be healthy.[3] Kissinger continued to believe, however, that the Soviets had been deeply involved. In recounting his September 25 meeting with Soviet Ambassador Anatoly
Dobrynin (who returned to Washington on the previous day, after
seven weeks of absence), Kissinger showed his skepticism of Soviet
claims not to have known of the Syrian plan: "He weakened his case

1. Henry Kissinger, *White House Years* (Boston: Little, Brown, 1979), p. 630.
2. Ibid., p. 631.
3. Interview with a State Department official.

considerably by reassuring me that Soviet advisors had left their Syrian units before the latter crossed the frontier!" Consequently, the Syrian debacle was a blow to the Soviet Union, "raising by another notch the growing Arab disenchantment with Moscow."[4] In view of the prevailing perception of a general Soviet forward thrust throughout the world, the Jordanian crisis was thus the first success in stemming this Soviet tide and beginning its reversal. In the global test of wills and prestige, the United States had scored an important victory by forcing a Soviet retreat in full view of the Soviet client states.[5]

Though success, like the crisis itself, was viewed predominantly in global terms, it also had a local expression. At long last, Hussein had successfully asserted control over his own territory. The Palestinian organizations, if not yet totally defeated, were doomed without Syrian or Iraqi support. The suppression of the terrorist organizations on Jordanian soil would enormously stabilize the Arab-Israeli front, while ending a serious threat to the existence of a moderate pro-Western regime whose participation in Arab-Israeli diplomacy was vital. A major roadblock in Arab-Israeli peace efforts had been removed.

How did policy-makers explain this success? Not surprisingly, they first credited the role of the United States: the firmness of the U.S. response, the cool crisis management of the Nixon-Kissinger team, and the successful communication of the determination and capability to act. Even administration officials normally critical of Kissinger cite the 1970 Jordanian crisis as a model of crisis management.[6]

A second reason for success, in the prevailing perception, was the activation of Soviet pressure on Syria. This again reflects the global focus, and in particular the assumption of a Soviet role in instigating the Syrian invasion. Given later evidence on Syrian independence of Moscow, this might be questioned. But most participants in the decision-making still felt it to be a factor, if only, as one later surmised, in preventing the Syrians from sending a second wave of armor across the border.[7]

Senior decision-makers apparently felt that local factors—splits in the Syrian government, the Israeli mobilization, and the surprising Jordanian military performance—were secondary at best. The role of

4. Kissinger, 1979, p. 631.

5. This theme is developed by Nadav Safran, *Israel: The Embattled Ally* (Cambridge: Harvard University Press, 1978), p. 455.

6. This was felt by all the participants interviewed, including Defense Secretary Melvin Laird, U.S. Ambassador to Jordan L. Dean Brown, Assistant Secretary of State Joseph Sisco, and a number of lower-ranking officials—some of whom generally had few kind words for Henry Kissinger.

7. Interview with Sisco.

internal dissension in Damascus, and General Assad's refusal to provide air cover to Syrian tanks, are scarcely mentioned by contemporary sources. One high-ranking intelligence source later indicated his belief that the Syrians made a serious error by intervening in a "half-assed" way, but offered no explanation for the lack of coherence in the Syrian effort. Only one of the participants interviewed spontaneously mentioned the splits in the Syrian government.[8]

Kissinger himself gives little credit to internal Syrian splits or to the impact of the Israeli mobilization at the Syrian border, though he does note that Hussein prevailed "by his own courage and decisiveness."[9] Some lower-ranking officials have given more credit to the Israeli role—in particular, noting that the crisis turned quickly when Israeli forces began to move.[10]

Nixon and Kissinger did, however, come out of the crisis with a new appreciation of Israel's willingness and capability to act on behalf of common American and Israeli interests in the Middle East. The availability of Israeli forces, when the adequacy of U.S. military capability was questionable, put new light on Israel's potential as a strategic asset. On September 25, Kissinger relayed to Rabin a message embodying the most far-reaching statement to date on the mutuality of interests between the two countries:

> The President will never forget Israel's role in preventing the deterioration in Jordan and in blocking the attempt to overturn the regime there. He said that the United States is fortunate in having an ally like Israel in the Middle East. These events will be taken into account in all future developments.[11]

Quandt emphasizes the same development, from a somewhat different (and more critical) perspective, in concluding that "the U.S.-Israel relationship came to be seen as the key to combating Soviet influence in the Arab world and attaining stability."[12]

The final factor in explaining American success in the crisis—the tenacity and tough performance of Jordan's king and armed forces

8. Interview with a senior intelligence official; interview with Samuel Hoskinson, NSC staff aide.

9. Kissinger, 1979, p. 631.

10. Interviews with Hoskinson and with William Hyland, NSC staff aide. This is supported by David Schoenbaum, "Jordan: The Forgotten Crisis (2)," *Foreign Policy*, 10 (Spring 1973), 171–181.

11. Quoted in Yitzhak Rabin, *The Rabin Memoirs* (Boston: Little, Brown, 1979), p. 189.

12. William B. Quandt, *Decade of Decisions: American Policy Toward the Arab-Israeli Conflict, 1967–1976* (Berkeley: University of California Press, 1977), p. 106. Quandt also emphasizes, on pp. 124–125, the neglect of local factors and the stress on global dimensions in Nixon-Kissinger perceptions during and after the crisis.

—was also accorded an important but secondary role in the minds of most policy-makers. In retrospect, some observers have assigned higher importance to the Jordanian performance, even arguing that the major value of the U.S. role was to encourage King Hussein to use his own forces fully.[13]

In the glow of success through which U.S. policy-makers viewed events in the post-crisis period, there seemed to be almost no problems remaining. This is particularly striking with regard to the hostages, whose fate had been obscured by the civil war in Jordan but who remained in captivity during this period. Though the main activities of policy-makers, at least on the bureaucratic level, were turned again to this problem following the resolution of the Syrian invasion, there is a striking lack of references to the hostages during this period in published and unpublished accounts by major policy-makers. The question of the hostages' fate was apparently dwarfed by the larger issues of state that still cast a lingering shadow over the post-crisis period.

Since no public statements were made by senior government officials during these six days, no content analysis of their images can be offered.

DECISION FLOW

The news of the Syrian withdrawal led to a return to normal procedures and routines in policy-making. WSAG ceased to meet on Middle East affairs; its attention was taken with the new Cuban crisis. Activity on the return of the remaining hostages fell again into routinized procedures on the lower levels of bureaucracy. No further military moves or signals in the Middle East were suggested or discussed.

As Kalb and Kalb have noted, the return to normalcy in Washington was marked on the evening of September 23 by such phenomena as the reappearance of Russians at cocktail parties throughout the city.[14] On the following day, Nixon marked the relaxation of the Presidential mood by going golfing with Secretary of State William Rogers, Attorney General John Mitchell, and AFL-CIO President George Meany.

13. Especially Quandt, 1977, p. 126: "American diplomacy, through a mixture of subtlety and restraint combined with visible force, had helped create a situation in which Jordan was able to cope with its own problems." Also: interviews with Sisco and Brown.

14. Marvin Kalb and Bernard Kalb, *Kissinger* (New York: Dell, 1975), p. 239.

The only major concern was to prevent unexpected actions from unraveling what had been achieved. This concern was directed principally toward Israel. As the State Department was increasingly reintroduced into the picture, Rogers expressed concern on September 23 over the backing and assurances given to Israel during the height of the crisis, and called attention to the danger of unauthorized Israeli action based on these understandings. Consequently, Assistant Secretary of State Joseph Sisco was asked to repeat to Rabin the American understanding that Israel would not move without further consultation. An Israeli assurance on this score was given later on the same day.[15] Further reassurance on the winding down of the crisis was embodied in King Hussein's statement on September 23 that the worst was over, and by the first cease-fire effort—on Jordanian terms —that same day. A cease-fire agreement was reached on September 25, although it did not take hold effectively; and on the same day, fifteen of the remaining hostages were rescued from a refugee camp in Jordan.

Further normalization was marked by the announced establishment of a new Jordanian government on September 26, and by Nixon going ahead with a previously planned trip to visit the Sixth Fleet on September 27. This trip was used to mark the successful conclusion of the crisis publicly and to laud the role of the Sixth Fleet in it.

The only loose end, apart from the hostages, remained the open commitments to Israel that had already stirred Rogers. By September 25, it was clear that the hour had now passed and that these arrangements, including U.S. approval of Israeli intervention and a guarantee against Egyptian or Soviet retaliation, were no longer relevant. Consequently, it was decided to revoke the verbal agreements reached only days earlier, and to put Israel on notice that any future Israeli action would have to be renegotiated (Decision 13). Accordingly, Israel was notified that:

> According to the latest available information, the forces which invaded Jordan have withdrawn to Syria. We believe that the steps Israel took have contributed measurably to that withdrawal. We appreciate the prompt and positive Israeli response to our approach. Because circumstances will be different if there is another attack, we consider that all aspects of the exchanges between us with regard to this Syrian invasion of Jordan are no longer applicable, and we understand that Israel agrees. If a new situation arises, there will have to be a fresh exchange.[16]

15. Kissinger, 1979, p. 630.
16. Ibid., p. 631.

On September 27, an Arab summit meeting agreed on an immediate cease-fire on terms that ratified the Jordanian victory over the Palestinian organizations. This cease-fire finally became effective on September 29 with the arrival of Arab League observers in Amman; and at the same time, the remaining hostages were released from the control of the hijackers. Calm returned to Jordan, with King Hussein now clearly in control. There was no longer any perception of threat to the United States, nor any situation requiring U.S. action, and the post-crisis period of the 1970 Jordanian crisis came to an end.

CHAPTER NINE

Decision-Making in the Jordanian Crisis

As CHAPTER FIVE tried to trace the impact of crisis conditions on decision-making in the Lebanese crisis of 1958, this chapter will summarize the evidence of the Jordanian crisis of 1970. Based on the above reconstruction of the three crisis periods, how did coping mechanisms and dimensions of choice change under varying levels of crisis-induced stress?

COPING MECHANISMS

Information Processing

As in 1958, the increased tension level of the pre-crisis period brought an increased demand for accurate and up-to-date intelligence. American officials were severely handicapped in dealing with the hijackers by the lack of firsthand intelligence, and they also sought reliable guidance in deciphering the intentions of Jordan, Syria, and Iraq (the latter two governments not having diplomatic relations with the United States). Sources of intelligence remained, however, essentially what they had been previously, and changes in information processing were slight. More intelligence was presented orally, particularly with CIA Director Richard Helms participating in meetings of the Washington Special Actions Group (WSAG).

WSAG also presumably played a role not filled in non-crisis situations by serving as an information "clearinghouse," comparing the various intelligence estimates and evaluating them for the President. But in fact the interposition of WSAG did not change the number or the identity of intelligence consumers, nor did it prevent Nixon or Kissinger from performing as their own intelligence evaluators. The two senior decision-makers were in any event forced to rely largely on their own intuitive judgments on such crucial questions as Jordanian or Syrian intentions, given the lack of hard data and the inability of WSAG itself to resolve conflicting estimates. (Helms declared, for example, that Hussein would not move against the Palestinians; Kissinger did not hesitate to second-guess this opinion, knowing that it was not based on hard data.)

During the crisis period, the perceived inadequacies of available intelligence became even more acute. According to one well-placed source, there was not even any clandestine reporting from Syria during this period. The course of fighting was covered by photographic and signal surveillance and by information from Jordanian and Israeli intelligence. As the fighting intensified, however, contact with Jordan became problematic; the U.S. Embassy in Amman was cut off, and Jordanian reporting became less helpful. The felt need for better information was demonstrated by the fact that, after September 20, Israeli Ambassador Yitzhak Rabin briefed Kissinger twice daily on the latest Israeli intelligence.

The consensus of participants in retrospect is that information on the military situation was better than the political analysis, though even on a military level there is some indication that adequate intelligence was one of the constraints on a U.S. air strike against the invading Syrian tanks. But on a political level, decision-makers felt a more severe lack of information regarding Syrian intentions, the influence of internal splits in the Syrian government, and the role of the Soviet Union in Syrian decision-making. Given the lack of authoritative sources, it was assumed that the internal Syrian splits, which had been known for some time, were not particularly significant in this case and that the responsibility of the Soviet Union for the Syrian incursion was a sound "working hypothesis" for U.S. policy, even if the Soviets were not the actual instigators. There is disagreement over whether or not this lack of information significantly impaired U.S. decision-making. The problem of information during the crisis is further illustrated by the report that President Nixon purposely avoided external communications, relying only on his own internal sources of information, in order not to be influenced by the "hot words" of television.

As the crisis intensified, therefore, the search for information became much more active but less systematic, with the use of ad hoc and extraordinary channels such as Israeli Ambassador Yitzhak Rabin and even, at one stage, direct radio contact with King Hussein. On the other hand, given the general paucity of information, American decision-makers did not seem to suffer from information overload.

The tendency to see external events as related to each other did increase with the crisis, especially after the Syrian intervention, which was immediately tied to Soviet relations in policy-makers' minds. On the other hand, reliance on past experience, as detailed in Chapters Six and Seven, was clearly high in all periods of the crisis (i.e., in dealing with hijackings no less than in reacting to Soviet "provocations"), and there are no clear grounds for establishing a correlation with tension levels. Also, decision-makers did demonstrate good sensitivity to information that contradicted their expectations during the peak of the crisis, particularly in reacting to the Syrian invasion.

There was more communication with other parties, and especially with Israel, Jordan, and the Soviet Union (though not with Syria, Iraq, or the PLO), as the crisis intensified.

During the post-crisis period, there was still a larger than usual amount of information being processed, but there was a much less frantic search for it, as the military situation had clarified. Information processing was more routine, and there was a pronounced tendency for all participants to interpret the outcome as a confirmation of their own basic beliefs and favored options regarding the crisis.

In summary, the 1970 case study provides confirmation of the following hypotheses on information processing:

3. The greater the crisis, the greater the felt need for information, the more thorough the quest for information, and the more open the receptivity to new information.

4. The greater the crisis, the more information about it tends to be elevated to the top of the organizational [decisional] pyramid quickly and without distortion.

5. The higher the stress in a crisis situation, the greater the tendency to rely upon extraordinary and improvised channels of communication.

6. In crises, the rate of communication by a nation's decision-makers to international actors outside their country will increase.

7. As crisis-induced stress increases, the search for information is likely to become more active, but it may also become more random and less productive.

8. As crisis-induced stress declines, the quest for information becomes more restricted.

9. As crisis-induced stress declines, receptivity becomes permeated by more bias.

10. The more intense the crisis, the greater the tendency of decision-makers to perceive that everything in the external environment is related to everything else.

The following two hypotheses on information processing are rejected for the 1970 Jordanian crisis:

11. The more intense the crisis, the less the sensitivity to, and learning from, negative feedback.

12. The more intense the crisis, the greater the tendency to an overabundance of new information (information overload) and a paucity of usable data on decision-making levels.

Regarding the following hypothesis, the evidence of the Jordanian case provides partial confirmation regarding cognitive rigidity, but contradicts the supposition on closure to new information (the same was the case, it may be recalled, with the Lebanese case):

1. The greater the stress, the greater the conceptual rigidity of an individual, and the more closed to new information the individual becomes.

Finally, the last hypothesis cannot be either confirmed or rejected for the 1970 case, since reliance on past experience was high in all periods of the crisis:

2. The greater the crisis, the greater the propensity for decision-makers to supplement information about the objective state of affairs with information drawn from their own past experience.

Patterns of Consultation

There were no basic changes in the scope or procedures of consultation during the pre-crisis period, but there was greater volume and speed, and more consultation took place in formal meetings. WSAG brought together those who would usually be consulted, or their representatives, on a daily basis. This meant that second-level advisors could still have an input, as when the opposition of State Department Arabists resulted in the suppression of a Presidentially-approved public warning to the hijackers.

Military advisors were also consulted more often. As hopeless as prospects seemed, military opinions were sought in some detail over possible rescue operations for the hijacked hostages.

As in 1958, decision-makers also began to close out outside consultation, focusing more narrowly on advice from within the executive branch. Congressional leaders were briefed once during the pre-crisis period, but this did not constitute "consultation" in any meaningful sense. The Nixon-Kissinger penchant for controlled private diplomacy increased the tendency to exclude external pressures; in 1970, at least, the insulation of the crisis was nearly total.

During the crisis period, there was likewise a flurry of consultation within the executive branch, though some Middle East experts felt (perhaps inevitably) that there was inadequate consultation with regional experts. The defense component of WSAG was more active, though not necessarily more influential, than during the pre-crisis period. Since the policy of the administration was to "mute" the crisis, there was no consultation of either Congressional leaders or other outside agencies. This was especially true of the peak crisis period, when the decision time was shortest; even the little outside consultation that had been carried out in earlier decisions was then absent.

In the post-crisis period, the level of consultation within the administration also decreased. The fact that special crisis-coordinating bodies dropped the Jordanian issue reduced the participation of some middle-level policy-makers. Consultation with external actors, and especially with Israel, remained at a high level, however.

Thus, of the seven hypotheses on patterns of communication, six are confirmed in the 1970 case:

13. The longer the decision time [in a crisis], the greater the consultation with persons outside the core decisional unit.

14. The greater the crisis, the greater the felt need for face-to-face proximity among decision-makers.

15. As crisis-induced stress increases, the scope and frequency of consultation by senior decision-makers also increase. (This was true only within the executive branch and with foreign governments.)

16. As crisis-induced stress increases, decision-makers increasingly use ad hoc forms of consultation.

17. As crisis-induced stress declines, the consultative circle becomes narrower.

19. The more intense the crisis, the less the influence of vested interests and other groups outside the bureaucracy.

One of our initial hypotheses is, however, rejected for the Jordanian crisis:

18. As crisis-induced stress declines, consultation relies heavily on ad hoc settings as high-level consultation reaches its peak.

Decisional Forums

The convening of WSAG at the onset of the pre-crisis period would appear to mark a significant change in decisional forums. But appearances exaggerate the change. WSAG was in essence a coordinating body, pulling together recommendations made by the departments represented in it and preparing final recommendations for the President. It was a decisional body only on secondary issues, and its input into policy depended on acceptance of its views by the President— who did not participate in WSAG meetings. Nixon's relation to WSAG was described in the following terms by Kissinger:

> The President is crucial in a crisis. He must be close enough to the process to give impetus to the ultimate decisions; yet he should not become so involved in the details that he precludes a thorough examination of alternatives. . . . [Nixon] did not pretend that he was exercising his responsibilities as Commander-in-Chief by nervous meddling with tactical details or formative deliberations; he left the shaping of those to the governmental machinery under my supervision.[1]

In choosing to act primarily by approving or rejecting recommendations of WSAG, Nixon was not acting especially differently from the non-crisis procedure of acting upon recommendations of the various departments. This was especially true in 1970, when the WSAG operation was backed up by institutionalized responses to the hijackings that had become routinized by repetition.

During the crisis period, the size of the decisional unit decreased as the perception of threat increased. During the pre-crisis period, WSAG, consisting of Kissinger, Moorer, Johnson, Sisco, Helms, and Packard, had met regularly and made decisions on areas within its competence; otherwise, it made policy recommendations that were taken up with the President by Kissinger. As the crisis intensified, WSAG came to meet almost continuously. But the decision-making focus passed almost completely to the daily meetings of the "principals": Nixon, Kissinger, Rogers, Laird, Helms, and Moorer. In the final stage of the conflict, as remarked, Kissinger conducted the crucial negotiations with Rabin single-handedly, and the final decisions were made by Nixon in consultation with Kissinger, sometimes without even the knowledge of other principals.

In 1970, the structure of the decision-making group also became less formal and fixed as stress increased. Decision-making passed to a higher level on the more important issues, but not through the formal NSC structure. The ultimate decision-making group in the crisis consisted of Nixon and Kissinger; the inputs of other top officials were drawn upon in an increasingly ad hoc fashion. There was clearly less use of regional expertise.

1. Henry Kissinger, *White House Years* (Boston: Little, Brown, 1979), p. 603.

As the crisis intensified, decision time shortened and group conflict seems to have been reduced. At the height of the crisis, the urgent need to save Hussein's regime seems to have removed some obstacles to consensus among the decision-makers. Though some continued to oppose the Israeli option, the perceived need for quick action after the Syrian invasion led others to accept an Israeli move as the least objectionable alternative.

The Joint Chiefs of Staff, initially not supporters of a military option, by and large supported the Israeli option in the end as a means of avoiding the need for U.S. action. With the Jordanian government seemingly about to fall unless there were quick outside support, military advisors saw Israeli action as the only feasible response.

Arabists in the State Department, who had regarded the Israeli option with distaste and suspicion, likewise came to regard Israeli intervention as the lesser of two evils. In this case, it was unwillingness to contemplate Hussein's fall, together with an awareness of the high cost of American intervention in terms of U.S.-Arab relations, that led to acquiescence to the emerging consensus.

As indicated, not all the decision-makers supported the final decision, which was in any event made by a much smaller circle. But by the time it was made, the time pressure and perceived need for decisive action helped to make the Israeli option appear "inevitable" —enough so, at least, that the decision remained surprisingly non-controversial afterwards.

Thus, eight of the thirteen hypotheses on decisional forums were confirmed in the 1970 Jordanian crisis:

20. The longer the crisis, the greater the felt need for effective leadership within decisional units.

24. Crisis decisions tend to be reached by ad hoc decisional units.

25. In high-stress situations, decision groups tend to become smaller.

26. In crises, decision-making becomes increasingly centralized.

29. The more intense the crisis, the greater the tendency of decision-makers to conform to group goals and norms, and the less the dissent within the group.

30. The more intense the crisis, the less the influence of "standard operating procedures."

31. The more intense the crisis, the greater the role in decision-making of officials with a general rather than a "parochial" perspective.

32. The more intense the crisis, the less the influence of vested interests in the bureaucracy ("bureaucratic politics").

The remaining five hypotheses on decisional forums are, however, rejected in the case at hand:

21. The longer the decision time, the greater the conflict within decisional units.

22. The greater the group conflict aroused by a crisis, the greater the consensus once a decision is reached.

23. The longer the amount of time available in which to make a decision, the greater will be the consensus on the final choice.

27. As crisis-induced stress rises, there is a heavy reliance on medium-to-large and institutional forums for decision.

28. As crisis-induced stress declines, there is a maximum reliance on large, institutional forums for decisions.

Alternatives: Search and Evaluation

In any Middle East crisis, as noted previously, it is "routine" to move the Sixth Fleet. In 1970, there was opposition to this movement as being counterproductive in the particular circumstances. Be that as it may, the option of *not* moving the Sixth Fleet was not carefully considered in this case, at least.

In 1970, as in 1958, there was a tendency to focus on military options. Rescue operations for the hijack victims were discussed at length despite the unfavorable prognosis, and the relative merits of Israeli versus U.S. intervention in Jordan were argued. There was little search for other options on the hijacking, because of the routinization of hijacking crises (negotiation through the Red Cross) and Nixon's "hard line" on the issue. Likewise, diplomatic options on Jordan were not pursued. But again as in 1958, there was sober calculation on those options that were considered, even though the issue of U.S. versus Israeli intervention was not resolved.

In the crisis period, it is clear that U.S. policy-makers tended to react instinctively on the larger issues facing them. As one high-level participant noted, the preoccupation in a crisis is with problems of the moment, which tend to close out larger analytical issues; decision-makers worry about hardware, infrastructure, and getting forces into place, and fall back on basic instincts on the larger questions.

In any event, as the perception of threat increased, U.S. policy-makers tended to devote more time to the consideration of military and strategic options than to public and private diplomatic moves. At the height of the crisis, proposals for diplomatic approaches directly to the Soviet Union or through the UN were rejected with little discussion. With the declaration of martial law and the outbreak of war in Jordan, American concern shifted to preventing outside intervention in the fighting. Middle-level options prevailed, as they had during the pre-crisis period: warnings were relayed via a public Presidential speech (September 16), an inspired leak of a Presidential briefing (September 17), and the first Sisco-Vorontsov meeting (September 18). In addition, further military moves were initiated (on the 15th) and announced (on the 17th).

At this stage, however, stronger military action was not considered, as the general appraisal in Washington was that Hussein could handle the Palestinian guerrillas if there were no outside intervention. The focus was on the prevention of such intervention, and there was no felt need to consider further alternatives unless and until Syria and/or Iraq actually intervened. When Syria invaded on September 19–20, the alternatives adopted were (1) to put maximum pressure on the Soviet Union to force Syria to withdraw, and (2) to prepare a credible military option in the event of Hussein's imminent collapse. The first course of action was carried out by a selective alert on September 19, daily Sisco-Vorontsov meetings, increasingly stern diplomatic notes, further military moves on September 21, and a public show of U.S.-Israeli cooperation. In the minds of the decision-makers, this show of determination was designed not only to galvanize the Soviet Union, but also to deter Syria directly and to encourage Hussein to fight; in addition, of course, the military moves could contribute to the actual military option.

The military option followed from the general aim of saving the Jordanian government, which was perceived to be in mortal danger. Most discussion revolved around the various alternatives within this general option. The initial tendency was to favor direct U.S. action, but, as indicated, this had to be put aside because of inadequate capability, as well as considerations of Arab and Soviet reactions and the opposition of U.S. allies. The focus thus shifted to consideration of U.S.-backed Israeli moves, with the debate centered on an air strike only (the preference of Hussein and most Middle East specialists in the U.S. government; a few even favored doing nothing rather than "letting Israel in"), or intervention by both air and ground. Eventually, the Israeli move was approved, by ground as well as by air if necessary, but subject to review at the last moment. This was backed by a U.S. commitment to neutralize Egypt and/or the Soviet Union.

Among the alternatives that were not considered at the peak of the crisis were (1) dealing directly with Syria, (2) diplomatic approaches to the Soviet Union (aside from the stern warnings that were transmitted), and (3) "going public" with the crisis. Direct dealings with Syria—difficult in any event, because of the lack of formal channels—were considered irrelevant, given the decision to hold the Soviet Union responsible for Syrian actions. Nixon instinctively rejected the idea of raising the issue in the Security Council (September 20), or of making a demarche to the Soviets (as Secretary of State Rogers proposed the following day), apparently because he felt the time had come to demonstrate resolve to the other side. "Going public" appealed to none of the policy-makers: dramatizing the conflict might make it more difficult for the other side to retreat, ran the risk of unpredictable responses, and was uncertain of gaining public support in any event.

In the evaluation of the alternatives, military options in particular were discussed intensively and with attention to all the ramifications. Sober judgments of military feasibilities—even painful judgments on American incapacity—were reached with the help of expert advice. The political and diplomatic consequences of various military courses of action were likewise argued and taken into account; the risks of using Israeli intervention to save Hussein were realistically assessed. According to reports, Nixon and Kissinger even "wargamed" the options on September 20, at the height of the crisis.[2] Nevertheless, in at least two respects, time pressure seems to have constrained the evaluation of alternatives: (1) time pressure seems to have led to a willingness to overlook, at least partially, the implications of intelligence, especially in regard to the assessment of Soviet moves and the Soviet role in Damascus; and (2) in the rush to prepare the Israeli option, little attention was paid to operationalizing the American guarantee that stood behind it, and thinking through all the implications of the guarantee given.

The Jordanian crisis seems to illustrate, in sum, the same "tactical rationality" that characterized the Lebanese crisis. There was less predisposition, as the crisis intensified, to reexamine basic assumptions or to search for new options. Attention was focused more on immediate problems and outcomes. There were some serious flaws in performance during the peak stress phase. Nevertheless, serious efforts were made to evaluate options and weigh consequences, and there was no strong tendency to act before relevant information was processed. Operational decisions involved a reasonably rational process in which costs and gains were soberly calculated.

During the post-crisis period, American policy-makers do not seem to have considered any further moves or signals, or any

2. "The Mid East: Search for Stability," *Time,* October 5, 1970.

measures to aid the hostages. They were careful to cancel the American commitments to Israel that might have encouraged Israel to upset what had been achieved, but the very success of the American policy, as they perceived it, seems to have foreclosed either a search for or an evaluation of additional alternatives.

The results confirm, therefore, ten of the thirteen hypotheses on the consideration of alternatives:

33. As stress increases, decision-makers become more concerned with the immediate than the long-run future.

34. The greater the reliance on group problem-solving processes, the greater the consideration of alternatives.

35. During crisis, the search for alternatives occupies a substantial part of decision-making time.

36. The relationship between stress and group performance in the consideration of alternatives is curvilinear (an inverted U)— more careful as stress rises to a moderate level, less careful as stress becomes intense. (In the 1970 case, the consideration of alternatives was only slightly less careful under peak stress.)

37. Despite the rise in stress, choices among alternatives are not, for the most part, made before adequate information is processed; that is, there is not a tendency to premature closure.

38. As time pressure increases, the choice among alternatives does not become less correct.

42. As crisis-induced stress declines, the search for options tends to become less extensive than in all other phases of the crisis period.

43. As crisis-induced stress declines, the evaluation of alternatives reaches its maximum care, more so when time salience is low.

44. The more intense the crisis, the greater the tendency of decision-makers to narrow their span of attention to a few aspects of the decision-making task ("tunnel vision").

45. The more intense the crisis, the more likely that decision-makers will be forced to make a clear choice rather than postponing choices or drifting into policy.

Two additional hypotheses appear to be confirmed *in part* in the Jordanian crisis:

39. Decision-makers do not generally choose among alternatives with an inadequate assessment of their consequences.

41. As crisis-induced stress increases, the evaluation of alternatives becomes less careful. (This was not true for moderate increases in stress, but was true for the period of peak stress.)

The last hypothesis is rejected on the basis of the evidence presented above:

40. As crisis-induced stress increases, the search for options tends to increase.

DIMENSIONS OF CHOICE

Pre-Crisis Period

Four major decisions were made during the first period of the Jordanian crisis:

1. On September 7, President Nixon confirmed a hard-line policy toward the hijackers.

2. On September 9, Nixon ordered a number of preparatory military moves.

3. On September 11, the United States adopted a comprehensive anti-hijacking program.

4. On September 12, Nixon authorized increased aid to Israel.

The hijacking of the airliners was, in one form or another, the *core input* of all four decisions, though the last decision involved anticipated consequences of the hijacking within Jordan.

The *cost* in all four decisions was perceived by decision-makers to be low.

The perceived *importance* of the first decision was clearly Important (3), while Decisions 2 and 4 were only Consequential (2), and Decision 3 seems to have been regarded by decision-makers as Marginal (1).

Two of the decisions (2 and 3) seem to have involved only one issue-area (Military-Security) in terms of *complexity,* while Decision 1 involved both Military-Security and Political-Diplomatic issues, and Decision 4 involved Military-Security and Economic-Developmental.

The *systemic domain* of Decision 1 was Global and Bilateral; Decision 4 was Regional and Bilateral; Decision 2 was primarily Bilateral in terms of expected reverberations; and Decison 3 was Domestic.

The dominant *process* of Decision 1 was Affective, with some Routine elements. Decision 2 was clearly Routine. Decisions 3 and 4 appear to have been primarily Rational, with some affective influence in the former.

In three of the Decisions—2, 3, and 4—the *activity* implied was to act, and it involved physical action. In Decision 1, the thrust was to act verbally but to delay physical action.

In terms of *novelty,* only Decision 3 involved a significant departure from precedent and past choices.

The dominant *coping strategies* in the pre-crisis period were similar to those in the Lebanese crisis. All four decisions involved *operational code* beliefs; all but Decision 2 involved *satisficing* behavior; all but Decision 3 used *historical models;* and all but Decision 4 made significant use of *ideology.* Decision 2 (military preparations) seems to have involved a measure of *incrementalism,* and Decision 1 was characterized by an attempt to *avoid value trade-offs* (in arguing that a tough anti-hijacking stance actually had the best chance of saving hostages' lives).

Crisis Period

There were eight identifiable major decisions in the crisis period:

5. On September 15, Nixon approved further measures of military readiness.

6. On September 17, the President again confirmed demonstrative military movements.

7. Also on September 17, the President speeded up aid to Israel.

8. On September 20, the President approved a higher state of alert for the airborne brigade in West Germany.

9. Later on September 20, the President approved further military movements.

10. Also on September 20, Nixon endorsed an Israeli air strike against Syrian forces in Jordan.

11. On September 21, Nixon approved Israeli ground action against Syrian forces.

12. On September 21, Nixon reportedly also approved an American guarantee of Israel against retaliation by other states (there is some doubt about the inclusion of this decision; see above, pp. 171–173).

The number and variety of *core inputs* increased during the crisis period. Policy-makers were moved by impending or actual conflict in Jordan (Decisions 5 and 6), by anticipation of needed Israeli support (Decision 7), by Syrian intervention (Decision 8), by Jordanian requests (Decisions 9 and 10), and by Israeli pressure (Decisions 11 and 12).

The *cost* of the first five decisions (5–9) remained low, but the last three (10–12) were clearly seen as high in terms of anticipated losses.

As for *importance,* most of the military moves (Decisions 5, 6, and 8) seem to have been regarded by decision-makers as Important (3), though the last such move, in response to the Syrian invasion (Decision 9), was seen as Significant (4). Decision 7, on aid to Israel, was only Consequential (2). The three decisions regarding Israeli intervention (10–12) were clearly Decisive (5).

In terms of *complexity,* all eight decisions involved both the Military-Security and the Political-Diplomatic issue-areas.

The *systemic domain* of decisions in the crisis period also increased. Decisions 5 and 6 involved three expected levels of reverberations (Global, Regional, and Bilateral), while Decision 7 seems to have involved Regional and Bilateral levels only. The remaining five decisions, however, all appear to have involved four levels: Global, Superpower, Regional, and Bilateral.

The dominant decisional *process* associated with crisis-period decisions was Rational in all cases except Decisions 5 and 6 (on military moves), which were Routine.

In every case the *activity* implied was to act, and in the first five decisions the action was physical. The important decisions at the peak of the crisis, however, were either verbal and physical (Decision 10) or entirely verbal (Decisions 11 and 12).

The *novelty* of the decisions also increased, with Decisions 8, 9, 10, 11, and 12 all significantly innovative in contrast to precedents.

In terms of *coping strategies,* again *historical models* and *operational codes* seemed most dominant, with both accompanying every decision except Decision 11 (endorsing Israeli ground action). *Satisficing* behavior seems clearly present in Decision 7 (aid to Israel) and in the three peak crisis decisions (10–12). *Incrementalism* and *ideology* were clear elements in all the military readiness moves (Decisions 5, 6, 8, and 9). The three peak crisis decisions (10–12) also involved the *avoidance of value trade-offs* in one sense or another.

Post-Crisis Period

The *core input* of the single decision in this period—the decision to cancel the understandings with Israel—was basically bureaucratic pressure. The *cost* was perceived by decision-makers as low; the *importance* was perceived as Marginal (1); the *complexity* was moderate, with two issue-areas involved (Military-Security and Political-Diplomatic); and the *systemic domain* was Bilateral only. The *process* was Rational, *activity* was verbal action, and *novelty* was present. The only *coping strategy* was invocation of the *operational code.*

Hypotheses

Of the seventeen hypotheses linking stress levels to decisional choices, thirteen are confirmed by the above evidence:

46. As crisis-induced stress begins to rise, the number and variety of core inputs to decisions increase sharply.

47. As crisis-induced stress declines, the number and variety of core inputs are reduced.

48. When decision-makers operate under stress, they assess their decision as costly.

49. When decision-makers operate under low or declining stress, they perceive their decisions as of small cost.

50. As crisis-induced stress rises, decision-makers tend to perceive their decisions as more and more important.

51. As crisis-induced stress declines, the perceived importance of decisions declines from the levels in all other phases of the crisis period.

52. As crisis-induced stress rises, the complexity of issue-areas involved steadily rises.

56. As crisis-induced stress rises, the selected option tends to be chosen by rational calculus and analysis of the issues, rather than by a process of bargaining and compromise.

57. As crisis-induced stress declines, decision-makers resort mainly to rational procedures to ultimate choice.

58. As crisis-induced stress rises, there is a tendency for decisions to be continuously active.

59. As crisis-induced stress rises, the activity implied by the decisions moves from physical to verbal.

61. As crisis-induced stress rises, there is a steady increase in resort to choices without precedent.

62. As crisis-induced stress declines, unprecedented choices remain at their peak.

The remaining four hypotheses are rejected for the 1970 Jordanian crisis:

53. As crisis-induced stress declines, the number of issue-areas involved in decision-making reaches its maximum.

54. In situations of peak crisis-induced stress, the heretofore steadily-broadening systemic levels of anticipated reverberations from decisions become narrower.

55. As crisis-induced stress declines, systemic domain rises from the peak crisis phase.

60. As crisis-induced stress declines, there is a sharp increase in decisions to delay or not to act.

PART III

THE YOM KIPPUR WAR

CHAPTER TEN

1973: 6 October to 12 October

THE GLOBAL and regional environment of the 1973 crisis differed considerably from that of 1970. Globally, the international system had moved from confrontation to detente. During the intervening years, the American opening to China and a flurry of U.S.-Soviet agreements had established a new structure of international relations. A strategic arms limitation agreement (SALT I) had been concluded, and the United States had withdrawn its troops from Vietnam. It seemed that a new era of superpower cooperation might be dawning. With both parties committed to wide-ranging consultation, U.S.-USSR cooperation even in areas of contention such as the Middle East did not seem impossible.

There was also less concern about Soviet involvement in the Middle East. Nasser's successor, Anwar Sadat, had suppressed pro-Soviet elements within his own government and, in July 1972, had sent home most of the Soviet military "advisors" in Egypt. There was a quiet renewal of U.S.-Egyptian contact, institutionalized in a so-called "back channel" of communications directly between Sadat and the White House. There seemed to be less instability and more unity in the Arab world, symbolized by the closer relationship between Sadat and King Feisal of Saudi Arabia. U.S. Middle Eastern diplomacy therefore tended to focus more directly on the issues of the Arab-Israeli conflict. Increased Arab unity also had other implications: the growing power of OPEC, and increasing concern over both oil prices and the use of oil as a political weapon. U.S. Middle Eastern policy since the 1970 crisis—and in large part as a direct result of that crisis—tilted toward the Kissinger school of thought on the maintenance of Middle Eastern stability. Gradualism rather than

comprehensiveness became the guiding principle of diplomatic
efforts, and a more modest U.S. role was envisioned. American diplomacy focused on the pursuit of "interim" agreements, particularly
regarding the Suez Canal, though even this proved elusive. Between the United States and Israel, a "partnership" of sorts developed, and there was less tendency to exert pressure on Israel through
the manipulation of arms supplies. The prevailing view held that
the status quo could be maintained until Arab states accepted the
American negotiating framework, including recognition of Israel and
a binding peace treaty.

This view assumed, of course, that Arab military options—either
all-out war as in 1967, or a limited war of attrition as in 1969–70—
had been effectively closed. The Egyptian-Syrian attack on the 6th
of October, 1973, challenged these assumptions and posed a severe
challenge to U.S. policy not only in regional terms but ultimately on
the superpower level as well. For the United States, the pre-crisis
period began with the war itself, which was unanticipated in Washington, and lasted until a collapse of cease-fire efforts, combined with
a growing sense of Israeli desperation, created a crisis atmosphere in
the minds of U.S. decision-makers.

DECISIONS AND DECISION-MAKERS

There were five major decisions in the 1973 pre-crisis period:

Decision Number	Date	Content
1	6 October	President Nixon ordered the eastward movement of certain units of the U.S. Sixth Fleet in the Mediterranean.
2	6 October	The President approved the recommendation of the Washington Special Actions Group (WSAG) that the United States promote a cease-fire on the basis of the *status quo ante.* [1]
3	6 October	The President confirmed WSAG's delineation of a "low-profile" U.S. policy on the military resupply of Israel, combined with efforts to dissuade the

1. Henry Kissinger, *Years of Upheaval* (Boston: Little, Brown, 1982), pp. 471–472;
William B. Quandt, *Decade of Decisions: American Policy Toward the Arab-Israeli
Conflict, 1967–1976* (Berkeley: University of California Press, 1977), p. 173; Marvin
Kalb and Bernard Kalb, *Kissinger* (New York: Dell, 1975), p. 522.

		Soviet Union from resupplying its clients.[2]
4	9 October	The President approved a WSAG recommendation that the United States modify its position on resupply, granting Israeli arms requests "in principle," but withholding U.S. military transport.[3]
5	10 October	Kissinger decided to accept "in principle" a Soviet proposal for a cease-fire-in-place.[4]

There were also several moves designed to implement these basic decisions. As part of the effort to achieve a cease-fire, Nixon exchanged letters on October 7 with Soviet leader Leonid Brezhnev, agreeing on mutual restraint in the Middle East crisis. He also agreed to call a meeting of the UN Security Council on October 8, and pushed for adoption of a cease-fire resolution in that forum (without pressing for an immediate vote). As part of the resupply policy, the U.S. government permitted disguised El Al planes to begin carrying supplies to Israel on October 7; and on October 10–12, efforts were made to arrange for civilian charters to carry promised supplies to Israel.

The 1973 decision-makers included many who had been prominent in the 1970 crisis. First and foremost were Nixon and Kissinger, the latter now functioning as Secretary of State as well as Assistant to the President for National Security Affairs. Admiral Thomas Moorer, Chairman of the Joint Chiefs of Staff, and Joseph Sisco, Assistant Secretary of State for Near Eastern and South Asian Affairs, were also participants in both crises. But James Schlesinger was now Secretary of Defense, William Clements was now Deputy Secretary of Defense, and William Colby had recently been appointed Director of the Central Intelligence Agency. Another new figure in a top policy position was Kenneth Rush as Deputy Secretary of State.

As in 1970, the Washington Special Actions Group (WSAG) was the core crisis management group, but again Kissinger was the major link between WSAG and the President. Thus, decisions were usually confirmed in direct consultations between Kissinger and Nixon, and this dyad was most often the actual "decisional unit." In attendance

2. Kalb and Kalb, p. 522; interviews with two senior legislative aides in the U.S. Senate; Kissinger, 1982, p. 478.

3. Kissinger, 1982, pp. 495–496; Quandt, 1977, pp. 176–177; The Insight Team of the London Sunday Times, *The Yom Kippur War* (Garden City, N.Y.: Doubleday, 1974), p. 274; Kalb and Kalb, pp. 528–529; interviews with Department of Defense officials.

4. Kissinger, 1982, p. 498; other sources as in note 3, above.

at most WSAG meetings were Kissinger, Schlesinger, Moorer, Colby, Rush, Sisco, Clements, and Brent Scowcroft, Military Assistant to the President.[5]

PSYCHOLOGICAL ENVIRONMENT

Attitudinal Prism

The basic perceptual universe of Washington decision-makers in 1973 did not differ essentially from that of 1970. The following elements of the 1970 psychological environment, identified in the previous chapter, were particularly relevant in the 1973 crisis:

1. *Global Focus.* The tendency to read local developments primarily as a function of superpower relations was at least as pronounced as in 1970. This was expressed in the absence of area experts or expertise on the upper levels of decision-making.[6] Kissinger's own listing of American interests in the area, as recounted immediately after the 1973 war to Egyptian journalist Mohammed Hassanein Heikal, focused on strategic interests, Soviet relations, and detente, and touched upon local and regional factors only in the last three of seven points.[7]

2. *Redefinition of the American Role in the World.* In the post-Vietnam atmosphere, opposition to extensive American commitments still ran high, and the administration sought to rely more on local allies and client states whose interests ran parallel to those of the United States. As many observers remarked, Israel was in many ways an almost perfect test case for application of this "Nixon Doctrine," especially in light of the 1970 experience.[8]

3. *Emphasis on Credibility.* The Nixon administration believed by this time that it had already successfully demonstrated its resolve to the Soviet Union on several occasions, but the necessity of maintaining this credibility remained a top priority.

5. Quandt, 1977, p. 173.

6. Interviews with L. Dean Brown, U.S. Ambassador to Jordan, and with a senior intelligence official. The senior intelligence official argues, however, that the contribution of key figures such as Kissinger was precisely this global perspective, and that in the 1973 crisis Kissinger did not overdo the global focus, which was necessary for rising above parochial concerns.

7. Quoted in Edward R. F. Sheehan, *The Arabs, Israelis, and Kissinger: A Secret History of American Diplomacy in the Middle East* (New York: Reader's Digest Press, 1976), p. 53.

8. This was particularly remarked by observers hostile to Israel; see, for example, Barry Rubin, "U.S. Policy, January–October, 1973," *Journal of Palestine Studies,* 3 (Winter 1974), 99.

4. *Concern for Stability in the Arab-Israeli Conflict.* As before, policy-makers feared Middle Eastern hostilities as a threat to American interests and to world peace. But in partial contrast to 1970, the United States was generally forthcoming on arms delivery to Israel, based on the *belief that Israeli military superiority was the key to stability.* Also, the creation of Israeli confidence in the United States was considered a necessary part of ongoing diplomatic efforts. The President reportedly felt that Israelis must see the United States as a reliable partner during crisis, and Kissinger felt that "if we refused aid, Israel would have no incentive to heed our views in the postwar diplomacy."[9]

However, the victory of this school of thought was by no means complete. Nixon himself tempered his support of Israel when it conflicted with his aim of improving relations with Arab states: his pursuit of the opening to Egypt was particularly important. Concern over Arab control of oil essential to the West was also a factor (see below).[10] There was, moreover, continuing anti-Israel feeling in the bureaucracy. Many area experts would have welcomed the Israeli loss of part or all of the occupied territories. There was resentment over "undue Jewish influence" in the executive and legislative branches, Israeli access to officials and information, the constant stream of Israeli officials through Washington, and the "co-option" of U.S. intelligence.[11] Israeli demands for arms resupply during the 1973 crisis were seen by top military advisors as "extravagant."[12] As to the influence of countervailing domestic pressures on the administration, and especially the threat of Israeli and Jewish spokesmen to "go public" during the 1973 crisis, this was not a weighty threat; by all accounts, Kissinger and other officials knew that maximum pressure was already being exerted.[13]

5. *Image of Arab Irrationality.* Despite improvement in relations with Arab states, there was still considerable apprehension of unpredictability and extremism in Arab behavior. Kissinger himself admitted that "I am afraid of Arab romanticism," fearing that Arabs

9. Quandt, 1977, p. 172; Kissinger, 1982, p. 478.

10. Richard Nixon, *RN: The Memoirs of Richard Nixon* (New York: Grosset and Dunlap, 1978), pp. 921–922.

11. Interviews with Admiral Thomas Moorer, Chairman, Joint Chiefs of Staff; Major General Gordon Summer, Jr., Director of Near Eastern and South Asian Affairs, Department of Defense; and with a senior State Department official.

12. Interview with Moorer.

13. Interviews with Simcha Dinitz, Israeli Ambassador to the United States; I. L. Kenen, Director, America-Israel Public Affairs Committee; and with a senior State Department official.

might expect too much out of his planned peace initiative in the Middle East.[14] Middle East experts in the bureaucracy, remembering the events of 1967, feared violent anti-American outbursts in the Arab world if war should break out. Connected to this perception was the judgment that Arabs were incapable of the sustained and systematic effort necessary for modern war. A 1971 CIA handbook reported that the Arab fighting man "lacks the necessary physical and cultural qualities for performing effective military services." The CIA's postmortem on the intelligence failure in the 1973 war points out that "there was ... a fairly widespread notion based largely (though perhaps not entirely) on past performances that many Arabs, as Arabs, simply weren't up to the demands of modern warfare and that they lacked understanding, motivation, and probably in some cases courage as well."[15]

6. *Belief in Private Diplomacy.* The Nixon administration's tendency to solitary, centralized decision-making, and its distrust of the foreign policy bureaucracy, were even more pronounced in 1973. Nixon and Kissinger consulted even less with subordinates and outsiders than they had previously; the Chairman of the Senate Foreign Relations Committee, for example, never saw the President (in part because the Vietnam War had so completely disrupted executive-legislative relations).[16] Kissinger's domination of the foreign policy-making machinery also limited the play of differing bureaucratic interests and perspectives. William Quandt, a participant in the 1973 decision-making process, observed that "bureaucratic politics was barely in evidence, so tight was Kissinger's control over the policy-making machinery."[17]

7. *Centrality of Detente.* Since policy-makers tended to adopt a global focus, the state of U.S.-Soviet relations was the key to much else. In 1970, the Soviets were seen as ruthless opportunists who were challenging the United States on many fronts. There was no basic change in this view three years later, but the prevalent percep-

14. Sheehan, p. 55.

15. Quoted in the leaked report of the Pike Committee: "The CIA Report the President Doesn't Want You to Read" (excerpts from a report of the House Select Committee on Intelligence), *Village Voice*, February 16, 1976, p. 30.

16. Interview with Senator William Fulbright, Chairman, Committee on Foreign Relations.

17. Quandt, 1977, p. 204. Quandt also concluded that "for all practical purposes, he [Kissinger] and Nixon made policy during the next several weeks [after October 6], with occasional inputs from Defense Secretary Schlesinger" (p. 171). There was one countervailing result from Kissinger's assumption of the role of Secretary of State: some State Department experts were drawn more directly into the policy-making process (interview with Helmut Sonnenfeldt, National Security Council staff). But this was still in the context of an increasingly centralized decision-making process.

tion was that the Soviet offensive had been checked, and that as a result the Soviets had been forced to moderate their thrust and cooperate with the United States on matters of mutual interest. "Detente" was seen as a major achievement of the administration, and as a large factor in its overwhelming 1972 electoral victory. In place of the apprehension that had characterized relations with the Soviets previously, there was now a mild euphoria; the Soviets seemed to be on the run around the world, or at least were behaving themselves. It was assumed that in the Middle East they would be helpful or at least quiet.[18] This did not necessarily extend to believing that the Soviet Union would sacrifice its relations with its Arab clients for the sake of detente, or even to help head off a war. As some participants later stressed, it was still assumed that the Soviets would act in their own interests and would exploit any situation that arose.[19] And as Kissinger repeatedly warned: if it came to a test, the United States would never allow a victory to be achieved by "Soviet arms" in the Middle East.[20] But nevertheless, in late 1973, U.S. decision-makers did not see themselves being tested any longer by the Soviet Union; rather, they credited themselves with having achieved a general improvement in superpower relations that needed to be nurtured and expanded. They expected consultation and some cooperation from the Soviet Union on problems in the Middle East as well as elsewhere.

8. *Cognizance of the Oil Weapon.* By 1973, official Washington had begun to recognize the growing importance of oil not only economically, but as a potential political weapon as well. Already in January 1973, an NSC memo had asked bluntly: "Can we still import in the 1980's if there is no resolution of the Arab-Israel dispute by then?"[21] In the background was the growing assertiveness of OPEC on matters of oil price and supply, and increasing hints from Arab members of OPEC about the possible use of oil as a weapon on Arab-Israeli issues. But while these issues were recognized and discussed, the dangers were not yet considered critical. In fact, evidence indicates that on matters of oil pricing, U.S. policy-makers even encouraged the OPEC price hikes that took place in the 1971–1973 period, believing that the United States would gain econom-

18. Interview with an NSC staff aide.
19. Interviews with William Hyland, Bureau of Intelligence and Research, Department of State, and with Samuel Hoskinson, National Intelligence Officer for the 1973 War; Kissinger, 1982, pp. 469–470.
20. See, for example, the conversation with Heikal cited in Sheehan, pp. 53–55; this is also stressed repeatedly by Kissinger, 1982 (for example, pp. 468, 494, 519–520).
21. Insight Team, pp. 251–253.

ically from (moderately) higher oil prices in the final balance, and that conciliation of oil-producing states was the best and most practical course in any event.[22]

The control of oil supply as a means of Arab political pressure was recognized more clearly as a threat, even if the likelihood of such an event was still rated as minimal. Again, signals warning about such moves had been available from early in 1973. Sheikh Ahmed Zaki Yamani, Saudi Minister of Petroleum, indicated during an April 1973 visit to the U.S. that Saudi Arabia would not carry out a needed increase in oil production simply out of good will. This followed warnings from King Feisal himself, and the major oil-producing companies had already been galvanized into activity designed to influence U.S. policy in the direction preferred by the Saudis.[23] These warnings were not taken seriously, for several reasons. In the first place, the lessons of 1956 and 1967 seemed to indicate that an oil embargo would not work. The Arab states could not cooperate with each other, the Saudis did not appear to be as committed as they would have to be for a successful embargo, and Arab oil could theoretically still be replaced.[24] The global focus of Kissinger and others at the top also tended to result in the de-emphasis of local inputs. Finally, raw intelligence that stressed Saudi intentions to use oil as a weapon—mostly from CIA and National Security Agency (NSA) sources—were not reflected in final intelligence reports, which tended to rely on embassy reporting, which in turn stressed continuity and cooperativeness in Saudi policy.[25] Thus, despite the general apprehension of anti-U.S. actions in the Arab world should a Middle Eastern war erupt, the danger of an effective oil embargo against the United States or the West was not high on the list of concerns of most policy-makers.

9. *Growing Divergence from Allies on the Middle East.* Though

22. See the article by V. H. Oppenheim, "Why Oil Prices Go Up (1)—The Past: We Pushed Them," *Foreign Policy,* 25 (Winter 1976–1977), 24–57. Oppenheim argues that this approach continued during the 1973 war, with a mild reaction to OPEC price hikes, praise of OPEC "moderation," and rejection of European "get-tough" suggestions. See also Peter R. Odell, *Oil and World Power,* 5th edition (New York: Penguin, 1979), pp. 215 ff.

23. Interview with James Akins, U.S. Ambassador to Saudi Arabia; Sheehan, pp. 66–68; Steven Spiegel, *The War for Washington: The Other Arab-Israeli Conflict* (forthcoming). The Chairman of ARAMCO relayed a message from Faisal in May; during the summer, Mobil ran ads in the *New York Times,* and the President of Socal sent a letter to stockholders.

24. Interview with Akins.

25. Seymour Hersh, "Senate Report Criticizes U.S. Intelligence on Oil Embargo," *New York Times,* December 21, 1977. Kissinger's own account, extremely detailed and with the advantage of hindsight, makes almost no reference to oil during this period of the crisis.

the United States and its West European allies had often pursued separate courses in the Middle East, the growing importance of oil (upon which Europe was more dependent) and the American tendency to see the Middle East in global terms (as a function of detente) made these differences more critical by 1973. The divergent interests of the United States and other NATO countries, and the lack of a common Middle East policy, were both glaringly revealed by the Yom Kippur War, which converted the "Year of Europe" into a period of confrontation.[26]

As a result of these perceptions, the prevailing conception among top U.S. policy-makers was that the risk of hostilities in the Middle East was low. It was assumed that, despite their presumed "irrationality," Arab states would not dare to attack Israel, even in a "limited war" scenario. Arab leadership was considered incapable of unified or decisive action, and Sadat in particular was dismissed as a buffoon. The Arab states, blocked militarily and absorbed in domestic problems, were thought to be seeking diplomatic recourses, giving Kissinger ample time to pursue new negotiating possibilities. Oil was seen as a problem only with regard to eventual world energy shortages; it was not an immediate political problem, was not linked directly to the Arab-Israeli conflict, and the threat of an oil embargo was not taken seriously. Given Soviet interests in detente, it was not considered likely that the Soviet Union would support rash Arab actions, and U.S.-Soviet cooperation seemed a viable basis for Middle Eastern diplomacy.[27]

This conception was backed by a number of recent experiences:

1. The humiliating Arab defeat in 1967 and the lack of military success in the 1969–1970 war of attrition.

26. See especially Linda Miller, *The Limits of Alliance: America, Europe, and the Middle East,* Jerusalem Papers on Peace Problems, No. 10 (Jerusalem: Hebrew University, 1974), pp. 5–12.

27. Kissinger, 1982, pp. 459–467; interviews with Akins; General George Brown, Chief of Staff, U.S. Air Force; and Seymour Weiss, Director of Politico-Military Affairs, Department of State (DOS); Quandt, 1977, pp. 170–171; Matti Golan, *The Secret Conversations of Henry Kissinger: Step-by-Step Diplomacy in the Middle East* (New York: Bantam, 1976), p. 144–145; Insight Team, pp. 128–129; Sheehan, pp. 66–80. G. Matthew Bonham, Michael J. Shapiro, and Thomas L. Trumble, "The October War: Changes in Cognitive Orientation Toward the Middle East Conflict," *International Studies Quarterly,* 23 (March 1979), 21–28, carried out a simulation based on pre-war interviews with twelve officials and predicted much the same attitudes, including the unlikelihood of Arab surprise attack, with the interesting difference that NSC officials and DOS Middle East specialists predicted that the Soviets would help bring the fighting to an end in the event of war, while intelligence officers in DOS and Department of Defense (DOD) officials had more negative appraisals of Soviet involvement —representing both views that prevailed (at different times) during the war.

2. The humiliation of Syria in 1970, which led to replacement of a "rash" Syrian government with a more cautious leadership.

3. The refusal of the USSR to supply certain types of advanced weaponry to Egypt, which seemed to show a high Soviet regard for detente and a strong distaste for military adventures in the Middle East, in addition to seriously limiting Arab military capability.[28]

4. Egyptian expulsion of Soviet military advisors in 1972.

5. A "war scare" in May 1973, in which the CIA accepted the Israeli appraisal that the Egyptians were bluffing and was vindicated over other analysts who took the alarm more seriously.[29]

6. The very stress put on oil as a weapon by some Arab spokesmen, though not taken seriously by the United States, seemed to diminish yet further the military threat, since it seemed to indicate an Arab focus on diplomatic, political, and economic methods of achieving goals.

7. Similarly, even the direct warnings—such as Feisal's and a blunt statement made by Brezhnev at the San Clemente summit in June 1973—were seen as efforts to increase U.S. pressure on Israel, and thus as also indicating a renewed focus on diplomacy rather than a serious threat of war.

The appraisal of Arab threats that prevailed in Washington has been admirably summarized by Kissinger himself in a reported conversation with Golda Meir after the war:

Do you remember what we all thought before the war?—that we never had it better, and therefore there was no hurry? We and you were both convinced that the Arabs had no military option which required serious diplomatic action. Instead of doing something we joked about the shoes the Egyptians left behind in 1967.

Do you remember when I reported to you on my meeting with Hafez Ismail in Washington? What did I do in those conversations? I talked with him about the weather and every subject in the world just so we wouldn't get to the subject the minister thought most important. I played with him. I toyed with him. My aim was to gain time and to postpone the serious stage for another month, another year. . . .

You know what? I remember now that Ismail told me several times that the present situation could not continue. He asked me whether the United States did not understand that if there weren't some agreement then there would be war. He expressed surprise that the United States didn't do something about it. . . .

There wasn't even a slight smile on my face but in my heart I

28. See the discussion of this point in Harvey Sicherman, *The Yom Kippur War: End of Illusion?* (The Foreign Policy Papers, Vol. 1, No. 4; Beverly Hills and London: Sage Publications, 1976).

29. Interviews with an NSC staff aide and with a senior intelligence official; Kissinger, 1982, p. 461.

laughed and laughed. A war? Egypt? I regarded it as empty talk, a boast empty of content. He invited me to come visit Egypt. Maybe because he read my thoughts and was hoping that in a meeting with Sadat I would understand the situation as it really was. But I did not dream of a trip to Cairo. Who is Sadat? We all thought that he was a fool, a clown. A buffoon who goes on stage every other day to declare a war. We were convinced that he was a passing episode. That his days were few.[30]

These perceptions prevailed up to the morning of the war itself. Only days before the Egyptian-Syrian attack, Kissinger held a meeting with Arab foreign ministers at the United Nations in New York, emerging with the strong feeling that Arab states were primarily interested in pursuing diplomatic moves and that he had several months in which to work.[31] More importantly, American intelligence consistently minimized the implications of Egyptian and Syrian military preparations, of which they had ample evidence. Consider the following excerpts from intelligence reports of October 3 and October 6, which were later released by the Pike Committee:

Syria-Egypt. The movement of Syrian troops and Egyptian military readiness are considered to be coincidental and not designed to lead to major hostilities. *DIA Intelligence Summary,* October 3, 1973.

Egypt. The exercise and alert activities underway in Egypt may be on a somewhat larger scale and more realistic than previous exercises, but they do not appear to be preparing for a military offensive against Israel. *Central Intelligence Bulletin,* October 5, 1973.

Egypt. The current, large-scale mobilization exercise may be an effort to soothe internal problems as much as to improve military capabilities. Mobilization of some personnel, increased readiness of isolated units, and greater communication security are all assessed as parts of the exercise routine. . . . There are still no military or political indicators of Egyptian intentions or preparations to resume hostilities with Israel. *DIA Intelligence Summary,* October 6, 1973.

Israel-Egypt-Syria. Both the Israelis and the Arabs are becoming increasingly concerned about the military activities of the other, although neither side appears to be bent on initiating hostilities. . . . For Egypt a military initiative makes little sense at this critical juncture. . . . Another round of hostilities would almost certainly destroy Sadat's painstaking efforts to invigorate the economy and would run counter to his current efforts to build a united Arab political front, particularly among the less militant, oil-rich states.

30. Quoted in Golan, pp. 144–145. Kissinger's own account of the meeting (1982, pp. 215–216) is more circumspect but not essentially contradictory.
31. Kissinger, 1982, pp. 460, 464.

For the Syrian president, a military adventure now would be suicidal. *Central Intelligence Bulletin,* October 6, 1973.

The Watch Committee met in special session at 0900 on October 6, 1973, to consider the outbreak of Israeli-Arab hostilities. . . . We can find no hard evidence of a major, coordinated Egyptian/Syrian offensive across the Canal and in the Golan Heights area. Rather, the weight of evidence indicates an action-reaction situation where a series of responses by each side to perceived threats created an increasingly dangerous potential for confrontation. The current hostilities are apparently a result of that situation. . . . It is possible that the Egyptians or Syrians, particularly the latter, may have been preparing a raid or other small-scale action. *Special Report of the Watch Committee,* October 6, 1970.[32]

In light of the prevailing conception, particular signals were also misread consistently. For example, the significance of the deployment of Soviet SCUD missiles in Egypt, as a deterrent to deep strikes by the Israeli Air Force in case of hostilities, was missed completely.[33] And when the Soviet Union evacuated its dependents from Cairo and Damascus on October 4, the action was seen as a sign of political strain between the Soviet Union and its clients rather than as an indication of impending hostilities.[34]

There were also some extenuating circumstances behind the intelligence failure. A PLO attack on Russian Jewish emigrants in Austria, which fortuitously took place on September 28, diverted attention from the Middle East itself and created a fear of Israeli reprisal action that served as a ready explanation for Arab military preparations.[35] In addition, the views of the U.S. intelligence community were reinforced by the strong judgment of Israeli intelligence—which would certainly be sensitive to any real danger—that Arab military action was unlikely and that military preparations were a bluff.[36]

It has been argued that the preconceptions of U.S. intelligence analysts were not the major source of intelligence failure. Instead, it

32. U.S. House of Representatives, Select Committee on Intelligence, *Hearings Before the Select Committee on Intelligence,* September 11, 12, 18, 25, 30, October 7, 30, 31, 1975 (Washington, D.C.: U.S. Government Printing Office, 1975), pp. 680–681.

33. Interview with a senior intelligence official.

34. Interview with an NSC staff aide; Kissinger, 1982, p. 465.

35. Kissinger, 1982, pp. 463–464.

36. The reliance on Israeli intelligence was emphasized by Richard Nixon in his interview with David Frost, *New York Times,* May 13, 1977; see also Kissinger, 1982, pp. 459–467; Kalb and Kalb, p. 514; interviews with Moorer and with Ray Cline, Director of Intelligence and Research, Department of State; interviews with an NSC staff aide and senior intelligence officials. Some observers pointed out that the lack of U.S. intelligence sources in Egypt and Syria tended to increase reliance on Israeli intelligence.

is suggested, the structure of information processing was at fault: decision-makers at the top were either not asking the right questions or were not listening to the answers. It is pointed out that the State Department had in fact predicted a Middle East war already in May, though, to be sure, the prediction had not specified a date for the actual eruption of hostilities.[37]

It seems clear overall, however, that U.S. intelligence estimates in 1973 were in fact shaped by the "conception" outlined above, whether this happened in the analysts' own minds, or by way of the distortion of the intelligence system, or both. In fact, both of these things seem to have happened. In any event, the official postmortem of the intelligence failure concluded that "certain substantive preconceptions . . . turned the analysts' attention . . . toward political indications that the Arabs were bent on finding non-violent means to achieve their objectives and away from indications (mainly military) to the contrary."[38]

As a result of this conception, the initial reaction to the war was that Israel must have initiated it. This mirrored the traditional preoccupation with Israeli preemption, which seemed the only logical scenario for the initiation of a Middle Eastern war (and which was made more plausible by apprehension of the Israeli reaction to the PLO attack in Austria).[39] The first American intelligence reports, and the first WSAG meeting at 9:00 A.M. on October 6, concluded that Israel must have struck first.[40] Kissinger also believed this at first; his initial phone conversations with Israelis indicated as much, as did a rather unusual cable to King Feisal stating his certainty that Israel had started the attack.[41]

37. Interviews with Cline and with a senior State Department official; see also Cline's testimony before the Pike Committee (*Hearings Before the Select Committee on Intelligence*, op. cit., pp. 656–657) and Cline, "Policy without Intelligence," *Foreign Policy*, 17 (Winter 1974–1975), 121–135. Kissinger (1982, pp. 462, 464) emphasizes the shortcomings of the State Department estimates.

38. Pike Committee, *Hearings*, p. 639.

39. According to some reports circulating in Washington, the United States had an informal agreement with Israel during the 1971–1973 period that provided Israel with heavy armament in return for a commitment not to initiate hostilities (interview with a legislative staff aide). Bonham et al., in drawing an aggregate cognitive map of four Middle East country directors in the State Department based on 1972 interviews, show a strong and consistent belief that Israel would strike first in the simulated conditions of the 1973 war—corresponding closely to the beliefs actually held by the bureaucracy in the first few hours of the war (G. Matthew Bonham, Michael J. Shapiro, and George J. Nozicka, "A Cognitive Process Model of Foreign Policy Decision-Making," *Simulation and Games*, 7 (June 1976), 145–146.

40. Interview with a senior intelligence official; Quandt, 1977, pp. 170–171; Kissinger, 1982, pp. 450–458.

41. Insight Team, pp. 128–129. Kissinger (1982, p. 458) says, however, that by 9:20 A.M., he had "long since" resolved any doubt that Egypt and Syria were attacking.

When it became unmistakably clear that Egypt and Syria had struck first, decision-makers made a minimal cognitive adjustment. They recognized that the Arabs had indeed initiated the war, but concluded that doing so was a grievous error: Egypt and Syria would quickly be smashed. Policy-makers expected a short war, a replay of 1967.[42] They were again reinforced in this by Israeli perceptions: Israeli representatives conveyed no sense of urgency, having been ordered to reassure the United States that they would defeat the Arab forces within a very few days. Arms resupply was requested, but on a very small scale and with no stress on immediate transport.[43] In addition, a clumsy Soviet effort to obtain a quick cease-fire showed that Moscow also expected and feared an Arab military debacle, thus further confirming the likelihood of an impending Israeli military triumph.[44]

Perceptions of Soviet policy in the Middle East, and its relationship to detente, also changed slowly under the impact of the war. The Kremlin's disagreement with Sadat over the advisability of an immediate cease-fire, and its procrastination in negotiations with the United States, created some initial confusion over the Soviet role. But it quickly became apparent from intelligence data that the Russians had known in advance of the attack (as a new look at the October 4 evacuation of Soviet dependents also indicated).[45] This raised the question of Soviet complicity in the attack, and the implications of that complicity for detente. Again, decision-makers made a minimal adjustment in their beliefs. Some observers charge that there was a tangible anxiety in the State Department and CIA, inspired from above, to show minimal Soviet complicity in order to save detente.[46] Be that as it may, the dominant tendency was to accept the evidence that Soviet leaders had known of the impending attack, but to conclude that they had neither approved nor inspired it. In this view, the Soviets had been placed in a dilemma: they wanted to maintain their credibility with their clients, but also to avoid another Arab military fiasco and a direct confrontation with the United States. Thus, they had not informed the United States, and had given some support to the attack—but they had not provided all the support requested by their Arab clients, and they were not (as observers sensed early in the

42. Interviews with Cline, Weiss, NSC staff aides, and a senior intelligence official; Kissinger, 1982, pp. 455, 471–472.

43. Interview with Cline; Moshe Dayan, *Story of My Life* (New York: William Morrow, 1976), p. 511.

44. Insight Team, p. 269; Kissinger, 1982, pp. 497–498.

45. Interviews with Hyland; General George Keegan, Chief of Intelligence, U.S. Air Force; and a senior intelligence official; Kissinger, 1982, pp. 469–470.

46. Interviews with Keegan and with a second senior intelligence official.

war) wholeheartedly behind what they viewed as a risky adventure at best. In evidence, one could cite their hasty support of a cease-fire effort and even the evacuation of their dependents, which could have been intended to demonstrate their dissociation from the Egyptian and Syrian actions. One could not expect the Soviets to do more than this, it was argued; informing the United States would have totally undercut their own clients. Nevertheless, on the whole, Soviet actions did show concern for the survival of detente.[47]

It was therefore possible to recognize Soviet knowledge of and support for the Arab attack, but to see it within the bounds of detente. Decision-makers were annoyed at Soviet behavior but not totally alienated. According to a senior intelligence official, Soviet behavior until October 23 was as expected; in any event, Kissinger himself had no specific complaints about Soviet behavior through the morning of October 9.[48] Like other policy-makers, Kissinger recognized very quickly that the Soviets had known of Arab intentions, but he considered their behavior predictable in the circumstances of a situation that had a certain momentum of its own. This basic perception was not changed by subsequent events, as Kissinger himself testified a year later:

> It gives the Soviets too much credit to believe that they can unleash a Middle East crisis by themselves. . . . I do not believe they wanted a war in 1973. What I believe happened was that in an ongoing relationship with Arab countries, they were not prepared to give up that relationship, and so everybody last year slid into a situation that was unforeseen and not sufficiently controlled.[49]

Nixon's view of Soviet complicity was similar, but with more anti-Soviet nuances. In his memoirs, Nixon refers to the Soviet role as "an even more disturbing question mark" than the war itself, and as illustrative of the limits of detente. He further speculates that

> the Soviets may have gone even further and directly urged the Arabs to attack, lured by the tantalizing prospect that they might actually win a quick victory over the Israelis if they could combine surprise with their vastly superior numbers. The Soviets might also have assumed that the domestic crisis in the United States would

47. Interviews with Sonnenfeldt and with a senior State Department official; Quandt, *Soviet Policy in the October 1973 War* (Santa Monica, Calif.: Rand Corporation, 1976), pp. v–viii, 7–12; Kissinger, 1982, pp. 469–470.

48. Kissinger, 1982, p. 494; interviews with Cline and with a senior intelligence official; Quandt, 1976, p. 16.

49. U.S. Senate, Committee on Foreign Relations, *Hearings on United States Relations with Communist Countries* (Washington, D.C.: U.S. Government Printing Office, 1974), p. 248. Kissinger's testimony was on September 19, 1974. See also Kalb and Kalb, pp. 523–524.

deflect or deter us from aiding Israel as much or as fast as we had in the past.[50]

Kissinger did not seem to fear at this stage that the Soviets were either testing the United States or exploiting domestic difficulties, but he did fear the immediate consequences of Soviet-supported Arab adventurism. The anticipated Israeli victory would, in the prevailing view, cause widespread anti-American moves in the Arab world, close the carefully cultivated U.S. opening to Egypt, and— should it reach major dimensions—tend to draw the Soviets into a salvage operation on behalf of Egypt and Syria, in which case the United States could not remain neutral. The war also seemed to endanger any chances of promoting peaceful negotiations in the Arab-Israeli conflict within the foreseeable future. As Kissinger later told Sadat:

> I had been planning to move toward a settlement perhaps by late in 1974. I did not think the time would be ripe until then. So when I first heard the news, I thought: "The Arabs are going to get another bloody nose. And that will end the chances of getting anywhere in the life of this Administration." I saw my last chance fade of pulling off a settlement.[51]

The outbreak of war thus did not bring about changes in basic perceptions, but only some adjustments to new events. By October 9 (the fourth day of the war), however, some basic perceptions began to change. The first major change was *a perception of diminished Israeli military superiority.* It was obvious that there was to be no quick Israeli victory, and that Arab defeat was not imminent. Thus, there was even less urgency to the immediate situation than had appeared on the first day of the war. The failure of the first Israeli counterattack on Monday, October 8, and the surprise over the large amount of military equipment employed by the Arabs and their demonstrated capability to use it, were both apparent by this time. Decision-makers did not yet see that there was any danger to Israel; the Israelis would as usual win the war, but this time it would take longer and be somewhat more costly.[52] Israeli requests by this time shifted from eventual to immediate resupply, but a corresponding

50. Nixon, pp. 921, 941.
51. Insight Team, p. 253. See also Sheehan, p. 33; and Quandt, 1977, pp. 171–172. Kissinger (1982, p. 468) describes his feelings on the first day of the war: "If Israel won overwhelmingly—as we first expected—we had to avoid becoming the focal point of all Arab resentments."
52. Interview with General George Brown; Kalb and Kalb, p. 528; Kissinger, 1982, pp. 491–494.

sense of urgency developed only gradually among American policy-makers. Some Air Force planners in the Pentagon began early in the week to make preliminary preparations for a possible airlift of supplies to Israel; and by Wednesday, October 10, there were clear perceptions among Congressional leaders that Israel had a real and urgent military need. But the full extent of Israeli needs was appreciated and acted upon by decision-makers in the executive branch only at the end of the week.[53]

Another modification in attitudes during the first week of the war was *the perception of an active Soviet challenge.* The Soviet failure to warn the United States before the war might be excused, but actions taken during the war itself forced a revision of detente-centered attitudes. Of some importance was the October 9 letter from Brezhnev to Algerian President Boumedienne, in which the Soviet leader urged Arab states to lend full support to the Egyptian and Syrian effort. The letter may in fact have been intended to excuse the Soviets themselves from not doing more to aid their Arab clients, and in any event the Soviets had apparently not intended to release the text of the message. But the reaction in Washington was sharp.[54] In the background was a series of signals on the extent of actual Soviet support, including a sealift that had obviously been prepared prior to the war, and signs of military preparations and alerts within the Soviet Union. But most important was the massive Soviet airlift to Cairo and Damascus that began on October 10, and the report the next day that three Soviet airborne divisions had been put on alert.[55] Even then, the shift in American attitudes was not sudden or total: on October 11–12, the United States and the Soviet Union were still cooperating in a cease-fire effort; and as late as his press conference on Friday, October 12, Kissinger was still publicly defending Soviet behavior as "less provocative, less incendiary, and less geared to military threats" than it had been during the 1967 war.[56]

But the most basic attitudinal change after October 8 was *the perception of a new basis for Arab-Israeli diplomacy.* Washington had initially feared a new Arab humiliation that would set back

---

53. Interviews with Keegan and with a legislative aide; see also Golda Meir, *My Life* (London: Weidenfeld and Nicolson, 1975), p. 430; Kissinger, 1982, pp. 512–513.

54. Quandt, 1976, pp. 16–17; Kissinger, 1982, p. 494.

55. Kalb and Kalb, pp. 529–532; Kissinger, 1982, pp. 497, 504.

56. *Department of State Bulletin (DSB)*, October 29, 1973. On the shift in attitudes toward the Soviet Union generally, see also Quandt, 1977, pp. 174–184; and Nadav Safran, *Israel: the Embattled Ally* (Cambridge: Harvard University Press, 1978), p. 480. Also, interviews with General George Brown, Dinitz, Hoskinson, Hyland, Sonnenfeldt, Colby, Moorer, and Edward Luttwak (Consultant, Department of Defense).

diplomatic efforts, but it now appeared that there was a new military balance that favored diplomacy. As one close observer of Kissinger's thinking summarized:

> On October 8 and 9, however, Kissinger's views began to change. After initial success on the Golan Heights, the Syrians were beginning to falter, but the Egyptians had crossed the Suez Canal, destroyed the Bar-Lev line, and now were entrenched several miles deep inside the Sinai Desert. The Israelis had lost numerous tanks and aircraft, along with the legend of their invincibility; Kissinger was amongst the first to sense that the strategic balance was shifting away from them. He had no mind to restore it straightaway, because he recognized instinctively that the new balance tendered him an exquisite chance to use the war as an extension of diplomacy. If he allowed neither side to win decisively, then he might manipulate the result to launch negotiations, and—ultimately—to compose the Arab-Israel quarrel. All of Kissinger's ensuing moves must be understood in this perspective.[57]

This new orientation was reinforced by the tendency to regard the Arabs with renewed respect, given their unexpected military success and the loss of unquestioned Israeli military superiority. There was apparently some tendency to regard Israel as a declining power, to project future wars as being even less favorable to Israel, and accordingly to view the Arabs favorably as the ascending force. Tied to this was the idea that regaining their self-respect on the battlefield would enable Arab states to be more forthcoming in diplomatic negotiations—an attitude which made pro-Arab actions seem almost pro-Israeli.[58] In addition, as military appreciations changed, Kissinger and his advisors grasped the politcal aims of the Egyptian-Syrian "limited war" strategy; this was not a rash military move to reconquer territory, but was designed as a shock to get diplomacy moving. As Kissinger said in his October 12 press conference:

> If the Arab objective was, as is sometimes stated, to emphasize the fact . . . that permanent stability cannot be assumed in the Middle East and that there is an urgency in achieving a negotiated settlement or that it is important to achieve a negotiated settlement, then it would be our judgment that that point has been made.[59]

57. Sheehan, p. 32.

58. Gil Carl AlRoy, *The Kissinger Experience: American Policy in the Middle East* (New York: Horizon, 1975), pp. 71, 86; interview with a senior intelligence official. AlRoy (p. 95) extends this thesis to argue that Kissinger deliberately sought to weaken Israel as part of his overall strategy for creating military stalemate as a basis for diplomacy; the weight of evidence would indicate, however, that Kissinger simply saw no serious threat to Israel until the end of the first week of the war. See the discussion of the airlift controversy below, pp. 234–237, and Kissinger, 1982, pp. 512–513.

59. *DSB*, October 29, 1973; on the understanding of Sadat's strategy, see Kissinger, 1982, pp. 460, 481–482, 499–500.

Thus, diplomacy may not have been torpedoed by the war, but may even have been enhanced. This implied, however, an entirely new conception of negotiations: negotiations based not on Israeli military strength and deterrence, but on mutual vulnerability and stalemate. Each side could expect at least partial satisfaction of its demands, but not more than that: the day of expecting Arab states to "face reality" on Israeli terms had passed. As one official put it:

> We saw the opportunity. We had been frustrated with the earlier negotiations. It became clear that Israel's military security didn't create a clear negotiating climate. The October war was seen as something new—something we can take advantage of.[60]

The "partial satisfaction" idea was a return to one of Kissinger's basic precepts of successful international negotiation (see Chapter Six, above.) Kissinger later stated this explicitly in his conversation with Heikal:

> If we want to solve a critical conflict, the point we start from must be the point at which each party feels it has obtained something and that to stop there is not a defeat for it. Such a situation was offered us at the end of the first half of October. Egypt had crossed the Suez Canal, penetrated the Bar-Lev line and advanced some kilometers into Sinai east of the pre-October 6 cease-fire line. Israel had succeeded in checking the Syrian attack—which had been strong and intense—in the Golan, and advanced some kilometers northward from the pre-October 6 cease-fire line. Thus each side had obtained some part of what it wanted even if it had not obtained all it wanted. This then was the time to stop fighting and seek a solution by political methods.[61]

In his memoirs, Kissinger writes regarding the events of October 9–10 that "theoretically, the best outcome was an Israeli victory that pushed back the Arabs without producing an Arab debacle."[62]

Nixon has also put on record his belief in an inconclusive military outcome as the key to future diplomacy:

> As far as the American position was concerned, I saw no point in trying to impose a diplomatic cease-fire that neither side wanted or could be expected to observe. It would be better to wait until the war had reached the point at which neither side had a decisive military advantage. Despite the great skepticism of the Israeli

---

60. Quoted in Bonham, Shapiro, and Trumble, p. 16. Bonham and his associates (pp. 15–16) argue that the belief in Israeli strength as the key to stability was salvaged by "differentiation": the concept was maintained for Israeli *military* strength, but not for Israeli intelligence. This does not seem persuasive; other evidence points to a fundamental shift away from relying on Israeli strength and deterrence of war at all; even the quotations offered by Bonham et al. themselves (p. 16) reflect a more basic revolution in thinking. See also Safran, pp. 502–505; Insight Team, pp. 254–260, 273.

61. Sheehan, p. 57.

62. Kissinger, 1982, p. 494.

hawks, I believed that only a battlefield stalemate would provide the foundation on which fruitful negotiations might begin. Any equilibrium—even if only an equilibrium of mutual exhaustion—would make it easier to reach an enforceable settlement.
Therefore, I was convinced that we must not use our influence to bring about a cease-fire that would leave the parties in such imbalance that negotiations for a permanent settlement would never begin.[63]

This new perception of the value of military stalemate helps account for the relative restraint toward Soviet actions, even as the perception of aggressive Soviet designs grew. Whatever the Soviets did, it was important to American policy-makers to end the war in a way that made it possible to work with Arab leaders, and especially with Anwar Sadat. It was important, therefore, not only to contain the Israeli victory, but also to avoid a total polarization that would tend to draw the Arabs back to Moscow. Thus, while detente became less influential in guiding American attitudes toward the Soviet Union itself, restraint was reinforced by other considerations of a more regional character.[64]

Images

The personalities of Richard Nixon and Henry Kissinger dominated American decision-making in 1973 even more than in 1970. Kissinger was now Secretary of State as well as Presidential Assistant for National Security Affairs. William Rogers and Melvin Laird were both gone. The new Secretary of Defense, James Schlesinger, was still settling into his new role. William Colby was also new at the helm of the CIA.

Nixon's personal images have already been summarized: a tactical and political view of detente (seen in 1973 in his quicker condemnation of the Soviet Union, relative to Kissinger), stress on personalities in diplomacy, a confrontational view of politics, a belief in insulated crisis management, admiration of boldness in action, and ambivalent feelings about American Jewish pressure ("I owe nothing to the American Jewish community," he reportedly told a state governor).[65] But in 1973 another important element was added to Nixon's personal perspective: the growing domestic preoccupations that

63. Nixon, p. 921.
64. Interview with an NSC staff aide; Kissinger, 1982, p. 498.
65. Insight Team, p. 265. Nixon's ambivalent feelings about Jews, discussed in Chapter Six, above, are described more fully by Kissinger (1982, pp. 202–203), who says that "Nixon shared many of the prejudices of the uprooted, California lower-middle class from which he had come."

were to lead eventually to the end of his presidency. In Nixon's own words:

> The immensely volatile situation created by the unexpected outbreak of this war could not have come at a more complicated domestic juncture. [Vice President Spiro] Agnew was beginning the final plea-bargaining negotiations that would lead to his resignation, and I was faced with the need to select his successor. The media were slamming us with daily Watergate charges, and we had just begun reviewing the subpoenaed tapes in preparation for reaching a compromise with the Special Prosecutor in the unfortunate but likely event that the court of appeals ruled against us. And Congress was pushing to assert its authority by passing a far-reaching bill to restrict the President's war powers. All these concerns would be interwoven through the next two weeks. Just as a crisis in one area seemed to be settling down, it would be overtaken by a crisis in another area, until all the crises reached a concerted crescendo as we neared the brink of nuclear war.[66]

The President's preoccupation reduced his role in crisis decision-making, though he made or at least approved final decisions on all major questions. There has also been suspicion that Watergate-related difficulties created an incentive for Nixon to act more decisively, but the weight of evidence cited below casts doubt on this supposition—in large part precisely because his role was usually limited to approving recommendations made by others.[67]

Nixon made only two public statements on the Middle East during the pre-crisis period. The first was at a brief joint appearance with Kissinger on Monday morning, October 8. In this appearance, Nixon typically stressed the importance of quietly gathering diplomatic support, rather than trying a "grandstand play," in seeking to stop the fighting; this simply reiterated his general philosophy of crisis management.[68] The second statement, on October 10, during remarks presenting the 1973 National Medal of Science Awards, consisted primarily of a reminder of U.S. dependence on foreign oil—showing that this was already on the minds of policy-makers.[69]

Kissinger's personal images have also been summarized: a "classical" view of history and international relations; belief in international stability by balance, negotiation, and imperfect satisfaction of all parties; stress on the linkage of diplomacy and military force;

---

66. Nixon, p. 922.

67. This is confirmed in Kissinger's description of Nixon's role as confirmer of decisions: "He was too distracted to shape the decisions before they reached him" (Kissinger, 1982, p. 470).

68. U.S. President, *Public Papers of the Presidents of the United States: Richard Nixon, 1973* (Washington, D.C.: U.S. Government Printing Office, 1975), pp. 848–849.

69. Ibid., p. 858.

cultivation of an image of relentlessness in crisis; belief that Middle East diplomacy required the reduction of the Soviet role rather than detailed U.S. proposals; and belief that strengthening Israel would secure Middle East stability in the near future.[70] To this could be added the uncertain implications of Kissinger's Jewishness, which does not seem to have played a large role in the earlier crisis.

Although the 1973 crisis, unlike 1970, directly involved Arab-Israeli conflict, Kissinger's Jewish origin seemed to play no greater role than before. Although some argue for his genuine feeling as a Jew, they concede that Kissinger conducted himself as an American, and the overall consensus accords with Golda Meir's conclusion:

> As for his being Jewish, I don't think it either aided or hindered him in all those months of negotiation. But if he was emotionally involved with us, such an involvement never reflected itself, for one moment, in anything he said to us or did on our behalf.[71]

As already indicated, Kissinger's image of Israeli strength as the key to stability in the Middle East was challenged by the course of the 1973 war. As his biographers recount, "Kissinger felt a growing conviction that Israel was pursuing a foolish, short-sighted policy, clinging to Arab lands that brought little security and tremendous resentment."[72] Thus, the time had come, in his eyes, to make the kind of serious effort toward a negotiated settlement about which he had earlier been quite dubious.

Regarding the administration's domestic distractions, there is evidence that Kissinger felt the need to demonstrate that foreign policy could be conducted despite Watergate—that the American government must appear decisive not for domestic political reasons, but because of the likely Soviet and world reaction to any appearance of debilitating internal instability. (This was consistent with his general tendency to see foreign policy as a function of the U.S.-Soviet relationship.) Kissinger reportedly concluded his first WSAG meeting with the "thought that the worst outcome for the United States would be to appear crippled by the domestic crisis over Watergate."[73]

Another element in the picture is Kissinger's image of himself as a peace-maker. He had previously been known for his position that

70. For a similar summary, see Sheehan, pp. 15–20.
71. Meir, p. 444. Among those who felt that Kissinger was influenced by his Jewishness was I. L. Kenen, Director of the America-Israel Public Affairs Committee (the "Jewish lobby") (personal interview).
72. Kalb and Kalb, p. 592.
73. Quandt, 1977, pp. 172–173. Also, interview with Cline.

"I will never get involved in anything unless I am sure of success. . . . I hate failure." And he had argued on these grounds that "the Middle East isn't ready for me."[74] This of course changed with the perception of new military and diplomatic options created by the war, and Kissinger was led to invest considerable personal prestige and credibility in complex Middle East negotiations.

Kissinger made two public statements during the pre-crisis period, in addition to his brief joint press conference with the President on October 8. In a previously scheduled speech at the Pacem in Terris Conference on October 8, he delivered one line on the Middle East situation, aimed at the Soviet Union, which indicated that even then his belief in Soviet innocence was not total:

> Our policy with respect to detente is clear: we shall resist
> aggressive foreign policies. Detente cannot survive irresponsibility
> in any area, including the Middle East.[75]

Kissinger's second statement, and by far the more significant, was made in his press conference on Friday, October 12.[76] This appearance confirms, in particular, two of the images already outlined:

1. *Soviet Responsibility.* The Soviets were seen as still behaving within the bounds of detente. As quoted previously, Kissinger described Soviet behavior as "less provocative, less incendiary, and less geared to military threats" than in 1967. In addition, he referred specifically to his earlier warning in saying that "we also do not consider that Soviet actions as of now constitute the irresponsibility that on Monday evening I pointed out would threaten detente." On the matter of Soviet foreknowledge, Kissinger argued that so long as the Soviet Union did not encourage the attacks ("that would have to be treated by us as a very serious matter"), their failure to inform the United States was "a different problem" and by implication less serious.

2. *The Need to Pursue Negotiations.* Kissinger stressed that the Arabs had successfully made the point that stability in the Middle East could not be assumed, and he reflected a new urgency to U.S. promotion of diplomatic efforts. As explained, this reversed his previous view that diplomatic stalemate worked in favor of American interests.

In addition, a number of other themes were confirmed in the October 12 press conference:

3. *The Urgency of a Cease-fire.* Kissinger defined the immediate American aim as ending hostilities as soon as possible, with the

74. Sheehan, p. 18.
75. *DSB*, October 29, 1973.
76. Ibid.

proviso that they be ended "in such a manner that they would contribute to the maximum extent possible to the promotion of a more permanent, more lasting solution in the Middle East."

4. *Military Balance.* Kissinger's presentation reflected no sense of impending victory by either side, but rather a fairly static view of the military situation. Thus, there was no urgency to the question of resupplying Israel; in fact, Kissinger declined to comment on that issue.

5. *The Need for a Consensus.* In discussing efforts to end the war, Kissinger still emphasized the importance of achieving the cooperation of all parties as the prerequisite to a cease-fire, especially in the framework of efforts in the Security Council: "We have therefore placed more stress on attempting to crystallize a consensus than we have on going through a battle of resolutions and counter-resolutions."

6. *The Dangers of a Great Power Confrontation.* Kissinger referred again to the analogy of the Balkans in 1914, calling the Middle East "an area where [there are] local rivalries that have their own momentum that will draw in the great nuclear powers into a confrontation that they did not necessarily seek or even necessarily start." Obviously, Kissinger was still concerned with the global implications of the Middle East War.

DECISION FLOW

In the period prior to October 6, U.S. policy-makers were concerned with three principal aims in the Middle East: preventing a Middle East war, promoting a new basis for negotiation, and reducing Arab dependence on the Soviet Union while maintaining America's detente with the Soviet Union. Corresponding to these basic aims were three policy concepts that guided operational decisions:

1. The deterrence of war by maintaining Israeli military strength, in return for an understanding that Israel would not initiate military action.

2. The initiation of a new round of talks, on the assumption that, with the closure of military options, Arab states would be ready to try diplomacy. This was expressed in Kissinger's efforts, only days before the war, to get agreement on "proximity talks" between the two sides.

3. The cultivation of the new opening to Egypt which had begun earlier in 1973 with secret meetings between Kissinger and Hafez Ismail ("Sadat's Kissinger"), and with the establishment of a "back-channel" of communication between

the two governments, tied in with the projected diplomatic effort.[77]

As indicated, these policies remained unchallenged up to the outbreak of the war. The last National Intelligence Estimate prior to the war was on May 17, 1973.[78] There was no reevaluation, for example, of the growing evidence of changed Saudi intentions regarding the use of oil as a political weapon: such evaluations as were made did not reach the top levels of the policy-making process.[79]

During the month of September, Egyptian and Syrian military preparations were interpreted either as normal maneuvers or as movements reflecting Arab apprehension of an Israeli strike. Intercepts and agency reports to the contrary were either minimized or ignored.[80] For example, King Hussein of Jordan passed on to one American ambassador, and apparently to other sources, reports that Syria was planning an attack. This information was relayed to Washington, but was not taken seriously in view of the overwhelming assumption that neither Egypt nor Syria would attack.[81] No alarms were sounded, therefore, by the September 13 air battle in which between eight and thirteen Syrian MIGs were downed by the Israeli Air Force (the event which Michael Brecher identified as the trigger to the pre-crisis period for Israel).[82] On September 24, the CIA spotted deviations in the Egyptian and Syrian maneuvers that indicated offensive intentions. On September 25, the shipment of surface-to-surface missiles from the Soviet Union was detected by American intelligence. At this time, Israeli intelligence was asked for its evaluation and responded with a reassuring report. The tendency of American intelligence was not to second-guess optimistic Israeli evaluations, since it was assumed that Israel would tend, if anything, to be *overly* alarmist about Arab military movements.[83] During the

77. U.S. policy in the 1970–1973 period is summarized in Quandt, 1977, pp. 119–164, and Safran, pp. 448–475. On Ismail's visit and the opening to Egypt, see Kissinger, 1982, pp. 210–216, 223–337; and Sheehan, pp. 23–25.

78. Cline, p. 134.

79. According to the Stevenson Committee, there were CIA agent reports and National Security Agency (NSA) intercepts that included accounts of war and oil embargo plans made at Feisal-Sadat meetings, but which were not included in the final reports. See Hersh, *New York Times,* December 21, 1977.

80. Interviews with Keegan and with two other senior intelligence officials; see the discussion in Kissinger, 1982, pp. 459–467, especially pp. 465 and 467.

81. Interview with a senior diplomatic official.

82. Brecher, *Decisions in Crisis: Israel, 1967 and 1973* (Berkeley, Los Angeles, and London: University of California Press, 1980), p. 51.

83. Interview with Walter Smith, Chief of Political Section, U.S. Embassy in Israel. See also Kalb and Kalb, pp. 512 ff.; and Tad Szulc, *The Illusion of Peace: Foreign Policy in the Nixon Years* (New York: Viking, 1978), p. 727.

week prior to the war, a number of other disturbing signals were received, including the Soviet evacuation of dependents from Cairo and Damascus on October 4. Kissinger later reported asking for American and Israeli intelligence assessments three times during this week, and receiving on each occasion the same reassuring answer.[84] Even on the morning of October 6, as cited previously, the Watch Committee declared *after* hostilities had commenced: "We can find no hard evidence of a major, coordinated Egyptian/Syrian offensive across the Canal and in the Golan Heights area."[85]

The evening before the war began, an urgent Israeli message had been sent to Washington—but attached to it was an intelligence estimate that did not mention the possibility of an Arab attack. Consequently, while the two messages were relayed to Kissinger in New York, they were not considered urgent enough to be brought to his immediate attention, and he saw them only on the following day.[86] The Israeli government apparently knew of the imminent attack from 10:00 P.M., October 5, Washington time,[87] possibly from U.S. sources.[88] But Kissinger himself received this message only at 6:15 A.M., October 6, less than two hours before the attack began. During the remaining time, he made valiant efforts to head off the impending conflict, reassuring Egypt and Syria, ironically, that Israel did not intend to attack—the most likely scenario for war, given his prevailing perceptions. There are accounts of a direct Kissinger threat to Israel designed to deter such action. But Israeli and U.S. participants both testify that the Israeli government had already decided on a policy of non-preemption, and conveyed this information through U.S. Ambassador Kenneth Keating in Tel Aviv.[89]

The outbreak of war occasioned no great sense of urgency in the executive branch or Congress. The lack of urgency was reinforced by the Israeli confidence projected during the first two days of fighting.

84. Kissinger, 1982, pp. 463–467; this was confirmed by official Israeli sources, which recorded requests for Israeli evaluations on October 1, 3, and 5. See Motti Raz, "The Decision-Making Process at the Pre-crisis Phase of the 1973 War, September 26–October 6, 1973" (Master's thesis, Hebrew University, 1975).

85. *Village Voice*, February 16, 1976, p. 30.

86. Kissinger, 1982, p. 466.

87. Dayan, p. 459; Brecher, 1980, p. 195.

88. Insight Team, p. 128.

89. The accounts of Kissinger's warning are in Kalb and Kalb, pp. 519–521; and Insight Team, pp. 127–129. But Kissinger's own account (1982, pp. 451, 477) and accounts based on personal interviews with Keating make it clear that there was no need to warn Israel, since Golda Meir informed the U.S. Ambassador that a decision not to pre-empt had already been taken; see Spiegel (forthcoming); Brecher, 1980, pp. 196–201; and Abraham Wagner, *Crisis Decision-Making: Israel's Experience in 1967 and 1973* (New York: Praeger, 1974), pp. 148, 158. See also Abba Eban, *An Autobiography* (New York: Random House, 1977), pp. 501–503.

Nixon himself, who had been spending the weekend at Key Biscayne, decided that there was no need to return to Washington before his scheduled return on Sunday night. Another indication of prevailing conceptions in Washington was the fact that for several hours the idea that Israel must have initiated hostilities still prevailed in official circles. Even after hard evidence had forced a change in this view, policy-makers continued to base their assessments on a belief in Israeli superiority. The Washington Special Action Group (WSAG) met during the morning, and again in the evening under Kissinger's chairmanship following his return to Washington. WSAG recommended routine moves in the U.S. Sixth Fleet, in accord with normal practice during Middle East crises. These moves were carried out in a routine fashion (Decision 1).[90]

According to one observer in the WSAG meetings, "there was very little controversy or argument during any of the meetings."[91] No basic changes were made in the objectives that had applied before the war. The objectives as outlined were simply adjusted to the exigencies of war, as can be seen by comparing them with a later Kissinger statement of the three "major concerns" that occupied the United States upon the outbreak of war:

1. The concern with preventing war became a concern with containing hostilities so that "the Middle East would not play the role of the Balkans in 1914, in which local rivalries produced a catastrophe from which Europe never recovered. . . ." This meant preventing a humiliating Arab defeat that would create the risk of Soviet intervention, possibly bring about the fall of Sadat, and damage the cause of Arab moderation generally in a spate of leftist coups. Therefore, from the beginning, Kissinger sought to avoid a total Israeli victory.[92]

2. The objective of promoting negotiations still survived despite Kissinger's initial pessimism. "From the outset," Kissinger later wrote, "I was determined to use the war to start a peace process." The U.S. sought to end the war "in such a manner that in the diplomacy that would follow the war, we would be able to talk to all of the parties involved. . . ."[93] To the extent possible, diplomatic openings would be salvaged, and in particular it was important to preserve the possibility of working with Anwar Sadat.[94]

3. The aim of reducing the Soviet role in the Middle East was translated, in the immediate circumstances, into a determination

90. Kissinger, 1982, pp. 455, 475.
91. Quandt, 1977, p. 170.
92. Interviews with Colby and Moorer; Safran, p. 478; Kissinger, 1982, pp. 468 ff.
93. Kissinger, 1982, p. 468.
94. Interview with Quandt; Sheehan, pp. 32–33.

that the "post-war evolution would not be determined by
military success primarily, especially by military success growing
out of a surprise attack and achieved with Soviet arms."[95] In
practice this meant preventing an Israeli defeat, which was not a
concern in the early days of the war when a quick Israeli victory
was expected. But there was also another side to U.S.-Soviet
relations. Kissinger and other Washington policy-makers hoped
to salvage detente as much as possible, conceivably by ending
the war with a show of U.S.-Soviet cooperation.[96]

To this, one might add the protection of American interests in the
Arab world, though the absence of the expected anti-American reactions and the general disbelief in the oil weapon meant a low priority
for this objective; the overwhelming weight of evidence indicates
that it was not a great concern.[97]

Thus, in sum, Kissinger

wanted the fighting stopped after Israel reversed the initial Arab
gains but before it inflicted a total defeat on its enemies. . . . The
problem was how to achieve this finely tuned result. At the outset
of the war, Kissinger estimated Israel would need two days to
mobilize and commit its reserves and two or three more days to
defeat the Arabs completely. He therefore wanted the cease-fire to
take effect sometime in the fourth day, October 10, and was
satisfied when he obtained the Soviets' agreement in principle late
in the night of the seventh, just before the expected Israeli
counter-offensive was to come into full swing.[98]

Or in the words of another observer:

A basic strategy was already set. The United States, expecting a
short war in which Israel would quickly prevail, hoped to be in a
strong position with Israel and the Soviets for post-war diplomatic
moves. In addition, Kissinger wanted to avoid a confrontation with
the Arabs. For the moment, the United States would adopt a low
profile, developing a position on the cease-fire that would soon be
seen as balanced. The viability of this policy depended upon a
quick Israeli reversal of the military situation and Soviet restraint.
For the next two days these conditions seemed to hold.[99]

95. Apart from the citation in note 93, above, all Kissinger quotations of the three
"major concerns" are from the news conference of December 27, 1973. *DSB*, January
24, 1974; see also Kissinger, 1982, pp. 467–468.
96. Interviews with Weiss and with a legislative staff aide; Kalb and Kalb, pp.
523–524.
97. For stress on concern with oil, see Insight Team, p. 356. Evidence to the
contrary: interviews with Hyland; Weiss; David Korn, Country Director, Lebanon,
Jordan, Syria, and Iraq, Department of State; Michael Van Deusen, Staff Aide, House
International Relations Committee; a National Security Council staff aide; and a senior
House legislative aide.
98. Safran, p. 478.
99. Quandt, 1977, p. 173; this was confirmed in interviews with participants.

Given the common assessment of the military situation, the only pressing concern of American policy-makers was to prevent the impending Arab defeat. It was estimated that the war could be allowed to run its course for a few days, and only then would its termination become urgent. In the meantime, the United States would adopt a low-profile posture, concentrating on laying the groundwork for the cease-fire that was considered inevitable. There would be no visible direct involvement. In addition, the United States government would resist pressures to denounce the Soviet Union.[100]

Thus, two immediate policy options were adopted. The first of these was to promote a cease-fire to return to the *status quo ante* (Decision 2).[101] This was not seen as a pro-Israeli move, since it was assumed that Israel would soon repulse the Arab attack. At that point, a cease-fire on the basis of pre-war lines would contain the Israeli victory and avert any Soviet move while preserving U.S. relations with Egypt and Syria. In the meantime, there was no need to push the proposal, pending Israel's expected counter-offensive. "Let the boys play awhile," Kissinger is reputed to have said.[102]

The other policy was to restrain resupply to Israel, likewise based on the expectation that the war would be over before shipments could arrive, and that there was therefore no need to antagonize the Arab states or spark large-scale Soviet resupply efforts (Decision 3).[103] Also, there were certain understood advantages to ending the war with Israel still needing resupply and thus dependent upon the United States.[104] "Low-profile" guidelines were delineated, meaning that Israel would get items already in the "pipeline," while any additional requests would be handled individually and without urgency. In any event, Israel was at this stage asking only for some speeding up of pipeline items and a small amount of consumables (particularly Sidewinder antiaircraft missiles) in order to "establish the flow" and prevent the development of an embargo mentality.[105] American policy-makers tried to extend the policy of restraint on resupply to both sides, through an understanding with the Soviet Union; according to one report, Kissinger and Dobrynin exchanged

---

100. Safran, pp. 478–479; Kalb and Kalb, pp. 523–524; interview with Weiss.
101. Kissinger, 1982, pp. 471–472.
102. Insight Team, p. 257.
103. Kissinger, 1982, p. 478.
104. Interview with an NSC staff aide.
105. Kissinger, 1982, pp. 477–478; interviews with Dinitz and Luttwak. Apparently a memo setting out U.S. resupply guidelines was formulated on Sunday or Monday (interviews with two legislative aides).

a verbal agreement on the first day of the war that both sides would keep hands off.[106]

The first two days of the war were occupied largely with unhurried consultations. American diplomats consulted, in the first place, with other UN Security Council members regarding the terms for a cease-fire, but there was no push to convene the Council before an agreed basis for such a resolution had been established. There were also continuous consultations with Israel and with Egypt. In the Egyptian case, Kissinger relayed the message that the United States would not allow Israel to occupy more Arab territory, while warning the Egyptians about the expected Israeli counterattack and urging them to accept a cease-fire on a *status quo ante* basis before it was too late.[107]

There were also contacts with other Arab states, designed to contain the war and head off the feared anti-U.S. actions that had erupted in the 1967 war. For example, there was a constant stream of messages to Jordan urging the government of that country to keep out of the war, or at least to limit its involvement in it.[108]

The preoccupations of American policy-makers during the early days of the war are illustrated by maneuvers over the Jackson-Vanik amendment, which was at that time pending before a House Committee. The administration had tenaciously fought the amendment, which stipulated that the Soviet Union would recieve most-favored-nation trading status only after granting the right of free emigration. Kissinger was later accused of attempting to link this matter to the Middle East war by inspiring Jewish leaders to approach Senator Henry Jackson and request the shelving of the amendment.[109] The weight of evidence from those closest to these transactions would indicate that the linkage was less direct; though Kissinger did try to get the cooperation of Jewish leaders in his fight against the Jackson-Vanik amendment, and while some Jewish leaders did in fact approach Jackson (unsuccessfully) at this time, it was only after the war had been terminated that a direct linkage was established—that is, Kissinger did not, during the early days of the war, make resupply of Israel explicitly conditional on American Jewish cooperation regarding the Jackson-Vanik amendment.[110] Nevertheless, the entire

106. Golan, p. 41. In his approach to the Soviet Union, Kissinger reportedly stressed that the United States would be restrained in its response to Israeli arms requests (interview with Sonnenfeldt). In his memoirs, Kissinger makes no mention of an agreement with the Soviets.
107. Kissinger, 1982, pp. 475–476; Heikal, 1975, pp. 33–34.
108. Interview with L. Dean Brown; Kissinger, 1982, pp. 494, 506.
109. Golan, pp. 54–57; interviews with two legislative aides.
110. Interviews with Kenen and with a senior legislative aide.

incident, even in its more modest interpretation, bears witness to the continuing tendency of Kissinger to deal with the Middle East in a superpower framework.

On October 7, Kissinger allowed the American position on a cease-fire—that it should be on a *status quo ante* basis—to be made public. The proposal was, as expected, rejected by Egypt, Syria, and the Soviet Union. American policy-makers concluded that only Israeli military success, which was still expected momentarily, would bring the other side around. Israel itself, of course, also wanted to reverse the military situation before a cease-fire came into effect. Kissinger and Israeli Foreign Minister Abba Eban had already agreed that the time was not yet ripe for a Security Council move to end the war.[111] Kissinger also met on Sunday, October 7, with Israeli Ambassador Simcha Dinitz, who had just returned to Washington from Israel. At this meeting, Dinitz presented a request for some two hundred tons of small arms and consumables, to be sent by air only in case of emergency. The modesty and routine nature of the request served to confirm the prevailing assessment in Washington regarding Israel's military superiority. At the same time, Kissinger informed Dinitz that Israel could pick up Sidewinder missiles and bomb-racks in an El Al plane at a Virginia naval base during the night. This followed from an earlier directive, within the framework of the low-profile resupply policy, allowing unmarked El Al planes to land in the United States to pick up items cleared for delivery to Israel.[112]

In the evening, another WSAG meeting was held, at which a CIA estimate was presented projecting that Israel would regain the initiative on the following day and win the war by the end of the week. Following the meeting, Kissinger had a long talk with President Nixon, who had finally returned to Washington from Key Biscayne. There was also, the same evening, an exchange of letters between Nixon and Brezhnev, in which both sides pledged mutual restraint in the Middle East war and agreed upon the convening of the

111. Insight Team, p. 257; Eban, p. 506; see Kissinger's own account of the general effort to delay a Security Council meeting (Kissinger, 1982, pp. 471–483).

112. Kissinger, 1982, pp. 480, 485–486; Kalb and Kalb, p. 522; Golan, pp. 45–47. The question of El Al landing rights is part of the Kissinger-Schlesinger controversy over whether, and by whom, the resupply of Israel was delayed. According to Kissinger (1982, p. 486) and Kalb and Kalb (pp. 525–526), the Defense Department delayed meeting the initial request for El Al landing privileges, and Kissinger intervened to get the supplies moving. Others argue that, regarding the loading of items already cleared for export, Israeli planes needed no special permission to land beyond routine FAA clearance; Schlesinger, accordingly, did not reject any Israeli request, and in fact the military not only did not oppose the use of El Al planes, but actually preferred that solution to the resupply problem. Interviews with General George Brown, Luttwak, and Sumner.

Security Council—even though, without prior agreement on terms of a cease-fire, such a meeting was bound to be no more than *pro forma.*[113]

On October 8, the military estimates still remained favorable to Israel; a joint report by the CIA and DIA (Defense Intelligence Agency) predicted that Israel would turn the tide on the Golan Heights by Tuesday night, October 9. In Kissinger's view, "the strategy seemed to be in train."[114] This being the case, diplomatic delay in negotiations with the Soviet Union seemed to fit American purposes, since every passing hour presumably reduced the difference between a cease-fire in place (the Soviet demand) and a return to the *status quo ante* sought by the United States.

Later intelligence during the day reinforced this attitude; at the daily WSAG meeting, the CIA reported that Israel had virtually completed reconquest of the Golan. As Kissinger remarked, "by the end of the third day of the war we went to bed expecting a repeat of the Six Day War of 1967."[115]

As arranged, the Security Council also met late on Monday, October 8. Ambassador John Scali, presenting the American position, made no effort to assess blame, but presented a rather conciliatory statement which, in line with declared American policy, called for a cease-fire on a *status quo ante* basis. But, as its clients were still in a favorable military position, the Soviet Union did not want a cease-fire on this basis, and therefore (in coordination with the Soviets) no resolution was offered.[116] Kissinger, "less as a threat than as an artist's flourish on a nearly completed canvas," delivered that same evening at the Pacem in Terris Conference his veiled warning which has already been quoted.[117]

But early on Tuesday, October 9, the American policy was badly shaken by new information. Dinitz woke Kissinger up twice, at 1:45 A.M. and at 3:00 A.M., to raise urgent resupply requests. At 8:20 A.M., Kissinger reports, he met Dinitz and Mordechai Gur, the Israeli military attaché, and was "shocked" to hear that Israel had lost some five hundred tanks. Obviously, previous estimates had been badly mistaken: "Israel stood on the threshold of a bitter war of attrition that it could not possibly win. . . ."[118] Another sign of Israel's panic was Israeli Prime Minister Golda Meir's urgent suggestion, relayed

113. Szulc, 1978, pp. 730–731. The CIA estimate is reported in Quandt, 1977, pp. 173–174.
114. Kissinger, 1982, p. 486.
115. Ibid., pp. 488–489, 491.
116. *DSB*, November 12, 1973; Kissinger, 1982, pp. 487, 489.
117. Kissinger, 1982, p. 491.
118. Ibid., p. 492.

by Dinitz, that she visit Washington to plead for emergency assistance. Not wishing to dramatize U.S. cooperation with Israel at this juncture, Kissinger deflected the suggestion.[119]

This changed perception of the military situation led to a complete rethinking of American policy. As later described by Kissinger to the Egyptians:

> Two days later there was still violent fighting in Sinai; our information about your mobilization for war had been wrong, and it is clear that our ideas about your ability for war had also been wrong. I asked for the Pentagon's reports on the progress of the fighting and more than once I asked them: what exactly is going on in the Middle East? Their answer was that the picture looked very different from our previous ideas. I received report after report on your operation of crossing the Suez Canal, and on your soldiers' and officers' will to fight, and on the tank battles in the desert. And the fighting was still going on. I said at the time that circumstances had now become favorable for a cease-fire. . . . I contacted the Soviets; perhaps I have also told you that I sent a message to Cairo. My proposal at that time was for a cease-fire in place. . . .[120]

A number of other pressures contributed to this recasting of American thinking. There were reports of an increased number of Soviet ships en route to Syria and Egypt, and also an increase in the number of Soviet warships in the Mediterranean.[121] The note from Brezhnev to Algerian president Boumedienne, cited above, was also made public on Tuesday. In fact, the note was probably a reaction to the collapse of the Syrian front, where Israel had carried out its only successful counterattack, and to the carrying out of Israeli air attacks in Damascus itself. Thus, by October 9 an anomalous situation existed in which the United States reacted to the lack of Israeli success on the Egyptian front, while the Soviet Union reacted primarily to the fact of Israeli success on the Syrian front.

Israeli requests also became much more urgent, moving from demands for eventual resupply to demands for immediate resupply. While unmarked Israeli airplanes had begun landing at American bases on Tuesday, it was clear that the capacity of this airlift would be grossly inadequate for Israel's military needs.[122] On Tuesday morning, Dinitz pressed for an additional list of crucial war materiel. Congressional pressure in support of Israeli requests also increased

119. Ibid., p. 493.
120. From the conversation with Heikal, quoted in Sheehan, p. 56.
121. Kalb and Kalb, p. 528.
122. Kissinger, 1982, p. 501; Quandt, 1976, p. 19. The disguise of Israeli planes did not work effectively: on the following day (October 10), the *Norfolk Ledger Star* reported the loading of El Al Boeing 707s in Norfolk; and on October 11, the Associated Press reported that shipments were being taken from a number of U.S. bases by Israeli planes.

during the day. There was not yet much pressure, however, from the outside; it was only on Tuesday night that Ambassador Dinitz met with American Jewish leaders and informed them of the serious nature of Israel's resupply needs.

All of these pressures came together with the perception analyzed above, that a military stalemate could be made to work in favor of American interests. The result was a change in American strategy to fit the newly appreciated circumstances. Instead of waiting for Israel to reverse the military situation, at which point the United States would intervene to contain the dimensions of the Israeli victory, an effort would be made to end the war without an Israeli victory. If the war could be terminated before the "balance" was upset, the danger of either an Israeli or an Arab defeat would be avoided. This would also provide the best basis for diplomacy after the war, especially if the war left the Arabs with some gains and ended with Israel needing resupply. It would also be the best policy for preserving U.S. interests in the Arab world. Thus, the one immediate objective—ending the war at an indecisive stage with Israel needing resupply—in fact embodied and focused more sharply the objectives already outlined.[123]

In light of the new situation, WSAG met in two emergency sessions before noon on Tuesday, October 9, to reconsider the American position on cease-fire efforts and resupply.[124] Recommendations on both topics were presented to Nixon by Kissinger and subsequently put into effect. The new departures adopted were:

1. Concessions to Israeli arms requests were made, but within the framework of the "low-profile" policy already adopted (Decision 4). Later in the day on October 9, Dinitz was informed of the American decision to meet nearly all Israeli requests for resupply, and to guarantee replacement of all losses. The significance of this "decision," however, was limited by the fact that Israel was expected to transport any released items with its own extremely limited airlift capability. Kissinger claims that there was not yet, at this stage, any talk of an American airlift, and he points out that "we also strove for a low profile in the method of resupply; we were conscious of the need to preserve Arab self-respect."[125]

---

123. In addition to sources cited in notes 55–60, above, see Edward N. Luttwak and Walter Laqueur, "Kissinger and the Yom Kippur War," *Commentary*, 50 (September 1974), 38–39.

124. Kissinger, 1982, pp. 493–495.

125. Ibid., pp. 495–496; interviews with General George Brown and with Luttwak; Insight Team, p. 274; Kalb and Kalb, pp. 528–529; Nixon, p. 922. It should also be stressed that Israel did not ask directly for an airlift; see the article by Mordechai Gazit, Director-General of the Israeli Prime Minister's Office, "An American Initiative," *Jerusalem Post*, October 9, 1981.

2. The call for a cease-fire was renewed, but on the basis of a cease-fire-in-place rather than a cease-fire to return to the *status quo ante* (Decision 5). The Israeli threat to additional Arab territory had receded, and a military stalemate appeared to offer a good basis for future negotiations and the strengthening of U.S.-Arab relations. Another factor was that the Soviet Union, which had insisted, along with the Arab states, that a cease-fire must be accompanied by some form of Israeli commitment to total withdrawal from occupied territories, indicated on the following day (October 10) a willingness to accept a simple, unconditional cease-fire-in-place. This made it hard for the United States to oppose such a proposal. Kissinger claims, however, that he still sought some restoration of the pre-war situation, "so I decided [on October 10] to accept the Soviet proposal 'in principle' to inhibit a Soviet diplomatic offensive at the UN, but to delay its implementation long enough to test the latest Israeli prediction of victory within forty-eight hours on the Syrian front."[126]

On October 10, as a massive Soviet airlift to Syria and Egypt began, an effort was launched to charter civilian American aircraft to carry supplies to Israel; this effort continued until October 12. These moves were designed to meet some of the Israeli demands, while incurring the least damage to the "low-profile" guidelines and to U.S.-Arab relations, all in the expectation or hope that the war would be concluded before harder choices would have to be made.[127] As Safran summarizes the thinking at the time:

> Kissinger continued to believe that Israel could win unaided and was afraid that providing it with massive amounts of arms would encourage it to prolong the fighting until total victory, besides provoking the Soviet Union and the oil-producing Arab states.[128]

In light of subsequent controversy over "who delayed the airlift," it might be useful to describe the agreed-upon policy in the words of the two chief protagonists:

> Kissinger: "Throughout the first week we attempted to bring about a moderation in the level of outside supplies that were introduced into the area. . . ."[129]

---

126. Kissinger, 1982, p. 498; interviews with Dinitz, Luttwak, Hyland, and three members of the NSC staff; Quandt, 1977, p. 179; Insight Team, p. 280.
127. Kissinger, 1982, p. 501.
128. Safran, p. 481; the *New York Times*, on October 11, reported that the administration officially did not want to encourage Israel, through promises of resupply, to carry on a long war of attrition.
129. *DSB*, November 12, 1973.

Secretary of Defense James Schlesinger: "The United States delayed, deliberately delayed, the start of its resupply operations hoping that a cease-fire could be implemented quickly."[130]

During the October 10–12 period, these modified policies were themselves gradually undermined as a sense of crisis was created in Washington by a number of new factors. In the first place, the Soviet airlift, the first signs of which had been received early on October 10, had by the next day reached "massive" proportions. Additionally, the Soviet Union had on the same day alerted three of its own airborne divisions—both actions perhaps being, as indicated, reactions to events on the Syrian front.[131]

Second was the growing pressure from Israel and Israel's supporters, and the growing recognition that Israel might indeed be in serious trouble, as opposed to simply being delayed in the achievement of inevitable victory. More was at stake here, in other words, than simply the length of the war.

A third factor was continuing evidence that the Egyptians were not ready for a standstill cease-fire even though the United States by October 12 had begun to push the idea with greater seriousness.[132] Also adding to the tension at this time was the resignation of Vice President Spiro Agnew on October 10. For the following two days, President Nixon's attention was focused upon the choice of a successor, which was announced on October 12, following a full day's deliberation in the seclusion of Camp David.[133]

The growing pressure for the resupply of Israel placed the administration in a somewhat difficult position. The previous motives for delaying such an operation remained valid, and in addition it was felt that any visible resupply effort at this stage would damage the delicate cease-fire effort. On the other hand, the various airlift options had been discussed on a military level as early as Sunday, October 7. The Joint Chiefs of Staff had informed Kissinger that three options on airlifting equipment were available. First was the El Al option, which was already being carried out but which had very limited potential. Second was the idea of chartering civilian cargo planes, and an effort in this direction was carried out during the October 10–12 period. Finally, there was the option of using U.S. military transport planes, which would clearly be the most effective method

130. *DSB*, November 19, 1973.
131. Kissinger, 1982, p. 504. Sicherman (pp. 48–49) attributes this Soviet boldness to American eagerness for a cease-fire-in-place and reluctance to resupply Israel, which in his view encouraged the Soviet Union to expand and exploit the war.
132. Kissinger, 1982, pp. 509–511.
133. Szulc, 1978, pp. 732–733.

of transport, but also the most costly in political terms. Nevertheless, the use of U.S. military transport was from the outset favored by some military advisors, including Chairman of the Joint Chiefs of Staff Admiral Thomas Moorer, since it accorded more with military notions of efficiency and control.[134]

There were also some technical issues and problems involved in the choice of resupply methods. Military advisors later complained that civilians thought of airlift operations as simple technical problems, while in reality such operations could hardly be implemented at a moment's notice, especially when the numbers and types of equipment to be delivered were themselves in constant flux. This point is important in light of the subsequent accusations that technical problems were used as a cover for political decisions. While this may have been the case in some instances, not all "technical problems" were imaginary.[135]

Nevertheless, as the subsequent report of the Comptroller General phrased it, the basic delay in mounting a military airlift was a "troublesome problem" that had nothing to do with military or technical issues. The problem was delay in the political decision on the U.S. role in delivering the equipment that was promised. The tendency of U.S. policy-makers was first to seek out low-cost answers to this question, and to adopt the more politically risky course only after pressures had mounted. The technical problems were to some extent foreseen, and preparations were undertaken to meet them; in particular, General George Brown, Chief of Staff of the U.S. Air Force, had already authorized the breaking out of supplies in depots and their transport and loading, before a final decision on the method of transport was made.[136]

Through Friday, October 12, the aim of preserving a low American profile guided all decision-makers in the White House, National Security Council, Department of State, and Department of Defense. The problem as seen by nearly all of those involved was how to respond to Israeli pressures and prevent an Israel defeat with the least damage to U.S.-Arab relations and to cease-fire efforts. By Wednesday, when it became clear that the El Al option was inadequate, the idea of civilian charters was floated.[137] On the same day,

134. Interviews with Weiss and Moorer.
135. Interviews with Moorer, Sumner, and Sonnenfeldt.
136. Comptroller General of the United States, *Report to Congress: Airlift Operations of the Military Airlift Command During the 1973 Middle East War* (Washington, D.C.: General Accounting Office, 1975), pp. 2, 7, 15; see also the Air Force reply on p. 64. Interviews with General George Brown and Admiral Elmo Zumwalt, Chief of Naval Operations.
137. See the summary of this period in Spiegel (forthcoming).

Secretary of Defense Schlesinger canceled a noon meeting with Israeli Ambassador Dinitz, as he had no answer to the Israeli questions
on the method of transport. The effort to secure civilian charters to
carry equipment to Israel was pursued unsuccessfully for two days.
Some observers have charged that the entire scheme was a subter-
fuge designed to further delay the resupply operation, following the
decision "in principle" on Tuesday, which had created the need for
a new cover story.[138] However, those close to Kissinger insist that the
effort was intended seriously, and that Kissinger himself genuinely
felt that the Department of Defense was dragging its feet on the
matter. Apparently, the central problem was that the civilian charter
scheme had simply not been thought through and involved complications that were not readily or quickly resolved.[139]

But, in any event, the effort to secure charter planes did not serve
as a cover story for aircraft which could fly themselves to Israel. This
involved primarily Phantom jets that were ready for delivery in St.
Louis. Although transport was not a problem, only small numbers—
on the order of three planes every two days—were released during
the first week of the war, and these were basically pipeline items.
The issue of the release of aircraft reflects the fact that the entire
resupply operation was first and foremost a matter of policy, of protecting the U.S.'s "low profile," which a visible resupply operation,
either by American military airlift or by the release of large numbers
of fighter aircraft, would seriously endanger.[140]

By Friday the 12th, pressures had mounted yet further. In the
evening, Ambassador Dinitz was finally able to meet with Pentagon
officials, but was unable to get the commitments for immediate resupply that he was seeking. It was also freely stated at the meeting
that the entire resupply operation was circumscribed by political
considerations. Dinitz emerged from the meeting in an angry state
of mind, but, as it turned out, this was to be the last major effort to
preserve a low-profile policy, and the last expression of the perceptions that prevailed during the pre-crisis period.[141]

138. Interviews with Weiss and Luttwak.
139. Interviews with Sonnenfeldt and other NSC aides; interview with Dinitz;
Kissinger, 1982, pp. 501–502. Testimony from the Defense Department also emphasizes the seriousness of the effort and the difficulties of getting civilian airlines to take
the risk of entering a war zone unless certain legal steps (primarily a declaration of
emergency) were met (interviews with General George Brown and Richard Peyer,
Near Eastern and South Asian Affairs, Department of Defense).
140. Interviews with General George Brown and Luttwak; Kissinger argues (1982,
p. 491) that the supply of Phantoms was severely limited by the availability of aircraft.
141. Kalb and Kalb, pp. 535–537; interviews with Dinitz and Sumner.

The entire airlift issue has been obscured by debate between partisans of Schlesinger and Kissinger over "who delayed the airlift." The account written by Marvin and Bernard Kalb, which is sympathetic to Kissinger and is based on sources close to him, paints a picture of consistent Pentagon obstruction of Kissinger's efforts to secure the release of supplies to Israel.[142] In this version, Defense Department officials used the excuse of technical problems to justify what was essentially the obstinacy of an anti-Israel clique. As we have seen, however, there were genuine technical problems, which may not have been appreciated fully on the civilian side. But generally there was no large-scale obstruction on political grounds, beyond that dictated by general policy: the Department of Defense was not delaying the implementation of decisions made in the White House. As it was later put by various observers, "Schlesinger's shoes were nailed to the floor," or "his hands were tied." It is clear that when orders were given, supplies were moved. The failure to move supplies was a matter of policy. Regarding the civilian charters, it is clear that the military was generally not enthusiastic about the scheme, and Kissinger may have genuinely thought that there was purposeful delay of the operation. But this overlooks the real problems of chartering civilian aircraft to enter a war zone, and it also overlooks a military dislike of the scheme that has nothing to do with anti-Israel prejudices, but which simply reflects the preference of military men for a military airlift. The real source of delay is again demonstrated in the issue of the Phantoms, where no transport problem existed. As with other equipment, the rate of release of these aircraft was calibrated very carefully by guidance furnished from the White House.[143] In sum, even Kissinger's most loyal partisans admit that the Kalb and Kalb account is unfair to Schlesinger.[144]

The critics of Kissinger, however, go even further, charging that the Secretary of State was using the Pentagon as a scapegoat, forcing Defense Department officials to maintain an elaborate pretense and play the villain in order to relieve pressure on the White House and bring about a stalemated result on the battlefield that could be obtained only by withholding necessary equipment from Israel. In this connection, it is claimed that Kissinger succeeded in manipulating Ambassador Dinitz so that the latter himself came to believe that the

142. Kalb and Kalb; Kissinger's version is less harsh toward the Pentagon while still presenting a picture of his own general sympathy to Israel's requests.
143. Interviews with General George Brown, Luttwak, Quandt, Sumner, Weiss, Zumwalt, a senior State Department official, and a legislative aide.
144. Interview with NSC staff aides.

Pentagon was responsible for delaying a military airlift, and that the idea of chartering civilian cargo planes was a deliberate ruse that succeeded in deflecting pressures during a crucial two days. It is further argued that the Defense Department and Schlesinger himself, far from opposing an airlift to Israel or even supporting Kissinger's policy, were actually pressing for an airlift while the Secretary of State was still fighting to preserve his low-profile policy.[145]

But this version is also exaggerated. Kissinger may indeed have found it convenient in some cases to deflect Israeli pressure by passing the buck to the Department of Defense. As he admits, "when I had bad news for Dinitz, I was not above ascribing it to bureaucratic stalemates or unfortunate decisions by superiors."[146] But it is clear that he believed the Defense Department to be dragging its feet on at least the effort to obtain civilian aircraft, which he favored as a method of obtaining resupply at a low political cost. Also, Kissinger did not conceal his basic policy orientation from Dinitz. By Tuesday or Wednesday, the Israeli ambassador had been informed of the American intention of preserving a low profile on resupply operations, and the charter scheme was presented in that context.[147] It also seems clear that Kissinger was not aiming to obtain a stalemate simply by manipulating supply operations. Obviously, American policy-makers wanted to avoid a humiliating Arab defeat, and they saw some benefits in maintaining a certain degree of Israeli dependence upon American largesse. But during the latter part of the first week of the war, there was no need or possibility of "fine-tuning" a military stalemate; the main focus was on trying to end the fighting before a crushing defeat of either side would become likely.[148] Thus, there were no orders to the Pentagon to go slowly in delivering goods that had been promised—there simply were no orders to do more than was being done.[149]

It is also apparent that the Defense Department was not basically opposed to the policy being followed. Military advisors supported the maintenance of a low profile, were hesitant on having American planes enter a war zone, and were not convinced until late in the

145. See Szulc, 1978, pp. 735–738; and Szulc, "Is He Indispensable? Answers to the Kissinger Riddle," *New York*, July 1974, pp. 33–39. On Dinitz, see Golan, pp. 50–51. For a summary of this debate, see John G. Stoessinger, *Henry Kissinger: The Anguish of Power* (New York: Norton, 1976), pp. 184–185.

146. Kissinger, 1982, p. 485; interviews with Dinitz and with NSC staff aides.

147. Interview with Dinitz.

148. Interviews with Hoskinson and with Joseph Sisco, Assistant Secretary of State for Near Eastern and South Asian Affairs.

149. Interviews with General George Brown, Sumner, Luttwak, and other Defense Department officials.

week that Israeli needs were as great as portrayed. Indeed, Dinitz describes the attitude of Defense Department officials at the Friday night meeting as "gloating," and there was certainly no absence of hostility to Israel within the Defense Department.[150]

The basic point, then, is that the "delay" was due to policy and not to bureaucratic obstruction. Furthermore, the entire issue involves a period of some seventy-two hours, which in terms of mounting a complicated military operation is not a very lengthy "delay."[151] The entire controversy seems to have been grossly exaggerated: what remains, after everything else has been excluded, is mainly a matter of personal rivalries and animosities. There was no real "culprit," in the final analysis.[152]

There is also controversy over how committed the U.S. government was to the cease-fire effort on October 10–12. Some observers claim that Kissinger made resupply of Israel conditional on that government's acceptance of a cease-fire-in-place. Others, equally well-placed, deny that any such linkage was made. According to Israeli Ambassador Simcha Dinitz, Kissinger even discouraged Israel from accepting a cease-fire on October 12—in opposition to his public stance.[153] One detailed study that has tried to sort out the facts concludes that the cease-fire proposal was meant seriously, but that it was peripheral rather than central to Kissinger's strategy; the effort was worth trying, but it was not the centerpiece of U.S. policy.[154] Kissinger's own account would tend to confirm this, in that he describes the effort as serious but not carried out urgently.

By October 12, in any event, the cumulative effect of several developments forced another important shift in American thinking. The Soviet airlift helped to change the dominant view of Soviet behavior, which was now seen as a violation of detente. Egyptian coolness to the cease-fire proposal indicated that Arab military aims were not yet satisfied and that there would be no cease-fire, and no diplomatic opening, until it had been made clear that nothing more could be gained on the battlefield. There was also pressure, from Israel and domestically, for immediate resupply, though it appears

150. Interviews with Dinitz and with an NSC staff aide.
151. This is a point stressed by the Israelis most intimately involved; see Eban, pp. 517–518; interview with Dinitz.
152. This conclusion is confirmed by some of the participants less involved in the rivalries, such as Moorer and Sisco (personal interviews).
153. Among those claiming that resupply of Israel was linked to the cease-fire: Quandt, 1977, p. 179; interviews with two members of the NSC staff; Insight Team, p. 280. Denying this version are Dinitz, Luttwak, Hyland, another member of the NSC staff (personal interviews), and Kissinger himself (1982, pp. 496, 498, 501, 509).
154. Spiegel (forthcoming).

that this pressure was not decisive in itself.[155] However, by October 12, decision-makers began to feel that Israel was in real danger: Egypt was deploying for a second-stage offensive, and Israel's dwindling stocks made defensive or offensive planning impossible. There was apprehension about what a desperate Israeli government, with a "very short nuclear option," might do. A triumph of Soviet arms seemed possible, increasing the likelihood of a U.S.-Soviet confrontation. Only with regard to Arab reactions were cognitive concepts unchanged; while U.S. action was thought by some to raise the danger of an oil embargo, this fear was generally not prominent.[156]

Nevertheless, on October 12, U.S. decision-makers clearly began to perceive, for the first time, a threat to American values that involved a possibility of involvement in hostilities and that required a response within a limited time. This marks, therefore, the end of the pre-crisis period, just as these same changing perceptions were leading to the consideration of options that had thus far been consistently put aside.

155. Both Dinitz and Kenen point out (in personal interviews) that Kissinger was aware that the Jewish lobby was already fully extended and that the threat of "going public" was less awesome than some commentators believe. In any event, the decisions made by Nixon and Kissinger can be explained almost without reference to inputs from outside the bureaucracy, even though the White House was bombarded by Congressional and other figures during the first week of the war. One must also bear in mind that the pro-Israeli pressures were countered by opposed viewpoints; Kalb and Kalb (p. 525) mention in particular the pressure from oil companies to avoid any action that would lead to an oil embargo. Interestingly enough, the influence of the oil companies also seems to have been minimal during the crisis; Akins reports that the memo on a meeting of oil company executives with the President (prepared by Kissinger's office) indicated a total lack of impact on the bureaucracy, while Dinitz reports that Kissinger at one point delayed for two days a message from the oil companies to the President (personal interviews with Akins and Dinitz). On the whole, available evidence—including other interviews—supports Quandt's conclusion that "the key decisions of the crisis . . . were not responses to domestic politics . . ." (Quandt, 1977, p. 203).

156. Policy-makers were aware, however, that Egypt had publicly urged Saudi Arabia on October 10 to halt oil production if the United States moved to replace Israel's losses in equipment. *New York Times,* October 11, 1973.

CHAPTER ELEVEN

1973: 12 October to 25 October

IN OCTOBER 1973, U.S. policy-makers had planned their policy on the basis of conditions best suited for ending the war at the end of the first week. However, the end of the first week of war brought a heightening, not a lessening, in the perceptions of crisis.

The Israeli army had advanced into Syrian territory, but was still stalled on the southern front. The Egyptian army was obviously preparing a second-stage offensive, while Israeli defense forces were unable to plan for either defensive or offensive action, due to the insecurity of supplies. Efforts to achieve a cease-fire in the war had failed, and it was obvious that the test of arms would determine the next stage of the conflict. There was the increasing possibility that a "victory of Soviet arms" might be achieved. The Soviet airlift to Egypt and Syria remained in full swing, and was accompanied by evidence of a sealift that obviously had been initiated before the outbreak of violence. There was fear of a desperate Israeli action, reinforced by the tone of Prime Minister Golda Meir's message to President Nixon on October 12. Policy-makers felt that the Arabs needed to be shown that they could not achieve their ends on the battlefield or through Soviet assistance. There were also mounting pressures to act, both from domestic sources concerned about Israel's safety, and from those circles traditionally concerned with American responses to the Soviet Union.

There was therefore a perception of a real danger to American interests; the achievement of an Israeli military advantage, if not an outright victory, was no longer regarded as simply a matter of time. There was also a new urgent note in the situation, as Israeli supplies of essential war materiel began to run low and some needs obviously had to be met immediately. Clearly, this also increased the risk of closer American involvement, since military supply could easily lead to other actions. The United States came closer to confronting the Soviet Union, particularly given the feeling that an Arab victory or threat of victory—and desperate Israeli actions designed to circumvent this—might indeed force Washington to take even more drastic measures than simple military resupply.

Thus, crisis conditions existed from late on October 12, despite Kissinger's "non-crisis" conference held earlier on the same day. The United States was forced into a new orientation toward the Middle East war, involving new decisions and a series of interactions that eventually culminated in one of the most alarming U.S.-Soviet confrontations of the nuclear age. The crisis did not abate until the war itself was finally halted, ending a period of high tension that lasted two weeks and involved some of the most dramatic crisis decisions of the Cold War.

DECISIONS AND DECISION-MAKERS

There were nine discernible decisions made by U.S. policy-makers during the 1973 crisis period:

Decision Number	Date	Content
6	13 October	Kissinger and Schlesinger decided on interim measures to aid Israel, including the dispatch of ten C-130s and the transport of supplies to the Azores.
7	13 October	President Nixon ordered a full-scale U.S. military airlift direct to Israel.
8	19 October	The President submitted to Congress a formal request for $2.2 billion in military aid to Israel.
9	19 October	Nixon authorized Kissinger to accept an invitation to fly to Moscow for urgent consultations.
10	21 October	Kissinger agreed to a joint U.S.-Soviet cease-fire proposal to be submitted to the UN Security Council.
11	23 October	Nixon and Kissinger resolved to prevent the destruction of the Egyptian Third Army; Nixon conveyed this commitment in a note to Sadat, and Kissinger relayed verbal warnings to Israel.

12	24 October	Nixon confirmed Kissinger's recommendation that the U.S. reject Sadat's plea for American and Soviet forces to supervise the cease-fire.
13	24–25 October	A rump "NSC" meeting decided to put most American forces on heightened alert and to dispatch a firm diplomatic note to Soviet Chairman Leonid Brezhnev.
14	25 October	Nixon approved U.S. acceptance of Security Council Resolution 340, establishing a UN Emergency Force without troop contributions from the major powers.

The major decision-makers were the same as in the pre-crisis period. The Washington Special Actions Group (WSAG) remained active, but there was a tendency for the focus to move to top-level consultations. Since President Nixon was distracted by matters relating to Watergate, including the "Saturday night massacre" on October 20, this also affected procedures. Nixon confirmed all major decisions, but was more remote from the daily deliberations; there were no formal, large-scale meetings with the President. This also meant an enlarged role for General Alexander Haig, his Chief of Staff (and, by virtue of his former position as Kissinger's deputy, a natural link to key foreign-policy advisors). There was an even greater impact on the role of Kissinger himself, who became in some cases the key figure in the decision-making process. In any event, the conversations between Nixon and Kissinger became the central focus of decision-making, and the Nixon-Kissinger dyad could be described as the key decisional unit. In one case (the negotiation of a cease-fire in Moscow), Kissinger was even authorized to make the final decision by himself.

PSYCHOLOGICAL ENVIRONMENT

Attitudinal Prism

By October 10, the mood of the Israeli Cabinet was one of extreme emergency, even though it was later seen to have been a less alarming situation than was perceived at the time. Israel was rapidly running out of consumable war materiel such as tank shells, and was forced to suspend any offensive operations for the near future. It was obvious by this time that Israeli aircraft alone could not transport an adequate amount of the materiel made available, and that the United States must take a more active role in its delivery. The fact that the Soviet airlift was in full swing did nothing to calm feelings in Jerusalem. As indicated, the full force of these feelings was conveyed to U.S. decision-makers.[1] Whether American policy-makers agreed with the Israeli perception or not, they were forced to recognize that the Israelis felt themselves in real danger, and the Israeli mood therefore became an important part of their psychological environment. But apart from these considerations, and apart from the force of pressures exerted within the United States, there was also serious apprehension of the consequences of Israeli leaders losing confidence generally in the United States. In the final analysis, there was *fear that Israel might take desperate action* that would upset American diplomatic designs and intensify the crisis, perhaps even creating the risk of a global confrontation. Some observers have stressed the importance of a general presumption in Washington that Israel had, or could quickly acquire, a nuclear option:

> Kissinger, along with a few people at the top government echelons, had long known that Israel possessed a very short nuclear option which it held as a weapon of last resort, but he had not dwelt much on the issue because of the remoteness of the contingency that would make it relevant. Suddenly, on October 12, 1973, the scenario of an Israel feeling on the verge of destruction resorting in despair to nuclear weapons, hitherto so hypothetical, assumed a grim actuality. The Secretary of State, whose policy had been inspired by the desire to preserve detente and by fear of the chaotic consequences of a total Israeli victory, did not need much pondering to imagine the catastrophic consequences of Israel's taking that road.[2]

There was therefore considerable external pressure to act, apart from the *perception of the immediate military situation.* And this perception of the military situation was itself changing. There were some policy-makers who continued to doubt the real need of an emergency resupply, but by late on October 12, Kissinger himself

1. See the accounts in Shlomo Aronson, *Conflict and Bargaining in the Middle East: An Israeli Perspective* (Baltimore and London: Johns Hopkins University Press, 1978), pp. 178–180; Henry Kissinger, *Years of Upheaval* (Boston: Little, Brown, 1982), pp. 507–513; Edward N. Luttwak and Walter Laqueur, "Kissinger and the Yom Kippur War," *Commentary,* 50 (September 1974), 34.

2. Nadav Safran, *Israel: The Embattled Ally* (Cambridge: Harvard University Press, 1978), p. 483; see also Aronson, pp. 178–179. Two high-ranking sources in the Department of State have confirmed that the U.S. government believed that Israel possessed nuclear weapons, but they assert that the role of this perception in the 1973 crisis was "not crucial" (personal interviews). Kissinger himself, in his memoirs, does not mention the topic.

had concluded that Israel was in danger. This was reinforced by Israel's ready acceptance of a cease-fire-in-place, in contrast to its earlier refusal to consider a cease-fire that did not restore the *status quo ante*. It was also brought home by the somber note from Golda Meir to Nixon, which spoke of the issue of Israeli survival and hinted that Israel might have to use "every means" at its disposal under the circumstances. In addition, Ambassador Dinitz met Kissinger late in the evening, delivering a note that warned of "very serious consequences" if the United States did not initiate a resupply operation quickly. In Dinitz's perception, Kissinger was very deeply affected at this meeting by the stark description of the military situation and the need of immediate resupply in order to plan any military operations.[3] According to a later account by Defense Secretary Schlesinger, Kissinger called him on Friday night with a very grave report on Israel's situation: "To say the least, he was a little bit concerned."[4]

This was matched by a *shift in attitudes towards the Soviet Union*. As outlined above, the original inclination in Washington was to take a relatively benevolent view of Soviet actions and intentions. Even the full-scale Soviet airlift did not cause a rapid reversal of this attitude; it was at first interpreted as a response to the deterioration of the Syrian military situation on October 8 and 9, a perception backed by the fact that on the first day of the airlift the An-12 transports (twenty-one of them) flew only to Syria.[5] Thus, the initial American reaction was limited to private efforts to persuade the Soviet Union to shut off the resupply, rather than public protest, under the apparent assumption that the Soviet action was an isolated matter and not a reflection of its basic policy thrust toward the war.[6]

But by the end of the week, a more sinister interpretation of Soviet behavior became current. First of all, the Soviet airlift had not only continued and expanded, but was also accompanied by a large-scale sealift, which obviously had been set in motion before the war and could not be regarded as a response to the shifting tides of battle.

3. Kissinger, 1982, pp. 512–513; Safran, pp. 482–483; William B. Quandt, *Decade of Decisions: American Policy Toward the Arab-Israeli Conflict, 1967–1976* (Berkeley: University of California Press, 1977), pp. 182–183; Marvin Kalb and Bernard Kalb, *Kissinger* (New York: Dell, 1974), p. 533; interview with Dinitz. Regarding doubts on the real need of emergency resupply, I had interviews with a National Security Council staff aide and with a senior intelligence official.

4. Interview with Schlesinger, *Jewish Telegraphic Agency Daily Bulletin,* July 1, 1974.

5. Quandt, *Soviet Policy in the October 1973 War* (Santa Monica, Calif.: Rand Corporation, 1976), pp. 18–19; Kissinger, 1982, p. 497.

6. Kissinger, 1982, pp. 447–499; the failure of the effort to secure Soviet agreement to end their airlift was revealed a week later by Schlesinger: *New York Times,* October 19, 1973.

Also, while not as dramatic as the airlift, the sealift was of greater scope and more significant militarily. American policy-makers, in some accounts, were in fact more impressed by the sealift than by the airlift.[7]

There was also a growing sense that American restraint was encouraging further Soviet moves. The Soviets, it was thought, might be acting more freely because of *their* perception that the United States had decided to do nothing that might endanger detente. This was reinforced by reports of stepped-up efforts in the airlift and the sealift, with Soviet personnel apparently driving tanks directly to the battlefields, and by the fact that the Soviets now announced their opposition to any cease-fire that was not linked to withdrawal to the 1967 lines.[8] Nixon was especially struck by the "menacing tone and intention" of a Soviet message received late on October 12, *before* the onset of the U.S. airlift, which not only accused the United States prematurely of massive resupply of Israel, but even referred to a rumor that 150 American pilots were being sent to aid in the Israeli war effort.[9] Thus, the Soviets appeared not only capable of exceptional hypocrisy, but seemed to be increasingly emboldened by the very moderation of U.S. statements and policy.

The prevailing mood in Washington, by the time the United States airlift was launched, was that the detente framework had been tried but had proved itself ineffective as a method of resolving the Middle East imbroglio. The Soviets seemed to be working outside the detente framework, pursuing their own aims without reference to it. There was therefore a strong need to show that the United States could match the Soviets, and even humiliate them by dominating the military situation and taking away the initiative that they had assumed.[10] This was directed also at the Arabs, but given the tendency to interpret regional events in a global perspective, there was an inclination to blame the Soviet Union for the Arab unwillingness to accept a cease-fire. Decision-makers felt that pressure on the Soviet Union was essential to achieve the basic aim of ending the war. An airlift to Israel might be needed because of real shortages in Israeli

7. Interview with an NSC staff aide.

8. Good expressions of this view can be found in Harvey Sicherman, *The Yom Kippur War: End of Illusion?* (Foreign Policy Papers, Vol. 1, No. 4; Beverley Hills and London: Sage Publications, 1976), pp. 44–49; and Robert Freedman, "Detente and Soviet-American Relations in the Middle East during the Nixon Years," paper presented to the Eighth National Convention of the American Association for the Advancement of Slavic Studies, October 8, 1976, p. 29.

9. Richard Nixon, *RN: The Memoirs of Richard Nixon* (New York: Grosset and Dunlap, 1978), p. 927.

10. Interviews with NSC staff aides; Kissinger, 1982, pp. 518–519.

war materiel, but it would be made all-out because of the desire to match and even overwhelm the Soviet airlift.[11]

The implication of this thinking was that Soviet behavior would change when Israel, with U.S. support, managed to reverse the military situation and again pose a credible threat to Arab states. Kosygin's quick trip to Cairo on October 16th, following the first Israeli operations on the west bank of the Suez Canal, seemed to confirm this: the Russians were apparently aware that the high-water mark for the Arabs had passed, and they were trying to get Sadat to accept a cease-fire (they were also presumably impressed, by this time, by the size of the U.S. airlift).[12] From that moment on, the American perception was that the Russians were likely to become increasingly anxious about the fate of their clients, and thus increasingly likely to act in desperation themselves. There was therefore considerable sensitivity to Soviet signals, and a quick positive response to Brezhnev's October 19 suggestion of a face-to-face meeting between top officials of the two countries.[13]

At this point, some underlying goals in U.S.-USSR relations, which had been put aside though never totally rejected, were reasserted. Detente had not proved to be the key to dealing with the Middle East crisis, and the United States had been forced to act outside the detente framework in countering Soviet actions. But by the end of the second week of the war, U.S. officials were again cautioning journalists that reports of the death of detente were greatly exaggerated.[14] There was still hope of preserving the essentials, including the capability of containing confrontations—such as that occasioned by the Middle East war—within an overall relationship of mutual restraint. Even after the shocks of the first week of the war, the change in perceptions of Soviet aims and actions was not total—which left room for policy-makers to be surprised by the events that took place during the night of October 24–25.

Thus, despite the quick adaptation to changed military conditions and a much less sanguine view of Soviet activities, the basic cognitive framework still embodied a *focus on the "global" elements* of the crisis, interpreting events as a function of U.S.-Soviet rivalry. Increased stress led, in essense, to reemphasis of a Nixon-Kissinger predisposition of long standing. Even the airlift to Israel was

11. Kissinger, 1982, p. 515; interviews with NSC staff aides; see also the report on administration attitudes in the *Christian Science Monitor,* October 15, 1973.

12. Interview with William Hyland, Bureau of Intelligence and Research, Department of State.

13. Kissinger, 1982, pp. 534, 538, 542; Kalb and Kalb, p. 544.

14. *New York Times,* October 18, 1973.

conceived in part as a signal to the Soviet Union. In seeking the ceasefire, the same American preoccupation with superpower relations, and the accompanying "illusion of superpower control," was apparent (and it soon became clear that both superpowers had underrated the obstinance of local forces). During the peak period, there was some adjustment of focus with Israel, and clarification of misconceptions regarding local actors, but the alert obviously marked an even stronger emergence of the U.S.-USSR preoccupation in traditional Cold War terms (expressed markedly in the Nixon press conference of October 26). This was in fact the beginning of a process through which Kissinger used the outcome of the war to exclude the Soviet Union, by and large, from Middle East diplomacy.

Part of the changing attitudinal prism was the *perception of the positions and strength of pressure groups*. As the war continued, there was more chance for outside groups to mobilize and make their presence felt, and the administration felt a growing need to take their activities into account even if it was not greatly influenced by them.

The influence of the Jewish lobby during the pre-crisis period, for example, was minimal, as was shown in Chapter Ten. But as the first week drew to a close, and other perceptions shifted, the sense of growing pressure from pro-Israel forces contributed to the decision on a massive airlift to Israel. As Kissinger later explained to Mohammed Heikal, this pressure was in fact critical:

> You can of course imagine the internal pressure we came under to help Israel. When we could not cope with the internal pressure through a Security Council decision to cease firing, we began to help Israel.[15]

This clearly overstates the case, as might be expected in an administration apologia to an influential Arab figure. The general limitations of the pro-Israel network under crisis conditions still applied. Its main support was outside Washington and needed time to mobilize; and in crisis conditions, deliberations were generally secret and the bureaucracy better insulated, while the prominence of "global" considerations enabled the administration to push other factors aside.[16] Nevertheless, by the time of the airlift decision, some pressures had indeed impinged on the consciousness of senior policy-makers. One of these pressures was a projected speech by Senator Henry Jackson that would have accused the administration of delaying resupply of

15. Recounted by Heikal in *Al Ahram,* November 16, 1973.
16. On the general weakness of the pro-Israeli lobby in crisis periods, see Steven Spiegel, *The War for Washington: The Other Arab-Israel Conflict* (forthcoming).

Israel through spurious cover stories. This speech, projected for delivery on Monday, October 14, was purposefully leaked to administration officials, and had an impact described by one observer as "incredible."[17]

In addition to its awareness of the increasing anger of pro-Israel groups, the administration also perceived that Israeli cooperation in future diplomatic moves would depend in large part on the demonstration of American support during the crisis. Thus, the perception of the domestic costs involved in further postponing a resupply operation was reinforced by the perception of future costs in direct U.S.-Israeli relations (offset, to be sure, by perceptions of cost to U.S.-Arab relations if an airlift should be launched).[18]

Perceptions of *pressures and costs from the Arab side* underwent a curious evolution during the crisis period. As in the case of the pro-Israel pressure groups, the administration continued to close itself off from direct interventions: a group of high-ranking oil executives, for example, was refused a requested meeting with the President.[19] But the administration perceived some risk of Arab retaliation as it moved toward a decision to resupply Israel by military airlift. On October 12, Saudi Arabian Foreign Minister Omar Saqqaf reportedly met Kissinger and delivered an explicit warning of cuts in oil production and supply if there were direct American assistance to Israel.[20] U.S. intelligence had already predicted an Arab oil embargo toward the end of the first week of the war, and was of the opinion that a military airlift to Israel would serve as a trip wire in forcing Saudi Arabia to make this crucial move.[21] Nixon and Kissinger were thus reportedly informed of the risk, but were prepared to accept it in view of the greater risks seen in not responding to the Soviet challenge.[22]

When the American airlift did not trigger an Arab oil embargo, therefore, there was a relaxation of concern on this score. It appeared that Arab states were willing to overlook the aerial resupply of Israel, at least if this action could be seen as a response to Soviet action. This

17. Interview with a legislative aide.
18. Charlotte Saikowski, "Congressional and Israeli Pressure on Nixon," *Christian Science Monitor,* October 12, 1973.
19. Spiegel (forthcoming).
20. The Insight Team of the London Sunday Times, *The Yom Kippur War* (Garden City, N.Y.: Doubleday, 1974), p. 358. (This meeting is not mentioned in Kissinger's memoirs.)
21. Interview with Samuel Hoskinson, National Intelligence Officer for the 1973 War.
22. Quandt, 1977, p. 184; Kissinger (1982, p. 520) reports telling British Ambassador Lord Cromer that the attitude to Arab oil threats would be "defiance" and that on the airlift "we have no choice."

thinking was reinforced by Sadat's speech on October 16, which praised the United States for its constructive role in the diplomacy surrounding the war.[23] On the following day, Nixon met with four Arab foreign ministers; nothing in that conversation seemed to challenge the now-prevailing view that the use of the oil weapon was not imminent.[24]

This perception may have contributed to the decision to make a dramatic announcement, on October 19, of a $2.2 billion aid package to Israel—a move that in fact triggered the Arab oil embargo. According to one close observer, Kissinger himself later speculated that the size and publicity of the aid program might have pushed the Arabs too hard at the wrong moment.[25]

In any event, even those experts who expected a sharp Arab reaction to the aid program continued to doubt the ability of the Arab states to carry out an effective oil embargo with the required degree of unity. As outlined above, U.S. intelligence assessments tended to minimize the danger that the embargo threat represented to American interests.[26] Thus, even the declaration of the embargo was met with a reaction described by U.S. Ambassador to Saudi Arabia James Akins as "soporific"; there was no real sense of urgency in the first few days after the threat had materialized (in part, no doubt, because it was a month before effects of the embargo began to be felt).[27]

As outlined in Chapter Ten, there was also a *newly perceived framework for diplomacy in the Middle East,* based on the victory of neither side and a negotiated end to the war that would leave both sides dependent on future diplomatic moves (while leaving Israel still vulnerable and in need of continuing U.S. support). This is central to understanding the apparent shifts of American policy from passivity to active support of Israel and then to strong pressure on Israel: as perceptions of the military situation changed, the United States adjusted its specific policies in order to preserve the conditions seen as most conducive to future negotiations. The policy was, in the words of one analyst, neither pro-Israel nor pro-Arab, but pro-equilibrium.[28]

23. Quandt, "Kissinger and the Arab-Israeli Disengagement Negotiations," *Journal of International Affairs,* 9 (Spring 1975), 37; Kissinger, 1982, pp. 526–527, 536.

24. See the account of the meeting in Mohammed Heikal, *The Road to Ramadan* (New York: Ballantine, 1975), pp. 238–240; and Kissinger, 1982, pp. 534–536.

25. Quandt, 1977, p. 188.

26. Interview with William Colby, Director, Central Intelligence Agency.

27. Interview with James Akins, U.S. Ambassador to Saudi Arabia.

28. John G. Stoessinger, *Henry Kissinger: the Anguish of Power* (New York: Norton, 1976), pp. 189–190; see also Kissinger, 1982, passim.

This basic premise was also seen in the airlift decision, which was designed to restore a military balance that seemed to be threatened and to demonstrate to the Soviet Union and the Arab states that they could not secure their objectives by the weight of arms. It was also expressed in Kissinger's promise to Arab leaders that the United States would take a more active role in Middle East diplomacy, rather than accepting the Israeli approach of reliance on military deterrence as the key to eventual Arab diplomatic concessions. Thus, in his meeting with Arab foreign ministers on October 17th, Kissinger agreed with the analysis that the crisis was rooted in the lack of diplomatic progress, and assured the Arab diplomats that they had made their point. He promised a future U.S. diplomatic initiative based on a cease-fire that would take into account "the efficiency and valor of Arab arms."[29] This conception could be undermined by a humiliating Israeli defeat of the Arabs, just as Arab military success earlier had undercut incentives to negotiate. For this reason, perceptions of the military balance were an especially critical element of the U.S. psychological environment.

The prevailing attitude during the second week of the war, as later expressed by Helmut Sonnenfeldt, was one of *waiting for the Israelis to turn the war around.* For the moment, the United States and the Soviet Union each thought its own clients were doing satisfactorily, and that there was consequently no need to intervene directly.[30] The military situation was too fluid for a standstill cease-fire; and after the failure of previous cease-fire efforts, the feeling was that no solution could be found until there were decisive developments in the field. There was some hope that the military situation would reach a natural pause in a few days, creating an opportunity for another cease-fire effort. Despite the lack of success to date, there was optimism in the White House regarding the chances of reaching a U.S.-Soviet formula for a cease-fire, on this basis, in the near future.[31]

Earlier, Kissinger had reportedly told Saqqaf that "it would be better to wait for three or four weeks until the combatants had exhausted each other, after which time some settlement might be

29. Edward R. F. Sheehan, *The Arabs, Israelis, and Kissinger: A Secret History of American Diplomacy in the Middle East* (New York: Reader's Digest Press, 1976), pp. 34–35; Kissinger, 1982, pp. 534–536.

30. Interview with Sonnenfeldt; also expressed by Kissinger, 1982, p. 534.

31. Kissinger, 1982, p. 538. The prevailing thinking on the necessary conditions for a cease-fire and the chances for concluding one in the near future was clearly reflected in contemporary press accounts. See especially *New York Times,* October 15 and 18, 1973.

possible."[32] While this time scale had undoubtedly been reduced, there was still no great sense of urgency on October 18, when Israeli Foreign Minister Abba Eban consulted with Kissinger before returning to Jerusalem. At this time, Kissinger reported that the Soviet Union had still made no serious cease-fire proposals, and that this issue was therefore not yet operative. When urged to remember that time was now working in Israel's favor, Kissinger replied: "Certainly. I don't believe that anything will move unless all parties have some incentive for a balanced cease-fire."[33]

There is some evidence that the sanguine American attitude on the course of the fighting led to a slow response to changes in the military situation after the Israeli crossing of the Suez Canal on October 15. Having been misled before into expecting a quick Israeli victory, Kissinger and other policy-makers were understandably leery of intelligence reports of a turn in the tide of battle. This was supported by the attitudes of Egypt and Israel. Both were reacting to military developments in a low-key manner, Egypt because its top leadership was not informed of the impending military fiasco, and Israel because it was naturally playing for time. Thus, the prevailing impression, as late as October 19–20, was that the Israelis still had hard fighting ahead, and that a smashing victory was not imminent. As a result, in Safran's words, "Kissinger almost missed his aim of stopping the Israelis short of total victory...."[34]

Kosygin's quick trip to Cairo on October 16 did seem to indicate Soviet concern over Israeli operations west of the canal; but since there was no immediate change in the Soviet posture toward the United States, no danger signals were sensed in Washington. (Apparently, it took Kosygin two days to persuade the Egyptians of the gravity of the situation.) On the evening of October 18, Soviet Ambassador Anatoly Dobrynin presented a new Soviet cease-fire proposal that conceded nothing. Kissinger could only conclude from this that the Soviets were not yet disturbed by the military situation.[35] But finally, on the morning of the 19th, Kissinger received Brezhnev's invitation to fly to Moscow, or alternately to receive Gromyko in Washington, for "urgent consultations on the Middle East." It was now obvious that the Soviets were becoming anxious, a development that was in itself sufficient to make American leaders more anxious.

There is some disagreement, however, about the American reading of the military situation at this point. Some observers have argued

32. Heikal, 1975, p. 240.
33. Abba Eban, *An Autobiography* (New York: Random House, 1977), p. 524.
34. Interview with Hyland; Safran, pp. 485–486.
35. Kissinger, 1982, pp. 539–540; Kalb and Kalb, pp. 543–544.

that Kissinger thought that Israel was on the verge of a decisive victory, and thus rushed to accept Brezhnev's invitation in order to head off that development.[36] The weight of evidence, however, is that while a shift in Israel's favor was detected, there was no sense of an impending Israeli victory that needed to be headed off quickly and no preoccupation with ending the war to the exclusion of other aims. The trip to Moscow itself consumed forty-eight hours, and there seems to have been some feeling on the part of American policy-makers that an improved Israeli military position would in fact be useful in extracting better terms from the Soviets on the projected cease-fire proposal. In any event, achievement of a cease-fire had always been the immediate American aim, and it was felt that the war had already lasted too long. On the other hand, there still seemed to be some hard bargaining ahead. Nor was the cease-fire seen as a totally anti-Israel move; Israel had already agreed in principle to it, and simply urged Kissinger and other American leaders to take their time in achieving it.[37]

What was apparently not anticipated was the extent of Soviet anxiety and pressure that was evident when Kissinger arrived in Moscow, and the Soviet alacrity in making concessions that removed all existing roadblocks to a quick cease-fire agreement. Apparently, neither the United States nor Israel had in fact anticipated such quick Soviet acquiescence to terms that Moscow had up to that moment rejected out of hand. Kissinger's "haste" when he got to Moscow is explained, in retrospect, as in large part a reaction to this Soviet desperation and as a reflection of his continuing central *concern of avoiding a dangerous superpower confrontation.*[38]

Kissinger was clearly serious about ending the war, but given his global focus he may have misread his ability to control local events —including the behavior of the Israeli government, given its desire to consummate a military victory so close at hand. Kissinger's stop in Israel on the way back from Moscow left the impression that he had achieved control of the situation. In the words of one aide: "We thought we left behind us a very sobered Israeli military

36. For example, interview with David Korn, Country Director, Lebanon, Jordan, Syria, and Iraq, Department of State. See also Insight Team, pp. 370–373; and Matti Golan, *The Secret Conversations of Henry Kissinger: Step-by-Step Diplomacy in the Middle East* (New York: Bantam, 1976), pp. 74–77.

37. Interviews with a senior State Department intelligence official and with an NSC staff aide. See also Kalb and Kalb, pp. 544–545; Quandt, 1977, pp. 190–192; Safran, p. 486.

38. This is also confirmed by Israelis who dealt with Kissinger during this period, though Eban felt Kissinger could have traveled to Moscow "on the morrow rather than on the same day" without running an undue risk of Soviet reaction. Eban, pp. 525–526; interview with Dinitz.

establishment."[39] But Kissinger apparently paid little attention to the mechanics of the cease-fire, an attitude that encouraged some Israelis and others to conclude that he was not overly concerned about the cease-fire being implemented on schedule. According to one account, Kissinger "downplayed the importance of continued cease-fire violations in Tel Aviv, encouraging the Israelis to believe that they could get away with a few more days of fighting."[40] Kissinger himself admits that "I might have emboldened them; in Israel, to gain their support, I had indicated that I would understand if there was a few hours' 'slippage' in the cease-fire deadline while I was flying home...."[41] According to Matti Golan, Kissinger also noted pointedly that the Vietnamese cease-fire had not gone into effect at the agreed-upon time, seeming to give his Israeli hosts the go-ahead for another two or three days of fighting.[42]

Given his reaction to the failure of the first cease-fire, however, it is hard to argue that Kissinger purposely invited the continuation of the war. According to another source, the comment attributed to Kissinger by Golan was actually made by one of the Israeli military figures present.[43] There is no other reliable testimony that Kissinger encouraged Israeli exploitation of Arab cease-fire violations in the form of a full offensive threatening the destruction of the Egyptian Third Army. There is only some evidence that he was ready to tolerate minor Israeli gains in response to cease-fire violations. The most plausible interpretation of the American position was, again, that it represented a misjudgment regarding superpower control of a volatile local conflict with unpredictable actors and interactions. As expressed by the *London Times* Insight Team:

> Carving up the world between them, demonstrating that the United Nations was powerless without their prior agreement, confident that their *protégés* were utterly dependent on them, the two superpowers could not apparently permit themselves to think that Israeli and Arab soldiers and politicians might have wills of their own.[44]

But whatever the problems in Kissinger's perception of Israeli thinking and U.S.-Israeli relations, his reaction to the collapse of the

39. Quoted in Insight Team, p. 390.
40. Scott D. Sagan, "Lessons of the Yom Kippur Alert," *Foreign Policy,* 36 (Fall 1979), 176.
41. Kissinger, 1982, p. 569; see also Aronson, pp. 189–190.
42. Golan, p. 86.
43. Aronson, pp. 189–190; the Golan version is also denied by NSC staff aides (personal interviews).
44. Insight Team, p. 418.

cease-fire was sharp and instructive. He tended to credit the Egyptian and Syrian allegations of Israeli violations, to the point that Golda Meir called personally to protest: "You can say anything you want about us and do anything you want, but we are *not* liars. The allegations are *not* true."[45] But whether the Israelis shot first, or were simply responding on a large scale to Egyptian violations, the threat to the Egyptian Third Army in either case represented to Kissinger a threat to world stability and to his emerging diplomatic conception. In view of the American assurances to the Soviet Union on the cease-fire, Kissinger feared that the United States would appear duplicitous to Moscow. There would be a risk of global confrontation as the Soviets moved to keep their commitments to Sadat (commitments made to secure Egyptian consent to the cease-fire). The destruction of the Egyptian Third Army would disrupt the developing U.S.-Egyptian relationship and remove any incentive for Egypt to rely on U.S. diplomacy. *American credibility with the Arabs* was generally at stake in Kissinger's mind—as was also, perhaps, the survival of Sadat. In place of a negotiated stalemate with both sides dependent on the United States, there would be another humiliating defeat, with the loser too bitter to negotiate and the winner having little incentive. For all these reasons, the prevention of the destruction of the Third Army was perceived by senior U.S. policy-makers as a matter of critical importance. In addition, Kissinger was genuinely angry at the Israelis, assuming that he had an understanding with them on ending the war.[46]

Against this background, U.S. policy-makers, on the night of October 24–25, were led to the perception that Soviet intervention into the Egyptian-Israeli theater was not only likely but imminent. As Nixon explained at the time: "We obtained information which led us to believe that the Soviet Union was planning to send a very substantial force into the Mideast, a military force."[47] What events lay behind this perception?

The first important signal was the request, made by President Sadat himself, for intervention by the two superpowers to preserve the cease-fire ordered by the UN Security Council. Nixon responded to this request by sending Sadat a "straightforward message" that the United States would veto any such resolution in the Security Council

45. Golda Meir, *My Life* (London: Weidenfeld and Nicolson, 1975), p. 445. On his disbelief in Israel's innocence, see Kissinger, 1982, pp. 569, 571, 576.

46. Quandt, 1977, p. 194; interviews with NSC staff aides, a senior State Department official, and a Defense Department official; Kissinger, 1982, pp. 571, 573.

47. *Department of State Bulletin* (*DSB*), November 12, 1973.

and would oppose the dispatch of Soviet or American forces into the Middle East because of the impossibility of assembling an effective counterweight to indigenous forces, and, more importantly, because of the increased risks of direct Great Power hostilities in such a situation.[48] American apprehensions were, however, increased by a spate of coded messages between Cairo and Damascus and the intercept of direct requests sent by Sadat to Moscow asking for the intervention of Soviet troops.[49] There were also a number of military signals: four more airborne Soviet divisions were put on alert, making a total of seven, while Soviet transport planes were held ready at embarkation points and an airborne command was established in the southern parts of the Soviet Union. The staff of one airborne division was reportedly already deployed in Syria, as was an officer cadre for SCUD missiles in Egypt. With recent reinforcements, there were now a reported eighty-five Soviet ships in the Mediterranean.[50]

At this point, on the evening of October 24, President Nixon received a message from Soviet Party Chairman Brezhnev which warned that "if you find it impossible to act with us in this matter, we should be faced with the necessity to urgently consider the question of taking appropriate steps unilaterally."[51] In Nixon's own words, this message represented "perhaps the most serious threat to U.S.-Soviet relations since the Cuban Missile Crisis eleven years before."[52] It seemed apparent to all American decision-makers that the Soviets had not taken previous American statements and warnings on Great Power intervention seriously. At the same time, Kissinger and those around him were inclined to believe that the Soviets meant business, since in their perception the Soviet leadership was indeed capable of desperate action in order to prevent the total collapse of its client regimes.[53] This assessment was reinforced by Kissinger's perception of Soviet decision-making as slow and deliberate, with never more than one step at a time. Kissinger felt, given this image, that it was important to challenge the Soviets on as many fronts as possible in order to overload the Soviet decision-making system and keep control of the crisis. This meant, again, that the

48. Nixon, p. 938.
49. Heikal, 1975, pp. 260–261; interview with General George Keegan, Chief of Intelligence, U.S. Air Force.
50. Insight Team, pp. 409–410; CBS Reports, "The Mysterious Alert," January 17, 1974; interviews with Keegan and with a senior legislative aide; Nixon, p. 937; Kissinger, 1982, p. 584.
51. *New York Times,* April 10, 1974; Kissinger, 1982, p. 583.
52. Nixon, p. 938.
53. Kissinger, 1982, pp. 585, 587; Kalb and Kalb, p. 553; interview with an NSC staff aide.

Soviet signals had to be met with a firm, multifaceted American response.[54]

Contributing to the general frame of mind was the realization that this time, unlike earlier crises, the Soviet Union had undoubted military capability to intervene. This had been shown by its involvement in Egypt since 1970, among other things.[55] In the context, it was also felt that a token Soviet force, well within the Soviet capability, would suffice for the purpose at hand.[56]

Washington acted in the belief that midnight was the logical time for a Soviet move, and that for this reason the American response must be determined and executed within hours.[57] Furthermore, simultaneously with the delivery of the Brezhnev message, a report came in that a flight of Soviet AN-22 transport planes had taken off in the direction of Cairo.[58] The experts upon whom American decision-makers relied concluded, therefore, that there was a "high probability" of a unilateral Soviet move, and that Soviet troops were possibly already airborne. Kissinger himself later expressed the belief that there was a "three out of four chance" of Soviet intervention at that moment.[59] According to the estimate of Israeli Defense Minister Moshe Dayan, the American perception was that the Soviets would land an airborne division near Cairo and link up with Egyptian forces to drive Israel from the west bank of the canal.[60] There was apparently some disagreement with this appraisal. Defense Secretary Schlesinger later disputed the Kissinger version, claiming that some advisors had rated the probability of a Soviet move as relatively low.[61] This view was shared by Ray Cline, Head of the Bureau of Intelligence and Research in the State Department, who argued that Kissinger himself would have reacted differently if he had really thought that the Soviets were likely to send troops to Egypt.[62] The leaked Pike Committee report reinforces this in another fashion by

54. Aronson, p. 196; Kissinger, 1982, p. 587.
55. See discussion in Spiegel (forthcoming).
56. Interview with Colby; Quandt, 1976, pp. 31–34; Quandt, 1977, p. 197.
57. Interviews with Admiral Thomas Moorer, Chairman, Joint Chiefs of Staff, and with Seymour Weiss, Director of Politico-Military Affairs, Department of State; Kissinger, 1982, p. 587.
58. Kissinger, 1982, p. 589; Insight Team, pp. 409–410; CBS Reports; interview with Hyland. Heikal reports that King Faisal of Saudi Arabia relayed to Nixon the message, received from a panicky Saudi liaison officer in Cairo, that seven Russian divisions were on their way. Though Heikal attributes the U.S. alert to this report, there is no evidence that U.S. policy-makers paid any attention to it.
59. Kalb and Kalb, pp. 554–555, 563–564.
60. *New York Times,* January 26, 1975.
61. Kalb and Kalb, pp. 561–562.
62. Cline, "Policy without Intelligence," *Foreign Policy,* 17 (Winter 1974–1975), 133–134; interview with a senior State Department official.

referring to reliance on Israeli intelligence, which led some American experts into underrating the Soviet reaction to events on the battlefield.[63]

Whatever the perception of the Soviet move, there is also the question of how perceptions of the domestic and foreign contexts played a role in the crisis. One observer calls attention to *"tunnel vision"* in crises, which led policy-makers to neglect factors from the external environment that were not directly related to the crisis at hand, and explained their shock over the charges that the American alert was motivated by a desire to detract public attention from Watergate.[64] (The question of the influence of domestic political considerations will be discussed further in the following section.) In addition, American decision-makers did not expect the alert to be publicized so quickly and dramatically, but saw it rather as a quiet signal, to be picked up by the Soviet Union, that would appear in the press only after the event. This perception of the likely public reaction to a worldwide alert was based on past experience. As Kissinger recounted:

> At 6:30 A.M. Thursday morning, October 25—after three hours of sleep—I discovered that the American public had already learned of the worldwide alert of American forces. It was all over the morning news. I was shocked. This unexpected publicity would inevitably turn the event into an issue of prestige with Moscow, unleashing popular passions at home and seriously complicating the prospects of a Soviet retreat. It also showed the change in the discipline of our government in the three years since the Jordan crisis of September 1970. Then we had gone through similar alert measures; their extent had not become known until the crisis was already over, three days later.[65]

There were other elements of the psychological environment that may have been important to the decisions of October 24–25. In particular, one piece of information may have heightened perceptions of Soviet risk-taking: on October 22, U.S. intelligence detected neutron emissions from a Soviet ship passing through the Bosphorus. This led to an immediate suspicion that the ship was transporting nuclear weapons. The ship docked at Alexandria on the morning of

63. "The CIA Report the President Doesn't Want You to Read" (Excerpts from the Report of the House Select Committee on Intelligence), *Village Voice*, February 16, 1976, p. 30.

64. Interview with Colby; also, interviews with Moorer, Hyland, and NSC staff members.

65. Kissinger, 1982, p. 591; Richard Valeriani, *Travels With Henry* (Boston: Houghton Mifflin, 1979), p. 181; David Binder, "Action Was Downstairs, President Was Upstairs," *New York Times*, November 25, 1973.

October 25, and the available evidence indicates that this information was in the hands of decision-makers when the alert was decided upon. In the minds of some observers, this information was an element in that decision.[66] It is not clear, however, that the "nuclear ship" was in fact important to the alert of October 24–25. The detection system was not considered infallible; there was even controversy over whether the ship had been unloaded or not (with the weight of evidence indicating that the ship had returned unloaded when it sailed back to Nikolaev in early November). Thus, the incident was not regarded as hard fact and seems to have been overshadowed by the other Soviet military measures and by other direct evidence of a possible Soviet move. The testimony of those close to the decision-making is, by and large, that it played a minor role, if any, in decisions on the American response. Kissinger himself indicated the ambiguity of the prevailing assessment when he later stated that the U.S. had no "confirmed" evidence that the Soviet Union had ever introduced nuclear weapons into Egypt.[67]

There was, however, another confirmed piece of information that made U.S. decision-makers more sensitive to any reports of Soviet activities involving nuclear weapons. The Soviet Union had deployed SCUD missiles in Egypt before the war, a fact picked up by American intelligence, but there was no certainty regarding the type of warheads deployed with the missiles. The presence of these missiles in Egypt was regarded as a signal of Soviet commitment, and the United States leaked its knowledge of their presence back to the Soviet Union in an article that appeared in *Aviation Week* on October 22 (no reference was made to the warheads deployed with the missiles). There was a possible linkage here to the reported "nuclear ship"; in any event, U.S. decision-makers could perceive such a link. It is also possible that the presence of the SCUDs in Egypt contributed to the general feeling in Washington that the American

66. See reports in Kalb and Kalb, p. 557; Quandt, 1976, pp. 30–31; Quandt, 1977, p. 198. This was confirmed in interviews with participants, including Colby, Hoskinson, Hyland, Keegan, Admiral Elmo Zumwalt (Chief of Naval Operations), and a senior Air Force intelligence officer. The intelligence network responsible for the report is described by Bob Woodward, "Pentagon to Abolish Secret Spy Unit," *Washington Post,* May 18, 1977.

67. Interviews cited in note 66, above; see also discussions in Aronson, pp. 192–193; Quandt, 1976, pp. 30–31. Kissinger's statement, at a press conference on November 21, 1973, was a response to the first leaks on the Soviet "nuclear" ship; see *DSB,* December 10, 1973; *Washington Post,* November 21, 1973; and *New York Times,* November 22, 1973. The only reference in Kissinger's memoirs (1982, p. 584) is a general mention of "other ominous reports in especially sensitive areas."

response to the Soviet threat must include deterrent action on the nuclear level.[68]

There is also a question of the perception of military capabilities in the Middle East, and especially of the naval balance in the Mediterranean. Aronson reports the concerns of senior naval officers over the military risks in the Mediterranean, with Kissinger himself influenced by the dangers of escalation.[69] Kissinger, however, has denied that the senior policy-makers perceived a weakness in U.S. naval strength against the Soviets. In a statement made two years after the war, he said:

> I have seen statements that in 1973, the United States was affected in the conduct of the Middle East crisis by its fear of the Soviet Navy. This may have been true of our Navy; it wasn't true of our government. . . . We all suffered from the illusion that our navy was far superior to the Soviet Navy, and we conducted ourselves accordingly.[70]

One final element in the attitudinal prism was *growing anger directed against America's European allies.* The United States had been refused the use of European bases for the airlift to Israel, save for the consent of Portugal to the use of the Azores, and this had caused bitterness. Turkey was even allowing Soviet overflights over its territory to the Middle East. The feeling in Washington was that the NATO allies of the United States failed to see the war in a proper "global" perspective, and failed to credit the need for common action against the Soviet Union and for a common front on the oil question. U.S. allies seemed to be letting the side down on every score.[71] The extent of disillusionment can be seen in the Kissinger statement that

> One cannot avoid the perhaps melancholy conclusions that some of our European allies saw their interests so different from those of the United States that they were prepared to break ranks with the United States on a matter of very grave international consequence. . . .[72]

68. Insight Team, pp. 411–413. *Aviation Week and Space Technology* later claimed, in the November 5, 1973 issue, that the SCUDs were in fact nuclear-tipped. Aside from the ambiguous information on the Soviet ship, described above, no further supporting evidence or information on this claim has been uncovered. See the discussion in Yona Bandmann and Yishai Cordova, "The Soviet Nuclear Threat Towards the Close of the Yom Kippur War," *Jerusalem Journal of International Relations,* 5:1 (1980), 102–105.

69. Aronson, p. 195.

70. Statement at Southern Governors Conference, quoted in Valeriani, pp. 181–182.

71. Linda Miller, *The Limits of Alliance: America, Europe, and the Middle East,* Jerusalem Papers on Peace Problems, No. 10 (Jerusalem: Hebrew University, 1974), pp. 13–15.

72. Press conference of November 21, 1973, in *DSB,* December 10, 1973.

Images

The dominance of a few key figures in American policy-making makes it difficult to distinguish personal images from the "attitudinal prism" described above. This is especially true for Henry Kissinger. The matter is more complicated with Richard Nixon because of his distraction with domestic affairs.

The crisis period in the 1973 Middle East war corresponded with the peak of the fight over access to Presidential tapes in the Watergate affair, culminating in the "Saturday night massacre" on October 20 (while Kissinger was in Moscow). There is little doubt that Nixon's mind was to a great extent occupied by Watergate-related matters; Nixon says so himself in his memoirs, and it is reflected in the way his account intersperses events from the war with events on the fight over the tapes. This leads to the suspicion that Nixon, acting under high stress, was affected in his judgment and tended to overreact, as expressed especially in the DefCon 3 alert on October 24–25.[73] (DefCon, or Defense Condition, 3 is a middle-level military alert; DefCons range from 1, actual war, to 5, the lowest level of readiness.) But while Watergate undoubtedly contributed to the stress on the President himself, for the same reason Nixon's role in decision-making during this period, and especially on October 24–25, was largely limited to ratifying conclusions reached by others. The DefCon 3 alert was supported by all the President's chief advisors, who were stunned by the suspicion that domestic politics had been a factor in the decision.[74]

There is, however, another sense in which Watergate might have affected personal images that were influential in foreign policy-making, and that is in the felt need to demonstrate *to the Soviet Union* that domestic distractions had not impaired the American ability to act. This was apparently true for Nixon as well, whatever his role in decision-making; in later accounts, he laid stress on the need to keep the Russians from miscalculating because of Watergate, and concluded that he had succeeded in this aim.[75]

This was an even stronger element in Kissinger's perception of the situation. A recurring theme in Kissinger's thinking was that domestic problems should not be allowed to disrupt foreign policy.

73. Nixon gives a sarcastic account of these accusations in his memoirs, pp. 962–963.

74. Kissinger, 1982, pp. 596–598; this was confirmed by all interviewees who participated in the decision-making process, whatever their personal feelings about Nixon. Golda Meir (pp. 440–441) also rejects the domestic politics connection, arguing for the sincerity of Nixon's determination "not to give in to Soviet blackmail."

75. Press conference of October 26, 1973, in *DSB*, November 12, 1973.

It was important, therefore, to demonstrate that Watergate had not weakened the President's ability to act, and to show that the nation was still on course.[76] Kissinger was initially irritated at the distraction of the Saturday night massacre while he was in Moscow, and was upset at his subordinates for letting it interfere with his important foreign policy accomplishments (he apparently did not realize the domestic impact of the event until he reached London on Monday morning, October 22).[77] And while hotly denying that the decision on a nuclear alert had been influenced by "domestic reasons," Kissinger did warn that Watergate might help to tempt the Soviets into challenging the United States in the Middle East: "One cannot have crises of authority in a society for a period of months without paying a price somewhere along the line."[78]

Another continuing strong element in Kissinger's personal reactions was the recurring emphasis on the need to prevent a victory of "Soviet arms" in the Middle East. This was clearly seen in the airlift decision: "[Kissinger] was resolved not so much to rescue Israel as to teach the Russians a hard lesson."[79] Kissinger is described by a sympathetic observer as having a "chronic obsession" about Soviet guns not winning a war over American guns; in the Kalbs' account, he believed that a Russian victory in the Middle East would lead to domination of the area and possibly even Communization of Western Europe and Japan in five to ten years.[80]

As during the pre-crisis period, there were few public statements by either Nixon or Kissinger during the crisis period. In one of the few statements made, Nixon made it clear that the experience of the two previous Middle Eastern crises in this study was very much on his mind:

> If I were to describe our policy, I would say that it is like the policy that we followed in 1958 when Lebanon was involved, it is like the policy we followed in 1970 when Jordan was involved.[81]

76. Kissinger, 1982, passim.; Quandt, 1977, p. 203; CBS Reports; Spiegel (forthcoming).

77. Kissinger, 1982, p. 567; Valeriani, p. 135.

78. Press conference of October 25, 1973, in *DSB,* November 12, 1973. See also *New York Times,* October 26, 1973; and Quandt, 1977, p. 199. The same idea was expressed by Secretary Schlesinger in his press conference on October 26, 1973 (*DSB,* November 19, 1973).

79. Sheehan, pp. 33–34.

80. Ibid.; Kalb and Kalb, p. 564.

81. Remarks at Medals of Honor ceremony, October 15, 1973, in *DSB,* November 12, 1973.

But the most significant statements were made in the press conferences given by Kissinger on October 25, and by Nixon on October 26, to explain the alert of October 24–25. In fact, a comparison of the two conferences highlights the differences between Nixon and Kissinger in personal perceptions and style. Whereas Kissinger attributed the alert to "the ambiguity of some of the actions and communications and certain readiness measures" on the part of the Soviet Union, Nixon stated flatly that "we obtained information which led us to believe that the Soviet Union was planning to send a very substantial force into the Mideast—a military force." Kissinger, while arguing for a firm response, downplayed the dangers in the crisis and used conciliatory language aimed at the Soviets; his account of the diplomatic developments since the outbreak of war was dispassionate and restrained. Nixon, on the other hand, dramatized the risks and seriousness of the confrontation: "The most difficult crisis we had since the Cuban missile crisis of 1962."

All in all, the two accounts differed appreciably in tone and nuance, even while agreeing on the essential interpretation of events, thus lending credence to the view that Nixon's perceptions were influenced more by personal stress and were more politically flavored. As Kalb and Kalb explained the difference between the two perceptions:

> Actually, the President and the Secretary were on the same "wave-length" in their private judgments about Soviet conduct and motivation in the Middle East: they both regarded the possibility of a unilateral Soviet military move as a very real threat. But they spoke at different times in the crisis—and clearly with different motivations. Nixon spoke that night as a politician under attack, trying desperately to keep one step ahead of impeachment. He knew that the crisis was over by then, and that his more extreme comments would cost him little diplomatically—but they might help him with the American public. Kissinger had spoken as the nation's number one diplomat at the height of the crisis; he had to speak cautiously because he was trying to head off a big-power confrontation that could have led to a world war.[82]

DECISION FLOW

By October 12, several developments had converged in the minds of American decision-makers:

82. Kalb and Kalb, pp. 562–563.

1. There had been no success, after three days of efforts, in getting any measure of Soviet restraint on the resupply of Egypt and Syria.

2. The cease-fire effort had not succeeded. Israel had accepted a cease-fire-in-place, signaling a state of despair, and the Soviet Union had lent a measure of support to the effort, but Sadat had not accepted it despite its "favorable" terms—reflecting his military success.[83]

3. The military situation of Israel was increasingly critical, as evidenced by the frantic cable from Israeli Prime Minister Golda Meir. There was apprehension of a desperate Israeli action, including the possible introduction of nuclear weapons into the Middle East. In any event, the United States did not want a Soviet-supported victory or a serious threat to Israel to materialize.

4. Outside pressures for an immediate airlift of supplies to Israel were growing. Congressional pressure had increased steadily since Monday, October 8. There were vocal demands that the United States match the Soviet airlift, from anti-Soviet hawks as well as from pro-Israel forces, and the projected speech by Senator Henry Jackson on Monday, October 15, threatened to bring the debate to a head.[84]

The change in American thinking envolved in stages. Any bureaucracy takes time to turn around, and Kissinger still clung to the hope of ending the war early and maintaining a low profile until that point. But as it became clear that a cease-fire was not in the offing, due to the *success* of the Arab armies, another implication was gradually accepted: if the United States could not stop the war, then it must go all-out to change its direction.[85] By late on October 12, American decision-makers perceived a clear threat to values, a clear possibility of involvement in hostilities, and a limited time for response.

But the official American position was still unchanged as of the early evening of October 12. At that time, Ambassador Dinitz met with officials of the Department of Defense, who gave him little assurance on immediate shipment of consumables, by charter or otherwise, and offered replacement F-4 Phantom aircraft to Israel only at the rate of three every two days (with a pause after the first

83. Kissinger, 1982, p. 509; Insight Team, p. 275; Sheehan, p. 34; Golan, pp. 65–68.
84. Jackson reportedly used his control of NATO legislation wanted by the administration to force use of NATO stocks to aid Israel—thus not only ensuring quicker resupply of Israel, but also demonstrating the relevance of NATO forces to the Middle East and reducing anti-NATO sentiment in Congress (interview with a legislative aide).
85. Interviews with a senior State Department official and with an NSC staff aide. Kissinger (1982, p. 520): "Once a stalemate had become apparent . . . we moved decisively, even brutally, to break it."

three were dispatched). Schlesinger himself bluntly acknowledged the political considerations behind this grudging response to Israeli requests, explaining that the United States was still operating on a "low profile" in order to prevent Arab reaction.[86] The first decision was made later that same night, after Dinitz had conveyed to Kissinger his anger and frustration over the Pentagon meeting. Kissinger and Schlesinger, with Nixon's approval, decided on some interim steps in the immediate resupply of Israel: ten C-130s would be loaded with ammunition and sent directly to Israel, and other supplies would be hauled to the Azores in order to shorten the distance for Israeli pickup (Decision 6). The decision was based on the need to convince Egypt and Syria that prolonging the war would be of no benefit, and to demonstrate to both the Arabs and the Soviet Union that the United States could and would offset Soviet arms shipments. Kissinger himself, in elaborating the aims of the airlift to other policymakers at the time, laid stress on its function as a signal to the USSR more than as a reflection of genuine military need. The Soviets, he reportedly said, must be "run into the ground"; they must see that the U.S. could outperform them as military suppliers; "I wanted a demonstrative counter to the Soviet airlift."[87]

In fact, some observers felt that the military situation was largely irrelevant to the decision. They saw the decision as directed at the Soviets and the Arabs, and as a decision that might even have been taken in response to the sealift had there been no Soviet airlift. In any event, it is argued, the American airlift was not militarily essential and did little to influence the course of the war.[88]

But whatever the influence on the war in retrospect, the dominant perception at the time was that Israel did need the resupply desperately. With high attrition rates in equipment, impending shortages in vital materials, and an avalanche of requests for resupply from the front, Israeli military planners were unable to plan further operations without a secure source of resupply. The feeling of most observers was that the military situation was dominant in the decision, and that it was closely tied to the course of the war—at least in the sense that the resupply of Israel and the matching of the Soviet airlift were complementary motives.[89] In any event, given the

86. Kalb and Kalb, pp. 535–537; Golan, pp. 52–53.

87. Quandt, 1977, pp. 184, 187–188; Kissinger, 1982, p. 515.

88. Interviews with a senior State Department official, with an NSC staff aide, and with an intelligence official; Sheehan, pp. 33–34.

89. Interviews with Colby, Weiss, and Korn, with a senior State Department official, with a Department of Defense official, with a legislative aide, and with Walter Smith, Chief of Political Section, U.S. Embassy in Israel. General George Brown, Chief of Staff, U.S. Air Force, stressed the importance of both motives (personal interview).

convergence of all considerations, at this late stage there was little if any significant opposition from any quarter to some form of American airlift, either from the Defense Department or elsewhere.

There are some indications, however, that Kissinger himself still wanted to move slowly, and that Nixon's intervention was critical in making a decision for all-out resupply by U.S. military aircraft. There have been charges that Kissinger, on the following morning (October 13), was still pursuing low-profile options, the last of which was the scheme of transporting supplies by American airlift only as far as the Azores. Nixon, however, rejected this idea, in line with his usual tendency to reject halfway measures. The President felt that since the United States would be blamed for whatever airlift it instituted, it had best make the airlift impressive. Thus, he reportedly took this decision out of Kissinger's hands, telling him that he had had his chance to make such schemes work.[90] This is supported by Nixon's own recollections; as he later told David Frost, he had reacted to the low-profile proposals by cutting through the red tape: "I said, 'Look, I mean, it isn't going to fool anybody.' "[91] Nixon also recalled a Pentagon proposal, relayed by Kissinger, that the United States send only three C-5A military transport planes, on the grounds "that politically it would be perhaps dangerous for us to send a greater number and it would destroy the chances for negotiations in the future if our profile was too high"—to which Nixon's own response was that the United States would take as much heat for sending three planes as thirty, and he therefore ordered Kissinger to "send everything that flies."[92]

On the morning of October 13, WSAG assembled to consider how far to extend the interim measures and whether to use U.S. military aircraft. Nixon, prior to the meeting, gave his approval to a straightforward U.S. military airlift. With this guidance, WSAG decided on the use of the giant C-5As for the direct transport of supplies to Israel, the use of C-141s to move supplies from the Azores the rest of the way, and a sharp acceleration of Phantom deliveries (Decision 7).[93] Some technical problems remained: there was no logistics contin-

90. Interviews with two senior State Department officials, two NSC staff aides, two legislative aides, and with Edward Luttwak, Consultant, Department of Defense; Golan, pp. 59–61. Nixon's personal role in ordering the airlift into operation is also stressed by Golda Meir, pp. 430–431.

91. *New York Times,* May 13, 1977.

92. Ibid. In his memoirs (pp. 926–927), Nixon repeats this incident but portrays the proposal more sharply as a DOD proposal, without mentioning Kissinger's position on it. Kissinger (1982, p. 515) confirms Nixon's views on the subject.

93. Kissinger, 1982, pp. 514–515; Kalb and Kalb, pp. 539–540; Quandt, 1977, p. 183.

gency operation plan for Israel, the Israelis refused to stratify their priorities, and there were problems of landing and overflight rights. But again there was no question of the effort made once a Presidential directive was issued. Reports afterwards praised the Military Airlift Command for its outstanding job in overcoming obstacles, and in eventually moving 22,497 tons of supplies in fifty-one C-5s and one hundred and seventy-seven C-141s.[94]

The major remaining problem on October 13 was obtaining landing and refueling rights. The previous order had been to fly to Lajes Air Force Base in the Azores, but the United States now needed permission to use this base for refueling direct flights to Israel. The major problem in obtaining Portuguese coorperation was that a pending aid bill before Congress included an amendment limiting aid to Portugal, in reaction to criticism of Portuguese policy in Africa. Contacts with the Portuguese had in fact begun before the airlift decision was taken, and had met with a sticky response. Seymour Weiss, Director of Politico-Military Affairs in the Department of State, had called Senator Hubert Humphrey for assistance in killing the Portuguese amendment on the aid bill then before the Senate. President Nixon also sent a stiff note to the Portuguese early in the morning on October 13, and permission for refueling rights was finally received at 3:40 P.M.[95] Following this, the Secretary of Defense issued the final operational order for a full-scale Military Airlift Command airlift.[96]

American policy from this point was to pump in supplies until the military position shifted enough to create an incentive for a cease-fire. As Eban understood Kissinger's position on Saturday morning, October 13:

> [Kissinger] found the existing military position adverse to basic American interests. It gave the Soviet Union excessive prestige, and it contained no incentive for a cease-fire, still less for negotiations. Unless Israel improved its military position, American diplomacy had no basis on which anything could be built.[97]

The airlift was thus designed to help Israel regain the initiative, as well as to match Soviet actions. It was not, however, designed to enable Israel to score a total victory. Although Egypt finally rejected

---

94. Comptroller General of the United States, *Report to the Congress: Airlift Operations of the Military Airlift Command During the 1973 Middle East War* (Washington, D.C.: General Accounting Office, 1975), especially pp. 6–7, 64. Israel moved 5,500 tons in eight B-707s and B-747s.

95. Interviews with Weiss and with legislative aides; Quandt, 1977, p. 183; Kissinger, 1982, p. 520.

96. Comptroller General, pp. 5–6.

97. Eban, pp. 515–516.

the pending cease-fire proposal late on October 13, policy-makers clearly anticipated that such a proposal would come when the tide of battle had turned, and Israeli cooperation at that time would be expected. Kissinger urged Israeli restraint in territorial aims and warned that Israel could not expect to go back to the original lines without a protracted war, which the United States did not want.[98] The Israeli crossing of the Suez Canal on October 15 was expected to create a new situation, but the United States waited for others to take the initiative. This expectation seemed to be confirmed by Kosygin's trip to Cairo, unannounced but known in Washington, and by the increasing desire of the Soviet Union for more constant communication between the two governments.[99] Although the image of increasing Soviet moderation was somewhat marred by the maximalist proposal relayed by Dobrynin on October 18 (see above), it seemed in Washington that American tactics were working and that the point was rapidly approaching at which the United States and the Soviet Union could act together to end the war. As indicated, there was concern at the same time that the Soviets not feel impelled to act out of desperation; the result was "not so much a detailed bargaining over diplomatic points as a simple process in which American anxiety grew rapidly to match that of the Soviet Union...."[100]

At the same time, a decision was being forged on the total aid package to Israel. It was necessary to provide for arms already being shipped, and to deal with other Israeli requests. The complete Israeli request totaled some $3.2 billion, while administration estimates on basic Israeli needs were around $1 billion. When WSAG debated the question on October 16, Kissinger argued for a large aid package. In his mind, the United States had already done the damage to its relations with the Arab states, and there was little further risk on this score. The figure of $2.2 billion was apparently suggested in an NSC staff meeting as a "compromise"; in any event, Nixon himself opted for a high figure, consistent with his usual tendency to "do things big." The decisive considerations were the desire to reassure Israel and to retain some leverage for securing Israeli cooperation (for example, on a cease-fire), as well as the desire to impress the Soviets and to secure domestic political credit for the actions undertaken.

98. Kalb and Kalb, p. 541; also see the reports of the Kissinger-Eban meeting in *Washington Post,* October 14, 1973; *Christian Science Monitor,* October 15, 1973; and *New York Times,* October 15, 1973.

99. *New York Times,* October 20, 1973. Heikal reports that Kosygin was in favor of a cease-fire and that the Russians "were obviously in close touch over this with the Americans . . ." (Heikal, 1975, p. 237).

100. Insight Team, p. 367.

Finally, the large aid package also served to reassure the American military on replacement of items shipped to Israel.[101]

The public announcement of the $2.2 billion aid request being transmitted to Congress was made on October 19 (Decision 8). In retrospect, Kissinger himself reportedly wondered if the size, timing, and publicity of the request took adequate account of likely Arab reactions.[102] In any event, fear of an Arab oil embargo was apparently not a major factor at this time. There was a general tendency, as indicated, to minimize the risk of such an embargo, and this attitude had been reinforced by the Arab reaction to the airlift and by Sadat's moderate speech of October 16. In any event, no real actions were taken to prevent an embargo before the event: in particular, no strong messages were sent to Saudi Arabia.[103]

By the same day—Friday, October 19—the Soviet push for a cease-fire had triggered negotiations with the United States regarding the wording of a standstill cease-fire.[104] As these efforts stalled, Brezhnev extended his urgent invitation for Kissinger to fly to Moscow for face-to-face talks. Nixon and Kissinger consulted at once and decided immediately to accept the invitation (Decision 9).[105] The United States had been waiting for such a Soviet move, which would give it a chance to extract concessions on the terms of the cease-fire as the battle shifted in Israel's favor. Kissinger intended to push for direct Egyptian-Israeli talks as a part of the cease-fire terms, a measure useful in its own right but also of some help in mollifying Israeli dissatisfaction over a cease-fire that would deny them the fruits of military victory.

The decision to travel to Moscow was also justified to Israel as a chance to gain more time, given the time consumed by such a trip. This rationale, however, does not seem entirely convincing. As Quandt says, Kissinger went to Moscow not to gain time for Israel on the battlefield, but in order to obtain Soviet and Arab agreement for the kind of cease-fire best designed to serve as a basis for future diplomacy. Once the Soviets were pushing hard for a cease-fire, under the pressure of impending Arab defeat, it became necessary to move quickly in order to avoid Arab and Soviet humiliation and

101. Quandt, 1977, p. 188; Spiegel (forthcoming); Sheehan, pp. 69–70; interviews with I. L. Kenen, Director, America-Israel Public Affairs Committee; Michael Van Deusen, Staff Aide, House International Relations Committee; and with a legislative aide.

102. See especially Quandt, 1977, p. 188; and Sheehan, pp. 69–70. The issue is not raised in Kissinger's memoirs.

103. Interview with Akins.

104. Kissinger, 1982, pp. 539–542.

105. Nixon, p. 933; Kalb and Kalb, pp. 544–546; Kissinger, 1982, p. 542.

the temptation for a direct Soviet move. Kissinger also had to consider the broader implications for U.S.-Soviet relations, in order to prevent irreversible damage to detente and to preserve overall international stability: "The stakes were no longer confined to the Middle East; they were also global. If necessary, Kissinger was prepared to lean hard on the Israelis."[106]

This is not to say that Kissinger was calibrating the war precisely, trying to fine-tune the military outcome and reach a totally inconclusive result, despite later suspicions and charges that this is exactly what he was attempting. There were too many forces, too little accurate information, and too many rapid developments in the field for such precision. While decisions were being made, the major motivation, according to the testimony of those closest to the decision-makers (both pro-Kissinger and anti-Kissinger), was simply to avoid a total defeat of the Arabs, and to obtain the diplomatic situation most conducive to future diplomacy. Aside from the general idea of balance, the only specific area in which Kissinger seems to have sought an "inconclusive" result was in preventing the destruction of the Egyptian Third Army. Kissinger felt that this development would undercut his diplomacy in the most serious way, and this was a constant element in his actions in the days that followed. Other than that, the timing and nature of most of his actions on the cease-fire seem to have been dictated by political, and not military, circumstances.[107]

Kissinger flew to Moscow late on October 19, arriving at 7:30 P.M. on Saturday, October 20, Moscow time. While still airborne, he received the news that Saudi Arabia had declared an oil embargo against the United States, and he also received an unusual and unwanted "power of attorney" from Nixon which authorized him to make a final decision on his own in Moscow on any agreement to end the fighting.[108] Nixon's motives remain somewhat unclear: the situation was urgent, and rapid agreement might be seen as imperative, while Nixon and Kissinger were in agreement on the basic points and the President could trust Kissinger to consult on any problematic

106. Quandt, 1977, p. 191; this is generally confirmed in Kissinger's account, 1982, pp. 542–567. On the importance of detente, see also Nixon, p. 933; and Walter Laqueur, *Confrontation: The Middle East and World Politics* (New York: Bantam, 1974), p. 197.

107. Interviews with Hyland, Van Deusen, two senior State Department officials, and an NSC staff aide; Kissinger, 1982, pp. 571, 573; see also the column by James Reston in *New York Times,* October 19, 1973.

108. Kissinger, 1982, pp. 547–548; Kalb and Kalb, pp. 546–548. Kissinger did not want the full authority to make decisions, because it deprived him of the flexibility afforded by the need to consult Washington.

issues. But the shadow of Watergate also intrudes at this point; Nixon was at the time contemplating the firing of Archibald Cox (the Watergate special prosecutor) and the events that were to culminate in the "Saturday night massacre." However, as Nixon presents the issues, the Middle East was intruding on Watergate rather than vice versa, which was one of the reasons he was forced to fire Cox:

> I strongly felt that I could not allow Cox to defy openly a presidential directive. I thought of Brezhnev and how it would look to the Soviets if in the midst of our diplomatic showdown with them I was in the position of having to defer to the demands of one of my own employees.[109]

In any event, the result of Nixon's delegation of authority was to put the next decision in the hands of Kissinger, thus actually divorcing it from Watergate.

The Russians insisted on meeting with Kissinger immediately upon his arrival on the evening of October 20, confirming in Kissinger's mind that they were anxious for agreement. They were, however, not yet ready to make the concessions central to that agreement, but rather spent the first meeting in feeling out the American delegation. Kissinger, in his own words, "procrastinated" until 2:00 A.M., intending to play out the Soviets for a while.[110] On the following day, however, the Soviets quickly conceded the essential points: a simple cease-fire-in-place, linked to a call for direct talks. Considering this a diplomatic achievement of the first order, Kissinger agreed to the wording of what became UN Security Council Resolution 338 (Decision 10). He asked Nixon to appeal immediately to the Israelis for their acceptance of the proposal, and to instruct U.S. Ambassador to the UN John Scali to convene the Security Council.

On October 22, at 12:52 A.M., New York time, the Security Council adopted the cease-fire resolution exactly as drafted in Moscow. The cease-fire was to go into effect at 6:52 P.M., Middle East time, on the same day. On his way home, Kissinger stopped in Israel to assuage Israeli anger over the haste and lack of warning in the implementation of the cease-fire—a visit he later described as one of the most moving moments of his government service. What most impressed Kissinger was the obvious war-weariness among the people, combined with a pervasive sense of insecurity brought on by Israel's travails. "Its people were yearning for peace as can only those who have never known it," he observed; yet "Israel's insecurity was so

109. Nixon, pp. 932–934.
110. Kissinger, 1982, pp. 549–550; Valeriani, pp. 134–135.

pervasive that even words were daggers."[111] Israelis were especially uneasy about the possibility of secret U.S.-Soviet deals concluded at Israel's expense—a commentary on how Kissinger's global approach to the Middle East looked to them.

Kissinger claimed that his lack of communication from Moscow was due, in part, to apparent Russian interference with all American communications from there; he backed this up later in his memoirs with a detailed description of the difficulty of establishing radio contact from Moscow. The result was to give Israel eight hours, rather than twelve, before implementation of the cease-fire.[112]

Upon his return, Kissinger immediately faced a new intensification of the crisis. The cease-fire had failed to take hold effectively, the Israeli advance had resumed, and the Egyptian Third Army was again threatened. The Soviets made a strong protest to Washington, Brezhnev apparently believing that Israel could not continue the war without U.S. connivance. Nixon and Kissinger agreed that the United States had to make a strong effort to restore the cease-fire, and they specifically resolved to prevent the destruction of the Egyptian Third Army (Decision 11). In their perception, such a decisive defeat of Egypt would completely change the military and diplomatic picture, undermining the basis for negotiations now being painfully established, destroying American credibility with the Arabs, and incurring the risk of an extreme Soviet response, superpower confrontation, and the end of detente. On the other hand, U.S. action to rescue Sadat would help establish the impartiality of the United States as a mediator, secure the good will of Arab states, and preserve Soviet trust in American commitments.[113]

The decision was carried out in a number of moves. Kissinger delivered blunt verbal warnings to Dinitz, and worked with Dobrynin to arrange a second Security Council cease-fire resolution. (Resolution 339, calling for an immediate end of hostilities, a return to the October 22 positions, and the dispatch of UN observers, was adopted at 1:00 A.M., Washington time, October 24.) Nixon, who by this time was in frequent communication with Sadat, sent the Egyptian president a message on October 24, telling him that

111. Kissinger, 1982, pp. 560, 564–565.

112. Ibid. Israelis regarded this explanation with skepticism, to say the least; see Golan, p. 84.

113. Interviews with Weiss and with a senior State Department official; Kissinger, 1982, pp. 568 ff.; Kalb and Kalb, pp. 549–550; and Golan, p. 88. In his own analysis of American policy, Eban lays stress on U.S.-Soviet relations as the "more decisive calculation" in the move to prevent a total Egyptian defeat (Eban, p. 536).

Immediately on receipt of your message I instructed Secretary of State Kissinger to make urgent representations to the Israelis that the continuation of offensive military operations will have most serious consequences for the future of United States–Israel relations. . . . I want to assure you that the United States is unalterably opposed to offensive military action by Israel and is prepared to take effective steps to end them.[114]

But the second cease-fire did not resolve the crisis either. Israel claimed that it had encircled the Egyptian Third Army, there was some continued fighting, and the Soviets were obviously growing increasingly restless, given their apparent commitment to Sadat. Kissinger again warned Dinitz, stressing the need to allow supplies to reach the Third Army. During the day on October 24, tension rose as the Soviet moves outlined above led to the perception of a possible unilateral Soviet action. In mid-afternoon came Sadat's appeal to the superpowers. Kissinger immediately recommended to the President that he firmly rejected the request, reiterating the strong American opposition to any Soviet forces in the Middle East. The President confirmed this response, which was then relayed to Sadat and Dobrynin (Decision 12).[115]

The Soviets persisted, however. Dobrynin called Kissinger at 7:05 P.M., saying that the Soviets would support a Security Council resolution calling for a superpower (i.e., U.S.-Soviet) police force. Kissinger strongly reiterated American opposition to either Soviet or U.S. forces in the area. Then, at 9:25 P.M., came the Brezhnev note, quoted above, which seemed to threaten unilateral Soviet action and brought the crisis to a head.[116]

Kissinger immediately phoned Nixon, suggesting that the United States respond both politically and with military signals. Nixon agreed that a military signal, such as an alert, might be necessary, and the basic framework for a decision was thus laid. Kissinger then assembled three groups of American experts—in Soviet, Middle East, and UN affairs—to evaluate the latest intelligence and probable Soviet intentions. At 10:40 P.M., Kissinger convened a rump "NSC" meeting with only himself and Schlesinger as statutory members. (Since Kissinger held two jobs, it was said that the meeting consisted of Kissinger, Kissinger, and Schlesinger.) Moorer and Colby were present as statutory advisors, and General Brent Scowcroft was

114. Quoted by Heikal, 1975, pp. 257–258.
115. Kalb and Kalb, p. 552; Safran, p. 493; Quandt, 1977, p. 195.
116. Kissinger, 1982, pp. 581–583; Kalb and Kalb, pp. 553–554; Quandt, 1977, p. 196; Nixon, p. 938.

present as Kissinger's deputy. Nixon remained upstairs in the White House. There was no Vice Presidential participation and no Director of the Office of Emergency Preparedness, since both offices were vacant at the time.[117]

Given the indications of a likely Soviet move, the "NSC" decided on a strong response, recommending ("unanimously," as Kissinger took pains to point out) that U.S. military forces be put on DefCon 3 and that a strong message be sent by Nixon to Brezhnev. Haig apparently confirmed the decision for Nixon, and it was carried out during the night (Decision 13).[118] The message to Brezhnev said that unilateral Soviet action would produce "incalculable consequences." It pointed out that violations of the cease-fire were in fact decreasing, and made a conciliatory gesture by accepting the idea that some U.S. and Soviet personnel be attached as observers to a UN force that would not contain superpower contingents.[119]

It has been suggested that the alert was a signal to Israel as well as a response to a likely Soviet move. Given the ongoing pressure exerted by the United States on Israel regarding the issue of the Egyptian Third Army, the alert might be seen as an additional way of forcing Jerusalem to realize that the game was getting too serious. It also presumably provided Israel with a means of stopping without appearing to submit to Soviet pressure.[120] However, other observers, closer to Kissinger, deny that the alert was directed at Israel, at least as a primary motivation, stressing the focus on the perceived Soviet threat.[121] Even if the alert were not aimed at Israel, of course, it

117. Nixon, p. 938; Binder, *New York Times*, November 25, 1973. Kissinger (1982, p. 587) says that the internal records called the meeting a WSAG "Meeting of Principals." The difference is of no practical importance.

118. In Kissinger's account (1982, pp. 585, 587, 593), he and Haig decided initially not to awaken Nixon after Brezhnev's note arrived, and Haig handled "internal White House notifications" after that. Upon briefing Nixon in the morning, Kissinger records, "I did not know what conversations Haig had had with Nixon in the early hours of the morning."

119. Nixon's message is quoted in Nixon, pp. 939–940; see also Kissinger, 1982, pp. 589–591; Kalb and Kalb, pp. 554–556; Quandt, 1977, pp. 196–198; Binder; CBS Reports. In the CBS version, Nixon's ratification was not obtained until 3:00 A.M., three and a half hours after the first orders on the alert were issued. As noted, Schlesinger, in his press conference of October 26, indicated that some advisors thought the probability of Soviet forces being dispatched to the Middle East was "quite low" (*DSB*, November 19, 1973). Nevertheless, it is clear that the dominant perception rated chances of Soviet intervention somewhat higher, and that in any event all were agreed that precautionary moves were in order.

120. Interviews with Zumwalt, Smith, and a senior State Department official; Sheehan, p. 38; Tad Szulc, "Is He Indispensable? Answers to the Kissinger Riddle," *New York*, July 1974, p. 39.

121. Interviews with Moorer, Weiss, and an NSC staff aide.

might have been functional as a signal to the Israeli government, intended or not.

The question of whether the Soviet "nuclear ship" was a factor has been discussed above. As noted, there was a feeling in some intelligence circles that the ship was more important than other factors in the alert decision.[122] But, as also noted, those closest to the decision-making deny its importance. Although the information was apparently available, it was somewhat ambiguous; and the meaning of the Soviet action, even if accepted as fact, was not clear. There was considerable suspicion generally on Soviet motives and intentions, but overwhelmingly on the basis of other actions and evidence.[123]

It was therefore the Brezhnev note, in the context of Soviet military moves, that created the felt need for a firm American response.

Another question is why this particular form of response, global in scope, was adopted. The prevailing opinion is that policy-makers felt the need to underscore to the Soviets that the United States viewed their threat with the utmost seriousness, and was able to act despite Watergate (in line with the conclusion above that Watergate was influential, but as a response to external rather than internal considerations).[124] There is good evidence, however, that the alert was not intended by senior political decision-makers to be as dramatic as it turned out. What was conceived by them as a signal to the Soviet Union, to be picked up first by Soviet intelligence and only gradually to become public knowledge, was blazoned in headlines within hours, partly because of the prevailing political atmosphere.[125] Kissinger himself later admitted that the desired effect might have been better achieved by a selective alert of certain units, rather than by alerting all U.S. forces, but he continued to insist that some kind of alert was necessary. There was also some suggestion that "overreaction" could be a deliberate policy, at least in the sense that, given the gravity of the situation, Kissinger and others preferred erring on the side of overkill rather than inadequacy.[126]

Another question was whether the decision to use an implied threat of nuclear forces was influenced by the lack of conventional capability. The fear of heavy naval losses in the Mediterranean, in the

122. Interview with a senior intelligence official.
123. Interviews with Colby, Moorer, Sonnenfeldt, and NSC staff aides; Quandt, 1977, p. 198; see notes 66 and 67, above.
124. This is particularly stressed in the CBS Reports account, based on interviews with senior defense officials.
125. Interviews with Colby, Hoskinson, and NSC staff aides; Kissinger, 1982, p. 591.
126. For Kissinger's later observations, see CBS Reports; Insight Team, p. 415; Kalb and Kalb, p. 563. On deliberate overreaction, see also Sagan, p. 172.

belief that twenty-three Russian attack submarines were tracking U.S. surface ships at the peak of the crisis, has already been noted.[127] This has been discounted by senior military officials, but critics see the choice made as a reflection not only of the lack of options but also as a smoke screen to conceal what was, in essence, capitulation to Soviet demands that Israel be forced to stop. The nuclear alert presumably made it possible to do this without the appearance of capitulation, though it was itself meaningless, since the threat of nuclear war on behalf of Israeli military success was not credible in any event.[128]

The failure to foresee the likely public reaction, and to realize that such a military alert in such an atmosphere could not be kept quiet, has been attributed by some observers to inexperience and lack of understanding of the implications of a DefCon 3 alert among senior civilian decision-makers.[129] In this regard, it is possible that civilian decision-makers might have been misled by previous experience, as discussed above. Interestingly enough, the senior *military* decision-makers apparently expected the alert to become known quickly and to appear dramatic—but favored it for precisely that reason. In Admiral Moorer's view, it was essential that the message get to the Soviets quickly and publicly. The Joint Chiefs of Staff were consulted, and they agreed with the action contemplated, presumably without illusions about the implications of a worldwide DefCon 3 alert.[130] In any event, as noted, Kissinger was surprised to learn, at 6:30 A.M. on October 25, that the alert was already public knowledge. He was further dismayed by suggestions at his noon press conference that the alert had been motivated by a desire to distract the public from Watergate. The idea that Nixon used the crisis for political reasons was especially ironic in view of the fact—which could hardly be publicized—that Nixon had played little or no role in the night's events. As Kissinger notes laconically, it was an allegation that Nixon "knew better than his critics to have been inherently impossible."[131]

By late on October 25, the tension was beginning to lift. Early in the afternoon, the United States and the Soviet Union both supported passage of Security Council Resolution 340, which, in line with Nixon's earlier suggestion to Brezhnev, called for a UN Emer-

127. CBS Reports; Sicherman, p. 53.

128. Sagan, p. 172. For the thesis on capitulation, Sicherman, p. 53; and interview with Zumwalt.

129. For example, interview with Weiss. Another senior Defense Department official has cast doubt on whether Schlesinger, in particular, understood the implications of a DefCon 3 alert (personal interview).

130. Interviews with Moorer and with General George Brown.

131. Kissinger, 1982, pp. 597–598.

gency Force, without superpower participation, to police the cease-fire (Decision 14). At the same time, both the Egyptian-Israeli and Syrian-Israeli fronts had stabilized, and the fear of unilateral Soviet action had consequently receded.

Thus, with the war in fact ended, there was no longer a strong perception of likely American involvement in hostilities, or of the need to respond within a limited time. There was still a threat to American values in the continuing unstable situation left by the war, but there was no longer a felt need to deal with this threat in a crisis environment. The nuclear alert was terminated on the following day, October 26, marking the passage to the post-crisis period.

CHAPTER TWELVE

26 October 1973 to 18 January 1974

THE ACHIEVEMENT of an effective cease-fire on October 25, 1973, reduced the tension level in the 1973 Middle East crisis considerably. The U.S.-Soviet confrontation was defused, and an overwhelming victory by either side in the fourth Arab-Israeli war had been prevented. But this did not resolve the basic problem of the crisis as it had in 1970; the armies of the warring parties remained entangled, with a special problem on the southern front, where the Egyptian Third Army was entirely cut off. There was a continuing risk of renewed hostilities, which galvanized the United States into an active role to preserve the peace. This process took almost three months of peripatetic diplomacy, dominated by U.S. Secretary of State Kissinger, culminating in a disengagement agreement on the southern front that, at least for the United States, reduced threat perceptions to a non-crisis level.

DECISIONS AND DECISION-MAKERS

Decision Number	Date	Content
15	26 October	Kissinger, with the President's approval, launched a U.S. initiative aimed at saving the Egyptian Third Army and achieving a separation of forces agreement between Israel and Egypt.
16	7 November	Kissinger, after meeting with Egyptian President Anwar Sadat, decided to push for an immediate Egyptian-Israeli agreement on limited measures to stabilize the cease-fire, leaving the separation of forces for a later stage.

17	Mid-November	Kissinger began efforts to organize a multilateral peace conference at Geneva as a formal negotiating framework for future diplomatic moves.
18	Late November	Kissinger put pressure on Israel to slow down the bilateral Egyptian-Israeli negotiations at Kilometer 101 and to save serious disengagement proposals for the Geneva conference.
19	8 January	Nixon approved Kissinger's proposal, after talks with Israeli Defense Minister Moshe Dayan, that Kissinger travel to the Middle East to work out the basic elements of an Egyptian-Israeli disengagement agreement through U.S. mediation, prior to the reconvening of the Geneva conference.
20	12 January	Kissinger decided to attempt to complete an Egyptian-Israeli disengagement agreement while in the Middle East, and began his "shuttle diplomacy" between Cairo and Jerusalem.
21	18 January	President Nixon confirmed a series of U.S. assurances and guarantees to Israel and Egypt as part of the disengagement agreement.

The post-crisis period featured the same decision-makers as the crisis period, but the dominance of the diplomatic process and the choice of negotiating methods gave a peculiar prominence to the U.S. Secretary of State. Also, the return to routine decision-making in Washington meant a lessened role for those brought in by crisis procedures: members of the Washington Special Actions Group (WSAG), defense and military specialists, and intelligence officials. On the other hand, the role of lower-level bureaucrats was enhanced, especially in the State Department and among staff members in State and the National Security Council chosen to accompany Kissinger on his travels, such as Assistant Secretary of State Joseph Sisco (Under Secretary after January 8, 1974) and NSC Aide Harold Saunders.

PSYCHOLOGICAL ENVIRONMENT

Attitudinal Prism

Bonham, Shapiro, and Trumble, in a recent study, conclude that "there was almost no restructuring of beliefs" in the 1973 Arab-

Israeli war, and that the war "tends to support the view that people react to new information by fitting it into pre-existing structures without making any general adjustments."[1] Were the post-war perceptions of U.S. policy-makers in 1973 little changed, in fact, from those held before and during the conflict?

The answer depends on the level of thinking that is examined. On the level of basic values and aims, there was in fact great continuity during and after the war. The aims of preventing general war, containing Soviet influence in the Middle East, protecting the U.S. position in the Arab world, and supporting Israel's survival were no less important at the war's end than previously. The aims of promoting settlement of the Arab-Israeli conflict and securing access to oil were, if anything, of higher value after the war than before. On the other hand, concern about detente with the Soviet Union in the Middle East was clearly now of lower priority.

Likewise, on the level of immediate policy objectives, the end of the war brought a return to objectives pursued prior to the war, with allowance for changed conditions. Averting war again became a preoccupation, especially with the immediate danger of renewed hostilities. Promotion of negotiations was again at the top of the agenda, though the methods and projected venue had changed. Reduction of Arab dependence on the Soviet Union was again an immediate aim; now, however, there was less concern about cooperating with the Soviets in the Middle East and more apparent leverage to work with in excluding them.

However, on the level of perceptions of the external environment, a revolutionary change in beliefs about the Middle East international system took place in the minds of U.S. policy-makers during and immediately after the 1973 war. The Arab states, contrary to previous thinking, did have military options and had to be taken more seriously. They were capable of threatening U.S. interests, and the oil weapon in particular would now have to be factored into American policy on the Arab-Israeli conflict. At the same time, there was an Arab leadership with which the United States could work; towards Sadat in particular there was a radical change of mind.

Furthermore, the change of thinking that took place was supported by a striking consensus among decision-makers. There was broad agreement on policy outline and decisions—despite a broad range of conflicting sympathies, backgrounds, and bureaucratic in-

1. G. Matthew Bonham, Michael J. Shapiro, and Thomas L. Trumble, "The October War: Changes in Cognitive Orientation Toward the Middle East Conflict," *International Studies Quarterly*, 23 (March 1979), 3, 43.

terests, heated discussions over particular tactical choices, and the pressures of crisis conditions. As one close observer noted:

> Individuals from widely different backgrounds agreed on each of the major decisions.... Perhaps if the policies had been less nuanced, less complex, there might have been some overt dissension within the bureaucracy. The Nixon-Kissinger policy, however, could be seen as pro-Israeli, pro-Arab, pro-detente, or anti-Soviet, depending on what one was looking for. Those who disagreed with one element of policy were likely to support other aspects.[2]

The "new consensus" had, therefore, a broad base of support, and it is not surprising to find many elements of it reflected in the thinking and policies of post-Kissinger U.S. Middle Eastern policy. There were a number of specific elements in the new prevailing view of the Middle East:

1. *The Assumption that War Cannot Be Deterred by a Strong Israeli Military Position.* The September 1970 crisis had seemed to show that Israeli military power was one of the keys to stability in the Middle East, and U.S. policy had accepted the conception of deterrence, based on Israeli strength, leading to a political settlement as military options were convincingly closed. But the 1973 war showed that the military options were not closed. As Egypt's Mohammed Heikal noted regarding Kissinger, "in his estimate, the facts of power take precedence over all other factors and calculations relative to crises."[3] Arab states had demonstrated their ability to challenge the status quo by force; this shift in the power realities had to be recognized. The Arab success in achieving surprise, in launching coordinated attacks, in achieving Arab solidarity and Soviet support, and in successfully using the oil weapon for the first time all indicated a new military calculus in the Arab-Israeli theater, posing considerably greater risks when the political dissatisfaction of Arab states was high.

   One immediate consequence of this revised view was a continued sense of the dangers in the post-war situation. Though the termination of the war in a "balanced" fashion did, in the minds of U.S. policy-makers, create a more promising diplomatic climate, the way in which the forces of the two sides were entangled created a high risk of renewed hostilities at any

2. William B. Quandt, *Decade of Decisions: American Policy Toward the Arab-Israeli Conflict, 1967–1976* (Berkeley: University of California Press, 1977), pp. 204–205.

3. Quoted in Edward R. F. Sheehan, *The Arabs, Israelis, and Kissinger: A Secret History of American Diplomacy in the Middle East* (New York: Reader's Digest Press, 1976), p. 59. See also Sheehan's own observations, pp. 11–14; Quandt, 1977, p. 201; and Henry Kissinger, *Years of Upheaval* (Boston: Little, Brown, 1982), p. 565 et passim.

moment. This contributed to Kissinger's desire to produce some results at an early date, though he basically envisioned a negotiating process of several years and urged Arabs to be realistic about the time required to achieve meaningful diplomatic results. There was a temptation for Egypt, in particular, to renew hostilities in the south in order to "solve" the problem of the Third Army and the Israeli presence on the west bank of the Suez Canal. This created a sense of urgency for U.S. policy-makers.[4]

2. *The Belief that U.S. Interests Would Be Seriously Threatened if There Were No Movement in Middle East Diplomacy.* Given the perception that war could not be deterred by military balance alone, the corollary was that political progress was necessary in order to ensure stability, which was still seen as the key U.S. interest. This was reinforced by the presence of the oil weapon and by the still-pending oil embargo, which became a more important element in U.S. thinking during the post-crisis period (even though Kissinger showed himself sensitive to the image of the U.S. seeming to submit to oil blackmail, and claimed that he would have pursued an active role in Arab-Israeli negotiations in any event).[5] The perception of the necessity of progress in Arab-Israeli negotiations was also accompanied by a sense of greater opportunity for doing so than in the past. The prevailing sense was that now was the time, that all the necessary elements were finally present, and that such opportunities came only rarely. Everyone seemed to be looking to the United States, which was perceived as holding most of the cards.[6] And even a skeptic such as Heikal recognized that "Henry Kissinger is serious in his search for a solution."[7]

3. *The Belief that Diplomatic Movement in the Middle East Would Require a Central and Active U.S. Role.* That Arabs and Israelis unaided would not be able to bridge the enormous gap between their respective positions had long been an article of faith in Middle Eastern diplomacy. There was also a new disillusionment over the Soviet role, as well as reinforced skepticism regarding the potential contributions of either the United Nations or America's European allies (since resentment over the European lack of support lingered after the war and led the Nixon

    4. Quandt, 1977, pp. 212–213; Anwar El-Sadat, *In Search of Identity: An Auto-biography* (New York: Harper and Row, 1977), pp. 268–269; Kissinger, 1982, p. 601.
    5. Quandt, "Kissinger and the Arab-Israel Disengagement Negotiations," *Journal of International Affairs,* 9 (Spring 1975), 45. The growing impact of the oil embargo after the war in decision-making circles is noted by most of the participants interviewed.
    6. Interview with David Korn, Country Director, Lebanon, Jordan, Syria, and Iraq, Department of State; Quandt, 1977, pp. 207–208. Kissinger (1982, p. 750): "We had the stronger hand; we played it."
    7. Quoted in Sheehan, p. 59.

administration to the determination that European wishes would not be allowed to limit U.S. policy options in the Middle East).[8]

The position and power of the United States were regarded as unique, and the way in which the war was terminated seemed to give the United States credit with both sides as a potential intermediary. No other party was equipped to play this essential role, and therefore, in terms of its own interests and the interest of peace in the Middle East, there was no alternative to an activist U.S. policy that departed sharply from the "wait and see" posture of the preceding years. The United States would have to become dramatically committed to a solution of the Arab-Israeli conflict, or at least to meaningful steps in that direction.

4. *The Perception that Comprehensive or Multilateral Approaches Would Lead to Stalemate.* Kissinger in particular believed that linking initial diplomatic steps to the nature of a final agreement was a recipe for failure. He recalled the reception of the ill-fated Rogers Plan of 1969 as a case in point. It was simply premature to tackle the basic issues in the Middle East conflict; the problem would have to be divided into manageable segments, and a basis of trust built gradually by taking the more soluble issues and the more tractable parties first. Kissinger envisioned a step-by-step approach, mainly on a bilateral basis with the United States in the middle.

In the circumstances, this meant diplomatic methods that maximized the U.S.-Egyptian connection while minimizing the Soviet ability to disrupt. After a formal effort at a multilateral Geneva forum, shuttle diplomacy and disengagement agreements came to fit these purposes splendidly.[9] These lessons were reinforced in the minds of policy-makers by the apparent ease of the Egyptian-Israeli disengagement agreement; there was little need to apply pressure on either party, since each demonstrated a strong need for the agreement.[10]

5. *A New Perception of Israeli Vulnerability, and of the Necessity of Israeli Concessions as a Key to Diplomatic Progress.* A new picture of Israel had emerged by the end of the war. As Kissinger expressed it in December:

> The country has gone through a great psychological trauma. On October 5, its position was unassailable—militarily invulnerable, diplomatically untouchable. Three weeks later, all that had

8. On Europe see Linda Miller, *The Limits of Alliance: America, Europe, and the Middle East,* Jerusalem Papers on Peace Problems, No. 10 (Jerusalem: Hebrew University, 1974), p. 21.

9. Interviews with Korn and with Helmut Sonnenfeldt, NSC staff aide; Kissinger, 1982, pp. 799–805.

10. Sheehan, p. 112. On Kissinger's conception of step-by-step diplomacy, see Quandt, 1977, p. 209; and John Stoessinger, *Henry Kissinger: The Anguish of Power* (New York: 1976), pp. 190–193.

changed. It was heartbreaking to go there and see how totally
dependent Israel is on the United States.[11]

However "heartbreaking" the increased Israeli dependence
was, however, it was also seen as a means of exerting leverage in
the diplomatic battles to come, and thus represented an
important new perception in the situation. In the past, there was
a perceived common U.S. and Israeli interest in preserving the
status quo and in either preventing a war or in winning quickly.
This was undermined by the 1973 war, which also raised Israeli
aid demands and inflicted high costs on the United States in its
Arab relations and in its access to secure oil supplies. Israel now
had to take a new approach, as American policy-makers saw it,
based on the view that continued holding of Arab lands was, as
Kissinger put it, a "shortsighted" approach to security.[12]

Israeli leaders quickly discovered in post-war diplomacy that
the United States was no longer interested in the Israeli version
of *quid pro quo* bargaining over specific issues: "The United
States sought to trade off the Israeli assets for the establishment
and reinforcement of American influence in Egypt in order to
advance peace, avert war, and remove the Arab oil embargo."[13]
Pressure on Israel was already apparent as the war ended in
clashes over resupply of the Egyptian Third Army and in
imposition of the six-point agreement on November 11.
Kissinger, for example, was "incensed" over his talks with Golda
Meir on November 1, declaring in a WSAG meeting that the
reduction of Soviet influence and an end to the oil embargo
depended on U.S. pursuit of a moderate peace settlement.
Otherwise, he felt, Arab states would turn back to the Soviets.
Israel would therefore have to accept what the United States
considered reasonable: "Anger at Israeli intransigence was
genuine and would be displayed repeatedly in succeeding
months."[14] On December 13, Nixon reportedly told a group of
Governors: "The only way we're going to solve the crisis is to
end the oil embargo, and the only way we're going to end the
embargo is to get the Israelis to act reasonable. I hate to use the
word blackmail, but we've got to do some things to get them to
behave."[15]

6. *A New Perception of Egypt as the Key to Diplomatic Progress.*
The U.S. opening to Egypt preceded the Middle East war of
1973, but the full evolution in American thinking about Egypt
and Sadat came only with the first meeting between Kissinger

11. Richad Valeriani, *Travels With Henry* (Boston: Houghton Mifflin, 1979), p. 198;
also, Kissinger, 1982, pp. 560–567.

12. Shlomo Aronson, *Conflict and Bargaining in the Middle East: An Israeli Perspective* (Baltimore and London: Johns Hopkins University Press, 1978), pp. 169–170.

13. Nadav Safran, *Israel: The Embattled Ally* (Cambridge: Harvard University
Press, 1978), p. 508.

14. Quandt, 1977, p. 216. See also Matti Golan, *The Secret Conversations of Henry
Kissinger: Step-by-Step Diplomacy in the Middle East* (New York: Bantam, 1976), pp.
103–104; Kissinger, 1982, pp. 621–624.

15. *Washington Post,* December 22, 1973.

and Sadat on November 7. By all accounts, this meeting was crucial in recasting the U.S. diplomatic strategy in the Middle East. Sadat overruled his own advisors, accepting Kissinger's proposal to subsume the issue of a return to the October 22 lines in the framework of future disengagement talks, and accepted a temporary stabilization of the conflict (the six-point agreement) with only trivial changes. Sadat and Kissinger spent three hours in private discussing a common overall strategy in the area. Kissinger emerged with a view of Sadat as a statesman, not a clown: "From that meeting onward, I knew I was dealing with a great man."[16] Consequently, Kissinger grasped the chance to shape a new policy built more on regional forces—Egypt in particular—and less tied to global factors such as U.S.-USSR relations. As one of Kissinger's top aides later explained:

> Kissinger made a judgment at that first meeting with Sadat that this was a man on whom we could build our peace strategy. This was the only person who seemed to understand our conceptual approach. . . . He instinctively saw the qualities in the man and the opportunities in the situation, and in his mind, he made a decision on the spot. He was not hampered by preconceptions. He could make a very quick adjustment and exploit the moment, exploit the opportunity.[17]

The idea of a global arrangement covering the Middle East faded; Kissinger told the Israelis that Egypt would be the focus of his new approach, which was based on building a community of interest with local actors.[18] In other discussions with Israelis, Kissinger seemed to be "truly charmed" by Sadat, refusing to take seriously any evidence (such as continued Egyptian shelling of Israeli forces) that countered his belief in Sadat's moderation.[19] In Kissinger's view, Sadat had several advantages in the immediate post-war situation that he might have used to demand much more than an interim settlement. The fact that he did not do so showed him to be a man of vision.[20]

There is some evidence that Kissinger's assessment of Egypt's position in fact overrated the Egyptian bargaining position. Kissinger was consistently outguessed by the Israelis on whether Egypt would accept certain proposals, with the Israelis arguing that Sadat would consent because of military and economic pressures and Kissinger doubting that the Egyptian President was that desperate. The first case regarded proposals for military talks after the cease-fire, which the Egyptians immediately accepted despite Kissinger's feeling that they would not. A second occasion occurred when Sadat accepted the Israeli position on the six-point proposal in early November, and, as

16. Kissinger, 1982, p. 646.
17. Quoted in Valeriani, p. 253. Also: Sheehan, p. 50; interviews with two State Department Middle East specialists; Mohammed Heikal, *The Road to Ramadan* (New York: Ballantine, 1975), p. 263.
18. Aronson, pp. 200–204.
19. Golan, p. 172.
20. Aronson, p. 224.

Israeli foreign minister Abba Eban recounted, "Kissinger
magnanimously admitted Israel had shown a clearer perception
of Egyptian attitudes than the United States."[21] Finally, during
the January shuttle, the Egyptians again made a key concession
that Kissinger had predicted they would refuse.[22] To judge from
the evidence, Kissinger considered Egypt's position considerably
stronger than the Israelis did—and perhaps stronger than Sadat
himself did.

Also, there are indications that the focus on Egypt led to a
certain lack of attention toward other Arab states, at least the
non-oil-producing states. Kissinger apparently assumed that
Jordan, for example, could be dealt with in due time. Aside from
urging Israel to do something to strengthen Hussein on the West
Bank, he paid no immediate attention to the Israel-Jordan front,
for which he was criticized in some quarters.[23]

7. *The Perception of the Increased Importance of the Oil-Producing
Arab States.* Having failed to foresee the successful use of the oil
weapon, American policy-makers in the post-war period still
demonstrated no clear conception on how to deal with it. Nixon
and Kissinger maintained consistently that the energy problem
would exist even without the Middle East war, and would exist
after the oil embargo was lifted.[24] Yet, in fact, and despite their
formal disclaimers, the American policy-makers accepted the
linkage between oil and the Arab-Israeli conflict. Kissinger once
hinted publicly at countermeasures,[25] but basically the American
response was an assiduous cultivation of Saudi Arabia and other
oil-producing states. Kissinger visited Saudi Arabia in November
and December 1973, and initiated attempts to use the Saudi
need of U.S. technology as a *quid pro quo* in dealing with the oil
crisis. This led eventually to a vast commitment to building a
Saudi infrastructure.[26] In the estimation of the U.S. Ambassador
to Saudi Arabia, James Akins, the United States compensated for
its previous underestimation of the Saudis by tending, after the
oil embargo, to overestimate them—forgetting that it was
dealing with a small country, circumscribed by very real limits
and not in an overall position of strength.[27]

As mentioned in Chapter Ten, there were also claims that
the United States government had already adopted a policy of
quietly accepting price increases, which were seen as more of a

21. Abba Eban, *An Autobiography* (New York: Random House, 1977), p. 539.
22. Golan, pp. 93–94, 112, 164.
23. Sheehan, p. 100.
24. For example, Kissinger in his press conference on January 3, 1974, *DSB*,
January 28, 1974.
25. At his press conference on November 21, 1973, Kissinger said: "It is clear that
if pressures continue unreasonably and indefinitely, then the United States will have
to consider what countermeasures it may have to take. We would do this with enormous reluctance, and we are still hopeful that matters will not reach this point." *DSB*,
December 10, 1973.
26. Sheehan, pp. 75–76.
27. Interview with Akins.

threat to Europe than to the United States. According to these reports, this tendency was reinforced after the embargo by the push to improve relations with the oil-producing states, leading the administration to turn down European "get tough" proposals. Akins has claimed that Washington did not respond to his cables on possible Saudi interest in lower oil prices in early 1974, and that he eventually came to realize that Kissinger was not strongly opposed to high oil prices.[28] This is disputed by others, and the evidence is not conclusive, but it is at least apparent that any effort to roll back the huge price increases of October–December 1973, if it indeed existed, was a very low priority, and that this hesitation to battle the oil price increases was connected to a general tendency to follow a very solicitous policy toward Saudi Arabia and other oil-producing states.

8. *The Perception of the Decreased Importance of Cooperation with the Soviet Union in the Middle East.* Disillusionment with Soviet behavior during the war, culminating in the nuclear alert confrontation of October 24–25, led to a post-war attitude that detente was no longer the main yardstick of U.S.-Soviet relations in the Middle East, and that the United States should act so as to minimize the Soviet role in Middle Eastern diplomacy. There was no longer confidence that detente was effective in limiting local conflicts, and it seemed clear that Moscow would exploit such situations and might even act rashly—as it seemed to have acted in the Middle East war—during moments of crisis. There were obviously strict limits to the "global" approach in the Middle East.[29]

All this was reinforced by the opening to Sadat, who apparently pushed for a common U.S.-Egyptian strategy for expelling Soviet influence from the area.[30] Kissinger also saw that success in his diplomatic approach depended on minimizing the Soviet role, since Arab states would not accept partial agreements if the Soviets were putting their own schemes for a total settlement on the agenda. It therefore "certainly crossed his mind" that the shuttle style of diplomacy would limit Soviet ability to interfere, though he also recognized that the Soviets would have to be part of the process at some stage.[31]

This did not mean that Kissinger was now completely reversing his priorities and subordinating U.S.-USSR relations to U.S. interests in the Middle East. The global context of U.S. policy was still the basis of the Kissingerian world view, and the Middle East was only one element in the spectrum of U.S.-Soviet relations. In December, for example, Kissinger urged Israel to

28. V. H. Oppenheim, "Why Oil Prices Go Up (1)—The Past: We Pushed Them," *Foreign Policy,* 25 (Winter 1976–1977), 39–40, 42–43; interview with Akins.

29. See the discussion in Harvey Sicherman, *The Yom Kippur War: End of Illusion?* The Foreign Policy Papers, Vol. 1, No. 4 (Beverly Hills and London: Sage Publications, 1976), especially p. 75.

30. Sheehan, pp. 88–89.

31. Interview with Sonnenfeldt; Kissinger, 1982, pp. 747–749.

use its influence with American Jews in order to help defeat the Jackson-Vanik Amendment, which would in turn preserve detente and gain the cooperation of the Soviet Union elsewhere.[32] And while condemning Soviet actions during the war on the grounds that Moscow could not have "selective detente," Kissinger also reiterated that relations with the Soviet Union had to be judged across the board, and he later praised Soviet behavior at the two-day Geneva conference in December and in support of the January disengagement agreement.[33]

Was there a fundamental change? At the beginning of this section, I asked whether there was any basic restructuring of beliefs among U.S. policy-makers after the 1973 Middle East war. By differentiating the levels of conceptualization, my analysis shows fairly clearly that there *was* a restructuring of beliefs. While basic values and objectives remained essentially unchanged, perceptions of the external environment had shifted considerably by the post-crisis period. Beliefs about events and forces in the international system were characterized by fluidity and adaptation to new conditions; at the war's end, there was a watershed change in American policy-makers' perceptions of the Middle East and in their substantive policies toward the area. On the whole, and in contradiction to much of the psychological literature that postulates conceptual rigidity under crisis conditions, the perceptions in this case appear analytic, pragmatic, and rational.

Of course, if one probes deeply enough, there is a level on which few changes are likely: basic values do not change readily. But of what importance is this fact? Is it reasonable to expect radical changes of basic value systems in every crisis? So long as perceptions of the real world and operational decisions are sensitive to new information, is it significant that basic predispositions were not fundamentally restructured? Also, it is unrealistic to expect *all* beliefs to change; this assumes that in any crisis all previous beliefs will turn out to be incorrect. Bonham, Shapiro, and Trumble cite as evidence of continuity of beliefs the fact that from 43 to 89 percent of perceived relationships among policy-makers interviewed were perceived similarly before and after the war by the policy-makers interviewed. One could easily argue in reverse that a 57 (or even an 11) percent change in perceived relationships is in fact a revolutionary reordering of thinking.[34] Quandt, in this case a participant as well as an academic analyst, has summarized the change in the attitudinal

32. Golan, pp. 172–173.
33. See the Kissinger press conferences of December 27, 1973 (*DSB*, January 21, 1974), and January 22, 1974 (*DSB*, February 11, 1974).
34. Bonham, Shapiro, and Trumble, pp. 40–43.

prism of U.S. policy-makers following the 1973 Middle Eastern war in the following words:

> Crises, by their very nature, expose prevailing assumptions about reality in particularly acute ways. Faced with surprise, danger and uncertainty, decision makers act on the basis of previously formulated conceptions of reality. When reality no longer conforms to these images, and under great pressures of time and events, policy makers are likely to restructure their perceptions with extraordinary speed. Impending failure or danger, much like a hanging, clears the mind. Pieces of the puzzle are quickly rearranged, and new policies are tried. If the crisis is resolved successfully, the revised or restructured image is likely to endure for some time; lessons will be drawn; and a new policy framework will emerge and will guide action until the next failure or crisis. The October war was therefore doubly important as an object of study, for it revealed the underlying assumptions of American policy toward the Arab-Israeli conflict from 1970 to 1973 and produced a major revision of those assumptions within a very short period.[35]

Images

KISSINGER

The images revealed in public statements by Henry Kissinger, the dominant decision-maker in the post-crisis period, are an important index to the thinking described above as an attitudinal prism. Analysis of these statements generally confirms the attitudinal prism as described, with minor variations of emphasis and nuance due to personal idiosyncrasies. During the post-crisis period, Kissinger held six press conferences, delivered one address, and released one public statement. These documents include a total of 194 statements of belief, of which 181 (93 percent) fall into three major categories. Taking these categories in order:

Peace Negotiations. About half of Kissinger's statements (ninety-eight, or 51 percent) deal with the importance, methods, or substance of peace negotiations in the Arab-Israeli conflict, reflecting the new priorities in post-war perceptions. Taking the individual perceptions within this category specifically:

1. *Kissingerian Negotiating Methods* (forty-two statements). This includes statements spelling out the preferred role of the United States as a mediator making a major effort to help the parties narrow their differences, though not by imposing its own will on them (fifteen statements). A second group of statements

35. Quandt, 1977, p. 165.

expresses a recognition of the difficulties, calling attention to the need for a long slow process carried out in stages, with the Egyptian-Israeli disengagement agreement as a necessary first step; these statements constitute, generally, a defense of the gradualist approach to Middle East diplomacy (thirteen statements). Finally, other statements put a stress on not predetermining the results of diplomacy, and on the need to let negotiations develop without pushing particular proposals or procedures at an early stage (eleven statements).

2. *The Importance of Progress Toward a Final Settlement* (twenty-three statements). This includes statements that a military solution has been shown to be impossible, and expressions of the general importance of a peaceful resolution to the conflict, including the role and importance of the Geneva conference.

3. *The Elements of a Final Settlement* (fifteen statements). While refraining from spelling out particulars, Kissinger did mention certain basic guidelines that he viewed as essential to an Arab-Israeli peace: Israeli territorial withdrawals from areas occupied in 1967 (five statements), provisions for Israeli security (five statements), and possible guarantees by outside parties, including the United States (five statements).

4. *The Danger of a Renewal of Hostilities* (seven statements). This includes references to the dangerous situation left by the Yom Kippur War and the need to stabilize the cease-fire arrangements that ended it.

5. *Optimism on Future Negotiations* (five statements). In these declarations, Kissinger referred to changes wrought by the war that created new opportunities for diplomatic progress toward a final resolution, and he expressed some degree of optimism on the chances for success now as opposed to the past.

Energy. The second major area of concern for Kissinger in the post-war period, to judge from his public expressions, was energy issues, accounting for fifty-five (28 percent) of his statements. As indicated, this represented a sharp contrast with his earlier priorities and a clear reflection of the increasing impact of the oil embargo. The specific perceptions were:

1. *The General Nature of the Energy Crisis* (twelve statements). In these references, there was stress on the energy crisis as a long-term issue, predating the war and not a direct result of it, which would remain a crisis long after the results of the war were liquidated. The energy crisis was described as the result of national and worldwide trends on energy supply and demand, requiring the urgent action of the U.S. government with or without the immediate impetus of the oil embargo. Kissinger resisted efforts to explain the energy crisis as a function of U.S. political relations with the Arab world.

2. *Dangers of Uncoordinated Responses* (ten statements). Kissinger condemned the tendency of oil-consuming nations to engage in unrestrained competition for the oil available, claiming that such actions intensified the crisis for all concerned and prevented the development of an effective strategy for coping with it.

3. *The Embargo No Longer Justified* (ten statements). Kissinger repeated, in a variety of formulations, the idea that while the United States could "understand" the Arab oil embargo directed against it during the war, this embargo was no longer "appropriate" to circumstances after the war. He reminded his listeners that the United States was taking the lead in finding a diplomatic solution to the Arab-Israeli impasse, and thus deserved better treatment from the oil-producing states.

4. *The Impact of High Oil Prices* (nine statements). The quadrupling of oil prices by oil-producing states during the October–December 1973 period was described as a serious threat to the financial health and stability of the entire world, including the producing countries themselves. This threat must be met by all countries cooperatively, and Kissinger saw a common interest in stabilizing oil prices in such a way that both consumers and producers were protected and disruptions to the world economy minimized.

5. *The U.S. Policy in the Arab-Israeli Dispute Not Influenced by Pressure from Oil Producers* (five statements). Kissinger denied publicly that the United States was linking its stance in Arab-Israeli diplomacy and its response to the oil embargo— even when private statements indicated the contrary. The United States could not, in his publicly expressed view, make specific commitments on Arab-Israeli issues in order to get the embargo lifted, "because it would make our foreign policy then entirely subject to the producing nations' decisions and would set up an endless cycle."[36] (In another five statements, not expressly tied to energy issues, Kissinger asserted that U.S. policy generally would not be set by "pressures," but rather by national interests and the interest of world peace.)

U.S.-Soviet Relations. The third major focus in Kissinger's public expressions was the Soviet Union and U.S.-Soviet relations, both globally and in the Middle East. This accounted for twenty-eight statements, or 14 percent of the total. This represents less of a focus than before the war, reflecting the disillusionment with the Soviet Union, the greater attention paid to local factors, and the beginning of a diplomatic process focused on regional actors and excluding the Soviet Union. A breakdown of these perceptions also shows the continuing Kissinger perception of Soviet relations as a mixture

36. Press conference of January 3, 1974, *DSB,* January 28, 1974.

of conflict and cooperation, since negative and positive statements are of about equal frequency:

1. *A Negative View of the Soviet Role in the Middle East* (nine statements). In these statements, the Soviet Union is accused of seeking unilateral advantages in the Middle East, or is warned that if it remains uncooperative the United States will proceed in Middle East diplomacy without Soviet participation, or references are made generally to the desirability of reducing Soviet influence in the area.

2. *The Importance of Cooperation with the Soviet Union* (eight statements). On the other hand, Kissinger made an almost equal number of references to the importance of cooperation with the Soviet Union in pursuing American goals in the area, given the importance of the Soviet Union in the Middle East and its ability to obstruct any arrangements negotiated if it is not included in the negotiating process.

3. *The Importance of Preventing Superpower Clashes* (six statements). Despite the diminished focus on detente, Kissinger still called attention to the need of preventing conflict between the United States and the Soviet Union in the Middle East, as well as the overriding concern of preventing nuclear war as an outgrowth of embroilment in local rivalries.

4. *The Continuing Importance of Detente* (three statements). Though remaining low-key and qualifying his remarks with a recognition of the limits of detente in dealing with such divisive issues as the Arab-Israeli conflict, Kissinger still made some mention of the continuing importance and validity of detente in overall U.S.-Soviet relations.

In concluding this picture of Kissinger's images, note should also be made of the items of low priority. There were only four references to Palestinians or the "Palestinian question" as an issue in the conflict, and only one to the "so-called Palestine Liberation Organization." There was only one mention of the role of the United Nations in Middle East diplomacy, and only one to disappointment over European behavior in the oil crisis. Similarly, there was one reference apiece to the goal of energy independence and the possibility of arms limitation in the area. Finally, there was only one hint of countermeasures against the Arab oil embargo, in a press conference on December 10, 1973, and even this mention was minimized at the next opportunity.[37]

37. Press conferences of November 21, 1973, and December 6, 1973, in *DSB*, December 10 and 24, 1973.

NIXON

Nixon's lower level of participation in American decision-making during the post-crisis period was reflected in the lesser number of public statements on the Middle East that he made during these days. There were references to the Middle East in two Presidential addresses, two public statements, one press conference, and two public letters signed by the President. These include a total of thirty-two statements of belief relevant to the Middle East, mostly along lines of themes already identified above:

1. The general nature of the energy crisis (nine statements).

2. The goal of U.S. energy independence (six statements).

3. The importance of progress toward a final settlement (six statements).

4. The necessity of common action on energy (corresponding to Kissinger's statements on the impact of high oil prices and the dangers of uncoordinated responses) (four statements).

5. The indispensable role of the United States as mediator (three statements).

6. The importance of preventing superpower clashes (one statement).

As compared to Kissinger, Nixon put much more stress on energy issues (nineteen of thirty-two statements, or 59 percent of all Middle East–related statements, as opposed to 28 percent for Kissinger). Also, there was much more stress on general issues, especially the goal of energy independence, which was scarcely mentioned by Kissinger. Kissinger focused more on specific aspects of the issue: ending the embargo, or not allowing linkage between energy and Arab-Israeli diplomacy.

Nixon also put less stress on peace negotiations—nine of thirty-two statements, or 28 percent as against 51 percent for Kissinger. And these statements tended to be more general than Kissinger's, focusing mostly on the importance of progressing to a final settlement or the general necessity of U.S. action, whereas Kissinger spelled out the role of the United States and devoted much more attention to methods and substantive elements of negotiations. Both of these issues (energy and peace negotiations) confirm a picture of Nixon remaining more in the background, focusing on general outlines and long-term issues, while Kissinger was intensely involved in specific policy problems and had more of a day-to-day perspective.

Finally, and curiously in view of his general reputation, Nixon seemed even less concerned with the Soviet Union than Kissinger was, making only one public mention of the Soviet role in the Middle East during the post-crisis period. One obvious explanation for this is that Nixon, like Kissinger, came out of the war more attuned to regional factors and less inclined to see the Middle East as a function of U.S.-Soviet relations. But this may also reflect the higher level of generality on which Nixon was dealing with the Middle East, and his continued distraction during this period with the aftermath of the "Saturday night massacre" and other Watergate-related troubles.[38]

DECISION FLOW

As can be deduced from the foregoing, the immediate policy aims of the United States in the post-crisis period were:

1. Removing the danger of a renewal of war.
2. Getting a diplomatic process under way, with the help of Sadat (and the Syrians if possible).
3. Reducing the Soviet role in the process (with less concern for detente, given the disillusionment of the war).
4. Ending the oil embargo.

Consequently, as indicated in the discussion of the attitudinal prism, U.S. policy-makers made a number of new departures in overall U.S. strategy.

To summarize:

1. There was a much more active American diplomatic role, pushing immediate stabilizing measures for the conflict. Since results were now more important, there was also an emphasis on realistic procedures: taking the easier issues first, avoiding public diplomacy, and not spelling out final peace plans or detailed American proposals publicly. Kissinger tried to avoid the "Rogers Plan" model, and the essence of this approach was precisely that initial diplomatic steps were *not* linked in any way to a final peace agreement, a technique that made his achievements possible, even though it was roundly condemned by the purists, who pointed out—as though it were *ipso facto* a

38. This is, as in the crisis period, reflected by Nixon's own account of Middle East events during these days, which is generally quite thin as history and is overwhelmed with detailed references to his political tribulations. See Richard Nixon, *RN: The Memoirs of Richard Nixon* (New York: Grosset and Dunlap, 1978), pp. 940–982.

major revelation of shortcoming—that the basic issues of the conflict were being postponed.[39]

2. New diplomatic methods were also employed. Negotiations were carried out more directly, in bilateral rather than multilateral forums, working with the more moderate parties first. The United States took an active middleman role, and the Soviet Union (as well as more recalcitrant Arab parties) were increasingly excluded.

3. The American diplomatic strategy was radically different. The United States now attempted to trade substantial Israeli concessions for an Arab agreement to stabilize the conflict, using as leverage the increased Israeli dependence on the United States. Kissinger was repeatedly quoted as telling Arab leaders that they could get weapons from the Soviet Union, but that only the United States could get them their territory back.[40]

4. Consequently, there was greater pressure on Israel and— formally or informally—linkage between military supply of Israel and Israeli cooperation with American-sponsored diplomatic efforts. (There had been such linkage in the past, but not generally during the 1970–1973 period, when Israel was seen as a strategic asset and Israeli deterrence of Arab attack as the key to stability.) Before the war, Israel and the U.S. had a common interest and policy in preserving the status quo and in preventing war or winning it very quickly; this was undermined by the Yom Kippur war.[41]

5. Egypt (and to some extent Saudi Arabia) became the focus of a vigorous American thrust into the Arab world. As Sheehan puts it, the United States for the first time had a "coherent Arab policy," based on a quasi-alliance with Cairo, the assumption that other Arab states would follow Sadat, avoidance of the Palestinian question, and the use of American technology as a *quid pro quo*.[42]

6. Finally, there was a much more active concern about access to oil, expressed in continuing efforts to appease the Saudis. Though there was no formal admission of a linkage between energy issues and the Arab-Israeli conflict, and the United States continued to separate the two issues in theory,[43] American policy accepted the linkage de facto and sought to trade

39. Quandt, 1977, pp. 208–209. Foremost among the "purists" were Sheehan, George Ball (in numerous writings), Zbigniew Brzezinski (in his pre–White House writings), and most of the State Department and DOD Middle East specialsts inter-viewed for this research.

40. For example, Kalb and Kalb, p. 567; Kissinger, 1982, p. 638.

41. Aronson, pp. 169–170; interview with Samuel Hoskinson, National Intelli-gence Officer for the 1973 War.

42. Sheehan, pp. 13–14; interview with William Hyland, Bureau of Intelligence and Research, Department of State.

43. See *DSB*, January 28, 1974; February 4, 1974.

progress on Arab-Israeli issues for better relations with
oil-producing states.

Thus, to a great extent, U.S. policy choices during this period were
a matter of general orientation rather than of discrete, identifiable
decisions. Furthermore, most elements were in place by the time the
war ended, and actions in the post-crisis period were therefore a
matter of fine-tuning and execution. For example, already at the
time of the first cease-fire (October 22), Kissinger informed the Israelis of his plans for a Geneva conference, under the chairmanship of
the United States and the Soviet Union, which would have an opening session before the Israeli elections at the end of the year.[44] In fact,
this is precisely what happened. But the predetermination of the
general strategy, and the central role of a single individual making
subtle tactical choices almost daily, make it difficult to single out
moments of "decision." It is difficult to say precisely when Kissinger
(and thus the United States) "decided" to push vigorously for a multilateral conference at Geneva as an initial negotiating step.

Nevertheless, some clear decision points can be identified. The
first of these was precipitated by the way in which the war ended.
The second cease-fire left the Egyptian Third Army encircled, and
Washington had already set a policy of preventing Israeli destruction
of this force in order to show Sadat the benefits of working with the
United States (Decision 11, Chapter Eleven).[45] The Israeli expectation, naturally, was to use this military advantage as a bargaining card
on such issues as the release of prisoners and post-war disengagement. The Egyptians, of course, demanded a return to the positions
held at the time of the first cease-fire, before the Third Army was
encircled. The United States wanted, minimally, to assure resupply
of the Third Army so that a new crisis would be averted, while
searching for a formula that would encompass both the preservation
of the Third Army and the issue of a return to the October 22 lines.

The issue of resupply was urgent already by October 26, as the
Soviets reportedly told the United States that they would resupply
the Egyptian Third Army on their own if Israel did not allow supplies
to reach it.[46] As Israeli Defense Minister Moshe Dayan has recounted, there were a series of telephone calls between Washington

44. Eban, pp. 532–533.

45. This policy was described by one participant in Washington Special Actions
Group (WSAG) discussions as using the Egyptian Third Army as a "pawn" in the
opening to Egypt (personal interview); see Kissinger, 1982, pp. 601–611.

46. The Insight Team of the London Sunday Times, *The Yom Kippur War* (Garden
City, N.Y.: Doubleday, 1974), p. 433; Walter Laqueur, *Confrontation: The Middle East
and World Politics* (New York: Bantam, 1974), p. 214; Moshe Dayan, *Story of My Life*
(New York: William Morrow, 1976), p. 544.

and Jerusalem during the day, with Washington adopting a tone "that could not be described as the acme of civility," and with Kissinger demanding that Israel open supply routes to the Third Army.[47] This pressure, a direct outgrowth of the policy initiated by Decision 11 during the crisis period, culminated in an American "ultimatum" involving a threat to allow the Soviets to resupply the Egyptians on their own, as Moscow had hinted that they might, or alternately for the United States itself to supply the Third Army.[48] In any event, Israel agreed to allow a one-time convoy of nonmilitary supplies to pass through its lines to the Egyptians. This provided a temporary respite, but left the basic problem unresolved.

Therefore, Kissinger, while attempting to find a temporary resolution to the problem of pressure on the Egyptians, also launched a diplomatic initiative to disentangle the two armies from the dangerous cease-fire lines created by the war, a step that would subsume the Third Army problem and Egyptian demands for a return to October 22 lines in a general stabilization of the southern front (Decision 15). The aim was to achieve a separation-of-forces or disengagement agreement that would straighten out the lines, reducing the vulnerability of both sides and the incentives for renewed hostilities, and providing a first step in post-war diplomacy. This would, in Kissinger's view, also produce a needed early negotiating success, avoid discussion of final borders, relieve pressures on the United States and Israel, and keep Sadat relying on U.S. mediation.[49]

In order to launch this effort, Kissinger offered to fly to Cairo on November 6, and on October 27 received word that Sadat had accepted this offer. Sadat also sent Ismail Fahmy, who was appointed Egyptian Foreign Minister on October 31 while in Washington, to

47. Dayan, p. 544; Kissinger, 1982, pp. 601–611.
48. The report of a U.S. threat to allow Soviet resupply of the Third Army appears in Israeli sources, especially Dayan (p. 544) and *Ma'ariv,* November 2, 1973, and in Insight Team, p. 433. Plans for U.S. resupply of the Egyptians, which would avert Soviet intervention, were confirmed in personal interviews with two high intelligence officials, by Kissinger himself (1982, pp. 604, 608, 623), and, in contrast to his later published account, by Moshe Dayan in a public lecture in December 1974, reported in the *New York Times* (December 20, 1974) and *Ma'ariv* (December 27, 1974). There has been some dispute over what Dayan actually said in this lecture, but all reported versions have him accusing the United States of threatening its own resupply (see letters from Donald Neff and Theodore Draper, *Commentary,* 60 (September 1975), 18–20, 22–24. Whether his later published version represents a correction of an earlier mistake or a covering up of an earlier indiscretion remains unclear. It is, of course, conceivable that the United States could have threatened Israel both with a Soviet resupply effort and with planning for a U.S. supply operation that would forestall the Soviets.
49. See Sheehan, p. 103; and Golan, p. 152. Kissinger's account is less clear on when the disengagement idea was first undertaken, but he mentions proposing it to Golda Meir on November 1 (1982, p. 623).

see Kissinger in the meantime. As Israeli Prime Minister Golda Meir was already present there, Kissinger began contacts with both, aimed at a broader agreement, in an intra-Washington "shuttle." By all accounts, the Kissinger-Meir exchanges and other meetings between the Israeli Prime Minister and the American officials were extremely acrimonious, due to the U.S. insistence on an end to the Israeli siege of the Egyptian Third Army with little in the way of a *quid pro quo*.[50] Nixon and Kissinger warned that Israel would receive no American aid if fighting resumed. (Throughout the post-crisis period, in fact, U.S. policy-makers explicitly linked continuing military aid to Israeli cooperation in political moves.)[51] They also made a definitive statement that the United States would resupply the Third Army itself, if necessary.

The Fahmy-Meir shuttle, October 29–November 4, did not produce agreement, and on November 7 Kissinger arrived in Cairo. The importance of his first meeting with Sadat as a turning point in his thinking has been described above. When Sadat accepted the idea of subsuming the issue of a return to the October 22 lines within the context of broader proposals for a general "straightening out" of the cease-fire lines, Kissinger decided on the spot to go for a more immediate agreement on stabilizing the cease-fire (Decision 16).[52] He immediately secured Sadat's consent to a six-point agreement opening up regular supply lines to the Third Army in return for an exchange of prisoners. Then, while proceeding himself to Jordan and Saudi Arabia, Kissinger sent Assistant Secretary of State Joseph Sisco and NSC Middle East expert Harold Saunders to Jerusalem to get Israeli consent. This was accomplished with some additional arm-twisting (in the words of one U.S. diplomat, the agreement was "rammed down Golda Meir's throat").[53] The six-point agreement was signed on November 11.

Having thus secured at least temporary stability, Kissinger returned to the broader aim of a general disengagement. For a number of reasons, he saw the convening of a Geneva peace conference as the next step. Though he did not regard a multilateral forum as the best venue for negotiating such agreements, he felt the need to establish a formal framework within which such steps as disengage-

50. See for example, Golan, pp. 105–111; Quandt, 1977, pp. 215–216; Marvin Kalb and Bernard Kalb, *Kissinger* (New York: Dell, 1975), pp. 567–570; Kissinger, 1982, pp. 619–624.

51. Dayan, pp. 553–554.

52. Kissinger, 1982, p. 641.

53. Personal interview; this is confirmed generally by Kissinger, 1982, pp. 653–654.

ment could be carried out. As he had earlier explained to Eban, Kissinger wanted to convene such a conference before the Israeli elections, though postponing substantive discussions until afterwards. (Apparently, Kissinger believed that holding such an opening session would, among other things, help the more moderate Labor Party in the Israeli elections.)[54]

Kissinger therefore inaugurated a full-fledged effort to organize the opening session of the Geneva conference before Christmas (Decision 17). The conference planning was coordinated with the Soviets, whose role as co-chairman would give them a formal function and a sense of being consulted without involving them in the ongoing bilateral diplomatic efforts. Kissinger was also in touch with Syria, with whom the United States had no diplomatic relations; he met the Syrian Ambassador to the United Nations in Washington in early November, and arranged a visit to Damascus as part of his second Middle East tour, in December, in order to secure Syrian participation in the conference.[55] There were other problems: Israel refused to sit down with the Syrians before the prisoner-of-war issue was settled, and there was the everpresent central issue of Palestinian representation. In the end, Kissinger met the Israeli opposition to PLO participation by promising that no other parties would be invited without the agreement of the initial participants, and the prisoner-of-war issue was solved by the Syrian decision not to attend the conference.[56]

In the meantime, Kissinger was forced to define the American position toward the direct Egyptian-Israeli talks that were making unexpected headway at Kilometer 101 on the Cairo-Suez Highway. These talks, begun on a military level in the framework of the cease-fire, had moved into an exploration of various ideas for a broad Israeli-Egyptian disengagement in Sinai. Israeli Major General Aharon Yariv and Egyptian Lieutenant General Abdel Ghany El-Gamasy had, by late November, come close to a meeting of minds on the general outline for a disengagement that was, in fact, quite similar to the one that was eventually achieved two months later. The question was how to relate these talks to the planned Geneva conference and to American diplomacy.

All sources agree that Kissinger reacted by putting pressure on the Israeli government to slow down the Kilometer 101 talks, leading to

54. Eban, pp. 532–533; Kissinger, 1982, pp. 747–749; on Israeli elections, see Golan, pp. 131–132.

55. Interview with Korn.

56. Kissinger, 1982, pp. 758–759; Golan, pp. 127–130; Sheehan, p. 108; Quandt, 1977, p. 222.

the withdrawal of Israeli offers and a collapse of the negotiations
(Decision 18).[57] There were a number of reasons for this action. The
Kilometer 101 talks had been seen as preliminary, their success was
in some respects unexpected, and the Israelis themselves (as well as
the Egyptians) were interested in involving the United States in
negotiations and establishing a negotiating model with direct U.S.
participation. Kissinger also felt, apparently, that U.S. credit for diplomatic achievements was important in getting the oil embargo
lifted. And while direct Egyptian-Israeli talks might work, Kissinger
felt that this model would not function with other parties (Israel-
Syria, Israel-Palestinians) and therefore was not a useful precedent.
He preferred rather to institutionalize a framework that had possibilities of leading further. Also, there was an incentive to save the
Egyptian-Israeli disengagement for Geneva so that negotiations
there might start with a success. Finally, Geneva itself might be
delayed if the conclusion of an Egyptian-Israeli disengagement be-
forehand led Syria to insist on an Israeli-Syrian disengagement as
well before a general peace conference.[58]

The end of the Kilometer 101 talks left the road clear for Kissinger. Early December was spent in putting together the Geneva
conference, which, as projected, met for a formal opening session on
December 21–22 and instructed Egypt and Israel to begin negotiations on a disengagement agreement. It was understood that substantive talks would begin only after the Israeli elections on December
31, and it was expected that most agreements would be worked out
informally with U.S. help and that only the finishing stages would
actually be negotiated at Geneva.[59]

The Israeli elections left the Labor Party in control, though by a
reduced margin. Immediately afterward, Dayan came to Washington and presented Kissinger with some new ideas on disengagement
that stirred American interest in making an immediate effort in that
direction. At Dayan's urging, and after consulting Sadat, Kissinger
planned another trip to the area in order to try to tie together the
elements of an agreement before reconvening Geneva; Nixon approved the trip on January 8 (Decision 19).[60] Kissinger arrived at

57. Golan, pp. 120–121; Sheehan, pp. 80–81; Quandt, 1977, p. 220; interviews with
State Department officials and NSC aides. Kissinger (1982, p. 752) records his opposition to the Kilometer 101 talks but not his pressure on the Israeli government.
58. Interviews with Simcha Dinitz, Israeli Ambassador to the United States; Walter
Smith, Chief of Political Section, U.S. Embassy in Israel; a senior State Department
official; two NSC staff aides. See especially the account in Quandt, 1977, p. 220; also,
Golan, pp. 120–121; and Sheehan, pp. 80–81.
59. Interviews with Sonnenfeldt and an NSC staff aide; Kissinger, 1982, pp. 747–
749.
60. Kissinger, 1982, pp. 803, 804-805.

Aswan to meet Sadat on January 11, and within one day was encouraged enough by Sadat's position that he decided to try to conclude the entire agreement while in the area (Decision 20).[61] Thus began the Egypt-Israel "shuttle," taking Kissinger back and forth three times over the next week and ending with the achievement of an Egyptian-Israeli disengagement agreement. Though not planned from the outset, the development of this technique was a natural outgrowth of Kissinger's outlook and predilections. Israeli Foreign Minister Abba Eban later referred to Kissinger's "taste for centralized reponsibility": the shuttle diplomacy magnified Kissinger's own role, leaving only a need for telephone and cable approval by the President, and with the rest of Washington cut out of the action— save for those in Kissinger's retinue.[62]

The method of shuttle diplomacy also met the felt need of making the U.S. role central and excluding the Soviets (in the words of one aide, Kissinger took personal delight in seeing the Soviets on the outside).[63] And, as before, Kissinger was quick to spot an opportunity and to move to exploit it in the most efficient fashion. This led some observers to conclude that the "miracle" of the Egyptian-Israeli disengagement was in Kissinger's making it seem miraculous, since it was in essence a "sure thing," given the strong need of both sides for stabilization.[64]

The conclusion of an agreement required a final decision on U.S. willingness to stand behind its terms. As part of the negotiating process, Kissinger promised—and Nixon confirmed—assurances to both parties. There was a ten-point memorandum of understanding between the United States and Israel, covering such points as UN peacekeeping troops not being withdrawn except by the agreement of both sides, promises of attention to Israeli defense needs, and assurances of diplomatic support under future circumstances. Nixon also sent letters to both sides covering agreed-upon force limitations in Sinai and U.S. reconnaissance to assure compliance. Sadat also received a U.S. promise to use its full influence to bring about the implementation of UN Security Council Resolution 242.[65]

With the conclusion of the disengagement agreement, the tension level dropped to the pre-war level. Though problems remained on the Syrian front, the fear of renewed full-scale hostilities dissipated,

61. Ibid., p. 811.
62. Eban, p. 558.
63. Interviews with Sonnenfeldt, Korn, and an NSC staff aide.
64. Gil Carl AlRoy, *The Kissinger Experience: American Policy in the Middle East* (New York: Horizon, 1975), p. 58.
65. Quandt, 1977, p. 228; *New York Times,* January 22, 1974; Kissinger, 1982, p. 840.

and there was no longer a sense of urgency. U.S. prestige benefited enormously from the disengagement, and the problems of the Middle East could now be approached on a more routine basis, free of a crisis atmosphere. The 1973–1974 Middle East crisis, from an American perspective, was a closed chapter.

CHAPTER THIRTEEN

Decision-Making in the Yom Kippur War

As in Chapters Five and Nine, I will now summarize the implications of our third case study for the questions posed at the outset. In other words, what was the impact of the 1973 crisis on the coping mechanisms used by decision-makers to deal with uncertainty and stress? And how did crisis conditions affect the nature of the choices made?

COPING MECHANISMS

Information Processing

The demand for more information was especially marked in the 1973 pre-crisis period. The dependence of U.S. policy on the outcome of the fighting led to extreme sensitivity to battlefield intelligence—a sensitivity made even more acute by the embarrassing failure to predict the war, which left official Washington in an initial state of confusion. There were efforts to find new information sources; for example, the U.S. Embassy in Israel began to receive hard and precise military briefings from Israeli officials by the third day of the war.

As in 1958 and 1970, more intelligence was presented orally than in non-crisis periods, with William Colby acting as a member of WSAG. But the difference in information processing was more marked in 1973. There was a flood of "raw" data to the top, and a significant acceleration of the entire information processing system. This expressed the greater sensitivity of U.S. policy to military outcomes on a rapidly moving and confused battlefield, a situation basically dissimilar from the first two cases. Communication became mostly "vertical," with little or no time for the "horizontal" circulation and analysis of information. As noted, this led to complaints that only Kissinger and a few select NSC aides knew the whole picture, and that they were in fact overloaded with a mass of information, much of it lacking the expert interpretation needed to put it into focus. In some ways, this begins to look like a description of information processing under *crisis* (rather than *pre-crisis*) conditions—and indeed the 1973 pre-crisis period, marked by a major conventional war, was perhaps closer to crisis conditions than the other two cases. But even here, it should be remarked, the information sources and procedures were largely unchanged from the non-crisis period; the entire process was simply speeded up.

During the crisis period, there was yet more demand for information. Kissinger himself demanded increasing quantities of raw and processed data. Lower-level participants felt perhaps an even greater need of information, due to the fact that the exclusively vertical flow of information to the top denied them "horizontal" access to information they considered necessary for their own analyses. As explained by William Colby: in a crisis, vertical communication becomes more important and horizontal communication is moribund. Large amounts of raw data, made available by modern technology, go to the top immediately; Kissinger may even have had *less* tendency to rely on this than others, as he tried to get analytic content as well, but this was difficult when there was less time. The intelligence community did not meet for formal estimates after war broke out; quick judgments were made by the CIA or the Defense Intelligence Agency (DIA) alone, or by Kissinger himself. Since only formal estimates guarantee that dissents and evaluation reached the top, the CIA and the State Department developed special procedures for advising the top of dissents.

The flood of raw data at the top, and the lack of time for preparation of accompanying evaluations, did, as suggested, present problems in making productive use of the information that was available. In the absence of formal analyses, and with analysts unable to compare notes, the choice of significant signals became more difficult. To quote the Pike report:

> The Defense Intelligence Agency, having no military contingency plan for the area, proved unable to deal with the deluge of reports from the war zone, and quickly found itself in chaos. CIA and INR [Bureau of Intelligence and Research, Department of State] also engulfed Washington and each other with situation reports, notable for their redundancy.
>
> Technical intelligence gathering was untimely, as well as indiscriminate. U.S. national technical means of overhead coverage

of the Middle East, according to the post-mortem, was "of no practical value" because of time problems. Two overflight reconnaissance missions, on October 13 and 25, "straddled the most critical phase of the war and were, therefore, of little use."[1]

The Pike report goes on to claim that "randomized" intelligence may have even contributed to the worldwide alert on October 24–25, in that U.S. policy-makers were putting too much weight on Israeli battle reports and thus failed to appreciate fully the circumstances that sparked the vociferous Soviet reaction.

In sum, the crisis period was characterized by an increased demand for accurate and up-to-date intelligence, by attempts to tap new and often unconventional sources of intelligence data, and by considerable changes in intelligence processing as well. In particular, there was a pronounced tendency to channel intelligence directly to the top of the decision-making hierarchy, often in the form of raw and unanalyzed data, and for senior officials to do their own intelligence evaluation (a procedure that proved, interestingly enough, to have "functional" results in 1958, in that it corrected prevailing misconceptions at the top, but which seems to have performed dysfunctionally in 1973).

The crisis also inspired an outpouring of direct and indirect communications with other parties: with the Soviet Union, with Israel, with moderate Arab states such as Jordan and Saudi Arabia, and even with Egypt. The Europeans felt dissatisfied with the amount of U.S. consultation, but they were contacted when problems arose (principally regarding the airlift). Contacts intensified along with the crisis; Kosygin's trip to Cairo led to even more intense exchanges between the U.S. and the Soviet Union, which had already been in fairly frequent contact. Following ten hours of fruitless negotiations over the hot line regarding the cease-fire, it was decided that only face-to-face contact would suffice, and Kissinger traveled to Moscow. On the night of the alert, the two countries were in constant contact. Communication to other parties was also characterized by extraordinary channels: the "back-channel" to Egypt, a direct phone link to Israeli Ambassador Dinitz (installed during the crisis), and transatlantic phone calls between Nixon and Israeli Prime Minister Golda Meir.

In the post-crisis period, the situation was distorted by Kissinger's personal domination of the diplomatic process. Though the amount of information required and generated was substantially greater than under non-crisis conditions, much of it was personally collected,

1. "The CIA Report the President Doesn't Want You to Read" (excerpts from a report of the House Select Committee on Intelligence), *Village Voice*, February 16, 1976.

analyzed, and used by Kissinger and his closest aides alone. By central-izing American diplomacy around his personal contacts with for-eign leaders, Kissinger guaranteed to himself a near monopoly on the information regarding the crucial diplomatic issues and the posi-tions of the negotiating parties. As this process has been described by an observer:

> Kissinger insisted on severe limits on the dissemination of information about the negotiations within the U.S. Government. In addition, by relying on many channels of communications, only he was privy to all the relevant information on the U.S. side.
> A small staff prepared papers for Kissinger prior to negotiations, but talks themselves were conducted frequently in complete private with Sadat, Assad or Mrs. Meir. On occasion others would be included, but Kissinger, on behalf of the President, was the only one to speak for the United States. He delegated responsibility to his deputies only by employing them to convey messages when he was unable to do so himself. To an extraordinary degree, then, Kissinger relied on the very broad authority granted him by Nixon to manage the entire American diplomatic effort. Hence the need for frequent trips to the area, since unless he was physically present the negotiations seemed likely to stall.[2]

The extent of this domination of the information process was illus-trated by Kissinger's inclination not to use American interpreters in his high-level negotiations, but rather to rely on the other side's interpreters, which meant one less American "cut in on the action." This tendency was also expressed in Kissinger's attempt to exclude U.S. Ambassador James Akins from his discussions with the Saudi Arabian leaders, an action that led Akins to threaten his resignation.[3] But clearly, Kissinger was the only American policy-maker with com-plete access to the details relevant to the negotiating process, a situa-tion made possible by his impressive capability of mastering the "minutest details of whatever problems he undertakes to solve," as testified to by Golda Meir herself.[4] One anomaly of this situation was that Kissinger practiced a policy of selective dissemination of infor-mation to the press, keeping the knowledgeable public better in-formed than in most comparable diplomatic negotiations, and thus building for himself a base of support in Congress and among the general public while minimizing the role of his own subordinates.[5]

2. William B. Quandt, "Kissinger and the Arab-Israel Disengagement Negotia-tions," *Journal of International Affairs,* 9 (Spring 1975), 42.

3. Richard Valeriani, *Travels With Henry* (Boston: Houghton Mifflin, 1979), pp. 103, 173.

4. Golda Meir, *My Life* (London: Weidenfeld and Nicolson, 1975), p. 443.

5. Quandt, 1975, p. 46.

In sum, the experience of 1973 seems to confirm the following hypotheses regarding information processing:

3. The greater the crisis, the greater the felt need for information, the more thorough the quest for information, and the more open the receptivity to new information.

4. The greater the crisis, the more information about it tends to be elevated to the top of the organizational [decisional] pyramid quickly and without distortion.

5. The higher the stress in a crisis situation, the greater the tendency to rely upon extraordinary and improvised channels of communication [and information].

6. In crises, the rate of communication by a nation's decision-makers to international actors outside their country will increase.

7. As crisis-induced stress increases, the search for information is likely to become more active, but it may also become more random and less productive.

9. As crisis-induced stress declines, receptivity becomes permeated by more bias.

10. The more intense the crisis, the greater the tendency of decision-makers to perceive that everything in the external environment is related to everything else.

12. The more intense the crisis, the greater the tendency to an overabundance of new information (information overload) and a paucity of usable data on decision-making levels.

Hypothesis 1, given the evidence for lack of examination of basic premises at the height of the crisis, is confirmed with regard to cognitive rigidity, but is clearly rejected with regard to closure to new information (it will be recalled that this was also the case in 1958 and 1970):

1. The greater the stress, the greater the conceptual rigidity of an individual, and the more closed to new information the individual becomes.

Two of the information hypotheses are rejected in the 1973 case:

8. As crisis-induced stress declines, the quest for information becomes more restricted.

11. The more intense the crisis, the less the sensitivity to, and learning from, negative feedback.

Finally, the hypothesis on past experience was untestable in 1973 (as in 1970), since reliance on the past seemed to be high, and perhaps equally high, during all periods of the crisis:

2. The greater the crisis, the greater the propensity for
decision-makers to supplement information about the objective
state of affairs with information drawn from their own past
experience.

Patterns of Consultation

As in 1958 and 1970, the patterns of consultation were not basically
altered in the 1973 pre-crisis period. There was no significant change
in the identity of persons consulted, though there were more consultations, carried out more quickly and in more formal, face-to-face
settings (the convening of WSAG brought together persons who
would usually be consulted, but this time in daily meetings). There
was also more "expert" input, since policy-makers needed informal
judgments on the course of the war as well as consideration of such
technical questions as military resupply operations.

There was also the beginning of the process of "closure" to outside
influences, as in the two previous crises. In 1973, other views could
not be as readily ignored, of course, given the much greater public
interest and pressure, but there is little to indicate that advice from
outside the executive branch was any more decisive in influencing
policy. Quandt's summary of domestic influences in 1973 is a good
statement for all three pre-crisis periods (and even more for the crisis
periods):

> Crisis periods, especially, tend to isolate policy makers from
> domestic pressures. Decisions are often made rapidly, before public
> opinion can be mobilized. Information is closely held, depriving
> interest groups of the means for effective action. The stakes are
> high and the public tends to be deferential to presidential
> authority, even when that authority has been weakened, as Nixon's
> had been.[6]

In the crisis period, there were even more complaints from officials within the administration of exclusion from the decision-making
process, but on the whole the weight of evidence still indicates that
there was more consultation within the executive branch as the crisis
intensified. For example, on the night of October 24, three groups
of experts were urgently convened to consider the response to the
threat of Soviet intervention. What can be said about the sense of
exclusion is that the process of consultation was clearly one-way, with
Kissinger and his closest aides receiving input from those consulted
but not making them part of the overall picture. As in 1970, there

---

6. Quandt, *Decade of Decisions: American Policy Toward the Arab-Israeli Conflict, 1967–1976* (Berkeley: University of California Press, 1977), p. 203.

was no meaningful consultation outside the executive branch, aside from purely *pro forma* gestures.

In sum, as the crisis intensified, there was increased consultation within the executive branch, but less consultation with outside parties. There was a growing tendency toward direct and informal contact, with more participation by military advisors, though this does not mean that they dominated the decision-making process. Nor did other subordinates consulted in the course of decision-making necessarily wield significant influence on the outcome; there was a pronounced tendency to seek the advice and support of subordinates in a narrow sense only, making use of their input but not making them full participants in the decision-making process.

In the post-crisis period, the dominant fact, again, was Kissinger's control of the American policy-making process. There was, consequently, a higher level of consultation with external parties with whom Kissinger was in direct contact, principally the governments of Egypt and Israel. There was not a high ongoing level of consultation with any other outside parties or elements of the decision-making structure—with the important exception again of those outside parties seen as essential to building a base of support for Kissinger's policies. In this sphere, Kissinger was assiduous in cultivating Congressional and other support by the practice of frequent "consultations," which in fact may have amounted to little more than briefings. According to one description of this process:

> Kissinger also sought to build domestic support for a new approach to the Middle East by consulting Congress frequently. Between trips to the Middle East, Kissinger made a point of briefing members of Congress in detail and of appearing before committees of the House and Senate. The success of this approach was such that it was virtually impossible to find a senator or congressman who had a critical word to say about Kissinger's role in the Arab-Israeli disengagement talks.[7]

When questioned on his "penchant for secrecy" and his "personalizing" of American policy during this period, Kissinger responded by stressing that he was working closely with the appropriate assistant secretaries responsible for the areas with which he was dealing.[8] All available evidence indicates, however, that this participation was largely formal in structure and content, and that the role of area experts in the consultative process during the post-crisis period was

7. Quandt, 1975, p. 46.
8. Press conference of December 27, 1973, *Department of State Bulletin,* January 21, 1974.

largely limited to those persons fortunate enough to be included among Kissinger's retinue.

These findings provide unqualified substantiation, therefore, for five of the seven hypotheses on patterns of consultation:

13. The longer the decision time [in a crisis], the greater the consultation with persons outside the core decisional unit.

14. The greater the crisis, the greater the felt need for face-to-face proximity among decision-makers.

16. As crisis-induced stress increases, decision-makers increasingly use ad hoc forms of consultation.

17. As crisis-induced stress declines, the consultative circle becomes narrower.

19. The more intense the crisis, the less the influence of vested interests and other groups outside the bureaucracy.

The remaining two hypotheses are only confirmed conditionally or in part. Hypothesis 15 was valid in 1973 only within the executive branch and with foreign governments; Hypothesis 18 is confirmed for ad hoc settings but rejected on consultation reaching its peak:

15. As crisis-induced stress increases, the scope of consultation by senior decision-makers also increases.

18. As crisis-induced stress declines, consultation relies heavily on ad hoc settings as high-level consultation reaches its peak.

Decisional Forums

As noted in the 1970 study, the convening of WSAG did not substantially change the decisional forums, since WSAG was basically a coordinating body whose recommendations could be accepted or rejected by Nixon (and Kissinger). To the extent that there was a departure from routine during the pre-crisis period, moreover, it was in the direction of greater centralization on the Presidential level (especially the Nixon-Kissinger dyad) and less decisive input from institutionalized channels such as WSAG.

Throughout the crisis period, the decision-making groups—WSAG, Nixon-Kissinger, or Kissinger alone—were small. But at crucial points, the weight shifted to the Nixon-Kissinger consultations. For example, on October 12–13, the real decision was made in advance of the formal meeting on the 13th, in a consultation between Kissinger and the President. And there is evidence that, on October 24, Kissinger and others had already agreed over the telephone on a military response—if not specifically an alert—before the so-called

"NSC meeting" convened. In fact, available records show only one meeting during the crisis that might be labeled as a true National Security Council meeting, and even that one was somewhat improvised and not the real locus of decision. Finally, Nixon's authorization for Kissinger to decide policy on his own in Moscow certainly qualifies the Secretary of State as a rather unique "ad hoc decisional unit."

Decision-making thus became increasingly centralized during the crisis period. Henry Kissinger, by virtue of holding the two positions of National Security Advisor and Secretary of State, ensured a domination of decision-making that was nearly total. As Quandt notes: "For all practical purposes he [Kissinger] and Nixon made policy during the next several weeks, with occasional inputs from Defense Secretary Schlesinger." Others describe the situation as a duumvirate, noting that only the NSC staff, in part, was in the picture, and that the Sisco-Atherton task force in the State Department, for example, was engaged in carrying out orders and not in planning. Most participants interviewed expressed, in one way or another, the thought that centralization is inevitable in a crisis: outside influences are closed out, bureaucratic politics cease to have an impact, and power flows to the top.

Thus, in 1973, as in 1958 and 1970, we see that the onset of the crisis period is characterized by (1) a decrease in the size of the decisional unit, (2) increasing centralization, with greater Presidential involvement and less real participation by lower-ranking officials, (3) fewer formal and institutionalized procedures and more ad hoc communication and consultation, and (4) a decision-making focus on the global perspective, with less representation of regional and military expertise.

However, while in 1958 and 1970 the post-crisis period was marked by a return to routine procedures with more decentralized decision-making and larger decisional units, 1973 saw a reversal of this pattern. The domination of the Secretary of State was above all expressed in the reduction of the decisional unit to a single person. The use of "shuttle diplomacy" was an almost perfect expression of this drive for centralization in the making of U.S. foreign policy. Even the role of the President himself was reduced from the crisis level; according to one report, while on his January mission to conclude an Egyptian-Israeli disengagement agreement, Kissinger did not even phone President Nixon until January 15, four days after the mission had begun and when an agreement was almost concluded.[9]

9. Marvin Kalb and Bernard Kalb, *Kissinger* (New York: Dell, 1975), p. 606.

Given these findings, we can confirm eleven of the thirteen hypotheses on decisional forums:

20. The longer the crisis, the greater the felt need for effective leadership within decisional units.

21. The longer the decision time, the greater the conflict within decisional units.

22. The greater the group conflict aroused by a crisis, the greater the consensus once a decision is reached.

23. The longer the amount of time available in which to make a decision, the greater will be the consensus on the final choice.

24. Crisis decisions tend to be reached by ad hoc decisional units.

25. In high-stress situations, decision groups tend to become smaller.

26. In crises, decision-making becomes increasingly centralized.

29. The more intense the crisis, the greater the tendency of decision-makers to conform to group goals and norms, and the less the dissent within the group.

30. The more intense the crisis, the less the influence of "standard operating procedures."

31. The more intense the crisis, the greater the role in decision-making of officials with a general rather than a "parochial" perspective.

32. The more intense the crisis, the less the influence of vested interests in the bureaucracy ("bureaucratic politics").

The remaining two hypotheses are, however, rejected in the 1973 case:

27. As crisis-induced stress rises, there is a heavy reliance on medium-large and institutional forums for decisions.

28. As crisis-induced stress declines, there is a maximum reliance on large, institutional forums for decision.

Alternatives: Search and Evaluation

In the pre-crisis period, there was more search for new options than in non-crisis periods, forced by the pressures of a rapidly changing full-scale military conflict. The United States shifted its diplomatic approach and adopted new positions on a cease-fire, and on Arab-Israeli diplomacy generally, by the third and fourth days of the war. During the following days, various options for low-profile resupply of Israel were pursued avidly—often at the cost of inadequate consideration of the difficulties involved (e.g., the impracticality of using chartered civilian cargo planes in war zones or of transferring equipment to Israeli control in the Azores). But this search for options was in large part a tactical flexibility designed to preserve the basic strategy in U.S. policy, which was pursued against growing resistance until the end of the week. Thus, on a fundamental policy level, there was considerably less "search for alternatives" than might appear from the above discussion. In essence, policy-makers were making minimal adjustments to new conditions. Within these limits, however, the options considered were generally evaluated carefully and thoroughly.

During the crisis period, there seems to have been a basic consensus on the major alternatives, which has been somewhat obscured by the debate over "who delayed the airlift." Extensive interviewing has shown that there was, in fact, little conflict between political and military decision-makers on the question of resupply of Israel. To some extent, there were indeed "technical problems" that delayed the airlift, especially with regard to the ill-fated but apparently sincere effort to charter civilian airplanes. But basically, U.S. policy during the first week of the Yom Kippur war was to maintain a low profile on resupply of Israel. There was no significant dissent from this policy, nor any open support for a U.S. military airlift, from any senior policy-makers, until perceptions of the military situation changed toward the end of the first week. The real technical problems were, to some degree, overplayed in order to protect the low-profile policy, thus laying the foundation for stories of Pentagon obstructionism. Likewise, on the level of basic assumptions and evaluation of major alternatives, there seems to have been inadequate consideration of the likely Arab response to either the airlift or the Israeli aid package, and a tendency to focus on the global aspects (U.S.-Soviet relations), to the neglect of local forces which in the end proved at least as problematic.

But on the tactical level, in 1973 as in the other cases, the search for and evaluation of alternatives seem to have been more rational and analytical. The airlift decision was preceded by a detailed examination of other options, all in the framework of the basic decision to maintain a low profile toward the conflict. It could be argued, on the other hand, that the implications of the military alert on October 24–25 were not adequately weighed, or that at least the possibility and consequences of public reaction to it were not foreseen. Given the possible validity of these conclusions, it still seems apparent that the decision-making process itself was carried out with considerable attention to the costs and gains of the various options and a careful reading of the relative risks of action and inaction.

Thus, in 1973 as in 1958 and 1970, the intensification of crisis led to a wider formal search for alternatives, but to some circumscribing of the consideration of certain alternatives. On the level of basic assumptions and predisposition, there seems to have been some tendency to close out certain options and in particular to focus on military options more than political or diplomatic alternatives. On the other hand, all three crises demonstrate a certain tactical rationality (with some lapses); there was a fairly careful weighing of the limited number of tactical options being considered.

The evidence at hand thus underlines the importance of cognitive factors in setting general policy aims. In none of the three crises does there appear to have been any tendency to analyze the basic assumptions upon which policy rested, and this in turn limited the consideration of major options. But while decisions on basic policy directions were firmly rooted in the perceptions and instincts of top policymakers, operational decisions were made on a more analytical basis. In these decisions, more open debate and disagreement took place, and subordinates played a more active role. With basic policy guidelines assumed, the deliberative machinery of decision-making focused on the practical problems of carrying out these aims. It should be noted, finally, that despite flawed perceptions, faulty intelligence, defective political-military coordination, and other shortcomings that characterized U.S. decision-making, in each case the immediate American aims were achieved.

The situation in the 1973 post-crisis period was more complex than in the other two crises. With a broad policy set, Kissinger demonstrated his skill in making subtle tactical shifts in response to changing conditions. Illustrations include his quick adaptation to the new possibilities presented by his meeting with Sadat, his quick adjustment to "shuttle" diplomacy, and his quick tactical decision to push the six-point agreement with Sadat in early November. The use of pressure on Israel was also delicately fine-tuned and coordinated with the basic American posture. On the other hand, Kissinger had been criticized for failure to consider seriously some of the more obvious alternatives to the overall strategy adopted. For example, the idea of using the threat of Israeli forces on the west bank of the Suez Canal to get the oil embargo lifted was given up in the very beginning of Kissinger's diplomacy. Kissinger's decision to slow down the Kilometer 101 talks could also be criticized as an insufficient weighing of the costs and advantages of establishing the precedent of direct Egyptian-Israeli diplomacy. On a broader basis, Kissinger's entire "crisis management" technique in Middle East diplomacy has been viewed by some observers as brilliant on a tactical level, but as not touching basic issues of the conflict, and as leading in fact to very limited results.

Of the thirteen hypotheses on consideration of alternatives, eight are confirmed by the evidence of U.S. decision-making in the 1973 Middle Eastern war:

34. The greater the reliance on group problem-solving processes, the greater the consideration of alternatives.

35. During crisis the search for alternatives occupies a substantial part of decision-making time.

36. The relationship between stress and group performance in the consideration of alternatives is curvilinear (an inverted *U*)— more careful as stress rises to a moderate level, less careful as stress becomes intense.

37. Despite the rise in stress, choices among alternatives are not, for the most part, made before adequate information is processed; that is, there is not a tendency to premature closure.

38. As time pressure increases, the choice among alternatives does not become less correct. [This is a tentative confirmation.]

43. As crisis-induced stress declines, the evaluation of alternatives reaches its maximum care, more so when time salience is low.

44. The more intense the crisis, the greater the tendency of decision-makers to narrow their span of attention to a few aspects of the decision-making task ("tunnel vision").

45. The more intense the crisis, the more likely that decision-makers will be forced to make a clear choice rather than postponing choices or drifting into policy.

Two hypotheses are confirmed only for the peak stress phase, and not for the crisis period as a whole:

33. As stress increases, decision-makers become more concerned with the immediate than the long-run future.

41. As crisis-induced stress increases, the evaluation of alternatives becomes less careful.

Hypothesis 40, in contrast, is confirmed for periods of higher stress but rejected in the peak stress phase:

40. As crisis-induced stress increases, the search for options tends to increase.

The final two hypotheses are rejected in an analysis of data from the 1973 case:

39. Decision-makers do not generally choose among alternatives with an inadequate assessment of their consequences.

42. As crisis-induced stress declines, the search for options tends to become less extensive than in all other phases of the crisis period.

DIMENSIONS OF CHOICE

Pre-Crisis Period

Five significant U.S. decisions were taken during this period of the 1973 Middle East crisis:

1. On October 6, elements of the Sixth Fleet were moved.

2. On the same day, policy-makers set a policy of seeking a cease-fire *status quo ante.*

3. Also on October 6, a policy of "low profile" in resupply of Israel was delineated.

4. On October 9, it was decided "in principle" to meet Israeli arms requests and replace war losses.

5. On October 10, the United States accepted "in principle" the proposal for a cease-fire-in-place.

In each of these decisions, there was a single dominant *core input,* either the outbreak of war (Decisions 1–3) or subsequent military developments (Decisions 4 and 5).

The *cost* of all five decisions was perceived to be low, and the *importance* was either Consequential (Decisions 1, 2, and 5) or Important (Decisions 3 and 4).

In terms of *complexity,* four of the decisions involved both Military-Security and Political-Diplomatic issues, while Decision 1 seems to have involved only Military-Security issues.

The *systemic domain* ranged from Regional only (Decisions 2 and 5), to Superpower and Regional (Decision 1), to Superpower, Regional, and Bilateral (Decisions 3 and 4).

The dominant *process* of Decisions 2–5 seems to have been Rational, while Decision 1 was Routine.

Regarding *activity,* the decision in three cases (1, 2, and 5) was to act, in one (Decision 3) to delay, and in one (Decision 4) to both act and delay. Two decisions (1 and 3) implied physical action, two decisions (2 and 5) implied verbal activity, and Decision 4 again implied both.

None of the decisions rated positively on *novelty.*

The *coping strategies* were predominantly *historical models, ideology,* and *operational codes,* all of which seem to have significantly entered into all five decisions. Decisions 2, 3, and 4 were also marked by *avoidance of value trade-offs,* Decisions 1 and 4 by *incrementalism,* and Decision 5 by *satisficing behavior.*

Crisis Period

To recapitulate, the nine major decisions of this period were:

6. Early on October 13, interim measures to aid Israel were taken.

7. Later on October 13, a full-scale military airlift to Israel was undertaken.

8. On October 19, a $2.2 billion aid request for Israel was submitted to Congress.

9. On October 19, Nixon authorized Kissinger to fly to Moscow.

10. On October 21, Kissinger agreed to a joint U.S.-USSR cease-fire resolution.

11. On October 23, Nixon and Kissinger resolved to prevent the destruction of the Egyptian Third Army.

12. On October 24, the United States rejected Sadat's plea for a joint U.S.-USSR force.

13. On the night of October 24–25, the United States put its forces on heightened alert in response to an intervention threat.

14. On October 25, the United States accepted a UN peacekeeping force without superpower troops.

The *core inputs* for these decisions were more varied: military developments, together with Israeli and domestic pressures, were instrumental in Decisions 6 and 7. Israeli pressure was critical in Decision 8, Soviet pressure in Decisions 9, 10, and 13, and Soviet and Egyptian pressure in Decision 12. An impending Egyptian military defeat was the important input for Decision 11, and the UN debate was the immediate stimulus to Decision 14.

Only three of the decisions (9, 10, and 14) were perceived to have low *costs.* Another four (6, 8, 11, and 12) must be rated as medium, and one (Decision 7) was clearly high in perceived costs. Decision 13 can be regarded as no less than *very* high on this scale.

The perceived *importance* of the decisions was no less than Important in any case: one decision (8) was rated on this middle level, with the others still higher. Decision 13 was clearly at the top of the scale (Decisive), while the remaining seven decisions were all Significant (i.e., between Important and Decisive).

All of the decisions involved both Military-Security and Political-Diplomatic issues, in measuring *complexity.* Decision 8 also brought in the Economic-Developmental issue-area.

Systemic domain was more extensive than in the pre-crisis period. Two decisions (6 and 7) could be said to involve all five levels of repercussions. Another five (Decisions 9–13) involved four levels: Global, Superpower, Regional, and Bilateral. Decision 8 also had an anticipated impact on four levels: Global, Regional, Bilateral, and Domestic. Decision 14 involved only Global, Superpower, and Regional reverberations.

The dominant *process* in Decisions 9, 10, 11, and 14 was clearly Rational; the remaining decisions appear to have been the result of a predominantly Rational process with strong Affective elements.

The *activity* of all decisions except Decision 12 was to act; the implied activity was physical in five cases (6, 7, 8, 12, and 13) and verbal in four (9, 10, 11, and 14).

Three of the decisions taken during the crisis period—6, 7, and 11 —seem to rate positively in terms of *novelty.*

The *coping strategies* fit the previous patterns: all nine decisions involved invocation of an *operational code,* all but one (Decision 8) were marked by *ideology,* and in all but three (6, 7, and 8) significant use was made of *historical models.* Five decisions (6–10) included a strong element of *avoiding value trade-offs,* and in one case (Decision 6) there seems to have been both *satisficing* behavior and *incrementalism.*

Post-Crisis Period

The seven decisions during the last period of the 1973 crisis were:

15. On October 26 and after, Kissinger launched an effort to stabilize the Egyptian-Israeli front.

16. On November 7, Kissinger decided to pursue the six-point agreement with Sadat.

17. In mid-November, Kissinger began organizing the Geneva conference.

18. In late November, Kissinger moved to slow down bilateral Egyptian-Israeli talks.

19. On January 5, Kissinger agreed to try working out an Egyptian-Israeli disengagement by personal mediation.

20. On January 12, Kissinger decided to try to conclude an agreement while in the Middle East.

21. On January 18, Nixon approved American assurances tied to the Egyptian-Israeli disengagement.

The *core inputs* of these decisions were: military instability in Decision 15, diplomatic opportunity or strategy in Decisions 16–18, Israeli proposals in Decision 19, and Egyptian or Israeli pressures in Decisions 20 and 21.

The perceived *costs* of all the decisions were low except for Decision 21, which appeared to be medium. In terms of *importance,* Decision 18 was seen as Consequential, Decisions 15, 16, 17, and 19 as Important, and Decisions 20 and 21 as Significant.

Five of the decisions involved two areas (Military-Security and Political-Diplomatic) on the scale of *complexity;* Decision 16 involved Military-Security only; and Decision 17, Political-Diplomatic only.

The *systemic domain* was more restricted than in the crisis period. The last two decisions had a perceived impact on three levels (Superpower, Regional, and Bilateral), but Decisions 15, 16, and 18 seem to have involved only the Regional and Bilateral levels. Decision 17 was important on the Global and Regional levels only, and Decision 19 on the Regional level alone.

All decisions were Rational in terms of process, and the *activity* implied in all cases was to act verbally. Four of the decisions (17, 18, 20, and 21) seem to rank high on *novelty.*

The *coping strategies* used included *ideology* and *operational codes* in all seven decisions, but only three of them (15, 19, and 21) were marked by significant reference to *historical models.* On the other hand, four of the decisions (17, 18, 20, and 21) involved *avoidance of value trade-offs.* Two (Decisions 16 and 19) were characterized by *incrementalism,* and one (Decision 16) by *satisficing.*

Hypotheses

Of the seventeen hypotheses on the linkage between crisis and dimensions of choice, ten are confirmed by the above evidence of the 1973 Middle East crisis:

46. As crisis-induced stress begins to rise, the number and variety of core inputs to decisions increases sharply.

48. When decision-makers operate under stress, they assess their decision as costly.

49. When decision-makers operate under low or declining stress, they perceive their decisions as of small cost.

50. As crisis-induced stress rises, decision-makers tend to perceive their decisions as more and more important.

51. As crisis-induced stress declines, the perceived importance of decisions declines from the levels in all other phases of the crisis period.

56. As crisis-induced stress rises, the selected option tends to be chosen by rational calculus and analysis of the issues, rather than by a process of bargaining and compromise.

57. As crisis-induced stress declines, decision-makers resort mainly to rational procedures to ultimate choice.

58. As crisis-induced stress rises, there is a tendency for decisions to be continuously active.

61. As crisis-induced stress rises, there is a steady increase in resort to choices without precedent.

62. As crisis-induced stress declines, unprecedented choices remain at their peak.

The remaining seven hypotheses are rejected in the 1973 case:

47. As crisis-induced stress declines, the number and variety of core inputs are reduced.

52. As crisis-induced stress rises, the complexity of issue-areas involved steadily rises.

53. As crisis-induced stress declines, the number of issue-areas involved in decision-making reaches its maximum.

54. In situations of peak crisis-induced stress, the heretofore steadily-broadening systemic levels of anticipated reverberations from decisions become narrower.

55. As crisis-induced stress declines, systemic domain rises from the peak crisis phase.

59. As crisis-induced stress rises, the activity implied by the decisions moves from physical to verbal.

60. As crisis-induced stress declines, there is a sharp increase in decisions to delay or not to act.

PART IV

CONCLUSIONS

CHAPTER FOURTEEN

The Components of Crisis

In Chapter One, "international crisis" was defined in terms of changes in three basic perceptions by a state's decision-makers: the perception of threat to basic values; the increased perception of the probability of war or involvement in military hostilities; and the awareness of finite time for response. It was also hypothesized that the pre-crisis period is marked by a change in only the first of these perceptions, that is, by a perception of a threat to basic values, but not by a perception of increased likelihood of hostilities or of limited time for response. To what extent do the three crises studied here fit this definition of crisis?

PRE-CRISIS PERIOD

Threat to Values

In 1958, the threat perceived by American policy-makers was far broader than the threat to Lebanon itself. As expressed by Secretary of State Dulles in cabled instructions to American diplomats:

> Lebanon has thus become test case for preservation of independence of small states and respect of their right to solve their internal problems by themselves. Because of international aspects of this issue problem has rightly come before UN and we believe it is up to Lebanese to exhaust all available UN remedies. We have given fullest support to UN efforts in Lebanon and have been gratified to note steps taken by other NATO members to assist UN. We believe every reasonable effort must be made to have UN succeed in Lebanon. We foresee most serious

consequences both for the Free World and the UN if UN should prove ineffective to cope with indirect aggression.[1]

Lebanon was therefore seen in the context of an overriding Communist threat and the threatened deterioration of the West's position. It was part of a series of threats posed by the Soviet strategy of undermining Western influence in the Third World. Consequently, policy-makers concluded that the United States must either help to contain the threat to Lebanon, or see it fall under a Nasserist domination that was either linked to Communism or served the purposes of Communist strategy. But since the primary threat was defined as external intervention in Lebanese affairs, it was regarded less seriously so long as no open invasion took place. It was not the instability of Lebanon in itself, but rather the exploitation of this instability that constituted a threat to basic American values.

Even though American lives, as well as "law and order" generally, were endangered in the hijackings in 1970, a more fundamental threat in the eyes of American decision-makers was the future of Jordan itself. As in 1958, there was apprehension of the collapse of a friendly regime, with the implication of expanded radicalism throughout the area and the consequent risk of a war triggered by Israeli or other reaction to these events. Likewise, the perception of such developments as a Soviet gain, given the global focus of American decision-makers, was of crucial importance. This was reinforced in 1970 by the perception that the Soviets were on the offensive in the area, and that American credibility was being tested. Events in Jordan also threatened the preservation of the recent cease-fire on the Suez Canal and the general future of Arab-Israeli talks, which were seen to depend upon the availability of a moderate negotiating partner in Amman. Thus, a great deal was at stake; as Henry Kissinger later recounted:

> The President turned to me. I replied that we faced two problems, the safety of the hostages and the future of Jordan. If the fedayeen could use Jordan as their principal base and in the process destroy the authority of the king—one of the few rulers in the region distinguished by moderation and pro-Western sympathies—the entire Middle East would be revolutionized. Two months after our peace initiative the military balance along the Canal would have been altered by cheating at the very moment that the political balance along the Jordan front would have been destroyed by force. We could not acquiesce in this by dithering on the sidelines, wringing our hands, urging the resumption of peace talks, and then proclaiming our impotence.[2]

1. Dulles to American Embassy, Paris, June 24, 1958, *Declassified Documents Reference System,* 1977 (Washington, D.C.: Carrollton Press, 1978).
2. Henry Kissinger, *White House Years* (Boston: Little, Brown, 1979), pp. 602–603.

In 1973, American decision-makers saw a war between Israel and Arab states as a threat to detente and equilibrium between the superpowers, to the future of Arab-Israeli diplomacy, and to the furtherance of good U.S.-Arab relations, which were of high value both on these issues and on others of interest to the United States. In addition, another overwhelming Israeli victory would, it was thought, endanger U.S. interests and influence throughout the Arab world and make more difficult the basic task of containing Soviet influence in the area. As part of this picture, the growing importance of oil could not be denied—and in one study prepared by Kissinger's National Security Council staff earlier in the year, it had been predicted that if war did break out in the Middle East, there was a "45% chance" that Arab oil supplies would be disrupted. The participation of Deputy Treasury Secretary William Simon in WSAG meetings at which oil supply was discussed also indicated this concern. It is clear, however, that it was not at this stage a major preoccupation in the minds of top policy-makers.[3]

In summary, therefore, it appears that in all three Middle East crises American decision-makers perceived serious, but finite, threats to basic American values.

Probability of Involvement in Hostilities

In 1958, American policy-makers made a point from the outset of keeping the door open for the use of force. But it appears that the primary motivation in doing so was deterrence, or at most keeping force available as a final resort. American policy-makers in Beirut and in Washington felt that American forces would not be needed, barring drastic changes in the Lebanese situation. It was assumed that the Lebanese army was capable of handling any significant internal threat, and that the major problem was neutralizing the threat of external intervention. Furthermore, these threats of external intervention were understood to involve the forces of the United Arab Republic, and not the more dangerous contingency of Soviet action. Dulles expressed the general mood when he said on May 20, in response to a question on the likelihood of the introduction of American forces, that "we do not have any present reason to anticipate that there will be the need for that."[4]

3. The intelligence estimate of 45 percent is reported in the Insight Team of the London Sunday Times, *The Yom Kippur War* (Garden City, N.Y.: Doubleday, 1974), p. 356. The low estimate of the fear of an oil embargo is supported by interviews with Hyland, Korn, Weiss, Van Deusen, an NSC staff aide, and a legislative aide.

4. *Department of State Bulletin,* June 9, 1958.

Likewise in the pre-crisis period of 1970, there was no real sense of likelihood of involvement in hostilities. A military rescue was considered impractical as a solution to the hijacking crisis, and the general crisis in Jordan, though anticipated, had not yet erupted. It was also felt that if such a crisis did develop, the Jordanian government would be able to meet the challenge if there were no external intervention. Behind this, the Nixon Doctrine signaled a diminished inclination to use American forces in such cases, and the constraints posed by Vietnam and the Cambodian incursion placed a special limit on American policy-makers. Thus, there was a strong tendency, at least among some officials, to favor the "proxy" use of Israeli forces, should military action seem necessary. Finally, there was some apprehension of a confrontation with the Soviet Union—as expressed in the frequent invocation of the 1914 Balkan analogy—but this was not an overriding fear during the pre-crisis stage.

In 1973, the initial assessment was that Israeli armed forces would quickly reverse the initial Arab success, and that there was no need to act in defense of Israel. It was also anticipated that any supplies sent would not arrive in time to influence the military outcome of the war. These assessments changed only toward the end of the first week. The principal danger felt by American policy-makers was the opposite: that an Arab defeat would drag in the Soviets, with the consequent danger of an American-Soviet confrontation. But even this was not felt to be imminent during the early days of the war, and there was some confidence that this confrontation could be handled in the framework of the U.S.-USSR detente. As the likelihood of an immediate Israeli victory receded after October 8–9, there seemed to be even less immediate danger of U.S. involvement, since the most plausible scenario projecting such involvement seemed yet more remote. The effect was to reduce even further the slight apprehension that had existed regarding involvement in military hostilities.

Therefore, in all three cases of American decision-making during the pre-crisis period of Middle East crises, the perception of the danger of involvement in military hostilities was slight to nonexistent.

Time Pressure

In the absence of a direct invasion, American policy-makers felt no great sense of urgency during the pre-crisis period of the 1958 Lebanese crisis. It was felt that Chamoun could handle matters, and that the crisis would in fact work itself out. Only one week before the full-fledged crisis developed, Secretary of State Dulles felt that "there was hope for a quieting of the civil strife and a lessening of the intervention under the influence of world public opinion and the careful system of observation."[5]

In 1970, the time pressure regarding the hijacking passed as the original deadline expired, and this aspect of the crisis became routinized. There was fear of escalation within Jordan, but so long as Hussein himself did not act, Washington felt no urgency. According to Defense Secretary Laird, a Syrian action in response to a Jordanian civil war—which might in turn require a quick American response —was considered 70 percent unlikely at this time. This probability seemed to rise, in his eyes, toward the end of the pre-crisis period, but still remained theoretical so long as there was no overt conflict in Jordan.[6]

Finally, in 1973 no urgency was felt when war broke out. There was no danger of Israeli defeat, in the minds of American decision-makers, and the opposite danger of a humiliating Arab defeat would, it was thought, take time to develop. In that case, of course, the Arab states and the Soviet Union would be the pleaders, and an American response would again be less sensitive to time considerations. This view was reinforced in the early stages of the war by Israeli requests that reflected no special sense of time pressure. During October 8–9, perceptions of the military situation changed; it became clear that Israel would not achieve a quick military victory. But, again, this did not create a greater sense of time pressure for U.S. policy-makers. To the contrary, the threat of a humiliating Arab defeat simply became less pressing. Policy-makers continued to believe in an Israeli victory, which would force them to act, but now felt that they had more time. On the other hand, Israeli requests for resupply became more urgent, though it was not until the end of the week that this forced a radical shift in American perceptions, since the NSC staff felt that the Israeli requests and sense of urgency were exaggerated.

Thus, in all three cases of American decision-making during Middle East pre-crisis phases, there was no sense of a finite time for American decisional response.

Consequently, in all three cases, I have been able to define a pre-crisis period that involved an increased perception of a threat to basic values, but not an increased perception of probable involvement in hostilities or of a finite time for an American response. For these cases, at least, this part of the theoretical framework is relevant and applicable.

5. Eleanor Lansing Dulles, *John Foster Dulles: The Last Year* (New York: Harcourt, Brace and World, 1963), p. 140.
6. Interview with Melvin Laird, Secretary of Defense.

CRISIS PERIOD

Threat to Basic Values

In 1958, the coup in Iraq led American policy-makers to fear the imminent demise of all moderate and pro-Western governments in the area. The event was viewed as a major victory for the forces of Nasserism and for the interests of the Soviet Union. It was feared that the Iraqi revolution would have a deleterious effect on the Arab-Israeli conflict, complicating any future diplomatic move, but even more importantly increasing the likelihood of further destabilization and violence in that theater. Above all, the loss of a major Western ally in this area of the world seemed a major blow to American prestige and to the general credibility of the United States as a supporter of moderate and pro-Western regimes throughout the region and the world.

In a more immediate sense, the events in Iraq led to the conclusion that the Lebanese government could no longer stand on its own; the impact of the Iraqi coup on the balance of forces within Lebanon, on the morale of pro-government forces, on the supply of aid that had previously been extended from Iraq, and on the rate of infiltration of hostile forces into Lebanon was thought likely to culminate in a decisive blow to President Chamoun and his government. Washington believed, on the basis of intelligence data, that the fall of the Iraqi government was part of a three-pronged plot that also included designs to topple Chamoun and the government of King Hussein in Jordan. This would leave the Soviet Union, it was feared, in a position to threaten oil routes from the major fields of the Middle East, and acquiescence in the fall of these three governments would constitute, in the words of American statesmen, a reward to acts of indirect aggression.

Finally, the sense of threat to basic values was reinforced by a general sense of growing anti-Americanism throughout the world, fueled by a series of recent incidents not connected to the Middle East, which also led President Eisenhower and other American policy-makers to view the impact of the Iraqi coup in terms of the worldwide position and stature of the United States.

In 1970, likewise, the threat to a specific friendly regime—in this case, Jordan—was seen as a harbinger of radicalization of the entire region, threatening the stability of the entire Middle East and posing a serious threat to American credibility on a global scale. There was also, as in 1958, serious apprehension of the impact on the Arab-Israeli conflict, with the loss of a moderate negotiating partner and the possibility, even more than in 1958, that the fall of the threatened government would inaugurate a chain of events dragging the entire region into war. The sense of being tested by the Soviet Union was even stronger than it had been twelve years previously, with Iraq and Syria seen as Soviet proxies being used to probe the will and credibility of the relatively untested American administration.

In 1973, the perception that Israel was in trouble also triggered a perception of threat to yet more basic and overriding values. A victory of Soviet arms in the Middle East, it was feared, would lead to the decline of Western influence in the area and in the world. It was felt that a military victory would lead Arab states to believe that their aims could be achieved by arms, thus undermining any future incentive to cooperate in diplomatic moves. Regarding Soviet relations, there were two perceived threats: on the one hand, it was feared that the Soviets would be emboldened by a lack of American response, while, on the other hand, American policy-makers did not want to sacrifice the achievements of detente because of events in the Middle East.

On a more immediate level, reaction to the sense of urgency felt by Israel was considered important to the future willingness of Israel to cooperate with American diplomacy. At the same time, the costs of any American action in terms of U.S.-Arab relations were more of a factor in the perceptions of American policy-makers than in the two previous crises. Finally, American policy-makers also perceived an overwhelming Israeli victory as a potential threat to basic American interests in the area, since it would undermine future diplomacy and close the promising American opening to Egypt; and in this light they interpreted the possible destruction of the Egyptian Third Army as a serious threat to American values.

American decision-makers thus perceived serious threats to American values—and, with minor variations, to almost the same values—in 1958, 1970, and 1973. In short, in all three cases, American policy-makers saw a threat to a friendly Middle Eastern regime as a serious challenge to critical regional and global interests of the United States.

Probability of Involvement in Hostilities

In 1958, the prevailing assessment in Washington was that the Lebanese rebels would win control in the civil war if no outside action were taken. It was felt that an army coup to displace Lebanese President Chamoun was likely at any moment, and that only the immediate establishment of an American military presence could forestall such an event. American involvement in hostilities was therefore regarded as highly probable, verging on inevitable. There was, however, little fear of involvement in hostilities with the Soviet Union, or of escalation of fighting beyond the Lebanese theater, given the limited Soviet logistical capabilities and the general nuclear stalemate between the two superpowers. There was, on the other hand, no clear sense of the likely extent of hostilities or the risks actually being run in Lebanon itself. Given uncertain knowledge regarding the reaction of the Lebanese army and other armed bodies within that country, American military planners feared the possibility of heavy fighting and thus decided on an American landing on the beach rather than in Lebanese ports.

In 1970, civil war in Jordan was regarded as a near certainty upon Hussein's declaration of intent to impose martial law. The question at this point became the reaction of Syria and Iraq, and behind that the possibility of instigation by Nasser's Egypt or by the Soviet Union. Behind these certainties lay the clear possibility of a spreading war that would involve the entire Middle East, including the explosive Arab-Israeli theater, and create a high risk of superpower confrontation. In this context, the use of American military forces was considered very seriously. And if the United States did not choose to intervene with its own forces, there was clear apprehension of a sharp Israeli reaction to the fall of the Jordanian government, including Israeli military action that would in itself force the hand of the United States. Related to this was the debate, later in the crisis, over the risks of Israeli ground action as opposed to air strikes. Israeli intervention on the ground would, in the minds of American policymakers, also increase the risks of a general Arab-Israeli conflict that would involve the United States directly or indirectly in hostilities.

In 1973, the need to save Israel from a conceivably mortal danger involved the possibility of at least indirect American involvement as an arms supplier under conditions of distress. Behind this was the threat of a desperate Israeli action, possibly involving the use of nuclear weapons, and the everpresent danger of a confrontation with the Soviet Union as the two superpowers maneuvered to support their respective clients. Later in the crisis period, this fear peaked with the perceived risk of Soviet intervention to save the Egyptian regime, a perception reinforced by a number of signals that converged to create almost a war atmosphere in Washington.

Thus, in all three crisis periods, there was a clear perception of possible American involvement in hostilities, ranging from the expectation of direct military intervention in 1958 to the role as arms supplier to Israel and neutralizer of the Soviet Union in 1973.

Time Pressure

In 1958, the sense of limited time to act, following the coup in Baghdad, was overwhelming. It was expected that the Lebanese army might stage a coup deposing President Chamoun at any minute, and that with each passing hour the situation in Lebanon and in the Middle East was slipping further out of control. As Eisenhower defined the situation, it was a "matter of hours, in which any action must be taken."[7] There was therefore no time to consider seriously such options as an appeal to the United Nations, until after urgent action had been taken.

In 1970, the outcome of the crisis clearly depended, from the onset of the crisis period, upon military outcomes. In such a situation, it was clear that events could turn rapidly and that any outside action designed to influence the outcome would be taken under the greatest time pressure. There was also the clear possibility of a Syrian action that, given the distances, could threaten Amman before outside intervention could become effective. Some breathing space was afforded to decision-makers by the fact that Israeli mobilization, which was seen as an essential warning and preliminary move in the crisis period, provided an opportunity for the Syrians to back down before the United States would have to decide whether to intervene. On the other hand, time pressures were pushed to the extreme on the night of September 20–21, following the initial Syrian incursions, when the United States received an urgent request from the Jordanian government for an air strike that in Hussein's view would be the only measure soon enough and effective enough to halt the collapse of his government.

In 1973, with the impending shortages of essential war materiel on the Israeli side, there was a genuine sense of urgency in Jerusalem that was communicated to decision-makers in Washington. Israeli policy-makers persuaded their American counterparts that no offensive or defensive planning was possible without the assurance, if not the actuality, of military resupply by air. The sense of sharp time pressures was also evident in the U.S. response to Soviet proposals to conclude a cease-fire, given the American interest in avoiding any desperate Soviet action on behalf of Egypt or Syria. Finally, time pressures peaked on the night of October 24–25, when it was concluded that Soviet action, if it were to come, would logically take

7. Dwight D. Eisenhower, *The White House Years: Waging Peace, 1956–1961* (New York: Doubleday, 1965), p. 270.

place around midnight of that same night—thus necessitating an immediate American signal of unmistakable strength and urgency.

Thus, in all three cases—and especially in 1970 and 1973, when military hostilities were already taking place—there was a sharply increased sense of time constraints in the minds of those responsible for U.S. policy.

Thus, the onset of all three crisis periods was marked by a sharpened sense of threat to basic values, by a clear perception of the possible involvement of the United States (at least indirectly) in hostilities that were either imminent or already taking place, and by a sharp sense of finite time for an American response. This therefore confirms, as in the previous section, the operational relevance of the crisis-period definitions posited in the theoretical framework.

POST-CRISIS PERIOD

Threat to Values

The fact that Lebanese rebel leaders had participated in the choice of General Fuad Chehab as the new President of Lebanon seemed to end the danger of a Nasserist takeover in that country in 1958. There was no more threat of a "domino" effect, in which the remaining moderate countries of the Middle East would be overwhelmed by a tide of radicalization. Firm U.S. action had led to an acceptable outcome, and was reflected in the toned-down threats from the United Arab Republic and the Soviet Union. The result represented a victory over "indirect aggression" across national borders and reduced the Lebanese problem to its internal dimensions. U.S. prestige had been greatly boosted by the American role in achieving this result, and the only threat to American status that remained was the possibility of embarrassment in the UN General Assembly debate scheduled for mid-August. In fact, however, the outcome of this debate and the compromise resolution adopted did not embarrass the United States, but rather helped to cover the extrication of American troops with no loss of face.

Likewise in 1970, there was a steep decline in the perceived threat to a moderate regime. With the Jordanian regime apparently now safe, American policy-makers no longer feared the collapse of a friendly regime and the consequent risk of a momentum bringing further radicalization to the entire region. The stability of the Middle East was preserved, and adventurism by radical regimes was shown not to pay. A smashing victory for the forces of Western influence and moderation had in fact been achieved, giving a tremendous boost to American credibility and inflicting on the Soviet Union the first serious reversal of its worldwide offensive during the Nixon administration. In addition, the forces of terrorism had been defeated, although the hostages still remained in the hands of the guerrilla forces until the end of the post-crisis period. The fate of the hostages was, in fact, the one remaining serious threat to values perceived by American decision-makers after the withdrawal of Syrian forces from Jordan.

In 1973, there was also a significant decline in perceived threats, but not to the same extent as in the two earlier crises. The threat of an overwhelming Arab defeat, bringing in its train the loss of diplomatic openings with Egypt and elsewhere, and of diplomatic flexibility generally, had been terminated. There was also no longer a threat of an even worse confrontation with the Soviet Union that might have spelled a total end to detente. Costs in U.S.-Arab relations had been contained by ending the war at this point, and there was now a significant chance for improvement in these relations, especially with Egypt. Policy-makers now tended to view American interests in the area more in relation to local forces, as was also the case in the 1958 post-crisis period (though not in 1970). The war was also ended in such a way as to avoid the total embitterment of U.S.-Israeli relations. On the other hand, there was a significant danger of the renewal of hostilities, which in itself might well upset all of the above achievements. American policy-makers perceived that unless some progress were made toward both the stabilization of the immediate situation and the building of a final peace settlement, American interests in the region might again soon be subjected to serious challenge. In addition, the continuation of the Arab oil embargo after the end of the war represented a threat to the United States that could not be ignored.

Probability of Involvement in Military Hostilities

Chehab's election in 1958 greatly reduced the perceived danger of American forces actually engaging in combat. It now seemed that an end to the Lebanese civil war was in sight, and the role of U.S. troops—which had fortunately remained a noncombat role—now seemed to be ended. It was now possible to contemplate an early withdrawal of the U.S. forces. The United States was determined to see President Chamoun serve out the remaining two months of his Presidential term, but this did not seem to risk hostilities, since it was unlikely that Chamoun, as a lame duck, would be challenged as he had been previously, and since the presence of whatever U.S. forces remained would be a deterrent to such actions.

In the Jordanian crisis, the need to consider either an American intervention or support of an Israeli intervention vanished with the Syrian withdrawal from Jordanian territory. It was clear in the minds of American policy-makers that the Jordanian army could handle the Palestinian fighting organizations without outside assistance. The major remaining concern regarding the expansion of hostilities was the possibility that Israel might, despite the Syrian withdrawal, decide to act on its own either in Jordan or against Syria. This likelihood was reduced by the explicit cancellation of understandings with Israel regarding American support for Israeli actions.

In 1973, there was also a sharp drop in the perceived possibility of American involvement in hostilities, but (again) to a lesser extent than in the other two crises. The end of the Soviet threat removed the danger of a direct U.S. action to counter any Soviet move in the area. On the other hand, the real possibility of a renewal in hostilities, particularly over the issue of the encirclement of the Egyptian Third Army, carried with it an attendant risk of the United States becoming involved in a new war as Israel's major arms supplier. This brought with it a strongly felt need to separate the forces of the two sides in order to stabilize the southern front and remove the danger of renewed warfare.

Time Pressure

In both the Lebanese and Jordanian crises, the onset of the post-crisis period was marked by an elimination of any sense of urgency. The election of Chehab in 1958 created a situation requiring no further urgent action by the United States, which was content to let the situation unfold. American withdrawal could proceed on schedule, and did so despite the September-October cabinet crisis; in fact, Ambassador McClintock waited several days before intervening as an intermediary in that dispute. On the diplomatic front, far from feeling any need for urgent UN debate or action, the United States engaged in leisurely diplomatic interchanges, which led the Soviets to accuse Eisenhower of purposely delaying action on this front.

The termination of the outside military threat in 1970 removed any felt need to act within a finite time. The situation was now such that time was operating in favor of American interests. The United States did not even demonstrate any sense of urgency toward the conclusion of a cease-fire between Hussein and the guerrillas, since it was clear that the military balance favored the regular Jordanian army. There remained the issue of the release of hostages, but in this case it was assumed that a solution to the problem would come about as a result of Hussein's establishing his dominance over the Palestinian organizations. In the end, this perception proved to be correct.

Again, the 1973 crisis presents a somewhat different picture. The end of the U.S.-Soviet confrontation had eliminated any sense of necessary actions within a finite time on that level. But there was a clear perception of the need to take diplomatic steps on the local level because of the unstable military situation. The issue of the Egyptian Third Army was especially urgent, since the need for re-supply would make the situation critical within a number of days. At the same time, Kissinger told his Arab interlocutors that diplomatic results could not be achieved immediately and emphasized the necessity of a step-by-step diplomatic process in dealing with basic issues. As Mohammed Heikal remarked regarding Kissinger's perceptions: "The importance of the time factor to us is different from the importance of the time factor to him. This is because we are under pressure from the present military, political and psychological situation, . . . whereas for him they are no more than memoranda written on paper, ideas, and possible subjects for discussion at the negotiating table."[8]

And while clearly feeling that the oil embargo represented a threat to the United States and necessitated a response, Kissinger consistently refused to establish a timetable for either American action on the subject or an Arab response to it.

CRISIS COMPONENTS: SUMMARY

To summarize the above discussion of American perceptions of threat, probability of hostilities, and finite time in the 1958, 1970, and 1973 Middle East crises:

During the *pre-crisis period,* U.S. decision-makers in the three crises experienced a serious but finite rise in their perceptions of threat to basic values. There was, however, little or no increase in perceptions of possible involvement in military hostilities, and in none of the three cases was there a pressing sense of finite time available for an American response.

During the *crisis period,* there were again sharply similar perceptions in all three crises. Threats to a friendly regime came to be

8. Quoted in Edward R. F. Sheehan, *The Arabs, Israelis, and Kissinger: A Secret History of American Diplomacy in the Middle East* (New York: Reader's Digest Press, 1976), p. 60.

regarded as a pressing challenge to American global and regional interests, and thus as a very serious threat to basic American values. There was a clear perception of likely involvement, directly and indirectly, in military hostilities. There was a sharp sense of time constraints governing the American response, given the apprehension of an impending military coup in 1958 and the fear of possible rapid developments in battles already being fought in 1970 and 1973.

During the *post-crisis period,* there was a sharply reduced sense of threat to basic values in 1958 and 1970, and a significantly reduced sense of threat in 1973. The perceived likelihood of military involvement was greatly diminished in the first two crises, and no notable sense of time pressure remained; again, the 1973 crisis differed somewhat, in that decision-makers still felt some possibility of military involvement and some time pressure, but both perceptions were still significantly below the crisis level.

These findings correspond to the definitions of periods within a crisis suggested in Chapter One. In other words, for all three crises, it is possible to delineate pre-crisis, crisis, and post-crisis periods in which the perceptions of threat, time pressure, and war probability fit the definitions of the three-stage model of international crisis behavior. This supports, therefore, the applicability of the model to at least some historical cases, and provides significant evidence for the relevance and utility of the ICB definition of crisis.

Two further observations on the periods and components of crisis might be offered. First, one factor that seemed to distinguish the pre-crisis periods from the crisis periods, in a shorthand way, was the feeling that it was not (yet) necessary for the United States to act directly. Although there was a definite sense of threat to American values, the direction of events was not yet seen as negative. In all three areas, local forces still seemed sufficient to meet the threat, whether it was the Lebanese army dealing with Lebanese rebels, the Jordanian army fighting an unaided PLO, or Israel against Egypt and Syria before the massive Soviet airlift.

The event, in each case, that changed this perception of local sufficiency and created the feeling that the United States must *now* act because the direction of events had become negative was what engendered the sense of likely involvement and time pressure and marked the onset of the crisis period. Statements that the United States "must do something," that "doing something is better than doing nothing," and that the "consequences of inaction" were worse than any other alternative provided a sure and sharp contrast in all three crises to the pre-crisis mood. As an index to the crisis period, the sense of the need to act—even if only in a cathartic mode—seems as reliable as the changes in the defined crisis components.

A second observation derives from an earlier effort to measure the relationship between *individual* crisis components (i.e., threat, time pressure, or war probability separately) and the intervening dependent variables.[9] In an analysis of crisis situations, it is very difficult *operationally* to isolate the impact of any one of the three variables. This is not because they are not analytically distinct; theoretically, any one of them could have an independent impact on decision-makers. But after the pre-crisis period, increases in perceived threat, time pressure, and war probability tend to occur simultaneously and to reinforce each other. The relationship of any one of them to a dependent variable is therefore likely to be describable in terms almost identical to those that describe the relationship of the other two to the same variable. The relationship of time pressure to the search for alternatives, for example, will be difficult to differentiate from the relationship of increased probability of war to the search for alternatives.

Conceptually, then, it would seem more economical to regard the three crisis components not as distinct independent variables but as different measures of a single independent variable, which could be called *intensification of crisis.* On a different level, the concept of *increased stress*—as a result of the intensification of crisis associated with an increased sense of threat, time pressure, and war probability —provides the same economy of a single independent variable (Brecher has generally defined his hypotheses in this way).[10] In either case, whether defined as more intense crisis or as increased stress, there seem to be strong operational grounds for employing a single independent variable in the study of crisis decision-making.

9. Alan Dowty, "The U.S. and the Syria-Jordan Confrontation, 1970," in Michael Brecher, ed., *Studies in Crisis Behavior* (New Brunswick, N.J.: Transaction Books, 1978), pp. 172–196.

10. Michael Brecher, *Decisions in Crisis: Israel, 1967 and 1973* (Berkeley, Los Angeles, and London: University of California Press, 1980), pp. 343, 375–378, 397–402.

CHAPTER FIFTEEN

Decisions in Crisis

MY CONCLUSIONS on crisis decision-making are organized in the following format:

1. A summary of evidence on coping mechanisms, based on Chapters Five, Nine, and Thirteen, including the testing of hypotheses defining the impact of crisis-induced stress on the ways decision-makers cope with crisis.

2. A summary of evidence on patterns of choice, again drawing from Chapters Five, Nine, and Thirteen, a final discussion of hypotheses concerning the impact of crisis-induced stress on decisional choice, and an analysis of the coping strategies used by decision-makers.

3. General observations on the implications of the results for theories of crisis decision-making, a delineation of new hypotheses and areas of exploration suggested by this study, and comments on the pattern of U.S. responses to Middle East crises as seen in the three cases at hand.

CRISIS AND COPING

Based on the discussions in Chapters Five, Nine, and Thirteen, and other observations from the case studies themselves, what is the evidence on changes in coping mechanisms over the three crisis periods?

Search for and Receptivity to Information

In the pre-crisis period, there was increased demand for information and the tapping of new sources in all three crises. In 1958 and 1970, there were no basic changes in information processing, though information was transmitted orally more often and moved more quickly to the top than before. This was somewhat more pronounced in 1973, which had more of the elements of a crisis situation, in that the entire information processing was speeded up.

During the crisis period, there was in all three instances a sharply increased demand for information and a serious effort to find new sources of information where existing sources were inadequate. Information processing was transformed, with information passing more quickly to the top, often in undigested form. This resulted in an abundance of raw, unevaluated intelligence at the top in 1958 and in 1973, though not in 1970, owing to the overall lack of firsthand information. Interestingly enough, this "overload" seems to have been functional in 1958, as Eisenhower learned from Murphy's cables to appreciate the subtleties of Lebanese politics, while it is described by participants as dysfunctional in 1973.

There was, generally, a return to routine information search and evaluation in the post-crisis period, reflecting less rapid political and military developments. Though much information was still channeled directly to senior decision-makers, there was less felt need to search for new information. The 1973 crisis is a partial exception to this, in that Kissinger's unique role guaranteed a continuation, and even increase, in the centralization of information search and evaluation. Ironically, while Kissinger tended to exclude large parts of his own bureaucracy, there was in the 1973 post-crisis period greater public dissemination of information, as he turned to the media and Congress to build support for his policies. A similar pattern of broader public dissemination of information in the post-crisis period can be observed in 1970.

There was also, in the 1970 and 1973 post-crisis periods, more bias in receptivity to new information, at least in part because of the centralization of the Kissinger system. On the other hand, the new receptivity to information on Lebanon, shown by Eisenhower in 1958, continued into the post-crisis period.

Looking at the crises as a whole, it is clear that increasing stress did not lead decision-makers to become more closed to new information. Other aspects of cognitive performance are more complex to judge. It seems clear that in certain respects—the tendency to interpret events as a function of Soviet relations, the resort to certain affective responses, and the clinging to unexamined basic goals—the heightening of tension was indeed accompanied by a certain cognitive rigidity. There was, during the peak of all three crises, a notable narrowing of attention span and a focus on a few key—usually tactical

—elements of the crises. There was a remarked tendency under high stress to see "everything as related to everything," in line with the global focus: the Iraqi coup was part of a three-pronged plot including Jordan and Lebanon; the Syrian invasion was Soviet-inspired; and Arab success in battle raised the spectre of "a victory of Soviet arms."

On the other hand, as argued in Chapter Twelve, a differentiation of levels of thinking demonstrates that this rigidity obtained primarily on the level of basic values and policy objectives, while perceptions of the environment and immediate policy choices proved to be —especially in 1973, but also in the other two cases—sensitive to external change and flexible in operation. Policy-makers proved willing to accept evidence that challenged prevailing perceptions on many issues, such as the nature of opposition goals in Lebanon, the likely costs of U.S. action in 1970, and the military balance during the 1973 war. (Kissinger, in particular, demonstrated quick adaptability to new conditions on several occasions in 1970 and 1973.) There was also sensitivity to negative feedback from policies carried out, as shown by the way policy-makers weighed the costs of negative reactions in decisions on aiding Lebanon, Jordan, or Israel. On the whole, then, there was no cognitive rigidity, but rather considerable adaptability, in analyzing situational factors and preferred strategies.

Consultation

In the pre-crisis period, the scope of consultation was not basically altered; there was no significant increase or reduction in the circle of persons normally consulted within the executive branch. As with information, however, there was some intensification of the process: greater volume and speed in consultation, with more face-to-face contact in meetings. The input of second-rank officials was still important, and there was, to some degree, more military participation (especially in 1970 and 1973, where full-scale military conflicts were being waged). On the other hand, one can already witness, in all three pre-crisis periods, the beginning of a tendency to close out consultation with individuals and groups, governmental and nongovernmental, outside the executive branch (apart from foreign governments). During the crisis period, there was increased consultation within the executive branch, less or no consultation with outside groups, and increased selective communication with other governments. The increased consultation within the executive branch was more direct and informal. This increased scope and frequency of internal consultation should not be taken to mean, however, that those consulted (including the military) had more influence on the decisions made. In fact, the opposite was usually the case, since senior decision-makers—usually the President and one top advisor—reserved decisions to themselves as tension rose and used the wider consultative forums more as sounding boards (e.g., Eisenhower's decision to intervene in 1958 and the numerous Nixon-Kissinger "end runs" around the bureaucracy in 1970 and 1973).

There was generally less internal consultation with the reduction of tension in the post-crisis period, marked by a return to routine procedures. Again, 1973 is a partial exception, with Kissinger's adoption of a diplomatic style that was anything but routine; aides traveling with the Secretary were consulted more, though those left behind were indeed consulted less than during the peak of the crisis. As suggested, the differences in 1973 may also reflect the fact that the tension level in the 1973 post-crisis period did not drop as much as in 1958 or 1970.

Consultation with outside groups did not drop and seems even to have increased—at least in 1970 and 1973—during the post-crisis period.

Decisional Forums

Decision-making procedures remained close to routine, institutionalized rather than ad hoc, during all three pre-crisis periods. The large meetings convened in 1958 do not contradict this, since such meetings were "routine" for Eisenhower and closely resembled formal NSC meetings. Likewise, in 1970 and 1973, WSAG did not represent a great departure from normal procedures, since it operated largely as a coordinating body transmitting recommendations to the President rather than as a decisional unit. The greatest departures from routine came in 1973, when a higher degree of centralization characterized the pre-crisis period—reflecting, perhaps, the fact that a major Arab-Israeli war was being fought, and the tension level was higher. One must also take into account, of course, the Nixon-Kissinger tendency to regard the bureaucracy as an adversary. Even before the onset of crisis in 1970 and 1973, there was a pronounced centralization of foreign policy decision-making, and thus one begins the examination of the impact of crisis from a base that is already high.

As can be clearly seen from the historical accounts, the passage to crisis in all three cases was marked by a decrease in the size of the decisional unit, further centralization of the decision-making process, a closing out of bureaucratic politics, more informal and ad hoc decisional forums, and greater dominance by decision-makers with a global rather than "parochial" (military, regional, etc.) perspective.[1]

At the same time, despite the exclusion of subordinates from participation in actual decision-making, there was a clear tendency to consensus on the choices made. The greater the crisis, the greater the tendency to accept strong leadership and to close ranks behind the President. There was surprisingly little disagreement within the executive branch on the decisions made at the peak of crisis: U.S. intervention in 1958; backing Israeli intervention on the ground in 1970; and the worldwide alert in 1973.

This tendency to consensus appeared strongest when the decision time was shortest, in 1973, but not in 1970 (it is difficult to draw conclusions regarding the Lebanese crisis in 1958, since there was little internal disagreement on any of the decisions reached). Only in the 1973 case, likewise, was it true that when there was more time available for decisions, and more conflict surfaced among decision-makers, there was greater consensus once decisions were reached (presumably since there was more opportunity to work out disagreements before the decision). This is seen in the airlift decision in 1973, which took more time, was characterized by greater conflict prior to the decision, but enjoyed greater consensus afterward than the decisions on Israeli ground intervention or the DefCon 3 alert.

During the post-crisis period, there was generally a return to normal decisional forums, with more participation by subordinates and more routine procedures. Again, this must be qualified for 1973, given the continuing centralization of the Kissinger diplomatic shuttle.

Search for and Evaluation of Alternatives

In the pre-crisis period, there was generally little or no search for new options and no fundamental reexamination of the way choices were defined. There was a definite tendency to focus on routine military moves as signals to other parties, rather than rethinking habitual responses (the United States *always* moves the Sixth Fleet

1. This is perhaps the most significant difference between the conclusions of this study and Brecher's analysis of Israeli crisis decision-making, in Michael Brecher, *Decisions in Crisis: Israel, 1967 and 1973* (Berkeley, Los Angeles, and London: University of California Press, 1980). Brecher finds an increase in the size of the decisional unit, less centralization, and more institutionalization, as stress increases. The contradiction seems to be attributable, at least in part, to the difference between a parliamentary system, with collective Cabinet responsibility, and a Presidential system with strongly-established traditions of executive preeminence in foreign policy and weak or nonexistent Cabinet authority.

at the outset of a Middle East crisis). In 1958 and 1970, this confined search for options extended to the tactical level, where few if any new options were sought; in 1973, there was greater tactical creativity (basically on the issue of how to get supplies to Israel without upsetting the low American profile).

Those options that were considered, however—with the exception of the more routine military moves—seem to have been evaluated carefully in all three crises. This applies to the cautious responses to the Lebanese government during May and June 1958, the consideration of responses to the airplane hijackings in 1970, and the careful weighing of alternative answers to Israeli requests for resupply during the first week of the 1973 war.

The onset of the crisis period brought about a pronounced lessening of reliance on routine procedures in all three crises. There was a wider *formal* search for options, but regarding the actual consideration of alternatives the picture is more mixed. In 1958, Eisenhower and Dulles were careful to make a complete survey of all plausible options before intervening in Lebanon, though some options were perhaps foreclosed by predisposition. In 1970, there was clearly not much more search for alternatives, but rather a fairly quick focus on a limited number of tactical choices. In 1973, there appears to have been a curvilinear relationship: more search for options in periods of higher stress, but some closure and circumscribing of the search during peak crisis (i.e., the alert decision). When a larger circle was involved in consultation or decision-making, as in the Lebanese intervention decision or the debate over resupply to Israel, there was likely to be a broader search for additional options.

Whether the search broadened or narrowed, there was likely, during periods of higher or peak stress, to be more focus on military options (including displays of force, etc.) than on political and diplomatic alternatives. In periods of peak stress, there was a definite diversion of attention from long-term goals to pressing immediate concerns (in 1970, this applied not just to the peak of the crisis, but to the entire crisis period).

However, the narrowing of focus was accompanied by a clear tactical rationality. As in the pre-crisis period, those alternatives actually considered were evaluated with reasonable care, though there were more lapses than in the pre-crisis period (at least in periods of peak stress). These lapses were expressed in such failures as inadequate assessment of consequences of the nuclear alert decision in 1973. But such shortcomings, to repeat, occurred mainly in periods of the highest tension, as minor deviations from a general pattern of rational calculus on the tactical level. Policy-makers did not, at the height of crisis, reexamine their basic beliefs, but their choice of options was based on analysis of costs and gains rather than on purely affective reactions or bureaucratic bargaining and compromise.

It is also evident that crisis conditions forced clear choices where the tendency, during the pre-crisis period, had been to delay or to make policy incrementally. This is particularly true of the Lebanese crisis, in which pre-crisis decisions had been uniformly to delay, but it is also true, to a great extent, of responses to the hijacking in 1970 and to Israeli resupply needs in 1973.

Finally, it can be argued that the decisions made under highest stress in the three crises were no less "correct" than those made under less pressing conditions. Despite flawed perceptions and other shortcomings, in each case the immediate American aims were achieved. Lebanon was stabilized with a non-Nasserist regime, Hussein survived after suppressing the PLO in Jordan, and the Yom Kippur War ended in a way that opened diplomatic vistas. In each case, U.S. policy was at least partly instrumental in achieving these results, even when this policy followed basic premises that could easily be criticized. Both Malcolm Kerr, analyzing the 1958 crisis, and William Quandt, speaking of 1970, make a strong case for the appropriateness of U.S. policy, even while criticizing the perceptions on which it was based.[2] A similar argument could be made for 1973.

In the post-crisis period, interestingly enough, there appears to have been in 1958 and 1973 a *broader* search for options, as policymakers turned to some of the background issues and broader perspectives submerged by the crises (1970 was an exception, as the degree of success apparently created the perception that no basic issues remained). But, once more, 1973 is something of an anomaly, due to the peculiar circumstances. The limits were essentially those of Kissinger's own capacities, since he completely dominated the process; many options were not considered, even though the search appears wider than it did during the peak phase of the crisis. In particular, the "tough" options—on the oil embargo, separation of forces, etc.—do not seem to have been seriously considered by Kiss-

2. Malcolm H. Kerr, "The Lebanese Civil War," in Evan Luard, ed., *The International Regulation of Civil War* (New York: New York University Press, 1972), p. 79; William B. Quandt, "Lebanon, 1958, and Jordan, 1970," in Barry M. Blechman and Stephen S. Kaplan, eds., *Force Without War: U.S. Armed Forces as a Political Instrument* (Washington, D.C.: Brookings Institution, 1978), pp. 119–127. Adam Garfinkle, in "United States Foreign Policy and the Jordan Crisis of 1970: A Cognitive Approach" (Ph.D. dissertation, University of Pennsylvania, 1979), pp. 315–316, makes a similar and persuasive argument about "substantially wrong assumptions" on the regional level but "admirable skill" on the U.S.-USSR level.

inger. On the other hand, as recounted earlier, Kissinger displayed a quick tactical adaptability in making use of opportunities as they arose in the diplomatic process—e.g., when he pursued the "option" of a quick disengagement agreement in January 1974.

The evaluation of the options considered was, as in previous periods, carried out carefully, with fewer lapses as time pressure and stress decreased. There was a notable increase of tactical subtlety in deliberations and decisions, especially in 1973.

Hypotheses

Based on this summary of the evidence regarding coping mechanisms during the various crisis periods, we can now proceed to a final test of the forty-five hypotheses posed in Chapter One regarding the impact of crisis-induced stress on coping mechanisms. The first twelve of these hypotheses dealt with *information* search and processing:

1. The greater the stress, the greater the conceptual rigidity of an individual, and the more closed to new information the individual becomes.

2. The greater the crisis, the greater the propensity for decision-makers to supplement information about the objective state of affairs with information drawn from their own past experience.

3. The greater the crisis, the greater the felt need for information, the more thorough the quest for information, and the more open the receptivity to new information.

4. The greater the crisis, the more information about it tends to be elevated to the top of the organizational [decisional] pyramid quickly and without distortion.

5. The higher the stress in a crisis situation, the greater the tendency to rely upon extraordinary and improved channels of communication [and information].

6. In crisis, the rate of communication by a nation's decision-makers to international actors outside their country will increase.

7. As crisis-induced stress increases, the search for information is likely to become more active, but it may also become more random and less productive.

8. As crisis-induced stress declines, the quest for information becomes more restricted.

9. As crisis-induced stress declines, receptivity becomes permeated by more bias.

10. The more intense the crisis, the greater the tendency of
    decision-makers to perceive that everything in the external
    environment is related to everything else.

11. The more intense the crisis, the less the sensitivity to, and
    learning from, negative feedback.

12. The more intense the crisis, the greater the tendency to an
    overabundance of new information (information overload) and
    a paucity of usable data on decision-making levels.

My findings support only part of Hypothesis 1. There was cognitive rigidity, but it was largely on the level of basic beliefs and policy objectives, especially in 1973. There was flexibility on the level of sensitivity to situational changes and adaptation of policy. The part of the hypothesis on closure to new information is rejected in all three cases.

Hypothesis 2 is difficult to assess. There seems to have been somewhat greater reliance on past experience during the peak phase of the 1958 crisis, but, generally, historical experience was important in all periods of all three crises. For 1970 and 1973, it is not possible to say with certainty whether this reliance was more important at the height of the crisis than earlier; it was high in all phases (see also the discussion of the use of historical models under "Coping Strategies" in the next section).

Hypotheses 3–6 are confirmed in all three crises. Hypothesis 7 is supported by the 1970 and 1973 studies, but not for 1958, when the search for information seems to have been more systematic and more productive.

Hypothesis 8, on the reduced quest for information in the post-crisis period, seems to hold true for 1958 and 1970 but not for 1973 (which is, as has been noted, something of an exception in the post-crisis period). Hypothesis 9, on the other hand, is supported by the 1970 and 1973 cases, but is rejected for 1958, when receptivity to new information remained relatively open and unbiased.

Hypothesis 10, from among those added to previous ICB hypotheses, is strongly supported by the evidence in 1958, 1970, and 1973. Hypothesis 11, in contrast, is not supported by the evidence in any of the cases.

Hypothesis 12 is supported only partly by the data for 1958 (when there was an abundance of raw data but no overload), is rejected for 1970 (when there was a general lack of raw or evaluated data), and is strongly supported by evidence in the 1973 crisis.

The seven hypotheses posed on patterns of *consultation* were:

13. The longer the decision time [in a crisis], the greater the
    consultation with persons outside the core decisional unit.

14. The greater the crisis, the greater the felt need for face-to-face proximity among decision-makers.

15. As crisis-induced stress rises, the scope and frequency of consultation by senior decision-makers broadens and also increases.

16. As crisis-induced stress increases, decision-makers increasingly use ad hoc forms of consultation.

17. As crisis-induced stress declines, the consultative circle becomes narrower.

18. As crisis-induced stress declines, consultation relies heavily on ad hoc settings as high-level consultation reaches its peak.

19. The more intense the crisis, the less the influence of vested interests and other groups outside the bureaucracy.

Hypothesis 13 is supported by the 1970 and 1973 cases, but not by the evidence from 1958 (when there was as much or more consultation when decision time was most limited).

Hypotheses 14–17 are supported in all three cases, with the qualification that Hypothesis 15 (broadening of the scope of consultation) is true only inside the executive branch and with other governments.

Hypothesis 18 is not supported by the findings on 1958 and 1970, and is supported in 1973 only in that consultation relied on ad hoc settings (it did *not* reach its peak).

Hypothesis 19 is strongly supported in all three cases.

There were thirteen hypotheses proposed at the outset regarding the linkage between crisis and *decisional forums:*

20. The longer the crisis, the greater the felt need for effective leadership within decisional units.

21. The longer the decision time, the greater the conflict within decisional units.

22. The greater the group conflict aroused by a crisis, the greater the consensus once a decision is reached.

23. The longer the amount of time available in which to make a decision, the greater will be the consensus on the final choice.

24. Crisis decisions tend to be reached by ad hoc decisional units.

25. In high-stress situations, decision groups tend to become smaller.

26. In crisis, decision-making becomes increasingly centralized.

27. As crisis-induced stress rises, there is a heavy reliance on medium-to-large and institutional forums for decisions.

28. As crisis-induced stress declines, there is a maximum reliance on large, institutional forums for decisions.

29. The more intense the crisis, the greater the tendency of decision-makers to conform to group goals and norms, and the less the dissent within the group.

30. The more intense the crisis, the less the influence of "standard operating procedures."

31. The more intense the crisis, the greater the role in decision-making of officials with a general rather than a "parochial" perspective.

32. The more intense the crisis, the less the influence of vested interests in the bureaucracy ("bureaucratic politics").

Hypothesis 20 is supported by all three case studies.

Hypotheses 21–23 are supported by evidence from 1973, but not by that from 1958 or 1970. In the 1958 case, it will be recalled, the level of disagreement was low in all decisions, whatever the time available. For that reason, Hypothesis 22 is not testable and Hypotheses 21 and 23 are rejected for 1958. All three are rejected for 1970.

Hypotheses 24–26 are supported by the evidence from all three crises.

Hypotheses 27 and 28 are rejected for all three cases, with the qualification that in 1958 there was a tendency to convene large meetings at the peak of the crisis, even though the decisions were not made in a large institutional forum.

Hypotheses 29–32 are all supported by the evidence in 1958, 1970, and 1973.

Finally, there were thirteen hypotheses dealing with the search for and the evaluation of alternatives:

33. As stress increases, decision-makers become more concerned with the immediate than the long-run future.

34. The greater the reliance on group problem-solving processes, the greater the consideration of alternatives.

35. During crisis the search for alternatives occupies a substantial part of decision-making time.

36. The relationship between stress and group performance in the consideration of alternatives is curvilinear (an inverted U)— more careful as stress rises to a moderate level, less careful as stress becomes intense.

37. Despite the rise in stress, choices among alternatives are not, for the most part, made before adequate information is processed; that is, there is not a tendency to premature closure.

38. As time pressure increases, the choice among alternatives does not become less correct.

39. Decision-makers do not generally choose among alternatives with an inadequate assessment of their consequences.

40. As crisis-induced stress rises, the search for options tends to increase.

41. As crisis-induced stress rises, the evaluation of alternatives becomes less careful.

42. As crisis-induced stress declines, the search for options tends to become less extensive than in all other phases of the crisis period.

43. As crisis-induced stress declines, the evaluation of alternatives reaches its maximum care, more so when time salience is low.

44. The more intense the crisis, the greater the tendency of decision-makers to narrow their span of attention to a few aspects of the decision-making task ("tunnel vision").

45. The more intense the crisis, the more likely that decision-makers will be forced to make a clear choice rather than postponing choices or drifting into policy.

Hypothesis 33 is partially supported by evidence from 1958 (there were still some long-term considerations at the peak of the crisis), seems to have been true *only* in the period of peak stress in 1973, and is wholly supported only by the 1970 case.

Hypotheses 34–37 hold true for all three crises, with a reservation regarding Hypothesis 36 for 1970, when group performance became only slightly less careful as stress became intense.

Hypothesis 38, following the discussion above, is tentatively confirmed for all three crises (with more conviction for 1970 than for the other two cases).

Hypothesis 39 seems to hold true to some extent for 1958 and 1970; consequences were assessed, with some lapses. It is, however, rejected for 1973, for which a stronger case for the inadequate assessment of consequences can be made.

Hypothesis 40 is confirmed for the 1958 crisis, is rejected for 1970, and for 1973 is curvilinear: confirmed in higher stress phases, but rejected in the peak stress phase.

Hypothesis 41 is confirmed in all three cases for the peak stress phase only; it is rejected in all three cases for periods of high, but less than peak, stress.

Hypothesis 42 is confirmed only by the data of the 1970 crisis; it is not supported by evidence from 1958 or 1973.

Hypotheses 43–45 are confirmed in all three case studies.

The results of the testing of hypotheses on coping mechanisms are summarized in Tables 1–4.

TABLE 1

HYPOTHESES ON CRISIS AND COPING: INFORMATION

Hypothesis	Lebanese Crisis, 1958	Jordanian Crisis, 1970	Yom Kippur War, 1973
1. Greater stress→cognitive rigidity, closure to information	Rigidity partially confirmed; closure rejected	Rigidity partially confirmed; closure rejected	Rigidity partially confirmed; closure rejected
2. Greater crisis→more reliance on past experience	Confirmed	High in all phases	High in all phases
3. Greater crisis→greater felt need for information, more search and receptivity	Confirmed	Confirmed	Confirmed
4. Greater crisis→more information to top, better transmission	Confirmed	Confirmed	Confirmed
5. Higher stress→extraordinary channels	Confirmed	Confirmed	Confirmed
6. More communication to international actors	Confirmed	Confirmed	Confirmed
7. Higher stress→active but random information search	Rejected	Confirmed	Confirmed
8. Decline in stress→more restricted information search	Confirmed	Confirmed	Rejected
9. Decline in stress→more bias in receptivity	Rejected	Confirmed	Confirmed
10. Greater crisis→everything related to everything else	Confirmed	Confirmed	Confirmed
11. Greater crisis→less sensitivity to negative feedback	Rejected	Rejected	Rejected
12. Greater crisis→more information overload	Partially confirmed	Rejected	Confirmed

TABLE 2
HYPOTHESES ON CRISIS AND COPING: CONSULTATION

Hypothesis	Lebanese Crisis, 1958	Jordanian Crisis, 1970	Yom Kippur War, 1973
13. Longer decision time→greater outside consultation	Rejected	Confirmed	Confirmed
14. Greater crisis→more need for face-to-face proximity	Confirmed	Confirmed	Confirmed
15. Higher stress→broader scope and more frequent consultation	Confirmed*	Confirmed*	Confirmed*
16. Higher stress→more ad hoc consultation	Confirmed	Confirmed	Confirmed
17. Decline in stress→narrower consultative circle	Confirmed	Confirmed	Confirmed
18. Decline in stress→heavy reliance on ad hoc settings, peak consultation	Rejected	Rejected	Ad hoc confirmed; Peak rejected
19. Greater crisis→less outside influence	Confirmed	Confirmed	Confirmed

*Only within the executive branch and with foreign governments.

TABLE 3

HYPOTHESES ON CRISIS AND COPING: DECISIONAL FORUMS

Hypothesis	Lebanese Crisis, 1958	Jordanian Crisis, 1970	Yom Kippur War, 1973
20. Longer crisis→greater felt need for leadership in decisional units	Confirmed	Confirmed	Confirmed
21. Longer decision time→greater conflict within decisional units	Rejected	Rejected	Confirmed
22. Greater group conflict→greater consensus after decision	Not testable	Rejected	Confirmed
23. Longer decision time→greater consensus on decision	Rejected	Rejected	Confirmed
24. Decisional units tend to be ad hoc	Confirmed	Confirmed	Confirmed
25. High stress→smaller decision groups	Confirmed	Confirmed	Confirmed
26. Crisis→increasingly centralized decision-making	Confirmed	Confirmed	Confirmed
27. Higher stress→heavy reliance on medium-to-large and institutional settings	Rejected*	Rejected	Rejected
28. Decline in stress→maximum reliance on large institutional forums	Rejected	Rejected	Rejected
29. Greater crisis→greater conformity to group norms, less dissent	Confirmed	Confirmed	Confirmed
30. Greater crisis→less influence of standard operating procedures	Confirmed	Confirmed	Confirmed
31. Greater crisis→greater role of general perspectives	Confirmed	Confirmed	Confirmed
32. Greater crisis→less influence of bureaucratic politics	Confirmed	Confirmed	Confirmed

* Use of large institutional settings, but not as a decisional unit.

TABLE 4
HYPOTHESES ON CRISIS AND COPING: ALTERNATIVES

Hypothesis	Lebanese Crisis, 1958	Jordanian Crisis, 1970	Yom Kippur War, 1973
33. Increased stress→more concern with immediate than long-run future	Partially confirmed	Confirmed	Confirmed for peak stress phase
34. Greater group problem-solving→greater consideration of alternatives	Confirmed	Confirmed	Confirmed
35. Crisis→substantial time in search for alternatives	Confirmed	Confirmed	Confirmed
36. Curvilinear relationship between stress and performance in consideration of alternatives	Confirmed	Confirmed*	Confirmed
37. Higher stress→choices *not* made before adequate information processed	Confirmed	Confirmed	Confirmed
38. Increased time pressure→choices *not* less correct	Confirmed (tentatively)	Confirmed	Confirmed (tentatively)
39. Alternatives *not* chosen with inadequate assessment of consequences	Partially confirmed	Partially confirmed	Rejected
40. Higher stress→more search for options	Confirmed	Rejected	Higher stress confirmed; Peak stress rejected
41. Higher stress→less careful evaluation of alternatives	Higher stress rejected; Peak stress confirmed	Higher stress rejected; Peak stress confirmed	Higher stress rejected; Peak stress confirmed
42. Decline in stress→less extensive search options than in all other pahses of crisis period	Rejected	Confirmed	Rejected
43. Decline in stress→most careful evaluation of alternatives	Confirmed	Confirmed	Confirmed
44. Greater crisis→narrower span of attention	Confirmed	Confirmed	Confirmed
45. Greater crisis→greater likelihood of clear choice rather than delay	Confirmed	Confirmed	Confirmed

*Consideration of alternatives is only slightly less careful under peak stress.

STRESS AND CHOICE

The second half of our research question, the impact of crisis-induced stress on the content of decisions, will now be examined. Following the discussions in Chapters Five, Nine, and Thirteen, I will summarize the application of the "dimensions of choice" and "coping strategies" frameworks to the decisions that have been identified.

Dimensions of Choice

The forty-nine decisions analyzed in the study of U.S. policy in the Middle East crises of 1958, 1970, and 1973 have been codified along the eight dimensions of choice proposed by Brecher.[3]

To recapitulate for the sake of convenience, these dimensions, and the procedures for coding them, are as follows:

Core Inputs:	The crucial stimuli to each decision as perceived by the decision-maker(s).
Costs:	The perceived magnitude of the loss(es) anticipated from the choice that was made—human (casualties); material (equipment and economic); political (deterrence credibility, alliance potential); and intangibles, such as morale and unity; these are coded as a qualitative composite: low, medium, or high.
Importance:	The perceived value of the decision at the time of choice, measured along a five-point ordinal scale: 5—decisive; 4—significant; 3—important; 2—consequential; 1—marginal.
Complexity:	The number of issue-areas involved in the choice, ranging from one to four—namely, Military-Security (M-S), Political-Diplomatic (P-D), Economic-Developmental (E-D), and Cultural-Status (C-S).
Systemic Domain:	The perceived scope of reverberations of the decision, ranging from Domestic alone to Bilateral, Regional, Superpower, and Global—any one or all of which may constitute the Domain.
Process:	The mental procedure associated with the selected options, as distinct—but not necessarily different—from the procedure attending the evaluation of all other options considered *prior* to choice; this is coded as Routine (following established procedures for a response to similar challenges); Affective (an assessment dominated by reliance on past experience,

3. Brecher, 1980, pp. 29–30, 380–381.

ideology, rooted beliefs, emotional preference, etc.); and Rational (a calculus based upon the measurement of costs and benefits, qualitatively and/or quantitatively).

Activity: The thrust of the decision; coded as to act, to delay, or to not act, and as to whether action or implied action is verbal or physical.

Novelty: The presence or absence of innovation, in terms of reliance on precedent and past choices; coded as yes or no.

The results of the earlier discussions in Chapters Five, Nine, and Thirteen can be bound in Tables 5–7. To summarize some of the more interesting findings: *Core inputs,* to some extent, increased in number and variety from the pre-crisis to the crisis period. There was a decline in core inputs during the post-crisis period, except in 1973, in which case, as already noted, there were fewer differences between the crisis and post-crisis periods.

Costs likewise were perceived as higher during the crisis period, and especially with decisions taken during peak stress (No. 5 in 1958, Nos. 10–12 in 1970, and Nos. 7 and 13 in 1973). They were perceived as low during the pre-crisis and post-crisis periods.

The *importance* of decisions, as perceived by the decision-makers, also varied by stress level. On a scale of 0–5, pre-crisis decisions averaged 2.2, crisis decisions averaged 3.8, and post-crisis decisions averaged 2.6. The variance was similar in all three crises.

The *complexity* of decisions, as measured by issue-areas, does not yield such clear patterns. Only in 1958 can there be said to be a significant increase in complexity during the crisis period as compared to pre-crisis decisions, and only in 1958 is there a significant change in the number of issue-areas involved in post-crisis decisions —and this is a decrease rather than the increase predicted by Hypothesis 53.

The *systemic domain* of the decisions did tend in all three crises to increase as stress rose, and to narrow during the post-crisis period. This is again not the direction postulated by the hypotheses.

The *mental process* associated with the decisions made was dominated by a rational calculus as stress increased, except in 1958, when the decision made at peak stress (to intervene) was largely affective (but, even here, other decisions made during the crisis period were generally made by a rational process). This tendency to rational procedures continued strongly in all three post-crisis periods.

The *activity* of choice, as stress increased, was in all three cases to be continuously active rather than to delay or to decide against action. There was, however, no clear pattern on physical as opposed

TABLE 5

DIMENSIONS OF CHOICE: LEBANESE CRISIS, 1958

No.	Decision Content	Core Inputs	Cost	Impor-tance	Complex-ity	Systemic Domain	Process*	Activity	Nov-elty
Pre-Crisis									
1	Set conditions for Lebanese intervention	Lebanese request	Low	3	M-S, P-D	R, B	Rational	Delay-verbal/physical	Yes
2	Support UN resolution	UN debate	Low	1	P-D	R	Routine	Act-verbal	No
3	No favorable response to Nasser	Egyptian "feeler"	Low	1	P-D	B	Affective	Not to act-verbal	No
4	Delay direct action	Military development in Lebanon	Low	3	M-S	R, B	Rational	Delay-physical	No
Crisis									
5	U.S. intervention in Lebanon	Iraqi coup; ideology	High	5	M-S, P-D	G, S-P R, B, D	Affective/Rational	Act-verbal/physical	Yes
6	Murphy sent to Lebanon	Need for coordination with Lebanon	Low	3	M-S, P-D	B	Rational/Routine	Act-verbal	No
7	No U.S. troops to Jordan	British pressure	Low	3	M-S, P-D	R, B, D	Rational	Not to act-physical	No
8	Reject Soviet summit proposal	Soviet proposal; oper-ational code	Medium	3	P-D	G, S-P, R	Rational/Affective	Act-verbal	Yes
9	Support election of Chehab	Murphy mission	Low	4	M-S, P-D	G, R, B	Rational	Act-verbal	Yes

10	Convene UN Security Council	Soviet pressure	Low	2	P-D	G, S-P	Rational/ Affective	Act-verbal	No
11	Recognize Iraqi government	Normalization in Iraq; pressure from allies	Low	2	P-D	B	Rational/ Routine	Act-verbal	No
12	Agree to General Assembly debate	Soviet pressure	Low	1	P-D	G, S-P	Rational	Act-verbal	No
13	Withdraw one battalion	Impending UN debate	Low	3	M-S, P-D	G, S-P	Rational	Act-physical	No
14	Mediate Lebanese cabinet crisis	Lebanese instability	Low	2	P-D	B	Rational	Act-verbal	No
15	Announce withdrawal of all forces	Successful transfer of power in Lebanon	Low	3	M-S, P-D	G, B	Rational	Act-physical	No

*Where two processes are listed, the first is considered dominant.

M-S = Military-Security
P-D = Political-Diplomatic
E-D = Economic-Developmental

G = Global
P-D = Political-Diplomatic

R = Regional
B = Bilateral

D = Domestic
S-P = Superpower

TABLE 6

DIMENSIONS OF CHOICE: JORDANIAN CRISIS, 1970

No.	Decision Content	Core Inputs	Cost	Impor- tance	Complex- ity	Systemic Domain	Process*	Activity	Nov- elty
Pre-Crisis									
1	No capitulation to hijackers	Airplane hijacking	Low	3	M-S, P-D	G, B	Affective/ Routine	Act-verbal; Delay- physical	No
2	Military preparations (sixth fleet)	Need to exert pressure	Low	2	M-S	B	Routine	Act-physical	No
3	Announce anti-hijacking program	Domestic reaction to hijackers	Low	1	M-S	D	Rational/ Affective	Act-physical	Yes
4	Increase aid to Israel	Anticipation of crisis in Jordan	Low	2	M-S, E-D	R, B	Rational	Act-physical	No
Crisis									
5	Further military readiness	Impending conflict in Jordan	Low	3	M-S, P-D	G, R, B	Routine	Act-physical	No
6	Further military moves	Outbreak of Jordanian civil war	Low	3	M-S, P-D	G, R, B	Routine	Act-physical	No
7	Speed up aid to Israel	Need for Israeli support	Low	2	M-S, P-D	R, B	Rational	Act-physical	No
8	Airborne alert	Syrian intervention	Low	3	M-S, P-D	G, S-P, R, B	Rational	Act-physical	Yes
9	Higher alert, military signals	Jordanian request	Low	4	M-S, P-D	G, S-P, R, B	Rational	Act-physical	Yes

10	Endorse Israeli air strike	Jordanian request	High	5	M-S, P-D	G, S-P, R, B	Rational	Act-verbal/ physical	Yes
11	Endorse Israeli ground action	Israeli pressure	High	5	M-S, P-D	G, S-P, R, B	Rational	Act-verbal	Yes
12	Guarantee Israel against retaliation	Israeli pressure	High	5	M-S, P-D	G, S-P, R, B	Rational	Act-verbal	Yes

Post-Crisis

13	Cancel understandings with Israel	Bureaucratic pressure	Low	1	M-S, P-D	B	Rational	Act-verbal	Yes

*Where two processes are listed, the first is considered dominant.

M-S = Military-Security
P-D = Political-Diplomatic

E-D = Economic-Developmental
G = Global

S-P = Superpower
R = Regional

B = Bilateral
D = Domestic

TABLE 7

DIMENSIONS OF CHOICE: YOM KIPPUR WAR, 1973

No.	Decision Content	Core Inputs	Cost	Impor-tance	Complex-ity	Systemic Domain	Process*	Activity	Nov-elty
Pre-Crisis									
1	Move Sixth Fleet	Outbreak of war	Low	2	M-S	S-P, R	Routine	Act-physical	No
2	Promote cease-fire *status quo ante*	Outbreak of war	Low	2	M-S, P-D	R	Rational	Act-verbal	No
3	Low-profile resupply of Israel	Outbreak of war	Low	3	M-S, P-D	S-P, R, B	Rational	Delay-physical	No
4	Israeli resupply "in principle"	Military developments	Low	3	M-S, P-D	S-P, R, B	Rational	Act and delay-verbal and physical	No
5	Promote cease-fire-in-place	Military developments	Low	2	M-S, P-D	R	Rational	Act-verbal	No
6	Interim measures to aid Israel	Military developments; Israeli and domestic pressure	Medium	4	M-S, P-D	G, S-P, R, B, D	Rational/ Affective	Act-physical	Yes
Crisis									
7	Military airlift to Israel	Military developments; Israeli and domestic pressure	High	4	M-S, P-D	G, S-P, R, B, D	Rational/ Affective	Act-physical	Yes
8	$2.2 billion Israeli aid request	Israeli pressure	Medium	3	M-S, P-D, E-D	G, R, B, D	Rational/ Affective	Act-physical	No
9	Kissinger to fly to Moscow	Soviet pressure	Low	4	M-S, P-D	G, S-P, R, B	Rational	Act-verbal	No

#	Decision	Context	Intensity		Issue	Scope	Motivation	Action	Novelty
10	Formulate joint U.S.-USSR cease-fire	Soviet pressure	Low	4	M-S, P-D	G, S-P, R, B	Rational	Act-verbal	No
11	Prevent destruction of Egyptian Third Army	Impending Egyptian defeat	Medium	4	M-S, P-D	G, S-P, R, B	Rational	Act-verbal	Yes
12	Reject Egyptian plea for U.S.-USSR to police cease-fire	Egyptian and Soviet pressure	Medium	4	M-S, P-D	G, S-P, R, B	Rational/ Affective	Not to act-physical	No
13	U.S. forces to DefCon 3	Soviet pressure	Very High	5	M-S, P-D	G, S-P, R, B	Rational/ Affective	Act-physical	No
14	Accept UN Emergency Force	UN debate	Low	4	M-S, P-D	G, S-P, R	Rational	Act-verbal	No

Post-Crisis

#	Decision	Context	Intensity		Issue	Scope	Motivation	Action	Novelty
15	Disengagement initiative	Military instability	Low	3	M-S, P-D	R, B	Rational	Act-verbal	No
16	Six-Point Agreement as temporary move	Opportunity	Low	3	M-S	R, B	Rational	Act-verbal	No
17	Push for Geneva Conference	Opportunity	Low	3	P-D	G, R	Rational	Act-verbal	Yes
18	Pressure to slow down K-101 talks	Diplomatic strategy	Low	2	M-S, P-D	R, B	Rational	Act-verbal	Yes
19	Push for Egyptian-Israeli disengagement prior to Geneva	Israeli proposals	Low	3	M-S, P-D	R	Rational	Act-verbal	No
20	Push for Egyptian-Israeli disengagement by shuttle	Egyptian pressure	Low	4	M-S, P-D	S-P, R, B	Rational	Act-verbal	Yes
21	Guarantees to Israel and Egypt	Israeli and Egyptian pressure	Medium	4	M-S, P-D	S-P, R, B	Rational	Act-verbal	Yes

*Where two processes are listed, the first is considered dominant.

M-S = Military-Security   B = Bilateral
P-D = Political-Diplomatic   D = Domestic
E-D = Economic-Developmental   S-P = Superpower
G = Global   R = Regional

to verbal action except in 1970, when decisions at peak stress (10–12) tended to be verbal. There was no observed reduction in the preference for continuous activity in the post-crisis period.

The *novelty* of decisions increased in all three crises during the crisis period, and remained high in the post-crisis period in 1970 and 1973, but not in 1958.

On the basis of these findings, seventeen hypotheses on stress and choice have been tested for each crisis. The hypotheses are:

Core Inputs

46. As crisis-induced stress begins to rise, the number and variety of core inputs to decisions increase sharply.

47. As crisis-induced stress declines, the number and variety of core inputs are reduced.

Costs

48. When decision-makers operate under stress, they assess their decision as costly.

49. When decision-makers operate under low or declining stress, they perceive their decisions as of small cost.

Importance

50. As crisis-induced stress rises, decision-makers tend to perceive their decisions as more and more important.

51. As crisis-induced stress declines, the perceived importance of decisions declines from the levels in all other phases of the crisis period.

Complexity

52. As crisis-induced stress rises, the complexity of issue-areas involved steadily rises.

53. As crisis-induced stress declines, the number of issue-areas involved in decision-making reaches its maximum.

Systemic Domain

54. In situations of peak crisis-induced stress, the heretofore steadily-broadening systemic levels of anticipated reverberations from decisions become narrower.

55. As crisis-induced stress declines, systemic domain rises from the peak crisis phase.

Process

56. As crisis-induced stress rises, the selected option tends to be chosen by rational calculus and analysis of the issues, rather than by a process of bargaining and compromise.

57. As crisis-induced stress declines, decision-makers resort mainly to rational procedures to ultimate choice.

Activity

58. As crisis-induced stress rises, there is a tendency for decisions to be continuously active.

59. As crisis-induced stress rises, the activity implied by the decisions moves from physical to verbal.

60. As crisis-induced stress declines, there is a sharp increase in decisions to delay or not to act.

Novelty

61. As crisis-induced stress rises, there is a steady increase in resort to choices without precedent.

62. As crisis-induced stress declines, unprecedented choices remain at their peak.

Conclusions on the testing of the hypotheses, drawn from the earlier discussions, are summarized in Table 8.

Coping Strategies

As elaborated in Chapter One, theorists have identified a number of strategies by which decision-makers may cope with stress:

1. Using a "satisficing" rather than an "optimizing" decision strategy.

2. Using the strategy of "incrementalism."

3. Deciding what to do on the basis of "consensus politics"—i.e., what enough people want and support—rather than attempting to master the cognitive complexity of the problem by analysis.

4. Avoiding value trade-offs, by persuading oneself that a policy which is best on one value dimension is also best for all other relevant values.

TABLE 8

HYPOTHESES ON STRESS AND CHOICE

Hypothesis	Lebanese Crisis, 1958	Jordanian Crisis, 1970	Yom Kippur War, 1973
46. Higher stress→increased number and variety of core inputs	Confirmed	Confirmed	Confirmed
47. Decline in stress→reduced number and variety of core inputs	Confirmed	Confirmed	Rejected
48. Under stress, assess decisions as costly	Confirmed	Confirmed	Confirmed
49. Decline in stress→low perceived cost	Confirmed	Confirmed	Confirmed
50. Higher stress→decisions perceived as more improtant	Confirmed	Confirmed	Confirmed
51. Decline in stress→decisions perceived as less important than in all other crisis phases	Confirmed	Confirmed	Confirmed
52. Higher stress→rise in complexity of issue-areas	Confirmed	Confirmed	Rejected
53. Decline in stress→number of issue-areas reaches maximum	Rejected	Rejected	Rejected
54. Peak stress→narrower systemic levels of anticipated reverberations	Rejected	Rejected	Rejected
55. Decline in stress→increase in systematic domain from peak phase	Rejected	Rejected	Rejected

56. Higher stress→selection option by rational calculus	Rejected*	Confirmed	Confirmed
57. Decline in stress→resort mainly to rational procedures	Confirmed	Confirmed	Confirmed
58. Higher stress→tendency to continuous activity in decisions	Confirmed	Confirmed	Confirmed
59. Higher stress→move from physical to verbal activity	Rejected	Confirmed	Rejected
60. Decline in stress→increase in decisions to delay or not to act	Rejected	Rejected	Rejected
61. Higher stress→increased resort to choices without precedent	Confirmed	Confirmed	Confirmed
62. Decline in stress→unprecedented choices remain at peak	Rejected	Confirmed	Confirmed

*Not supported by decision at peak of crisis, but supported by other decisions during crisis period.

TABLE 9

COPING STRATEGIES—LEBANESE CRISIS, 1958

Decision No.	Satisficing	Incrementalism	Consensus	Avoid Trade-offs	Historical Models	Ideology	Operational Code
Pre-Crisis							
1	X				X	X	X
2					X	X	X
3	X			X		X	X
4	X				X	X	X
Crisis							
5					X	X	X
6					X		X
7	X		X		X	X	X
8	X				X	X	X
9	X	X		X		X	X
Post-Crisis							
10	X				X	X	X
11	X				X		X
12	X			X	X	X	X
13		X		X	X	X	X
14					X	X	X
15				X	X	X	X

TABLE 10
COPING STRATEGIES—JORDANIAN CRISIS, 1970

Decision No.	Satisficing	Incrementalism	Consensus	Avoid Trade-offs	Historical Models	Ideology	Operational Code
Pre-Crisis							
1	X			X	X	X	X
2		X			X	X	X
3	X					X	X
4	X				X		X
Crisis							
5		X			X	X	X
6		X			X	X	X
7	X				X		X
8		X			X	X	X
9		X			X	X	X
10	X			X			
11	X			X			
12	X			X	X		X
Post-Crisis							
13							X

TABLE 11

COPING STRATEGIES—YOM KIPPUR WAR, 1973

Decision No.	Satisficing	Incrementalism	Consensus	Avoid Trade-offs	Historical Models	Ideology	Operational Code
Pre-Crisis							
1		X			X	X	X
2				X	X	X	X
3				X	X	X	X
4		X		X	X	X	X
5	X				X	X	X
Crisis							
6	X	X		X		X	X
7				X		X	X
8				X			X
9				X	X	X	X
10				X	X	X	X
11					X	X	X
12					X	X	X
13					X	X	X
14					X	X	X

TABLE 11
COPING STRATEGIES—YOM KIPPUR WAR, 1973 (*Continued*)

Decision No.	Satisficing	Incrementalism	Consensus	Avoid Trade-offs	Historical Models	Ideology	Operational Code
Post-Crisis							
15					X	X	X
16	X	X				X	X
17				X		X	X
18				X		X	X
19		X			X	X	X
20				X		X	X
21				X	X	X	X

5. Using historical models to diagnose and prescribe for present situations.

6. Relying on ideology and general principles as a guide to action.

7. Relying on "operational code" beliefs.

Based on the case studies and the above summaries of evidence on the forty-nine decisions in the 1958, 1970, and 1973 U.S. Middle East crises, an effort has been made to identify the coping strategies represented in each decision. Of course, more than one (and, in our sample, as many as five) of the coping strategies may be relevant to any given decision. Tables 9–11 summarize the findings on coping strategies for the forty-nine decisions, organized by historical crisis and by periods within crisis.

Several observations emerge from the application of this framework to our study:

1. The tendency toward "satisficing" decisions—solutions that are "adequate" but not "best"—is strong in two crises (1958 and 1973), but with no clear pattern except somewhat greater frequency in the pre-crisis period. This parallels the greater frequency of decisions to delay, or not to act, when stress is still low. But "satisficing" also appears at peak stress in 1970, when objective constraints did not permit "optimal" solutions.

2. The cases of "incrementalism" are largely instances of precautionary military moves or signals—such as the movement of the Sixth Fleet—which are an integral part of international communication in such crises (at least for the United States). Apart from this, incrementalism does not seem to be a common response in crisis.

3. As could be predicted from previous conclusions on the decline of bureaucratic politics during crisis, there is little tendency in these three cases to base a decision on consensus-building (in all three cases, the consensus follows the decision rather than the reverse).

4. Avoidance of value trade-offs, in which a preferred decision is rationalized by trying to ignore the costs that it entails, characterized some but by no means a majority of the decisions. If anything, it was more characteristic—not surprisingly—of the harder and more risky decisions made (at least in 1970 and 1973). But aside from these instances, there was generally a clear recognition of the trade-offs that preferred options entailed.

5. As has been repeatedly shown in previous chapters, the role of historical models, ideology, and operational codes ("a set of general beliefs about fundamental issues of history and central questions of politics as these bear, in turn, on the problem of

action"[4]) is strong across the board. This bears out, furthermore, our conclusions on the importance of basic beliefs and predispositions on the level of basic policy choices (though not on the level of situational perceptions or tactical choices).

GENERAL OBSERVATIONS

What are the implications of this study for existing theories of crisis decision-making, for possible new hypotheses and areas of exploration, and for observed patterns in American responses to Middle East crisis? The concluding sections of this chapter will deal, one by one, with these questions.

Crisis Decision-Making

The mixture of cognitive rigidity and tactical rationality that has been identified in this study, in the seemingly contradictory results of hypothesis testing, appears confusing at best. But a road map through the complexity has been provided, as shown in Chapter Twelve, by Bonham and Shapiro's differentiation of four levels of conceptual thinking in decision-making:[5]

Value concepts are abstract values that a decision-maker tries to satisfy. Such "values" are generally synonymous with the *basic aims* of a state; one would expect that they are often assumed rather than debated, and that they tend to remain stable over time.

Cognitive concepts are beliefs about events that occur in the international environment.

Affective concepts refer to immediate policy objectives, or the short-term aims of policy, as opposed to the long-term aims of value concepts.

Policy concepts are the alternatives or options from which policy choices are made.

As defined here, it is the value concepts and the affective concepts that tended to remain impervious to new inputs during the crises studied. Basic beliefs, ideology, affective factors, past experience, the "operational code," and other such aspects of "cognitive rigidity"

4. Alexander L. George, "The 'Operational Code': A Neglected Approach to the Study of Political Leaders and Decision-Making," *International Studies Quarterly*, 13 (June 1969), 191.

5. G. Matthew Bonham and Michael Shapiro, "Explanation of the Unexpected: The Syrian Intervention in Jordan in 1970," in Robert Axelrod, ed., *Structure of Decision: The Cognitive Maps of Political Elites* (Princeton: Princeton University Press, 1976), pp. 115 ff. ·

made themselves felt on the level of basic aims and policy objectives. The influence of such thinking was seen in the tendency to interpret local events as a function of global politics, to see linkages among all aspects of the external environment, to practice "tunnel vision" at the peak of crisis, to circumscribe the search for new options during the peak phase, to fail to weigh all consequences adequately, and to avoid value trade-offs and ignore costs.

Rigidity on this level was accompanied, however, by considerable flexibility in cognitive concepts (defined here as beliefs about events in the international environment) and policy concepts. Perhaps the archetype for this mixture was John Foster Dulles, with his fastidious logic on details and his total nonreceptivity to new ideas. In any event, decision-makers generally showed great receptivity to information, and in many cases—especially in 1958 and 1973—considerably transformed their perceptions of the external environment as a result. They were *not* insensitive to negative feedback; in fact, in anything involving cues from the environment, their behavior approached the rational model more than the affective. This tactical rationality extended to the analysis of alternatives. Once the options to be considered had been defined—admittedly by a largely cognitive process—the evaluation itself proceeded with a reasonable, and often impressive, focus on the costs and benefits of the courses being considered. There were more flaws in this performance during periods of the very highest stress—suggesting a curvilinear pattern in many respects—but a generally rational mode of analysis is never total proof against error or the occasional intrusion of emotions, ideologies, etc.—especially under high pressure.

This mixture of cognitive and rational processes may be linked to another observed feature of decision-making in the three crises: the centralization of authority and the reduction in the size of the decisional unit. Centralization, as noted, was accompanied by the reduced influence of standard operating procedures, bureaucratic politics, and other "pathologies" of group dynamics. But just as this development closed out the irrationality of group processes, so it enlarged the potential role of cognitive irrationality by making decisions more dependent on the mental processes of one or two individuals.

The shift to individual responsibility can in itself be, of course, a source of great variation and thus a complication to the study of crisis decision-making. A single individual may succeed in hewing to the dictates of rational procedure despite stress, or he may abandon himself totally to instinct and prejudice. The constraining influence of the group, which limits individual variation and establishes a "lowest common denominator," is much weaker under such circumstances. Decision-making may gain—as it seems to have done under Kissinger, especially in 1973—in clear direction, flexibility, and subtlety. Choices will be based on analysis of the issues, even if with a high affective component, rather than on bargaining and compromise. But the flaws are also those of a centralized, personalized system; the quirks of the central decision-maker will be closely reflected in the context of the decisions (as was the case, in fact, with Kissinger's failure to consider certain options and his other misjudgments in 1973). And the rational as opposed to the affective component of decisions may fluctuate widely from one instance to the next.

It can be inferred from much of what has been said that there are both functional and dysfunctional aspects to the changes in decision-making in the cases examined. As noted in Chapter One, most studies of foreign policy decision-making have tended to draw negative conclusions about the effect of crisis on coping and choice, being heavily influenced by cognitive psychological studies that focus on the performance of individuals under stress. Therefore, a number of hypotheses embodying the positive aspects of crisis, drawn largely from organizational theory, were deliberately added to the inventory.

Most of these hypotheses, as well as some others that also had positive implications for crisis decision-making, were confirmed by the evidence. The reduced role of standard operating procedures, bureaucratic politics, and other nonanalytic group processes has been mentioned. Nearly all of the information hypotheses (the exceptions being the "overload" and "random search" hypotheses) that were confirmed had positive implications regarding the search for and receptivity to information under stress. Even the fact that information was passed to the top more quickly, in undigested form, is also potentially functional; while it was apparently a problem in 1973, it was instrumental in "correcting" Eisenhower's perceptions in 1958. The increased role of decision-makers with a general rather than a "parochial" perspective was also a healthy corrective in certain ways.

Finally, the increased consultation, the more frequent face-to-face contact, and the reduction of pressures from interest groups and other extraneous influences could all be viewed positively. The same could be said for the way in which crisis pressures forced clear choices, pushing decision-makers out of "satisficing" or "drift" modes that sometimes characterized the pre-crisis period.

All of this should not be taken to mean that stress improved decision-making, but that crisis pressures often seem to be double-edged in their impact on the quality of decisions.[6] Since one of the major effects of crisis decision-making is to put more weight on the key decision-makers, perhaps this ambivalence is unavoidable. Much will hang on the cognitive performance of the man at the helm (an observation that is hardly novel).

One final observation concerns the post-crisis period, which has received little attention in studies of crisis decision-making. Putting together the confirmed hypotheses and other evidence on the period of declining stress, there does seem to be a pattern in the three cases with some rather interesting features. Among other things, passage from high to low stress was accompanied by a notable tendency to minimize problems and reinterpret "success." In 1958, it became possible to view the establishment of a neutralist Lebanese government as an achievement, which would have been unthinkable in earlier months. In 1970, the hostages were almost forgotten. And in 1973, Kissinger went out of his way to reassure Arab states that the United States "understood" the reasons for the embargo and was not contemplating a harsh response.

Generally, the "relief" of the post-crisis period seems to have reduced any inclination to consider "tough" options. With the major danger passed, the prevailing mood was one of conciliation and moderation. There was a willingness to reexamine basic suppositions, especially ones called into question by the crisis. There was also time and psychic energy to broaden the previously narrowed span of attention and to deal with larger issues that had not been on the agenda during peak stress (general Middle East problems in 1958; Arab-Israeli diplomacy in 1973). There was, at the same time, a definite tendency (at least in 1958 and 1973) to move to a greater focus on local and regional forces, in contrast to the generally globalist perceptions with which decision-makers had set out. In 1973, there was a move to "disaggregate" issues (particularly oil and the Arab-Israeli conflict), in reaction perhaps to the tendency under high stress to see linkages everywhere.

6. Ole Holsti, "Theories of Crisis Decision-Making," in Paul Gordon Lauren, ed., *Diplomacy: New Approaches in History, Theory, and Policy* (New York: Free Press, 1979), pp. 126–127, calls attention to other studies with more hopeful implications for crisis decision-making, including Howard H. Lentner, "The Concept of Crisis as Viewed by the United States Department of State," in C. F. Hermann, ed., *International Crises: Insights from Behavioral Research* (New York: Free Press, 1972), pp. 112–135; and Glen H. Snyder and Paul Diesing, *Conflict Among Nations: Bargaining, Decision Making, and System Structure in International Crises* (Princeton: Princeton University Press, 1977). Holsti himself (1979, p. 110) emphasizes the negative effects of crisis on performance.

All in all, then, there is enough evidence of distinctive behavior in the post-crisis period to justify the attention given to it in the ICB approach, and to suggest some of the patterns that seem to characterize this period of lower but still substantial tension.

Suggestions for New Hypotheses

The thoughts below will not be presented as finished propositions; they simply represent ideas raised by the three case studies that might be worth considering in future crisis studies.

1. *In Whose Favor Is Time Working?* As was suggested earlier, what seems to have distinguished the pre-crisis periods, on one level, was the sense that events were moving in a positive direction so long as no other outside party intervened. Local forces congenial to American interests were, so far, adequate to the occasion. It was when this assumption was shaken, in all three cases, that pre-crisis ended and crisis—characterized by the sense that the United States *must* act—began.

   So long as events are moving in a positive direction, delay and minimal response were options. This characterized pre-crisis decisions generally. It was also true for certain phases within the crisis period (after the U.S. intervention in 1958; after civil war erupted, but before the Syrian intervention, in 1970; and after the airlift in 1973) when events could be said to be moving in a positive direction. Generally, this was because of an action by the United States (or a U.S. client) that had "put the ball in the other court," and thus created a sense of some relaxation even in the midst of crisis. Of course, part of this mood may simply be *the catharsis of having acted,* which may in itself reduce the strains and pressures on decision-makers.

2. *A "Last Straw" Syndrome?* In finely balanced decisions, it is a common experience that one small additional stimulus, in itself of trivial importance, may trigger a decisive response. In crisis situations in which "provocations" have built up over time, creating a sense of frustration over repeated decisions not to respond, there may likewise be a tendency to regard a small incremental threat as one tipping the balance. If such a threat were to materialize without the buildup, it would not be deemed worthy of response—but in context it evokes the sense that "*this* time" there must be a response. Such may have been the case in 1958, with the repeated minor crises in Lebanon preceding the Iraqi coup, and similar feelings seem to have existed toward the Syrian invasion in 1970 and the receipt of Brezhnev's threatening message on the night of the DefCon 3 alert in 1973.

3. *The "Shock" Factor?* Brecher has shown, and this study bears out, that surprise is not a necessary defining characteristic of crisis (note, for example, the expectations of civil war in Jordan

in 1970). Nevertheless, it may play a role in shaping the response to crisis. The quick onslaught of the unexpected—the Iraqi coup in 1958, the Syrian invasion in 1970—seems to have left policy-makers more angry and frustrated than the same events would have done if anticipated. The sudden shock of unwelcome developments may in itself create a certain presumption toward action, if only as a cathartic response to the discomfort of having been unpleasantly surprised. Shock may also have an impact on unrelated beliefs, causing decision-makers to make wild surmises because it has uprooted some of the certainty of their conceptual universes (this seems to have happened in 1958, at least).

4. *Crisis as a Learning Experience?* In at least one of the case studies (the Lebanese crisis), the actions taken in the crisis brought new inputs to decision-makers that, in turn, modified some of the perceptions upon which the actions themselves had been based. In other words, the intervention in Lebanon brought American decision-makers into closer touch with Lebanese realities. Similar "learning experiences," or self-correcting feedback from decisions implemented, could be identified in the 1973 case.[7]

5. *"Success" as a Variable?* As will be noted below, all three crises were resolved "successfully" from the American point of view, and this sense of resolution clearly had an impact on the post-crisis period and on the way in which the crisis changed prevailing perceptions. It can be argued, ironically, that the bigger the success, the less the learning experience. The 1970 crisis was the most resounding "victory," and it led to the least adjustment in the perceptions of policy-makers (for example, it led to the least successful challenge to the tendency to view local conflicts as a function of global rivalries).

6. *A Theory of Background Factors?* It is commonplace to note that the historical context of decisions was important in shaping their content, yet the impact of the prevailing mood, in the cases at hand, stands out strongly enough to suggest the utility of more systematic attention to background factors that predispose decision-makers to action or to nonaction. In 1958 and 1970, for example, the state of U.S.-Soviet relations created a certain presumption in favor of strong responses, whereas the opposite was the case in 1973 (witness Kissinger's efforts to interpret

---

7. Richard Ned Lebow, in his thoughtful study of twentieth-century crises (*Between Peace and War: The Nature of International Crisis* [Baltimore: Johns Hopkins University Press, 1981], pp. 334–335), identifies the absence of learning—or more specifically, the insensitivity to information challenging prospects of success (labeled here "insensivity to negative feedback")—as the major distinguishing feature of crises that led to war, as opposed to those resolved peacefully. In the three crises studied here, it should be noted, the United States did avoid war, whether because of "learning" or other factors; it might be instructive to compare these cases with otherwise similar ones that did lead to American involvement in war.

Soviet actions generously). Similarly, international circumstances in 1970 and 1973 imposed a much stronger set of constraints on unilateral military action than those faced by Eisenhower and Dulles in 1958.

7. *The Superpower Variant?* In comparing these case studies to studies of decision-making in small or medium powers, it is clear that the crisis perspective of a superpower such as the United States is unique in certain respects. There is, first of all, the marked inclination, noted in every chapter of this book, to see local crises as a function of the global balance of power, whether in the ideological perspective of Eisenhower and Dulles or in the traditional Great Power view of Nixon and Kissinger. Of the nine triggering events identified in this book as marking the onset of periods within a crisis, only one was directed—in part— at the United States. The others, though not directed at the United States, were nevertheless felt from the superpower perspective to constitute an increase (or decrease) in threat to basic American values.

Also evident in these episodes is the tendency of both superpowers to assume that the other controls and is responsible for the behavior of its "clients." Thus, the United States blamed the Soviet Union for encouraging the Syrian invasion of Jordan, and the Soviets similarly assumed U.S. support for Israel's prolongation of the 1973 war. Both sets of assumptions could easily be challenged.

The United States and the Middle East

In addition to common features in the policy-making process, there are regularities in the content of American responses in 1958, 1970, and 1973. Four of these patterns can be briefly identified at this point, along with some speculation on their relationship to the decision-making process.

1. *Problems in Intelligence:* In all three cases, the key event in the crisis was unanticipated. The Iraqi coup in 1958, the Syrian invasion of Jordan in September 1970, and the Egyptian-Syrian attack of 1973 all caught policy-makers by surprise. In addition, inadequate information was a constraint on decision-making throughout all three crises, according to the testimony of participants. One should not demand the impossible of intelligence analysts; no one can foresee every contingent event. But it seems likely that the centralization of policy-making, the reduced representation of local expertise, and the tendencies to perceptual consensus all contributed to less effective use of the intelligence that was available than would have been the case otherwise. Good policy-making begins with reliable information where it counts, and in the cases examined it cannot be said that U.S. policy-makers always understood the Middle East.

2. *The Dominance of Global Perspectives:* We must note here
again that in all three cases, local and regional forces were seen
as a function of U.S.–Soviet relations. To be sure, in both 1958
and 1973, the United States turned, in the post-crisis period, to
an active diplomatic effort more tuned to local and regional
factors. But the initial perception was always global. To some
extent, of course, this is because the top decision-makers were
generalists, not specialists; local expertise tends to be closed out
as crisis decision-making is centralized. Insofar as the result is a
policy more effective on the U.S.-Soviet level (as argued, to some
extent, in all three crises), this is not entirely a negative
development. The problem seems to be finding the right
balance between global considerations and the appreciation of
local realities.

3. *The Lack of Political-Military Coordination:* Far from
dominating crisis decision-making, military spokesmen played
secondary roles in 1958 and 1973 and were influential in arguing
against direct U.S. military intervention in 1970. Military
advisors tended to complain, as a result, that civilian
policy-makers made decisions with inadequate attention to
military factors. In any event, political and military planning
often worked at cross-purposes, nearly leading to disaster in
Lebanon, and causing unnecessary complications in 1973. The
often noted American tendency to divorce military and political
considerations is reinforced by centralization of decision-making.
But as military constraints become more important in crisis
decision-making (and the trend from 1958 to 1973 was toward
greater limitations on U.S. capabilities in confrontations with the
Soviet Union), better integration and coordination would seem
imperative.

4. *The Achievement of Immediate Ends:* American policy-makers
may have a lucky habit of doing the right thing for the wrong
reasons; on the other hand, there may be some explanation for
the pattern. By converting Middle Eastern crises into U.S.-Soviet
confrontations, the United States puts emphasis on its strategic
military capabilities, where it is in a stronger position, rather
than on local capabilities that are often more problematic.
Moreover, holding the Soviet Union responsible for the behavior
of a local client may work even if the original assumption of
Soviet complicity was incorrect. It has been argued that as a
working hypothesis the assumption of Soviet responsibility may
be the best course of action whatever the Soviet role in
instigating the crisis; putting pressure on the Soviet Union is
likely to be more effective than trying to deal with the local
client.

Any implications drawn from these cases must be tentative. But
if the patterns described above should prove to be typical, what
should be our concerns regarding U.S. decision-making in future
Middle Eastern crises?

There is little need to comment on failures of intelligence or the tendency to define basic policy aims by instinct and belief rather than by open-minded examination of options. These are well-known problems, common to other areas of human endeavor, that have well-known if infrequently practiced solutions.

The tendency of U.S. policy-makers to do the right thing for the wrong reasons is, however, another kind of problem. It may work only so long as the United States has a large margin of power in which to err. When such a margin exists, an action based on a perception of global struggle may be incorrectly addressed, but may incidentally meet the needs of the situation.

In a situation of strategic parity between the superpowers, however, and with local military balances even more questionable from the U.S. perspective, such a margin for error may no longer exist. The risks will increase as the margin for error decreases, and actions that are based on misperceptions or ignorance of local conditions may no longer turn out happily in spite of everything. On the other hand, one can make a case that the "closing out" and centralization of decision-making may, on balance, be positive. Crisis decision-making needs a global context, though not exclusively global perceptions. Regional experts tend inevitably to feel that their advice is inadequately respected, but any policy-maker who tried to please all his ambassadors simultaneously would surely commit even more grievous follies. Furthermore, it was the regional experts in all three cases who failed to alert their superiors to impending crisis. The solution would not seem to be increasing the role of the regional experts, but rather improving the quality of their input. It is apparent, in the cases before us, that those responsible often failed to convey to top policy-makers an accurate sense of Middle Eastern realities.

Bibliography

(Multiple entries under one author are listed in reverse chronological order.)

THEORETICAL

ALLISON, Graham T. *The Essence of Decision: Explaining the Cuban Missile Crisis.* Boston: Little, Brown, 1971.

———. "Conceptual Models and the Cuban Missile Crisis." *American Political Science Review,* 63 (September 1969), 689–718.

———, and Morton H. Halperin. "Bureaucratic Politics: A Paradigm and Some Policy Implications." In R. Tanter and R. H. Ullman, eds., *Theory and Policy in International Relations.* Princeton: Princeton University Press, 1973, pp. 40–79.

BRECHER, Michael. *Decisions in Crisis: Israel, 1967 and 1973.* Berkeley, Los Angeles, and London: University of California Press, 1980.

———. "Toward a Theory of International Crisis Behavior." *International Studies Quarterly,* 21 (March 1977), 39–74.

———. *Decisions in Israel's Foreign Policy.* New Haven: Yale University Press, 1975.

———. *The Foreign Policy System of Israel.* New Haven: Yale University Press, 1972.

———, ed. *Studies in Crisis Behavior.* New Brunswick, N.J.: Transaction Books, 1979.

———, Blema Steinberg, and Janice G. Stein. "A Framework for Research on Foreign Policy Behavior." *Journal of Conflict Resolution,* 13 (March 1969), 75–101.

———, and Jonathan Wilkenfeld. "Crises in World Politics." *World Politics,* 34 (April 1982), 380–417.

BUTTERWORTH, R. L. *Managing Interstate Conflict, 1945–1974: Data with Synopsis.* Pittsburgh: University Center for International Studies, 1976.

FRYE, R. L., and T. M. Stritch. "Effects of Timed versus Non-Timed Discussion Upon Measures of Influence and Change in Small Groups." *Journal of Social Psychology,* 63 (1964), 139–143.

GEORGE, Alexander L. *Presidential Decisionmaking in Foreign Policy.* Boulder, Colo.: Westview Press, 1980.

———. "The 'Operational Code': A Neglected Approach to the Study of Political Leaders and Decision-Making." *International Studies Quarterly,* 13 (June 1969), 190–222.

———, and R. Smoke. *Deterrence and Defense in American Foreign Policy: Theory and Practice.* New York: Columbia University Press, 1974.

GUETZKOW, H., and J. Gyr. "An Analysis of Conflict in Decision-Making Groups." *Human Relations,* 7 (1954), 367–381.

HERMANN, Charles F. "Threat, Time, and Surprise: A Simulation of International Crises." In C. F. Hermann, ed., *International Crises: Insights from Behavioral Research.* New York: Free Press, 1972, pp. 187–214.

———. *Crises in Foreign Policy: A Simulation Analysis.* Indianapolis: Bobbs-Merrill, 1969a.

———. "International Crisis as a Situational Variable." In J. N. Rosenau, ed., *International Politics and Foreign Policy.* New York: Free Press, 1969b, pp. 409–421.

———, ed. *International Crises: Insights from Behavioral Research.* New York: Free Press, 1972.

HOLSTI, Ole R. "Theories of Crisis Decision Making." In Paul Gordon Lauren, ed., *Diplomacy: New Approaches in History, Theory, and Policy.* New York: Free Press, 1979, pp. 99–136.

———. *Crisis, Escalation, War.* Montreal: McGill-Queens University Press, 1972a.

———. "Time, Alternatives, and Communications: The 1914 and Cuban Missile Crises." In C. F. Hermann, ed., *International Crises: Insights from Behavioral Research.* New York: Free Press, 1972b, pp. 58–80.

———. "The 1914 Case." *American Political Science Review,* 59 (June 1965), 365–378.

———, and A. L. George. "The Effects of Stress on the Performance of Foreign Policy-Makers." *Political Science Annual,* 6 (1975), 255–319.

HOPPLE, Gerald W., and Paul J. Rossa. "International Crisis Analysis: Recent Developments and Future Directions." In P. Terence Hopmann, Dina A. Zinnes, and J. David Singer, eds., *Cumulation in International Relations Research,* pp. 65–97. Monograph Series in World Affairs, Volume 18, Book 3. Denver: University of Denver, 1981.

JANIS, Irving L. *Victims of Groupthink: A Psychological Study of Foreign Policy Decisions and Fiascos.* Boston: Houghton Mifflin, 1972.

———. "Groupthink." *Psychology Today,* November 1971, pp. 43–76.

———, and Leon Mann. *Decision-Making.* New York: Free Press, 1977.

JERVIS, Robert. *Perception and Misperception in International Politics.* Princeton: Princeton University Press, 1976.

LeBow, Richard Ned. *Between Peace and War: The Nature of International Crisis.* Baltimore: Johns Hopkins University Press, 1981.

LENTNER, Howard H. "The Concept of Crisis as Viewed by the United States Department of State." In C. F. Hermann, ed., *International Crises:*

Insights from Behavioral Research. New York: Free Press, 1972, pp. 112–135.

McCLELLAND, Charles A. "The Anticipation of International Crises: Prospects for Theory and Research." *International Studies Quarterly,* 21 (March 1977), 15–38.

―――. "The Beginning, Duration, and Abatement of International Crises: Comparisons in Two Conflict Arenas." In C. F. Hermann, ed., *International Crises: Insights from Behavioral Research.* New York: Free Press, 1972, pp. 83–105.

―――. "The Acute International Crisis." *World Politics,* 14 (October 1961), 182–204.

MARCH, James C., and H. A. Simon. *Organizations.* New York: John Wiley, 1958.

MILBURN, Thomas W. "The Management of Crisis." In C. F. Hermann, ed., *International Crises: Insights from Behavioral Research.* New York: Free Press, 1972, pp. 259–277.

MOFFITT, J. W., and R. Stagner. "Perceptual Rigidity and Closure as a Function of Anxiety." *Journal of Abnormal and Social Psychology,* 52 (1956), 350–357.

NAVEH, Hanan, and M. Brecher. "Patterns of International Crises in the Middle East, 1938–1975." *Jerusalem Journal of International Relations,* 2–3 (Winter–Spring 1978), 277–315.

PAIGE, Glenn D. "Comparative Case Analysis of Crisis Decisions: Korea and Cuba." In C. F. Hermann, ed., *International Crises: Insights from Behavioral Research.* New York: Free Press, 1972, pp. 41–55.

―――. *The Korean Decision.* New York: Free Press, 1968.

PRUITT, Dean G. "Definition of the Situation as a Determinant of International Action." In H. C. Kelman, ed., *International Behavior.* New York: Holt, Rinehart and Winston, 1966, Chapter 11.

ROBINSON, James A. "Crisis: An Appraisal of Concepts and Theories." In C. F. Hermann, ed., *International Crisis: Insights from Behavioral Research.* New York: Free Press, 1972, pp. 20–35.

SHAPIRO, Howard B., and M. A. Gilbert. *Crisis Management: Psychological and Sociological Factors in Decision-Making.* Arlington, Va.: Office of Naval Research, Advanced Research Projects Agency AD-A010 211, 1975.

SIMON, Herbert A. "Political Research: The Decision-Making Framework." In D. Easton, ed., *Varieties of Political Theory.* Englewood Cliffs, N.J.: Prentice-Hall, 1966, pp. 15–24.

SNYDER, Glenn H. "Crisis Bargaining." In C. F. Hermann, ed., *International Crisis: Insights from Behavioral Research.* New York: Free Press, 1972, pp. 217–256.

―――, and Paul Diesing. *Conflict Among Nations: Bargaining, Decision Making, and System Structure in International Crises.* Princeton: Princeton University Press, 1977.

STEIN, Janice Gross, and M. Brecher. "Image, Advocacy and the Analysis of

Conflict: An Israeli Case Study." *Jerusalem Journal of International Relations,* 1 (Spring 1976), 33–58.

————, and R. Tanter. *Rational Decision-Making: Israel's Security Choices, 1967.* Columbus: Ohio State University Press, 1980.

TANTER, Raymond. "International Crisis Behavior: An Appraisal of the Literature." *Jerusalem Journal of International Relations,* 3 (Winter–Spring 1978), 340–374.

GENERAL HISTORICAL

ABRAHAMSEN, David. *Nixon vs. Nixon: An Emotional Tragedy.* New York: Farrar, Straus and Giroux, 1976.

ALROY, Gil Carl. *The Kissinger Experience: American Policy in the Middle East.* New York: Horizon, 1975.

BECKER, Abraham S. *The Superpowers in the Arab-Israeli Conflict, 1970–1973.* Santa Monica, Calif.: Rand Corporation, 1973.

BELL, Coral. *The Diplomacy of Detente: The Kissinger Era.* New York: St. Martin's Press, 1977.

BETTS, Richard K. *Soldiers, Statesmen, and Cold War Crises.* Cambridge: Harvard University Press, 1977.

CHURBA, Joseph. *The Politics of Defeat: America's Decline in the Middle East.* New York and London: Cyrco Press, 1977.

DECLASSIFIED DOCUMENTS REFERENCE SYSTEM. Washington, D.C.: Carrollton Press.

DESTLER, I. M. *Presidents, Bureaucrats and Foreign Policy.* Princeton: Princeton University Press, 1972.

DICKSON, Peter W. *Kissinger and the Meaning of History.* Cambridge, England: Cambridge University Press, 1978.

DOWTY, Alan. "United States Decision-Making in Middle East Crises: 1958, 1970, 1973." *Middle East Review,* 12 (Spring 1980), 23–30.

EVRON, Yair. *The Middle East: Nations, Superpowers, and Wars.* New York: Praeger, 1973.

FREEDMAN, Robert. "Detente and Soviet-American Relations in the Middle East during the Nixon Years." Paper presented to the Eighth National Convention of the American Association for the Advancement of Slavic Studies, October 8, 1976.

GARDNER, Lloyd C., ed. *The Great Nixon Turn-Around.* New York: New Viewpoints, 1973.

HEIKAL, Mohammed. *The Sphinx and the Commissar.* New York: Harper and Row, 1978.

HOXIE, R. Gordon. *Command Decision and the Presidency: A Study in National Security Policy and Organization.* New York: Reader's Digest Press, 1977.

KALB, Marvin, and Bernard Kalb. *Kissinger.* New York: Dell, 1975.

MAZLISH, Bruce. *Kissinger: The European Mind in American Policy.* New York: Basic Books, 1976.

———. *In Search of Nixon: A Psychohistorical Inquiry.* New York: Basic Books, 1972.

MORRIS, Roger. *Uncertain Greatness: Henry Kissinger and American Foreign Policy.* New York: Harper and Row, 1977.

NIXON, Richard. *RN: The Memoirs of Richard Nixon.* New York: Grosset and Dunlap, 1978.

QUANDT, William B. "Lebanon, 1958, and Jordan, 1970." In Barry M. Blechman and Stephen S. Kaplan, *Force Without War: U.S. Armed Forces as a Political Instrument.* Washington, D.C.: Brookings Institution, 1978, pp. 222–288.

———. *Decade of Decisions: American Policy Toward the Arab-Israeli Conflict, 1967–1976.* Berkeley: University of California Press, 1977.

———. "United States Policy in the Middle East: Constraints and Choices." In Paul Y. Hammond and Sidney S. Alexander, eds., *Political Dynamics in the Middle East.* New York: American Elsevier, 1972, pp. 489–551.

RABIN, Yitzhak. *The Rabin Memoirs.* Boston: Little, Brown, 1979.

REICH, Bernard. *Quest for Peace: United States–Israel Relations and the Arab-Israeli Conflict.* New Brunswick, N.J.: Transaction Books, 1977.

SAFRAN, Nadav. *Israel: The Embattled Ally.* Cambridge: Harvard University Press, 1978.

SPIEGEL, Steven. *The War for Washington: The Other Arab-Israeli Conflict.* Forthcoming.

STOESSINGER, John G. *Crusaders and Pragmatists: Movers of Modern American Foreign Policy.* New York: Norton, 1979.

———. *Henry Kissinger: The Anguish of Power.* New York: Norton, 1976.

SZULC, Tad. *The Illusion of Peace: Foreign Policy in the Nixon Years.* New York: Viking, 1978.

U.S. DEPARTMENT OF STATE. *Department of State Bulletin.*

ZUMWALT, Elmo. *On Watch: A Memoir.* New York: Quadrangle Books, 1976.

THE 1958 CRISIS

ADAMS, Sherman. *Firsthand Report: The Story of the Eisenhower Administration.* New York: Harper and Brothers, 1961.

AGWANI, M. S. "The Lebanese Crisis of 1958 in Retrospect." *International Studies,* 4 (April 1963), 329–348.

———, ed. *The Lebanese Crisis, 1958: A Documentary Study.* New York: Asia Publishing House, 1965.

ALEXANDER, Charles C. *Holding the Line: The Eisenhower Era, 1952–1961.* Bloomington: Indiana University Press, 1975.

BERKOVITZ, Morton, P. G. Bock, and Vincent J. Fuccillo. *The Politics of American Foreign Policy: The Social Context of Decisions.* Englewood Cliffs, N.J.: Prentice-Hall, 1977.

BROWNE, Bernard G. "The Foreign Policy of the Democratic Party during the Eisenhower Administration." Ph.D. dissertation, University of Notre Dame, 1968.

CAMPBELL, John C. *Defense of the Middle East: Problems of American Policy.* New York: Harper and Brothers, 1960.

CHAMOUN, Camille. *Crise au Moyen-Orient.* Paris: Gallimard, 1963.

COPELAND, Miles. *The Game of Nations: The Amorality of Power Politics.* London: Weidenfeld and Nicolson, 1969.

CUTLER, Robert. *No Time for Rest.* Boston: Little, Brown, 1966.

DAYAL, Rajeshwar. "The 1958 Crisis in the Lebanon—the Role of the UN and the Great Powers." *India Quarterly,* 26 (April–June 1970), 123–133.

DIVINE, Robert A. *Eisenhower and the Cold War.* New York and Oxford: Oxford University Press, 1981.

DONOVAN, John, ed. *U.S. and Soviet Policy in the Middle East, 1957–1966.* New York: Facts on File, 1974.

DRUMMOND, Roscoe, and Gaston Coblentz. *Duel at the Brink: John Foster Dulles' Command of American Power.* Garden City, N.Y.: Doubleday, 1960.

DULLES, Eleanor Lansing. *American Foreign Policy in the Making.* New York: Harper and Row, 1968.

————. *John Foster Dulles: The Last Year.* New York: Harcourt, Brace and World, 1963.

EISENHOWER, Dwight D. *The White House Years: Waging Peace, 1956–1961.* Garden City, N.Y.: Doubleday, 1965.

GEORGE, Alexander, and Richard Smoke. *Deterrence in American Foreign Policy: Theory and Practice.* New York: Columbia University Press, 1974.

GURTOV, Melvin. *The United States Against the Third World.* New York and Washington, D.C.: Praeger, 1974.

HALPERN, Manfred. "The Morality and Politics of Intervention." In James Rosenau, ed., *International Aspects of Civil Strife.* Princeton: Princeton University Press, 1964.

HART, Parker T. "Tensions and U.S. Policy in the Near and Middle East." Address before the Foreign Policy Association of Pittsburgh, May 1, 1959. *Department of State Bulletin,* 40 (May 18, 1959), 117.

HEIKAL, Mohammed. *The Cairo Documents.* Garden City, N.Y.: Doubleday, 1973.

HOLSTI, Ole R. "Cognitive Dynamics and Images of the Enemy: Dulles and Russia." In David J. Finlay, Ole R. Holsti, and Richard R. Fagen, *Enemies in Politics.* Chicago: Rand McNally, 1967, Chapter 2.

HOOPES, Townsend. *The Devil and John Foster Dulles.* Boston: Little, Brown, 1973.

HOTTINGER, Arnold. "Zu'ama' and Parties in the Lebanese Crisis of 1958." *Middle East Journal,* 15 (Spring 1961), 127–140.

HUDSON, Michael. *The Precarious Republic: Political Modernization in Lebanon.* New York: Random House, 1968.

HUGHES, Emmet John. *The Ordeal of Power: A Political Memoir of the Eisenhower Years.* New York: Atheneum, 1963.

JUNBLAT, Kamal. *Haqiqat al-Thawrah al-Lubnaniyyah* [The Truth About the Lebanese Revolution]. Beirut: Dar al-Nashr al 'Arabiyyah, 1959.

KERR, Malcolm H. "The Lebanese Civil War." In Evan Luard, ed., *The International Regulation of Civil War.* New York: New York University Press, 1972, pp. 65–90.

———. "Lebanese Views on the 1958 Crisis." *Middle East Journal,* 15 (Spring 1961), 211–217.

KNEBEL, Fletcher. "Day of Decision." *Look,* 22 (September 16, 1958), 17–19.

LAQUEUR, Walter Z. *The Soviet Union and the Middle East.* New York: Praeger, 1959.

LYON, Peter. *Eisenhower: Portrait of a Hero.* Boston: Little, Brown, 1974.

McCLINTOCK, Robert T. *The Meaning of Limited War.* Boston: Houghton Mifflin, 1967.

———. "The American Landing in Lebanon." *U.S. Naval Institute Proceedings,* 88 (October 1962), 65–79.

MacMILLAN, Harold. *Riding the Storm, 1956–1959.* New York: Harper and Row, 1971.

MEO, Leila M. T. *Lebanon, Improbable Nation: A Study in Political Development.* Bloomington: Indiana University Press, 1965.

Minutes and Documents of the Cabinet Meetings of President Eisenhower (Microfilm). Washington, D.C.: University Publications of America, 1980.

Minutes of Telephone Conversations of John Foster Dulles and of Christian Herter (Microfilm). Washington, D.C.: University Publications of America, 1980.

MURPHY, Robert. *Diplomat among Warriors.* Garden City, N.Y.: Doubleday, 1964.

QUBAIN, Fahim. *Crisis in Lebanon.* Washington, D.C.: Middle East Institute, 1961.

SALIBI, K. S. *The Modern History of Lebanon.* New York: Praeger, 1965.

SHULIMSON, Jack. *Marines in Lebanon, 1958.* Washington, D.C.: Historical Branch, G-3 Division, Headquarters, U.S. Marine Corps., 1966.

SIGHTS, Albert P., Jr. "Lessons of Lebanon: A Study in Air Strategy." *Air University Review,* 16 (July–August 1965), 28–43.

STEWART, Desmond. *Turmoil in Beirut: A Personal Account.* London: Wingate, 1958.

THAYER, Charles W. *Diplomat.* New York: Harper and Brothers, 1959.

TILLEMA, Herbert K. *Appeal to Force: American Military Intervention in the Era of Containment.* New York: Crowell, 1973.

TWINING, Nathan. *Neither Liberty Nor Safety.* New York: Holt, Rinehart and Winston, 1966.

U.S. DEPARTMENT OF STATE, Bureau of Intelligence and Research. *World Strength of the Communist Party Organizations.* Annual Report No. 10. Washington, D.C.: Department of State, 1958.

U.S. PRESIDENT. *Public Papers of the Presidents of the United States: Dwight D. Eisenhower, 1958.* Washington, D.C.: U.S. Government Printing Office, 1958.

U.S. SENATE. *Hearings Before the Committee on Foreign Relations and the Committee on Armed Services on Senate Joint Resolution 19 and House Resolution 117.* Part I, January–February 1957. Washington, D.C.: U.S. Government Printing Office, 1957.

THE 1970 CRISIS

Interviews
(Positions are those held during the crisis.)

Granville Austin, Executive Assistant, Senator Clifford Case
L. Dean Brown, Ambassador to Jordan
Richard Helms, Director, Central Intelligence Agency
Samuel Hoskinson, National Security Council Staff
William Hyland, National Security Council Staff
U. Alexis Johnson, Under Secretary of State for Political Affairs
Robert Kubal, Country Director, Israel and Israel-Arab Affairs, Office of International Security Affairs, Department of Defense
Melvin Laird, Secretary of Defense
Admiral Thomas Moorer, Chairman, Joint Chiefs of Staff
G. Warren Nutter, Assistant Secretary of Defense for International Security Affairs
Robert Oakley, Advisor, U.S. Delegation to the United Nations
Robert Pranger, Deputy Assistant Secretary of Defense for Near Eastern and South Asian Affairs
Harold Saunders, National Security Council Staff
Talcott Seelye, Country Director, Lebanon, Jordan, Syria, and Iraq, Department of State
Joseph Sisco, Assistant Secretary of State for Near Eastern and South Asian Affairs
Walter Smith, Deputy Director, Egyptian Affairs, Department of State
Helmut Sonnenfeldt, National Security Council Staff
Admiral Elmo Zumwalt, Chief of Naval Operations

Other Sources

BONHAM, G. Matthew, and Michael Shapiro. "Explanation of the Unexpected: The Syrian Intervention in Jordan in 1970." In Robert Axelrod, ed., *Structure of Decision: The Cognitive Maps of Political Elites.* Princeton: Princeton University Press, 1976, pp. 113–141.

BRANDON, Henry. *The Retreat of American Power.* New York: Dell, 1973a.
——. "Jordan: The Forgotten Crisis (1)." *Foreign Policy,* 10 (Spring 1973b), 158–170.

Brown, Neville. "Jordanian Civil War." *Military Review,* 51 (September 1971), 38–48.

Dowty, Alan. "The U.S. and the Syria-Jordan Confrontation, 1970." In Michael Brecher, ed., *Studies in Crisis Behavior.* New Brunswick, N.J.: Transaction Books, 1978, pp. 172–196.

Evans, Rowland, and Robert D. Novak. *Nixon in the White House: The Frustration of Power.* New York: Random House, 1971.

Garfinkle, Adam Morris. "United States Foreign Policy and the Jordan Crisis of 1970: A Cognitive Approach." Ph.D. dissertation, University of Pennsylvania, 1979.

Kaplan, Stephen S. "United States Aid and Regime Maintenance in Jordan, 1957–1973." *Public Policy,* 23:2 (Spring 1975), 189–217.

Kissinger, Henry. *White House Years.* Boston: Little, Brown, 1979.

―――. "The Mid East: Search for Stability." *Time,* October 5, 1970, pp. 10–16.

Richardson, Elliot. "Nixon Behind the Scenes." *Newsweek,* February 1, 1971, pp. 16–17.

Schoenbaum, David. "Jordan: The Forgotten Crisis (2)." *Foreign Policy,* 10 (Spring 1973), 171–181.

Snow, Peter. *Hussein: A Biography.* New York: Robert B. Luce, 1972.

U.S. President. *Public Papers of the Presidents of the United States: Richard Nixon, 1970.* Washington, D.C.: U.S. Government Printing Office, 1970.

Van der Linden, Frank. *Nixon's Quest for Peace.* New York: Robert B. Luce, 1972.

Welles, Benjamin. "U.S.-Israeli Military Action in Jordan Was Envisioned." *New York Times,* October 8, 1970.

THE 1973 CRISIS

Interviews

(Positions are those held during the crisis.)

James Akins, U.S. Ambassador to Saudi Arabia
Morris Amitay, Legislative Aide to Senator Abraham Ribicoff
General George Brown, Chief of Staff, U.S. Air Force
L. Dean Brown, U.S. Ambassador to Jordan
Joseph Churba, Chief Middle East Analyst, Air Force Intelligence
Ray Cline, Director of Intelligence and Research, Department of State
William Colby, Director, Central Intelligence Agency
Simcha Dinitz, Israeli Ambassador to the United States
Senator J. William Fulbright, Chairman, Senate Foreign Relations Committee
Samuel Hoskinson, National Intelligence Officer for 1973 War
William Hyland, Bureau of Intelligence and Research, Department of State
Leslie Janka, National Security Council Staff
General George Keegan, Chief of Intelligence, U.S. Air Force
I. L. Kenen, Director, America-Israel Public Affairs Committee

David Korn, Country Director, Lebanon, Jordan, Syria, and Iraq, Department of State
Edward Luttwak, Consultant, Department of Defense
Admiral Thomas Moorer, Chairman, Joint Chiefs of Staff
Robert Oakley, Staff Member, U.S. Embassy in Lebanon
Ralph Ostrich, Manager, Strategic Assessments Department, BDM Corporation
Richard Perle, Legislative Aide to Senator Henry Jackson
Richard Peyer, Staff Member, Near Eastern and South Asian Affairs, Department of Defense
William Quandt, National Security Council Staff
Peter Rodman, Special Assistant to Henry Kissinger
Joseph Sisco, Assistant Secretary of State for Near Eastern and South Asian Affairs; after January 8, 1974, Under Secretary of State for Political Affairs
Walter Smith, Chief of Political Section, U.S. Embassy in Israel
Helmut Sonnenfeldt, National Security Council Staff
Phillip Stoddard, Deputy Director, Office of Research and Analysis, Near Eastern and South Asian Affairs
Maj. Gen. Gordon Sumner, Jr., Director, Near Eastern and South Asian Affairs, Department of Defense
Mark Talisman, Administrative Aide to Rep. Charles Vanik
Michael Van Deusen, Staff Aide, House International Relations Committee
Seymour Weiss, Director of Politico-Military Affairs, Department of State
Admiral Elmo Zumwalt, Chief of Naval Operations

Other Sources

ARONSON, Shlomo. *Conflict and Bargaining in the Middle East: An Israeli Perspective.* Baltimore and London: Johns Hopkins University Press, 1978.
ASTRACHAN, Anthony. "The October War at the United Nations." *Midstream,* 19 (December 1973), 46–62.
BANDMANN, Yona, and Yishai Cordova. "The Soviet Nuclear Threat Towards the Close of the Yom Kippur War." *Jerusalem Journal of International Relations,* 5:1 (1980), 94–110.
BINDER, David. "Action Was Downstairs, President Was Upstairs." *New York Times,* November 25, 1973.
BONHAM, G. Matthew, Michael J. Shapiro, and Thomas L. Trumble. "The October War: Changes in Cognitive Orientation Toward the Middle East Conflict." *International Studies Quarterly,* 23 (March 1979), 3–44.
———, Michael J. Shapiro, and George J. Nozicka. "A Cognitive Process Model of Foreign Policy Decision-Making." *Simulation and Games,* (June 1976), 123–152.
BROWNLOW, Cecil. "Soviets Poise Three-Front Global Drive." *Aviation Week and Space Technology,* 99 (November 5, 1973), 12–14.
CBS Reports, "The Mysterious Alert." January 17, 1974.

"The CIA Report the President Doesn't Want You to Read." (Excerpts from a report of the House Select Committee on Intelligence.) *Village Voice,* February 16, 1976, pp. 21–44.

CLINE, Ray. "Policy without Intelligence." *Foreign Policy,* 17 (Winter 1974–1975), 121–135.

COMPTROLLER GENERAL OF THE UNITED STATES. *Report to the Congress: Airlift Operations of the Military Airlift Command During the 1973 Middle East War.* Washington, D.C.: General Accounting Office, 1975.

DAYAN, Moshe. *Story of My Life.* New York: William Morrow, 1976.

DOWTY, Alan. "U.S. Decision-Making Under Stress: 1973." Paper presented at the World Congress of the International Political Science Association, Moscow, August 12–18, 1979a.

————. "The Impact of the 1973 War on the U.S. Approach to the Middle East." Paper presented at the International Conference on Turning Points in International Politics, Leonard Davis Institute for International Relations, Hebrew University, Jerusalem, Israel, July 9–11, 1979b.

DRAPER, Theodore. Reply to Donald Neff. *Commentary,* 60 (September 1975a), 22–24.

————. "The United States and Israel: Tilt in the Middle East?" *Commentary,* 59 (April 1975b), 29–45.

EBAN, Abba. *An Autobiography.* New York: Random House, 1977.

FINNEY, John W. "Officials Suspect Russians Sent Atom Arms to Egypt." *New York Times,* November 22, 1973.

GAZIT, Mordechai. "An American Initiative." *Jerusalem Post,* October 9, 1981.

GELB, Leslie. "Kissinger and Schlesinger Deny Rift in October War." *New York Times,* June 23, 1974a.

————. "House Ends Study of October Alert." *New York Times,* April 10, 1974b.

GHAREEB, Edmund. "The U.S. Arms Supply to Israel During the War." *Journal of Palestine Studies,* 3 (Winter 1974), 114–121.

GOLAN, Matti. *The Secret Conversations of Henry Kissinger: Step-by-Step Diplomacy in the Middle East.* New York: Bantam, 1976.

GRIFFITH, William E. "The Fourth Middle East War, the Energy Crisis, and United States Policy." *Orbis,* 17 (Winter 1974), 1161–1188.

HEIKAL, Mohammed. *The Road to Ramadan.* New York: Ballantine, 1975.

HERSH, Seymour. "Senate Report Criticizes U.S. Intelligence on Oil Embargo." *New York Times,* December 21, 1977.

HERZOG, Chaim. *The War of Atonement: October, 1973.* Boston: Little, Brown, 1975.

HORROCK, Nicholas M. "Signs of 1973 Mideast War Eluded U.S. Spy Agencies." *New York Times,* September 12, 1975.

THE INSIGHT TEAM OF THE LONDON SUNDAY TIMES. *The Yom Kippur War.* Garden City, N.Y.: Doubleday, 1974.

KASSIS, Jihad. "U.S. Foreign Policy-Making in Middle East Crises: The 1973–1974 Oil Embargo." Ph.D. dissertation, University of Notre Dame, 1981.

KISSINGER, Henry. *Years of Upheaval.* Boston: Little, Brown, 1982.

KOHLER, Foy D., Leon Goure, and Mose L. Harvey. *The Soviet Union and the October 1973 Middle East War: The Implications for Detente.* Miami: University of Miami Center for Advanced International Studies, Monograph in International Affairs, 1974.

LAQUEUR, Walter. *Confrontation: The Middle East and World Politics.* New York: Bantam, 1974.

LUTTWAK, Edward N., and Walter Laqueur. "Kissinger and the Yom Kippur War." *Commentary,* 50 (September 1974), 33–40.

MEIR, Golda. *My Life.* London: Weidenfeld and Nicolson, 1975.

MILLER, F. C. "Those Storm-beaten Ships, Upon Which the Arab Armies Never Looked." *U.S. Naval Institute Proceedings,* March 1975, pp. 18–25.

MILLER, Linda. *The Limits of Alliance: America, Europe, and the Middle East.* Jerusalem Papers on Peace Problems, No. 10. Jerusalem: Hebrew University, 1974.

NEFF, Donald. Letter to the Editor. *Commentary,* 60 (September 1975), 18–20.

ODELL, Peter R. *Oil and World Power.* 5th edition. New York: Penguin, 1979.

OPPENHEIM, V. H. "Why Oil Prices Go Up (1)—The Past: We Pushed Them." *Foreign Policy,* 25 (Winter 1976–1977), 24–57.

PERLMUTTER, Amos. "Crisis Management: Kissinger's Middle East Negotiations (October 1973–June 1974)." *International Studies Quarterly,* 19 (September 1975), 316–343.

QUANDT, William B. *Soviet Policy in the October 1973 War.* Santa Monica, Calif.: Rand Corporation, 1976.

———. "Kissinger and the Arab-Israeli Disengagement Negotiations." *Journal of International Affairs,* 9 (Spring 1975), 33–48.

RAZ, Motti. "The Decision-Making Process at the Pre-Crisis Phase of the 1973 War, September 26–October 6, 1973." Master's thesis, Hebrew University, 1975.

ROSTOW, Eugene V. "America, Europe, and the Middle East." *Commentary,* 57 (February 1974), 40–55.

RUBIN, Barry. "U.S. Policy, January–October 1973." *Journal of Palestine Studies,* 3 (Winter 1974), 98–113.

EL-SADAT, Anwar. *In Search of Identity: An Autobiography.* New York: Harper and Row, 1977.

SAGAN, Scott D. "Lessons of the Yom Kippur Alert." *Foreign Policy,* 36 (Fall 1979), 160–177.

SAIKOWSKI, Charlotte. "Congressional and Israeli Pressure on Nixon." *Christian Science Monitor,* October 12, 1973..

SHEEHAN, Edward R. F. *The Arabs, Israelis, and Kissinger: A Secret History of American Diplomacy in the Middle East.* New York: Reader's Digest Press, 1976.

SICHERMAN, Harvey. *The Yom Kippur War: End of Illusion?* The Foreign Policy Papers, Vol. 1, No. 4. Beverly Hills and London: Sage Publications, 1976.

SMITH, Terence. "Dayan Doubts That a New War Is Imminent." *New York Times,* January 26, 1975.

SZULC, Tad. "Is He Indispensable? Answers to the Kissinger Riddle." *New York,* July 1974, pp. 33–39.

ULLMAN, Marc. "La Paix de M. Kissinger." *L'Express,* October 29–November 4, 1973, pp. 55–57.

U.S. HOUSE OF REPRESENTATIVES, Committee on Foreign Affairs. *The United States Oil Shortage and the Arab-Israel Conflict, Report of a Study Mission to the Middle East from October 22 to November 3, 1973.* Washington, D.C.: U.S. Government Printing Office, 1973.

———, Select Committee on Intelligence. *Hearings before the Select Committee on Intelligence, September 11, 12, 18, 25, 30, October 7, 30, 31, 1975.* Washington, D.C.: U.S. Government Printing Office, 1975.

U.S. PRESIDENT. *Public Papers of the Presidents of the United States: Richard Nixon, 1973.* Washington, D.C.: U.S. Government Printing Office, 1975.

———. *Richard Nixon, 1974.* Washington, D.C.: U.S. Government Printing Office, 1975.

U.S. SENATE, Committee on Foreign Relations. *U.S. Oil Companies and the Arab Oil Embargo: The International Allocation of Constricted Supplies.* Washington, D.C.: U.S. Government Printing Office, 1975.

———. *Hearings on United States Relations with Communist Countries.* Washington, D.C.: U.S. Government Printing Office, 1974.

VALERIANI, Richard. *Travels With Henry.* Boston: Houghton Mifflin, 1979.

WAGNER, Abraham R. *Crisis Decision-Making: Israel's Experience in 1967 and 1973.* New York: Praeger, 1974.

WHETTEN, Lawrence L. *The Canal War: Four-Power Conflict in the Middle East.* Cambridge: MIT Press, 1974.

WOODWARD, Bob. "Pentagon to Abolish Secret Spy Unit." *Washington Post,* May 18, 1977.

Name Index

Subject Index

Activity, as dimension of choice: defined, 6, 355; hypotheses on stress and, 18, 363; in 1958, 104–5, 356–57 table; in 1970, 194–95, 358–59 table; in 1973, 318–19, 360–61 table
Ad hoc forms of consultation, 347
Advisory groups, 98
Affirmative concepts, 371
Air Force (U.S.), 215
Airlie House, 162
Airlift: British, to Jordan, 74; Soviet, 215, 245, 246; U.S., to Israel, 237–38, 251, 262, 305, 375
Algerian President, 215, 231
Alexandria, 258
Alternatives: in crisis periods, 100, 189, 313–14; in post-crisis periods, 101, 191–92, 314–15; in pre-crisis periods, 99, 189, 312, 342; impact of changing stress on, in crisis behavior model, 5, 9 fig., 15–17; testing of hypotheses on, 102, 192–93, 315–16, 353 table
American: aid to Israel, oil threat if, 249, 298; aims, 221, 314, 344; aircraft, 233; airlift, 232, 249, 265, 266, 342; airstrike, 156–57; alert, 258, 261, 274, 276, 276n, 342, 375; Ambassador to Jordan, 223; Ambassador to the United Nations, 52, 230; apprehensions, 256; and Arab ties, 329; assurances, 255, 319; attitudes, 170, 215, 252; bases, 156; commitment to Israel, 192; communications, 272; credibility with Arabs, 255, 272, 324, 333, 338;

diplomacy and diplomats, 200, 228, 244, 267, 294–95, 306, 329; European allies, 260, 282; forces, 117, 157, 159, 243, 256, 258, 325, 326; global interests, 336; ground forces, 72, 157, 330; initiatives, 119, 134; intervention, 61n, 155, 157, 188, 334; involvement in Middle East, 242, 277, 329, 330, 376n; Jews, 129, 218, 228, 232, 288; leaders, 87, 252, 253; military, 155, 156, 178, 236, 246, 260, 269, 330, 329, 378; negotiating framework, 200, 330; officials, 145, 298; perceptions, 247, 257, 302, 327; policy, 192, 273, 292, 326, 329; policy and the Yom Kippur crisis, 230, 250, 267, 289, 294, 309; policy-makers in the Jordanian crisis, 117, 124, 145, 191; policy-makers in the Yom Kippur crisis, 215, 218, 227–229, 238, 244, 246, 253, 284, 286, 288, 306, 323, 325, 328, 330, 334, 378; position, 232, 264, 314; prestige after Iraqi coup, 328; public opinion, 120, 258; responses, 327, 332, 335, 336, 337; responses to U.S.S.R., 241, 245–257, 259, 260, 275, 286, 291, 292, 327, 332, 335–336, 377; role in world, 202; statements on the Great Powers, 256
American interests, 221, 230, 250, 300, 329; and the 1970 hijackings, 122, 123, 145; in the Middle East, 178, 202, 283; threatened, 113, 203, 226, 241, 375
Amman, 138, 139, 140, 149, 164, 172n,

398